SPECTRUM®

Complete Learning + VIDEOS!

PARENT SUPPORT | VIDEO TUTORIALS | LANGUAGE ARTS | MATH | READING & WRITING

GRADE 3

Spectrum®

An imprint of Carson Dellosa Education
Greensboro, North Carolina

Spectrum®
An imprint of Carson Dellosa Education
PO Box 35665
Greensboro, NC 27425 USA

ISBN 978-1-4838-6522-5

01-052227784

Table of Contents

About *Spectrum Complete Learning + Videos*

When children get stuck on a homework problem or need extra help, they turn to you for help if they're at home. But as children get older and the topics get more challenging, it becomes harder to help. What do they need to know? Why do they have to learn it to begin with? How will you be able to help?

This is why *Spectrum Complete Learning + Videos* was created. This book will help you help your child navigate through third grade and give you the tools you need to make sure your child learns everything they need to know. Inside you will find:

Chapter Introductions

These introductions serve to answer *what*, *why*, and *how* about each topic being taught.

- *What* is this topic and what is my child expected to learn? This will include skill checklists to ensure your child gets the knowledge they need out of the chapter.
- *Why* is my child expected to learn this? This will include real-life application and explanation about how the lesson is a building block for future learning.
- *How* can I help? This will include helpful definitions, strategies, examples, and visual models for you and your child going into the workbook pages that follow.

solid figure: a three-dimensional object

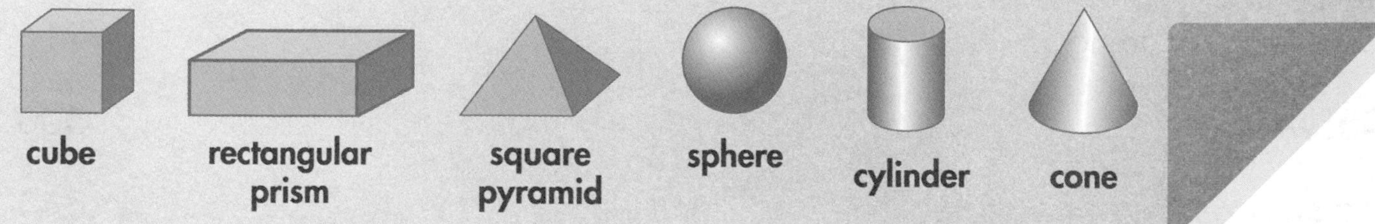

Free Videos

These free videos will act as your child's tutor for topics that might be a little trickier to master. The videos will show up as QR codes in the chapter introductions as well as on the applicable workbook pages. Not sure how to use a QR code?

- Open your smartphone's built-in camera app
- Point the camera at the QR code
- Tap the link that appears on your screen

Workbook Pages

These workbook pages give your child extra practice in each math and language arts topic that they are expected to learn in third grade. If your child gets stuck on a topic, look for a QR code on the page or flip back to the Chapter Introduction for helpful tips and strategies.

Answer Key

The Answer Key provides the answers to the workbook pages.

Passwords and Schedules

This section is just for you! Here you will find a place to store the many website passwords for your child as well as a seasonal schedule organizer.

Chapter 1: Addition and Subtraction

Basic Addition and Subtraction Facts and Beyond

Addition and subtraction are commonly used skills in daily life. Your child uses these skills to solve everyday problems, such as adding the cost of two milks at lunch or subtracting how many apples are left after they share one with a friend.

Your child uses their knowledge of basic facts when adding larger numbers. In the problem 24 + 13, they need to add the ones (4 ones + 3 ones = 7 ones) and then add the tens (2 tens + 1 ten = 3 tens). These facts enable them to find that 24 + 13 = 37. When your child sees a problem such as 93 – 71, they use basic facts to subtract the ones (3 ones – 1 one = 2 ones). Then they subtract the tens (9 tens – 7 tens = 2 tens). They find that 93 – 71 = 22.

Your child will also see problems that require them to regroup numbers, such as 71 – 12. Since you cannot subtract 1 – 2, your child needs to know to regroup 1 ten into 10 ones. Then they can subtract the ones (11 ones – 2 ones = 9 ones). This will leave them with 6 tens – 1 ten = 5 tens. 71 – 12 = 59.

Skill Checklist

- ☐ **Add and subtract through 20**
- ☐ **Add and subtract up to four-digit numbers with and without regrouping**
- ☐ **Add three or more numbers up to three digits**
- ☐ **Use addition to check subtraction answers and use subtraction to check addition answers**
- ☐ **Round numbers to the nearest ten or hundred**
- ☐ **Estimate addition and subtraction answers**

Chapter 1: Addition and Subtraction

Helpful Definitions

addend and sum:

addend →	5
addend →	+ 9
sum →	14

When there are three addends, it is helpful to use the "make a ten" strategy, when possible. For example, 2 + 8 = 10. When your child makes a ten, they can easily add the third number to the ten.

$$\begin{array}{r} {}^{1}\\ 12 \\ 8 \\ +16 \\ \hline 36 \end{array} \quad \begin{array}{l} 2 + 8 = 10 \\ 10 + 6 = 16 \end{array}$$

minuend, subtrahend, and difference:

minuend →	16
subtrahend →	− 9
difference →	7

Give your child chances to add and subtract basic numbers throughout the day. For example, ask: "What is the sum of the pages you read in the last three days?" or "What will be the difference if you give your brother 12 of your 18 stickers?"

regrouping: the process of rearranging groups in place value in order to add or subtract numbers

	Regroup 3 tens and 4 ones as 2 tens and 14 ones.	Subtract the ones.	Subtract the tens.	Subtract the hundreds.
534 − 218	5 ~~3~~2 ~~4~~14 − 218	5 ~~3~~2 ~~4~~14 − 218 = 6	5 ~~3~~2 ~~4~~14 − 218 = 16	5 ~~3~~2 ~~4~~14 (minuend) − 218 (subtrahend) = 316 (difference)

Draw models to help your child subtract the problem above. Dots can be used to represent ones, a line (or stick) to represent tens, a square to represent hundreds, and a cube to represent thousands (if needed). Since it is not possible to subtract 8 ones from 4 ones, 1 ten needs to be regrouped into 10 more ones. There are now 14 ones to subtract 8 ones from.

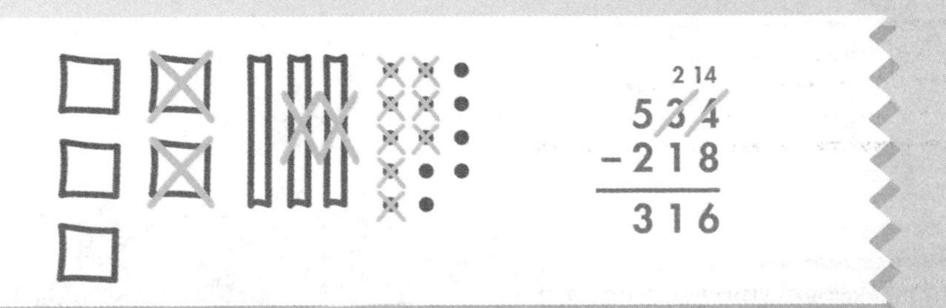

Adding Three Numbers

Chapter 1: Addition and Subtraction

Adding through 20

addend	3	→ Find the **3**-row.
addend	+ 8	→ Find the **8**-column.
sum	11	← The sum is named where the 3-row and the 8-column meet.

8-column

Addend

3-row

Addend

+	0	1	2	3	4	5	6	7	8	9
0	0	1	2	3	4	5	6	7	8	9
1	1	2	3	4	5	6	7	8	9	10
2	2	3	4	5	6	7	8	9	10	11
3	3	4	5	6	7	8	9	10	11	12
4	4	5	6	7	8	9	10	11	12	13
5	5	6	7	8	9	10	11	12	13	14
6	6	7	8	9	10	11	12	13	14	15
7	7	8	9	10	11	12	13	14	15	16
8	8	9	10	11	12	13	14	15	16	17
9	9	10	11	12	13	14	15	16	17	18

Add.

1. $2 + 3 = 5$
2. $7 + 9$
3. $2 + 5$
4. $1 + 7$
5. $0 + 3$
6. $9 + 5$
7. $7 + 2$
8. $3 + 3$
9. $9 + 0$
10. $6 + 5$
11. $0 + 7$
12. $8 + 5$
13. $4 + 3$
14. $2 + 9$
15. $7 + 7$
16. $5 + 6$
17. $5 + 9$
18. $0 + 6$
19. $0 + 0$
20. $8 + 3$
21. $8 + 6$
22. $6 + 1$
23. $5 + 3$
24. $4 + 8$

Chapter 1: Addition and Subtraction

Subtracting through 20

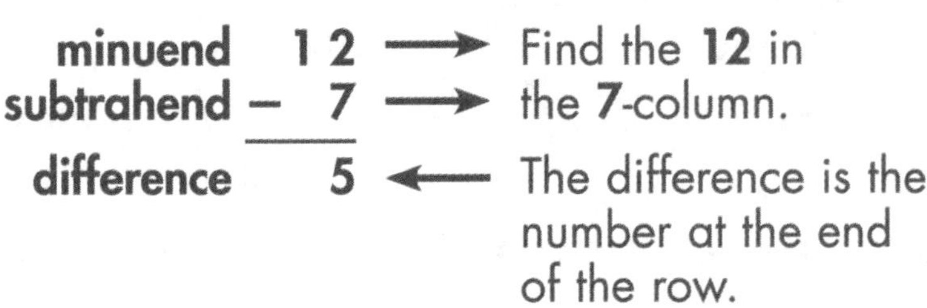

minuend 1 2 → Find the **12** in
subtrahend − 7 → the **7**-column.
difference 5 ← The difference is the number at the end of the row.

7-column

–	0	1	2	3	4	5	6	7	8	9
0	0	1	2	3	4	5	6	7	8	9
1	1	2	3	4	5	6	7	8	9	10
2	2	3	4	5	6	7	8	9	10	11
3	3	4	5	6	7	8	9	10	11	12
4	4	5	6	7	8	9	10	11	12	13
(5)	5	6	7	8	9	10	11	12	13	14
6	6	7	8	9	10	11	12	13	14	15
7	7	8	9	10	11	12	13	14	15	16
8	8	9	10	11	12	13	14	15	16	17
9	9	10	11	12	13	14	15	16	17	18

Subtract.

1. $7 - 2$ = 5 **2.** $6 - 0$ **3.** $5 - 4$ **4.** $11 - 6$ **5.** $16 - 9$ **6.** $13 - 8$

7. $6 - 3$ **8.** $9 - 6$ **9.** $5 - 2$ **10.** $8 - 0$ **11.** $18 - 9$ **12.** $9 - 7$

13. $7 - 2$ **14.** $3 - 0$ **15.** $8 - 2$ **16.** $7 - 4$ **17.** $10 - 3$ **18.** $9 - 2$

19. $14 - 3$ **20.** $3 - 2$ **21.** $19 - 3$ **22.** $13 - 5$ **23.** $13 - 8$ **24.** $17 - 4$

Chapter 1: Addition and Subtraction

Adding 2-Digit Numbers (no regrouping)

First, add the ones. Then, add the tens.

$$\begin{array}{r} 43 \\ +22 \\ \hline \end{array} \quad \begin{array}{r} 43 \\ +22 \\ \hline 5 \end{array} \quad \begin{array}{r} 43 \\ +22 \\ \hline 65 \end{array} \begin{array}{l} \text{addend} \\ \text{addend} \\ \text{sum} \end{array}$$

$$\begin{array}{r} 22 \\ +16 \\ \hline 38 \end{array} \begin{array}{l} \text{addend} \\ \text{addend} \\ \text{sum} \end{array}$$

First, add the ones.
Then, add the tens.

Add.

1. $\begin{array}{r} 23 \\ +16 \\ \hline 39 \end{array}$
2. $\begin{array}{r} 11 \\ +22 \\ \hline \end{array}$
3. $\begin{array}{r} 20 \\ +10 \\ \hline \end{array}$
4. $\begin{array}{r} 16 \\ +12 \\ \hline \end{array}$
5. $\begin{array}{r} 73 \\ +15 \\ \hline \end{array}$
6. $\begin{array}{r} 63 \\ +13 \\ \hline \end{array}$
7. $\begin{array}{r} 10 \\ +17 \\ \hline \end{array}$
8. $\begin{array}{r} 18 \\ +30 \\ \hline \end{array}$
9. $\begin{array}{r} 13 \\ +14 \\ \hline \end{array}$
10. $\begin{array}{r} 32 \\ +51 \\ \hline \end{array}$
11. $\begin{array}{r} 81 \\ +11 \\ \hline \end{array}$
12. $\begin{array}{r} 34 \\ +21 \\ \hline \end{array}$
13. $\begin{array}{r} 14 \\ +12 \\ \hline \end{array}$
14. $\begin{array}{r} 34 \\ +13 \\ \hline \end{array}$
15. $\begin{array}{r} 41 \\ +18 \\ \hline \end{array}$
16. $\begin{array}{r} 30 \\ +50 \\ \hline \end{array}$
17. $\begin{array}{r} 27 \\ +50 \\ \hline \end{array}$
18. $\begin{array}{r} 22 \\ +22 \\ \hline \end{array}$
19. $\begin{array}{r} 18 \\ +41 \\ \hline \end{array}$
20. $\begin{array}{r} 13 \\ +42 \\ \hline \end{array}$
21. $\begin{array}{r} 12 \\ +44 \\ \hline \end{array}$
22. $\begin{array}{r} 31 \\ +17 \\ \hline \end{array}$
23. $\begin{array}{r} 27 \\ +42 \\ \hline \end{array}$
24. $\begin{array}{r} 31 \\ +38 \\ \hline \end{array}$

Subtracting 2-Digit Numbers (no regrouping)

First, subtract the ones. Then, subtract the tens.

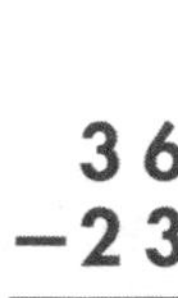

36	36	36	**minuend**
−23	−23	−23	**subtrahend**
	3	13	**difference**

Subtract.

1. 23 − 12 = 11
2. 86 − 22
3. 93 − 71
4. 30 − 10
5. 92 − 11
6. 48 − 16

7. 62 − 10
8. 83 − 13
9. 65 − 44
10. 54 − 12
11. 37 − 25
12. 88 − 32

13. 86 − 45
14. 92 − 70
15. 89 − 62
16. 75 − 62
17. 88 − 44
18. 90 − 60

19. 82 − 41
20. 57 − 36
21. 35 − 23
22. 65 − 43
23. 81 − 60
24. 42 − 30

Chapter 1: Addition and Subtraction

Adding 2-Digit Numbers (with regrouping)

Add the ones.
Regroup 12 as 10 + 2.

Add the tens.

$$\begin{array}{r} 37 \\ +25 \\ \hline \end{array} \qquad \begin{array}{r} 7 \\ +\ 5 \\ \hline 12 \end{array} \text{ or } 10 + 2 \qquad \begin{array}{r} {}^{1}\ \\ 37 \\ +25 \\ \hline 2 \end{array} \qquad \begin{array}{rl} {}^{1}\ & \\ 37 & \text{addend} \\ +25 & \text{addend} \\ \hline 62 & \text{sum} \end{array}$$

Add.

1. $\begin{array}{r} {}^{1}\ \\ 23 \\ +18 \\ \hline 41 \end{array}$	2. $\begin{array}{r} 76 \\ +15 \\ \hline \end{array}$	3. $\begin{array}{r} 13 \\ +77 \\ \hline \end{array}$	4. $\begin{array}{r} 36 \\ +16 \\ \hline \end{array}$	5. $\begin{array}{r} 19 \\ +62 \\ \hline \end{array}$	6. $\begin{array}{r} 29 \\ +19 \\ \hline \end{array}$
7. $\begin{array}{r} 27 \\ +36 \\ \hline \end{array}$	8. $\begin{array}{r} 52 \\ +39 \\ \hline \end{array}$	9. $\begin{array}{r} 36 \\ +28 \\ \hline \end{array}$	10. $\begin{array}{r} 30 \\ +50 \\ \hline \end{array}$	11. $\begin{array}{r} 56 \\ +27 \\ \hline \end{array}$	12. $\begin{array}{r} 59 \\ +13 \\ \hline \end{array}$
13. $\begin{array}{r} 54 \\ +27 \\ \hline \end{array}$	14. $\begin{array}{r} 53 \\ +28 \\ \hline \end{array}$	15. $\begin{array}{r} 28 \\ +17 \\ \hline \end{array}$	16. $\begin{array}{r} 13 \\ +19 \\ \hline \end{array}$	17. $\begin{array}{r} 39 \\ +17 \\ \hline \end{array}$	18. $\begin{array}{r} 56 \\ +14 \\ \hline \end{array}$
19. $\begin{array}{r} 62 \\ +19 \\ \hline \end{array}$	20. $\begin{array}{r} 27 \\ +18 \\ \hline \end{array}$	21. $\begin{array}{r} 26 \\ +55 \\ \hline \end{array}$	22. $\begin{array}{r} 18 \\ +13 \\ \hline \end{array}$	23. $\begin{array}{r} 72 \\ +18 \\ \hline \end{array}$	24. $\begin{array}{r} 37 \\ +17 \\ \hline \end{array}$

Chapter 1: Addition and Subtraction

Subtracting 2-Digit Numbers (with regrouping)

	Subtract the ones. Regroup 52 as "4 tens and 12 ones."	Subtract the ones.	Subtract the tens.	
	4 12	4 12	4 12	
52	~~5~~~~2~~	~~5~~~~2~~	~~5~~~~2~~	**minuend**
−19	−19	−19	−19	**subtrahend**
		3	33	**difference**

Subtract.

1. 2 10 ~~3~~~~0~~ −22 = 8	**2.** 22 −19	**3.** 53 −28	**4.** 41 −27	**5.** 92 −56	**6.** 86 −27
7. 83 −66	**8.** 62 −56	**9.** 51 −17	**10.** 34 −15	**11.** 46 −29	**12.** 57 −38
13. 72 −37	**14.** 82 −67	**15.** 64 −18	**16.** 86 −57	**17.** 41 −16	**18.** 53 −29
19. 24 −17	**20.** 60 −20	**21.** 86 −27	**22.** 93 −26	**23.** 52 −17	**24.** 47 −28

Chapter 1: Addition and Subtraction

Adding Three Numbers

Add the ones.

```
 23     3
 47     7  >10
+16    +6   + 6
            ---
            16 or 10 + 6
```

```
  1
 23
 47
+16
---
  6
```

Add the tens.

```
  1
 23   addend
 47   addend
+16   addend
---
 86   sum
```

Add.

1.	2.	3.	4.	5.	6.
13 + 26 + 45 = 84	7 + 29 + 56	16 + 23 + 25	27 + 7 + 34	6 + 13 + 29	10 + 30 + 50

7.	8.	9.	10.	11.	12.
22 + 31 + 45	19 + 21 + 32	29 + 16 + 15	13 + 15 + 25	42 + 21 + 8	26 + 23 + 35

13.	14.	15.	16.	17.	18.
11 + 30 + 42	27 + 16 + 9	4 + 7 + 8	34 + 16 + 41	16 + 23 + 35	29 + 31 + 25

19.	20.	21.	22.	23.	24.
82 + 5 + 9	33 + 47 + 12	86 + 5 + 2	18 + 32 + 16	46 + 29 + 16	53 + 21 + 15

Chapter 1: Addition and Subtraction

Adding 2-Digit Numbers

	Add the ones.	Add the tens.	
75 +66	1 75 +66 1 5 + 6 = 11	1 75 + 66 141	**addend** **addend** **sum**

Add.

1. 23 +95 118	**2.** 17 +86	**3.** 90 +50	**4.** 72 +46	**5.** 87 +23	**6.** 97 +65
7. 19 +75	**8.** 26 +93	**9.** 47 +58	**10.** 54 +59	**11.** 64 +94	**12.** 87 +27
13. 23 +79	**14.** 38 +81	**15.** 75 +86	**16.** 23 +92	**17.** 86 +41	**18.** 39 +82
19. 43 +71	**20.** 65 +39	**21.** 37 +82	**22.** 19 +83	**23.** 43 +62	**24.** 75 +95
25. 60 +40	**26.** 20 +87	**27.** 23 +97	**28.** 26 +85	**29.** 94 +45	**30.** 23 +63

Chapter 1: Addition and Subtraction

Subtracting 2 Digits from 3 Digits

	Subtract the ones.	To subtract the tens, regroup the 1 hundred and 2 tens as 12 tens.	Subtract the tens.	
125 − 84 ———	125 − 84 ——— 1	(12 over crossed-out 1 and 2) 125 − 84 ——— 1	(12 over crossed-out 1 and 2) 125 − 84 ——— 41	minuend subtrahend difference

Subtract.

1. 173 − 33 ——— 140	**2.** 121 − 60 ———	**3.** 195 − 44 ———	**4.** 122 − 11 ———	**5.** 147 − 53 ———	**6.** 182 − 90 ———
7. 143 − 62 ———	**8.** 180 − 70 ———	**9.** 119 − 15 ———	**10.** 123 − 12 ———	**11.** 186 − 65 ———	**12.** 187 − 42 ———
13. 154 − 13 ———	**14.** 127 − 83 ———	**15.** 187 − 67 ———	**16.** 135 − 42 ———	**17.** 115 − 24 ———	**18.** 171 − 60 ———
19. 132 − 51 ———	**20.** 177 − 43 ———	**21.** 192 − 71 ———	**22.** 186 − 92 ———	**23.** 134 − 72 ———	**24.** 125 − 45 ———

Chapter 1: Addition and Subtraction

Subtracting 2 Digits from 3 Digits

	Regroup 5 tens and 3 ones as 4 tens and 13 ones.	Subtract the ones.	Regroup 1 hundred and 4 tens as 14 tens.	Subtract the tens.	
153	4 13	4 13	14 13	14 13	
	1~~5~~~~3~~	1~~5~~~~3~~	~~1~~~~5~~~~3~~	1~~5~~~~3~~	**minuend**
− 65	− 65	− 65	− 65	− 65	**subtrahend**
		8	8	88	**difference**

Subtract.

1. 0 15 12 ~~1~~~~6~~~~2~~ − 73 = 89	**2.** 175 − 97	**3.** 182 − 94	**4.** 103 − 17	**5.** 116 − 39	**6.** 127 − 88
7. 174 − 95	**8.** 147 − 68	**9.** 132 − 65	**10.** 115 − 49	**11.** 107 − 39	**12.** 181 − 95
13. 101 − 75	**14.** 100 − 92	**15.** 127 − 79	**16.** 133 − 44	**17.** 142 − 73	**18.** 135 − 47
19. 141 − 63	**20.** 137 − 79	**21.** 142 − 73	**22.** 153 − 67	**23.** 155 − 96	**24.** 164 − 88

Chapter 1: Addition and Subtraction

Adding 3-Digit Numbers

	Add the ones.	Add the tens.	Add the hundreds.
755 +469	1 755 +469 4	1 1 755 +469 24	1 1 755 + 469 1,224

Add.

1. 123 +562 685	**2.** 982 +171	**3.** 342 +591	**4.** 782 +341	**5.** 123 +321	**6.** 681 +975
7. 862 +313	**8.** 900 +130	**9.** 720 +850	**10.** 931 +111	**11.** 823 +457	**12.** 547 +321
13. 861 +421	**14.** 862 +139	**15.** 431 +250	**16.** 782 +191	**17.** 751 +605	**18.** 871 +323
19. 791 +191	**20.** 144 +800	**21.** 192 +175	**22.** 257 +147	**23.** 203 +211	**24.** 541 +693

Chapter 1: Addition and Subtraction

Subtracting 3-Digit Numbers

Regroup 2 tens and 1 one as 1 ten and 11 ones. Then, subtract the ones.

Regroup 6 hundreds and 1 ten as 5 hundreds and 11 tens. Then, subtract the tens.

Subtract the hundreds.

$$\begin{array}{r} 621 \\ -259 \\ \hline \end{array} \qquad \begin{array}{r} {\scriptstyle 1\,11} \\ 6\not{2}\not{1} \\ -259 \\ \hline 2 \end{array} \qquad \begin{array}{r} {\scriptstyle 11} \\ {\scriptstyle 5\ \not{1}\,11} \\ \not{6}\not{2}\not{1} \\ -259 \\ \hline 62 \end{array} \qquad \begin{array}{r} {\scriptstyle 11} \\ {\scriptstyle 5\ \not{1}\,11} \\ \not{6}\not{2}\not{1} \\ -259 \\ \hline 362 \end{array} \begin{array}{l} \\ \\ \textbf{minuend} \\ \textbf{subtrahend} \\ \textbf{difference} \end{array}$$

Subtract.

1. $\begin{array}{r} {\scriptstyle 1\,11} \\ 3\not{2}\not{1} \\ -109 \\ \hline 212 \end{array}$	**2.** $\begin{array}{r} 745 \\ -152 \\ \hline \end{array}$	**3.** $\begin{array}{r} 639 \\ -150 \\ \hline \end{array}$	**4.** $\begin{array}{r} 830 \\ -710 \\ \hline \end{array}$	**5.** $\begin{array}{r} 626 \\ -146 \\ \hline \end{array}$	**6.** $\begin{array}{r} 457 \\ -309 \\ \hline \end{array}$
7. $\begin{array}{r} 729 \\ -321 \\ \hline \end{array}$	**8.** $\begin{array}{r} 657 \\ -451 \\ \hline \end{array}$	**9.** $\begin{array}{r} 386 \\ -107 \\ \hline \end{array}$	**10.** $\begin{array}{r} 411 \\ -305 \\ \hline \end{array}$	**11.** $\begin{array}{r} 486 \\ -109 \\ \hline \end{array}$	**12.** $\begin{array}{r} 311 \\ -121 \\ \hline \end{array}$
13. $\begin{array}{r} 983 \\ -652 \\ \hline \end{array}$	**14.** $\begin{array}{r} 971 \\ -572 \\ \hline \end{array}$	**15.** $\begin{array}{r} 876 \\ -357 \\ \hline \end{array}$	**16.** $\begin{array}{r} 549 \\ -360 \\ \hline \end{array}$	**17.** $\begin{array}{r} 721 \\ -144 \\ \hline \end{array}$	**18.** $\begin{array}{r} 958 \\ -637 \\ \hline \end{array}$
19. $\begin{array}{r} 256 \\ -142 \\ \hline \end{array}$	**20.** $\begin{array}{r} 347 \\ -139 \\ \hline \end{array}$	**21.** $\begin{array}{r} 725 \\ -196 \\ \hline \end{array}$	**22.** $\begin{array}{r} 863 \\ -692 \\ \hline \end{array}$	**23.** $\begin{array}{r} 980 \\ -532 \\ \hline \end{array}$	**24.** $\begin{array}{r} 720 \\ -500 \\ \hline \end{array}$

Chapter 1: Addition and Subtraction

Thinking Subtraction for Addition

To check
215 + 109 = 324,
subtract **109** from **324**.

$$\begin{array}{r} 215 \\ +109 \\ \hline 324 \\ -109 \\ \hline 215 \end{array}$$

These should be the same.

Add. Check each answer.

1. $\begin{array}{r} 157 \\ +212 \\ \hline 369 \\ -212 \\ \hline 157 \end{array}$

2. $\begin{array}{r} 719 \\ +182 \\ \hline \end{array}$

3. $\begin{array}{r} 312 \\ +105 \\ \hline \end{array}$

4. $\begin{array}{r} 213 \\ +519 \\ \hline \end{array}$

5. $\begin{array}{r} 306 \\ +215 \\ \hline \end{array}$

6. $\begin{array}{r} 120 \\ +170 \\ \hline \end{array}$

7. $\begin{array}{r} 710 \\ +398 \\ \hline \end{array}$

8. $\begin{array}{r} 357 \\ +249 \\ \hline \end{array}$

9. $\begin{array}{r} 712 \\ +363 \\ \hline \end{array}$

10. $\begin{array}{r} 714 \\ +291 \\ \hline \end{array}$

11. $\begin{array}{r} 312 \\ +\ 85 \\ \hline \end{array}$

12. $\begin{array}{r} 419 \\ +\ 57 \\ \hline \end{array}$

13. $\begin{array}{r} 300 \\ +547 \\ \hline \end{array}$

14. $\begin{array}{r} 591 \\ +120 \\ \hline \end{array}$

15. $\begin{array}{r} 612 \\ +319 \\ \hline \end{array}$

16. $\begin{array}{r} 425 \\ +125 \\ \hline \end{array}$

17. $\begin{array}{r} 411 \\ +120 \\ \hline \end{array}$

18. $\begin{array}{r} 247 \\ +259 \\ \hline \end{array}$

Chapter 1: Addition and Subtraction

Thinking Addition for Subtraction

To check
982 − 657 = 325,
add **657** to **325**.

$$\begin{array}{r} 982 \\ -657 \\ \hline 325 \\ +657 \\ \hline 982 \end{array}$$

These should be the same.

Subtract. Check each answer.

1. $\begin{array}{r} \overset{6}{\not7}\overset{12}{\not2}0 \\ -150 \\ \hline 570 \\ +150 \\ \hline 720 \end{array}$
2. $\begin{array}{r} 321 \\ -\ \ 83 \\ \hline \end{array}$
3. $\begin{array}{r} 125 \\ -\ \ 92 \\ \hline \end{array}$
4. $\begin{array}{r} 983 \\ -657 \\ \hline \end{array}$
5. $\begin{array}{r} 456 \\ -291 \\ \hline \end{array}$
6. $\begin{array}{r} 442 \\ -220 \\ \hline \end{array}$
7. $\begin{array}{r} 300 \\ -179 \\ \hline \end{array}$
8. $\begin{array}{r} 119 \\ -104 \\ \hline \end{array}$
9. $\begin{array}{r} 423 \\ -197 \\ \hline \end{array}$
10. $\begin{array}{r} 259 \\ -147 \\ \hline \end{array}$
11. $\begin{array}{r} 592 \\ -463 \\ \hline \end{array}$
12. $\begin{array}{r} 708 \\ -412 \\ \hline \end{array}$
13. $\begin{array}{r} 519 \\ -120 \\ \hline \end{array}$
14. $\begin{array}{r} 540 \\ -320 \\ \hline \end{array}$
15. $\begin{array}{r} 192 \\ -\ \ 86 \\ \hline \end{array}$
16. $\begin{array}{r} 710 \\ -447 \\ \hline \end{array}$
17. $\begin{array}{r} 683 \\ -419 \\ \hline \end{array}$
18. $\begin{array}{r} 712 \\ -307 \\ \hline \end{array}$

Chapter 1: Addition and Subtraction

Adding 3 or More Numbers (1- and 2-digit)

Add the ones.

Add the tens.

$$\begin{array}{r} 45 \\ 62 \\ +94 \\ \hline \end{array} \qquad \begin{array}{r} 5 \\ 2 \\ +4 \\ \hline \end{array} \quad \begin{array}{r} 7 \\ +\ 4 \\ \hline 11 \end{array} \text{ or } 10 + 1 \qquad \begin{array}{r} {}^{1} \\ 45 \\ 62 \\ +94 \\ \hline 1 \end{array} \qquad \begin{array}{r} {}^{1} \\ 45 \\ 62 \\ +\ 94 \\ \hline 201 \end{array}$$

Add.

1. 3, 6, +9 = 18	**2.** 7, 5, +8	**3.** 6, 12, +13	**4.** 8, 17, +19	**5.** 12, 32, +53	**6.** 8, 6, +2
7. 17, 93, +23	**8.** 16, 45, +92	**9.** 82, 18, +23	**10.** 7, 19, +57	**11.** 22, 86, +34	**12.** 50, 40, +60
13. 86, 93, +72	**14.** 23, 35, +62	**15.** 18, 35, +67	**16.** 86, 54, +83	**17.** 32, 49, +76	**18.** 13, 19, +23
19. 25, 66, +72	**20.** 81, 19, +83	**21.** 53, 42, +93	**22.** 13, 12, +14	**23.** 10, 20, +90	**24.** 82, 76, +54

Chapter 1: Addition and Subtraction

Adding 3 or More Numbers (3-digit)

	Add the ones.	Add the tens.	Add the hundreds.
231 457 +625	1 231 457 +625 3	1 1 231 457 +625 13	1 1 231 457 + 625 1,313

Add.

1. 1 1 522 367 +151 1,040	**2.** 868 321 +405	**3.** 150 200 +300	**4.** 701 231 +862	**5.** 986 105 +525	**6.** 129 318 +467
7. 803 623 +186	**8.** 545 309 +119	**9.** 868 740 +809	**10.** 132 195 +118	**11.** 200 300 +600	**12.** 180 240 +303
13. 861 757 +409	**14.** 863 404 +891	**15.** 731 356 +402	**16.** 865 591 +217	**17.** 238 405 +596	**18.** 898 777 +192
19. 341 127 +192	**20.** 864 425 +323	**21.** 127 291 +867	**22.** 205 876 +198	**23.** 712 490 +600	**24.** 750 400 +203

Problem Solving

Solve each problem.

SHOW YOUR WORK

1. Joe earned 135 dollars during his first week of work. He earned 213 dollars during his second week of work. He earned 159 dollars during his third week of work. How much money did Joe earn during the three weeks that he worked?

   Joe earned _____ dollars during his first week.

   Joe earned _____ dollars during his second week.

   Joe earned _____ dollars during his third week.

   Joe earned _____ dollars for all 3 weeks of work.

2. On the first floor of a 3-story apartment building, there are 186 apartments occupied. On the second floor, there are 175 apartments occupied. On the third floor, there are 182 apartments occupied. How many apartments are occupied in all?

   There are _____ apartments occupied on the first floor.

   There are _____ apartments occupied on the second floor.

   There are _____ apartments occupied on the third floor.

   There are _____ apartments occupied in all.

1.

2.

Chapter 1: Addition and Subtraction

Adding 4-Digit Numbers

	Add the ones.	Add the tens.	Add the hundreds.	Add the thousands.
3,746 +5,899	¹ 3,746 +5,899 5	¹ ¹ 3,746 +5,899 45	¹ ¹ ¹ 3,746 +5,899 645	¹ ¹ ¹ 3,746 +5,899 9,645

Add.

1. ¹ ¹ 7,865 +1,192 9,057	**2.** 8,654 +1,219	**3.** 4,320 +3,069	**4.** 3,543 +3,921	**5.** 4,293 +5,176
6. 6,405 +3,398	**7.** 1,982 +1,782	**8.** 7,083 +2,907	**9.** 4,325 +4,986	**10.** 6,057 +1,239
11. 8,761 +1,032	**12.** 2,305 +5,747	**13.** 3,050 +4,707	**14.** 6,932 +2,349	**15.** 5,437 +2,968
16. 1,718 +2,347	**17.** 7,923 +1,250	**18.** 4,523 +3,962	**19.** 5,431 +2,989	**20.** 7,986 +1,479
21. 1,119 +2,459	**22.** 7,239 +1,635	**23.** 2,450 +7,267	**24.** 6,527 +2,985	**25.** 5,431 +1,982

Chapter 1: Addition and Subtraction

Problem Solving

Solve each problem.

1. Two local high schools have 1,523 students and 1,695 students. How many students are there at both high schools together?

   One high school has ________ students.

   The other high school has ________ students.

   There are a total of ________ students at both high schools.

2. Monica started at an elevation of 1,200 feet for her hiking trip. She hiked up the mountain for 1,320 feet in elevation. How high did she hike?

   Monica started at ________ feet in elevation.

   She hiked ________ feet in elevation.

   She hiked up to an elevation of ________ feet.

3. Steve has a coin worth 1,050 dollars. He has another coin worth 1,072 dollars. How much are both coins worth?

   Both coins are worth ________ dollars.

SHOW YOUR WORK

1.

2.

3.

Subtracting to 4 Digits

	Subtract the ones.	Regroup 4 hundreds and 3 tens as 3 hundreds and 13 tens. Subtract the tens.	Regroup 5 thousands and 3 hundreds as 4 thousands and 13 hundreds. Subtract the hundreds.	Subtract the thousands.
5,437 −1,592	5,437 −1,592 5	3 13 5,~~4~~~~3~~7 −1,592 45	13 4 ~~3~~ 13 ~~5~~,~~4~~~~3~~7 −1,592 845	13 4 ~~3~~ 13 ~~5~~,~~4~~~~3~~7 −1,592 3,845

Subtract.

1. 7 16
9,~~8~~~~6~~5
−2,382
7,483
2. 7,528
− 792
3. 8,654
−3,993
4. 1,925
− 183
5. 1,876
− 982
6. 5,473
−3,591
7. 8,762
− 682
8. 7,945
− 963
9. 8,654
− 772
10. 7,846
−3,974
11. 6,932
−2,840
12. 1,389
− 794
13. 2,545
− 963
14. 7,863
−2,572
15. 8,121
− 640
16. 7,865
− 974
17. 3,456
− 661
18. 7,982
− 490
19. 8,163
−4,670
20. 4,325
−1,534

Chapter 1: Addition and Subtraction

Problem Solving

Solve each problem.

1. There are 2,532 students at the school. 1,341 are girls. How many are boys?

   There are ________ students.

   There are ________ girls.

   There are ________ boys.

2. In 2013, the average rent for a house was 1,250 dollars per month. In 1944, the average rent for a house was 495 dollars per month. How much higher was the rent in 2013 than in 1944?

   Rent in 2013 was ________ dollars per month.

   Rent in 1944 was ________ dollars per month.

   Rent in 2013 was ________ dollars per month higher than in 1944.

3. In the year 1986, Mrs. Olveras turned 103 years old. In what year was she born?

   In the year ________,

   Mrs. Olveras turned ________ years old.

   Mrs. Olveras was born in ________.

SHOW YOUR WORK

1.

2.

3.

Chapter 1: Addition and Subtraction

Rounding

The steps for rounding are:

1) Look at the digit one place to the right of the digit you wish to round.
2) If the digit is less than **5**, leave the digit in the rounding place as it is, and change the digits to the right of the rounding place to **zero**.
3) If the digit is **5** or greater, add **1** to the digit in the rounding place, and change the digits to the right of the rounding place to **zero**.

Round **5,432** to the nearest hundred. **4** is in the hundreds place. Look at the **3**. Do not change the **4**. **5,432** rounded to the nearest hundred is **5,400**.

Round each number to the nearest ten.

1. 963 960 **2.** 154 ________ **3.** 186 ________ **4.** 4,031 ________

5. 125 130 **6.** 3,452 ________ **7.** 8,657 ________ **8.** 7,987 ________

Round each number to the nearest hundred.

9. 8,765 ________ **10.** 986 ________ **11.** 3,250 ________ **12.** 7,913 ________

13. 507 ________ **14.** 1,349 ________ **15.** 842 ________ **16.** 4,370 ________

Round each number to the place named.

17. 8,576 hundreds ________ **18.** 1,930 hundreds ________ **19.** 364 tens ________ **20.** 1,543 tens ________

21. 1,886 hundreds ________ **22.** 765 tens ________ **23.** 863 hundreds ________ **24.** 86 tens ________

Chapter 1: Addition and Subtraction

Rounding

Round each number to the place named.

1. 543 tens ______

2. 867 hundreds ______

3. 479 tens ______

4. 962 tens ______

5. 5,678 hundreds ______

6. 9,654 tens ______

7. 4,432 hundreds ______

8. 1,605 tens ______

9. 592 hundreds ______

10. 86 tens ______

11. 5,432 hundreds ______

12. 981 tens ______

13. 4,932 tens ______

14. 9,651 hundreds ______

15. 596 hundreds ______

16. 720 hundreds ______

17. 1,081 hundreds ______

18. 7,090 tens ______

19. 7,446 tens ______

20. 1,143 tens ______

21. 4,599 tens ______

22. 3,923 hundreds ______

23. 5,103 tens ______

24. 638 hundreds ______

Chapter 1: Addition and Subtraction

Estimating Addition

Round each number to the highest place value the numbers have in common. Then, add from right to left.

194 + 76	→ 190 + 80 = 270	203 + 196	→ 200 + 200 = 400

$$\begin{array}{r} 194 \\ +\ 76 \\ \hline \end{array} \longrightarrow \begin{array}{r} 190 \\ +\ 80 \\ \hline 270 \end{array}$$

The highest place value for **194** and **76** is the tens place. Round **194** and **76** to the tens place. Add.

$$\begin{array}{r} 203 \\ +196 \\ \hline \end{array} \longrightarrow \begin{array}{r} 200 \\ +200 \\ \hline 400 \end{array}$$

The highest place value for **203** and **196** is the hundreds place. Round **203** and **196** to the hundreds place. Add.

Estimate each sum.

1. $\begin{array}{r} 25 \\ +36 \\ \hline \end{array}$ $\begin{array}{r} 30 \\ +40 \\ \hline 70 \end{array}$ **2.** $\begin{array}{r} 23 \\ +14 \\ \hline \end{array}$ **3.** $\begin{array}{r} 57 \\ +51 \\ \hline \end{array}$

4. $\begin{array}{r} 131 \\ +\ 42 \\ \hline \end{array}$ $\begin{array}{r} 130 \\ +\ 40 \\ \hline 170 \end{array}$ **5.** $\begin{array}{r} 165 \\ +\ 92 \\ \hline \end{array}$ **6.** $\begin{array}{r} 147 \\ +\ 97 \\ \hline \end{array}$

7. $\begin{array}{r} 147 \\ +362 \\ \hline \end{array}$ $\begin{array}{r} 100 \\ +400 \\ \hline 500 \end{array}$ **8.** $\begin{array}{r} 175 \\ +302 \\ \hline \end{array}$ **9.** $\begin{array}{r} 457 \\ +603 \\ \hline \end{array}$

10. $\begin{array}{r} 1{,}250 \\ +\ 347 \\ \hline \end{array}$ $\begin{array}{r} 1{,}300 \\ +\ 300 \\ \hline 1{,}600 \end{array}$ **11.** $\begin{array}{r} 5{,}786 \\ +\ 432 \\ \hline \end{array}$ **12.** $\begin{array}{r} 4{,}679 \\ +\ 578 \\ \hline \end{array}$

13. $\begin{array}{r} 1{,}562 \\ +3{,}492 \\ \hline \end{array}$ $\begin{array}{r} 2{,}000 \\ +3{,}000 \\ \hline 5{,}000 \end{array}$ **14.** $\begin{array}{r} 6{,}054 \\ +6{,}542 \\ \hline \end{array}$ **15.** $\begin{array}{r} 3{,}541 \\ +7{,}987 \\ \hline \end{array}$

Chapter 1: Addition and Subtraction

Problem Solving

Solve each problem by using estimation.

1. Kirima read 534 pages last week and 352 pages this week. About how many pages did Kirima read?

Kirima read about ________ pages.

2. Tim has 13 dollars. James has 15 dollars. About how many dollars do they have together?

Tim and James have about ________ dollars together.

3. Mr. Hwan had 532 dollars in his savings account before he made a deposit of 259 dollars. About how much money does he have in his savings account now?

Mr. Hwan has about ________ dollars in his savings account now.

SHOW YOUR WORK

1.

2.

3.

Chapter 1: Addition and Subtraction

Estimating Subtraction

Round each number to the highest place value the numbers have in common. Then, subtract from right to left.

236	→	240
− 49	→	− 50
		190

The highest place value for **236** and **49** is the tens place. Round **236** and **49** to the tens place. Subtract.

396	→	400
−287	→	−300
		100

The highest place value for **396** and **287** is the hundreds place. Round **396** and **287** to the hundreds place. Subtract.

Estimate each difference.

1. 56 − 43; 60 − 40 = 20

2. 49 − 12

3. 72 − 61

4. 986 − 59; 990 − 60 = 930

5. 760 − 32

6. 542 − 57

7. 543 − 290; 500 − 300 = 200

8. 943 − 457

9. 547 − 249

10. 3,247 − 843; 3,200 − 800 = 2,400

11. 4,560 − 493

12. 7,631 − 647

13. 8,798 − 4,453; 9,000 − 4,000 = 5,000

14. 9,476 − 2,652

15. 7,345 − 6,443

Chapter 1: Addition and Subtraction

Problem Solving

Solve each problem by using estimation.

1. Mateo had 39 dollars. He gave 23 dollars to Kim. About how much money does Fred have left?

   Mateo has about ________ dollars left.

2. There are 186 apartments in an apartment building. 92 are not rented. About how many apartments are rented?

   There are about ________ rented apartments.

3. Nora wants to buy a bicycle for 560 dollars. She has 430 dollars. About how much more money does she need to buy the bicycle?

   Nora needs about ________ more dollars to buy the bicycle.

4. At the theater, 98 adult tickets were sold. If 210 tickets were sold, about how many children's tickets were sold?

   About ________ children's tickets were sold.

SHOW YOUR WORK

1.

2.

3.

4.

Chapter 2: Multiplication

Understanding Multiplication Concepts

A building block toward learning multiplication is understanding repeated addition. Your child knows how to solve problems like 4 + 4 + 4 and 3 + 3 + 3 + 3. Help your child tie that knowledge to solving 4 × 3. All three ways of solving result in the answer 12. This conceptual knowledge is part of the foundation for learning multiplication facts.

Drawing simple pictures is a quick way to help your child understand multiplication concepts.

4 × 3 = 12

4 + 4 + 4 = 12 **3 + 3 + 3 + 3 = 12**

Then your child will be able to visualize the problems and eventually memorize the products. Once they have learned the basic multiplication facts, your child will be able to use multiplication in everyday life.

Skill Checklist

- ☐ **Understand multiplication facts as repeated addition**
- ☐ **Multiply numbers up to 9 × 9**
- ☐ **Multiply by multiples of 10**
- ☐ **Solve word problems using multiplication**

Chapter 2: Multiplication

Helpful Definitions

factors: numbers that are multiplied to get a product
For example, 2 and 5 are factors of 10.

2 × 5 = 10

product: the answer to a multiplication problem
For example, 24 is the product of 6 × 4.

factor	6
factor	× 4
product	24

Remind your child that multiplication is repeated addition.

6 × 4 is the same as 4 + 4 + 4 + 4 + 4 + 4 and 6 + 6 + 6 + 6.

Have your child draw pictures to solve multiplication facts. Another way to think of 6 x 4 is 6 groups of 4. Ask your child to draw a picture to show 6 groups of 4. The drawings do not need to be complex. Your child can simply draw circles or other shapes to show the problem.

Then they can count the total number of shapes to find the product.

multiples of 10: the product of numbers that are multiplied by 10, including 10, 20, 30, 40, 50, and so on

Help your child understand multiples of 10 by counting by tens. Point out that when they know the product of 2 × 3 = 6, your child can also solve 20 × 3 = 60. Help them understand that when multiplying by multiples of 10, they can "attach" a zero to the end of the product of the basic fact.

Video

Multiplication as Repeated Addition

Multiplying by Multiples of Ten

Chapter 2: Multiplication

Understanding Multiplication

two times seven

2 × 7 means 7 + 7

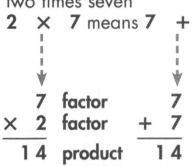

$$\begin{array}{rl} 7 & \text{factor} \\ \times\ 2 & \text{factor} \\ \hline 14 & \text{product} \end{array} \qquad \begin{array}{r} 7 \\ +\ 7 \\ \hline 14 \end{array}$$

five times three

5 × 3 means 5 + 5 + 5

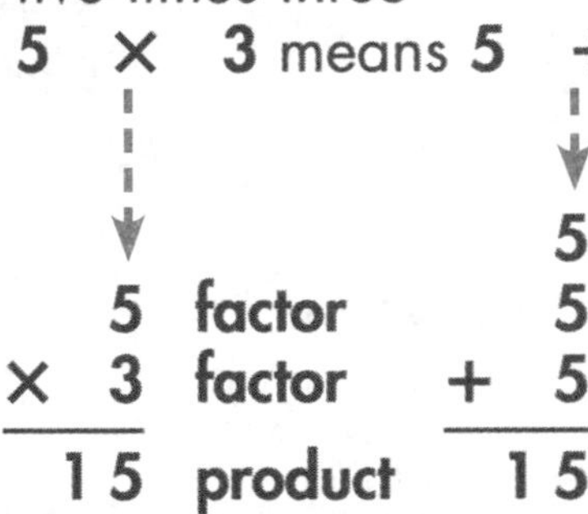

$$\begin{array}{rl} 5 & \text{factor} \\ \times\ 3 & \text{factor} \\ \hline 15 & \text{product} \end{array} \qquad \begin{array}{r} 5 \\ 5 \\ +\ 5 \\ \hline 15 \end{array}$$

Multiply. Write the corresponding addition problem next to each multiplication problem.

1. $\begin{array}{r} 3 \\ \times 2 \\ \hline 6 \end{array}$ $\begin{array}{r} 3 \\ +3 \\ \hline 6 \end{array}$
2. $\begin{array}{r} 7 \\ \times 2 \\ \hline \end{array}$
3. $\begin{array}{r} 6 \\ \times 2 \\ \hline \end{array}$
4. $\begin{array}{r} 9 \\ \times 2 \\ \hline \end{array}$
5. $\begin{array}{r} 8 \\ \times 2 \\ \hline \end{array}$
6. $\begin{array}{r} 2 \\ \times 2 \\ \hline \end{array}$
7. $\begin{array}{r} 1 \\ \times 2 \\ \hline \end{array}$
8. $\begin{array}{r} 5 \\ \times 3 \\ \hline \end{array}$
9. $\begin{array}{r} 6 \\ \times 3 \\ \hline \end{array}$
10. $\begin{array}{r} 3 \\ \times 3 \\ \hline \end{array}$
11. $\begin{array}{r} 2 \\ \times 3 \\ \hline \end{array}$
12. $\begin{array}{r} 1 \\ \times 3 \\ \hline \end{array}$
13. $\begin{array}{r} 4 \\ \times 3 \\ \hline \end{array}$
14. $\begin{array}{r} 7 \\ \times 3 \\ \hline \end{array}$
15. $\begin{array}{r} 2 \\ \times 4 \\ \hline \end{array}$
16. $\begin{array}{r} 4 \\ \times 4 \\ \hline \end{array}$
17. $\begin{array}{r} 1 \\ \times 4 \\ \hline \end{array}$
18. $\begin{array}{r} 5 \\ \times 4 \\ \hline \end{array}$
19. $\begin{array}{r} 9 \\ \times 4 \\ \hline \end{array}$
20. $\begin{array}{r} 8 \\ \times 4 \\ \hline \end{array}$
21. $\begin{array}{r} 3 \\ \times 4 \\ \hline \end{array}$
22. $\begin{array}{r} 4 \\ \times 2 \\ \hline \end{array}$
23. $\begin{array}{r} 5 \\ \times 2 \\ \hline \end{array}$
24. $\begin{array}{r} 8 \\ \times 3 \\ \hline \end{array}$
25. $\begin{array}{r} 9 \\ \times 3 \\ \hline \end{array}$

Chapter 2: Multiplication

Multiplying through 5 × 5

factor	3	→	Find the **3**-row.
factor	× 5	→	Find the **5**-column.
product	15	←	The product is named where the 3-row and the 5-column meet.

5-column ↓

3-row →

x	0	1	2	3	4	5
0	0	0	0	0	0	0
1	0	1	2	3	4	5
2	0	2	4	6	8	10
3	0	3	6	9	12	(15)
4	0	4	8	12	16	20
5	0	5	10	15	20	25

Multiply.

1. 2 ×5 = 10	**2.** 5 ×3	**3.** 1 ×3	**4.** 1 ×4	**5.** 3 ×4	**6.** 5 ×2
7. 0 ×5	**8.** 1 ×1	**9.** 3 ×5	**10.** 2 ×2	**11.** 0 ×3	**12.** 4 ×3
13. 4 ×4	**14.** 5 ×2	**15.** 4 ×5	**16.** 2 ×3	**17.** 5 ×5	**18.** 5 ×0
19. 4 ×2	**20.** 0 ×0	**21.** 3 ×3	**22.** 4 ×4	**23.** 3 ×2	**24.** 1 ×2
25. 0 ×2	**26.** 3 ×3	**27.** 2 ×4	**28.** 4 ×0	**29.** 3 ×2	**30.** 5 ×4

Chapter 2: Multiplication

Problem Solving

Solve each problem.

1. Ian has 4 bags. He puts 5 marbles in each bag. How many marbles are there in all?

   Ian________ has bags.

   Each bag has ________ marbles.

   There are ________ marbles in all.

2. Jennifer jumped over 3 rocks. She jumped over each rock 2 times. How many times did she jump in all?

   There are ________ rocks.

   Jennifer jumped over each rock

   ________times.

   She jumped ________ times in all.

Write a word problem to fit each number sentence. Solve.

3. $5 \times 1 =$ ________

4. $3 \times 4 =$ ________

SHOW YOUR WORK

1.

2.

3.

4.

Chapter 2: Multiplication

Multiplying through 5 × 9

factor	3	⟶	Find the **3**-row.
factor	× 7	⟶	Find the **7**-column.
product	21	⟵	The product is named where the 3-row and the 7-column meet.

7-column

3-row

×	0	1	2	3	4	5	6	7	8	9
0	0	0	0	0	0	0	0	0	0	0
1	0	1	2	3	4	5	6	7	8	9
2	0	2	4	6	8	10	12	14	16	18
3	0	3	6	9	12	15	18	(21)	24	27
4	0	4	8	12	16	20	24	28	32	36
5	0	5	10	15	20	25	30	35	40	45
6	0	6	12	18	24	30				
7	0	7	14	21	28	35				
8	0	8	16	24	32	40				
9	0	9	18	27	36	45				

Multiply.

1. $5 \times 0 = 0$

2. 3×9

3. 6×5

4. 1×4

5. 5×1

6. 6×3

7. 9×2

8. 8×5

9. 5×8

10. 0×0

11. 2×9

12. 3×4

13. 4×6

14. 7×3

15. 6×1

16. 7×2

17. 3×5

18. 4×1

19. 6×2

20. 5×5

21. 9×1

22. 2×4

23. 3×7

24. 7×0

25. 0×9

26. 3×6

27. 7×5

28. 5×6

29. 3×2

30. 4×2

Chapter 2: Multiplication

Multiplying through 9 × 9

factor 6 ⟶ Find the **6**-row.
factor × 8 ⟶ Find the **8**-column.
product 48 ⟵ The product is named where the 6-row and the 8-column meet.

8-column
6-row

×	0	1	2	3	4	5	6	7	8	9
0	0	0	0	0	0	0	0	0	0	0
1	0	1	2	3	4	5	6	7	8	9
2	0	2	4	6	8	10	12	14	16	18
3	0	3	6	9	12	15	18	21	24	27
4	0	4	8	12	16	20	24	28	32	36
5	0	5	10	15	20	25	30	35	40	45
6	0	6	12	18	24	30	36	42	48	54
7	0	7	14	21	28	35	42	49	56	63
8	0	8	16	24	32	40	48	56	64	72
9	0	9	18	27	36	45	54	63	72	81

Multiply.

1. 3 ×9 = 27
2. 7 ×6
3. 5 ×4
4. 7 ×9
5. 8 ×6
6. 5 ×0

7. 4 ×3
8. 8 ×5
9. 4 ×9
10. 3 ×0
11. 5 ×7
12. 2 ×9

13. 5 ×1
14. 4 ×6
15. 8 ×2
16. 6 ×8
17. 4 ×0
18. 0 ×9

19. 3 ×1
20. 6 ×4
21. 9 ×2
22. 3 ×4
23. 6 ×3
24. 5 ×6

25. 3 ×8
26. 3 ×6
27. 7 ×6
28. 9 ×9
29. 8 ×4
30. 5 ×3

Chapter 2: Multiplication

Problem Solving

Solve each problem.

1. Steven wants to buy 6 pieces of bubblegum. Each piece costs 5 cents. How much will he have to pay for the bubblegum?

Steven wants to buy ________ pieces of bubblegum.

One piece of bubblegum costs ________ cents.

Steven will have to pay ________ cents total.

2. There are 7 girls on stage. Each girl is holding 9 flowers. How many flowers are there in all?

There are ________ girls.

Each girl is holding ________ flowers.

There are ________ flowers in all.

Write a word problem to fit each number sentence. Solve.

3. $7 \times 5 =$ ________

4. $4 \times 9 =$ ________

SHOW YOUR WORK

1.

2.

3.

4.

Chapter 2: Multiplication

Multiplying by Multiples of 10

	Multiply **0** ones by **4**.	Multiply **7** tens by **4**.
$\begin{array}{r} 70 \\ \times\ 4 \\ \hline \end{array}$	$\begin{array}{r} 70 \\ \times\ 4 \\ \hline 0 \end{array}$	$\begin{array}{r} 70 \\ \times\ 4 \\ \hline 280 \end{array}$

Multiply.

1. $\begin{array}{r} 30 \\ \times\ 3 \\ \hline 90 \end{array}$
2. $\begin{array}{r} 20 \\ \times\ 1 \\ \hline \end{array}$
3. $\begin{array}{r} 10 \\ \times\ 9 \\ \hline \end{array}$
4. $\begin{array}{r} 60 \\ \times\ 4 \\ \hline \end{array}$
5. $\begin{array}{r} 80 \\ \times\ 2 \\ \hline \end{array}$
6. $\begin{array}{r} 70 \\ \times\ 7 \\ \hline \end{array}$
7. $\begin{array}{r} 40 \\ \times\ 5 \\ \hline \end{array}$
8. $\begin{array}{r} 50 \\ \times\ 8 \\ \hline \end{array}$
9. $\begin{array}{r} 90 \\ \times\ 6 \\ \hline \end{array}$
10. $\begin{array}{r} 40 \\ \times\ 2 \\ \hline \end{array}$
11. $\begin{array}{r} 80 \\ \times\ 5 \\ \hline \end{array}$
12. $\begin{array}{r} 60 \\ \times\ 8 \\ \hline \end{array}$
13. $\begin{array}{r} 90 \\ \times\ 2 \\ \hline \end{array}$
14. $\begin{array}{r} 10 \\ \times\ 5 \\ \hline \end{array}$
15. $\begin{array}{r} 20 \\ \times\ 7 \\ \hline \end{array}$
16. $\begin{array}{r} 50 \\ \times\ 3 \\ \hline \end{array}$
17. $\begin{array}{r} 70 \\ \times\ 3 \\ \hline \end{array}$
18. $\begin{array}{r} 30 \\ \times\ 5 \\ \hline \end{array}$
19. $\begin{array}{r} 20 \\ \times\ 4 \\ \hline \end{array}$
20. $\begin{array}{r} 10 \\ \times\ 3 \\ \hline \end{array}$
21. $\begin{array}{r} 90 \\ \times\ 4 \\ \hline \end{array}$
22. $\begin{array}{r} 70 \\ \times\ 9 \\ \hline \end{array}$
23. $\begin{array}{r} 60 \\ \times\ 2 \\ \hline \end{array}$
24. $\begin{array}{r} 50 \\ \times\ 5 \\ \hline \end{array}$

Chapter 2: Multiplication

Multiplying by Multiples of 10

Multiply.

1. $\begin{array}{r} 20 \\ \times\ 5 \\ \hline 100 \end{array}$ 2. $\begin{array}{r} 50 \\ \times\ 3 \\ \hline \end{array}$ 3. $\begin{array}{r} 10 \\ \times\ 3 \\ \hline \end{array}$ 4. $\begin{array}{r} 10 \\ \times\ 4 \\ \hline \end{array}$ 5. $\begin{array}{r} 30 \\ \times\ 4 \\ \hline \end{array}$ 6. $\begin{array}{r} 50 \\ \times\ 2 \\ \hline \end{array}$

7. $\begin{array}{r} 30 \\ \times\ 5 \\ \hline \end{array}$ 8. $\begin{array}{r} 10 \\ \times\ 4 \\ \hline \end{array}$ 9. $\begin{array}{r} 30 \\ \times\ 6 \\ \hline \end{array}$ 10. $\begin{array}{r} 20 \\ \times\ 2 \\ \hline \end{array}$ 11. $\begin{array}{r} 70 \\ \times\ 3 \\ \hline \end{array}$ 12. $\begin{array}{r} 40 \\ \times\ 3 \\ \hline \end{array}$

13. $\begin{array}{r} 40 \\ \times\ 4 \\ \hline \end{array}$ 14. $\begin{array}{r} 80 \\ \times\ 2 \\ \hline \end{array}$ 15. $\begin{array}{r} 40 \\ \times\ 6 \\ \hline \end{array}$ 16. $\begin{array}{r} 20 \\ \times\ 7 \\ \hline \end{array}$ 17. $\begin{array}{r} 50 \\ \times\ 6 \\ \hline \end{array}$ 18. $\begin{array}{r} 50 \\ \times\ 5 \\ \hline \end{array}$

19. $\begin{array}{r} 40 \\ \times\ 8 \\ \hline \end{array}$ 20. $\begin{array}{r} 90 \\ \times\ 0 \\ \hline \end{array}$ 21. $\begin{array}{r} 70 \\ \times\ 5 \\ \hline \end{array}$ 22. $\begin{array}{r} 40 \\ \times\ 9 \\ \hline \end{array}$ 23. $\begin{array}{r} 30 \\ \times\ 2 \\ \hline \end{array}$ 24. $\begin{array}{r} 10 \\ \times\ 8 \\ \hline \end{array}$

25. $\begin{array}{r} 70 \\ \times\ 2 \\ \hline \end{array}$ 26. $\begin{array}{r} 30 \\ \times\ 8 \\ \hline \end{array}$ 27. $\begin{array}{r} 20 \\ \times\ 9 \\ \hline \end{array}$ 28. $\begin{array}{r} 60 \\ \times\ 5 \\ \hline \end{array}$ 29. $\begin{array}{r} 80 \\ \times\ 6 \\ \hline \end{array}$ 30. $\begin{array}{r} 80 \\ \times\ 4 \\ \hline \end{array}$

Chapter 2: Multiplication

Problem Solving

Solve each problem.

1. Gary read 3 books with 60 pages each. How many pages did he read in all?

   There are ________ pages in each book.

   Gary read ________ books.

   Gary read ________ pages in all.

2. There are 4 classes at a school. Each class has 20 students. How many students are at the school?

   There are ________ students in each class.

   There are ________ classes.

   There are ________ students in the school.

3. Yolanda used up 4 rolls of stickers. If each roll has 30 stickers, how many stickers did she use in all?

   Each roll has ________ stickers.

   Yolanda used ________ rolls.

   Yolanda used a total of ________ stickers.

4. During a game, 2 teams play against each other. There are 10 players on the field for each team. How many players are on the field during the game?

   There are ________ players on the field.

SHOW YOUR WORK

1.

2.

3.

4.

Chapter 2: Multiplication

Problem Solving

Make a mental computation first. Then, solve the problem.

The PE teacher gave each team 6 basketballs and 6 tennis balls. If there were 5 teams, how many total balls did the PE teacher give out?

Each team gets 6 of each type of ball. I know that 6 times 5 is 30, so that is 30 basketballs and 30 tennis balls. Then, I can add the balls together, and 30 plus 30 is 60. So, there are 60 balls in all.

$$\begin{array}{r} 6 \\ \times\ 5 \\ \hline 30 \end{array} \qquad \begin{array}{r} 30 \\ +30 \\ \hline 60 \end{array}$$

Mental Computation: 60

Solve each problem.

1. Eight girls and 5 boys each have a button collection. Each girl has 8 buttons in her collection, and each boy has 4 buttons in his collection. How many buttons altogether do the boys and girls have?

   Mental Computation: ________

   The boys and girls have ________ buttons altogether.

2. There are 2 rows of 5 computers in each office. If there are 7 offices in the building, how many computers are in the building altogether?

   Mental Computation: ________

   There are ________ computers in the building.

SHOW YOUR WORK

1.

2.

Chapter 3: Division

The Relationship Between Multiplication and Division

Multiplication and division are inverse, or opposite functions in the same way that addition and subtraction are opposites. For example, if your child knows that 2 × 3 = 6, that will help them understand that 6 ÷ 3 = 2.

2 × 3 = 6  6 ÷ 3 = 2

Help your child understand how multiplication and division are related. For example, show them a multiplication problem using small items from your home. You can use cereal, small toys, or crayons. For 4 × 5 = 20, show your child 4 groups of items with 5 items in each group.

5  10 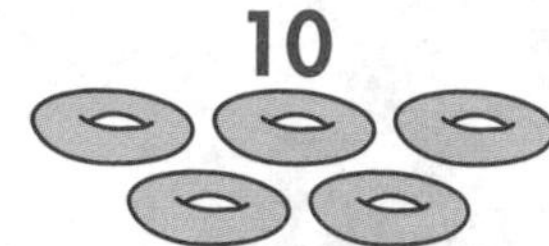 15 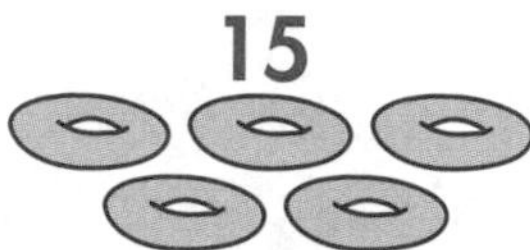 20 

Then relate the items to the problem 20 ÷ 5 = 4. For example, put the items back into a group of 20. Have your child divide the items into 5 groups. Help them to see there are 4 items in each group.

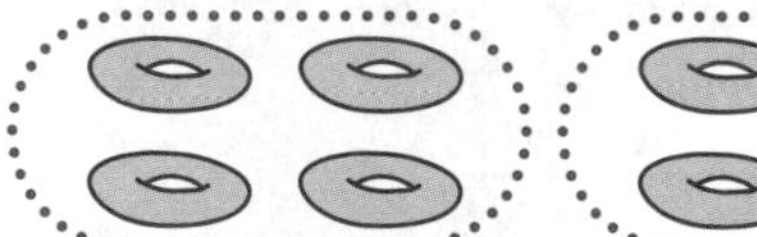 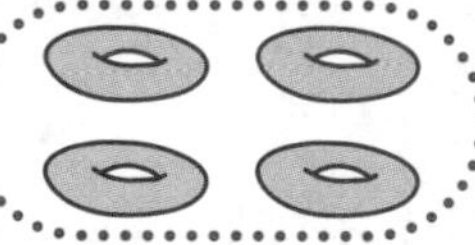 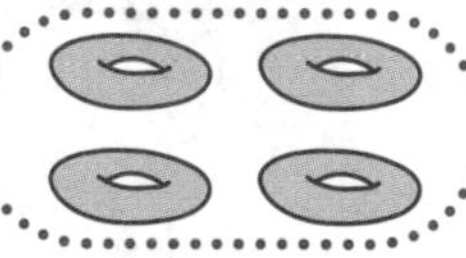 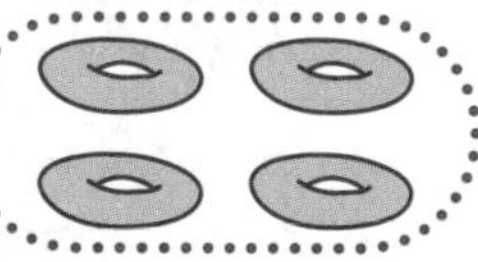 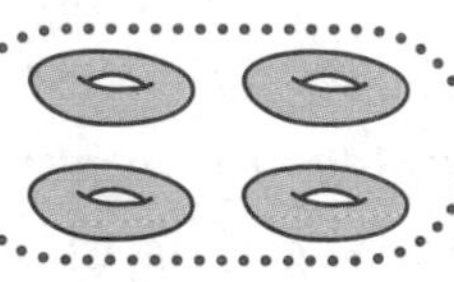

Using real items to show the problems will help your child have a clear understanding of multiplication facts and how they relate to division facts.

Skill Checklist

- ☐ **Understand the relationship between multiplication and division**
- ☐ **Divide numbers up to 81 ÷ 9**
- ☐ **Solve real-world problems using division facts**

Chapter 3: Division

Helpful Definitions

divisor, dividend, and quotient:

$$\begin{array}{r} 5 \leftarrow \text{quotient} \\ \text{divisor} \rightarrow 6\overline{)30} \leftarrow \text{dividend} \end{array}$$

$$30 \div 6 = 5$$

dividend ↗ divisor ↑ quotient ↖

Help your child understand that ÷ and $\overline{)\quad}$ mean the same thing by having them use both symbols. Write a multiplication fact, such as $5 \times 2 = 10$. Have your child write related division facts that go with the multiplication fact. Have them write the fact two ways, using each symbol: $10 \div 2 = 5$ and $2\overline{)10}$ with 5 above. Help your child understand that both equations are read "10 divided by 2 is equal to 5."

fact family:

Help your child understand the relationship between multiplication and division by having them use fact families.

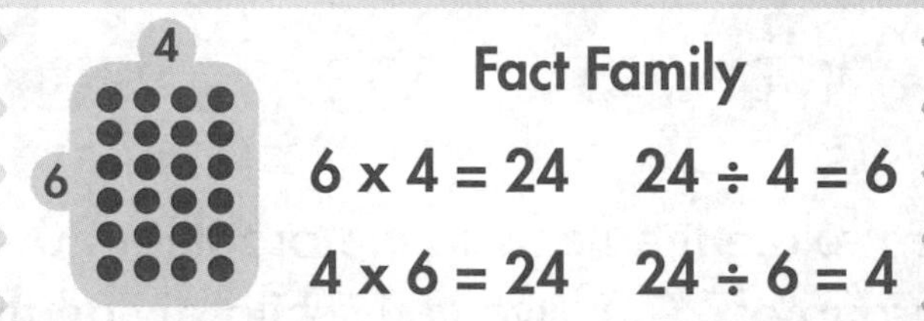

Help your child use a multiplication table to learn division facts. For example, point to the answer shown where the 9 and 5 meet on the chart: 45. Ask your child to tell or write a division fact that has 45 as the dividend. Show your child how to move their finger up the 9 column. Then ask them to determine the quotient of 45 ÷ 9.

Multiplication Table

	1	2	3	4	5	6	7	8	9
1	1	2	3	4	5	6	7	8	9
2	2	4	6	8	10	12	14	16	18
3	3	6	9	12	15	18	21	24	27
4	4	8	12	16	20	24	28	32	36
5	5	10	15	20	25	30	35	40	45
6	6	12	18	24	30	36	42	48	54
7	7	14	21	28	35	42	49	56	63
8	8	16	24	32	40	48	56	64	72
9	9	18	27	36	45	54	63	72	81

Video

Division and Multiplication

Solving Division Problems

Chapter 3: Division

Understanding Division

$\overline{)}$ means divide.

divisor → $3\overline{)18}$ ← dividend, with 6 ← quotient

$\begin{array}{r}6\\3\overline{)18}\end{array}$ is read "**18** divided by **3** is equal to **6**."

$\begin{array}{r}3\\4\overline{)12}\end{array}$ is read "**12** divided by **4** is equal to **3**."

In $\begin{array}{r}3\\4\overline{)12}\end{array}$, the divisor is **4**, the dividend is **12**, and the quotient is **3**.

÷ also means divide.

10 ÷ 2 = 5

dividend (10) **divisor** (2) **quotient** (5)

10 ÷ 2 = 5 is read "**10** divided by **2** is equal to **5**."

6 ÷ 3 = 2 is read "**6** divided by **3** is equal to **2**."

In **6 ÷ 3 = 2**, the divisor is **3**, the dividend is **6**, and the quotient is **2**.

Complete each sentence.

1. $\begin{array}{r}2\\6\overline{)12}\end{array}$ is read "12 divided by 6 is equal to 2."

2. $\begin{array}{r}3\\8\overline{)24}\end{array}$ is read "____ divided by 8 is equal to ____."

3. In $\begin{array}{r}2\\4\overline{)8}\end{array}$, the divisor is ____, the dividend is ____, and the quotient is ____.

4. In $\begin{array}{r}5\\7\overline{)35}\end{array}$, the divisor is ____, the dividend is ____, and the quotient is ____.

5. 20 ÷ 5 = 4 is read "____ divided by 5 is equal to ____."

6. 27 ÷ 9 = 3 is read "____ divided by 9 is equal to ____."

7. In 15 ÷ 3 = 5, the divisor is ____, the dividend is ____, and the quotient is ____.

8. In 14 ÷ 2 = 7, the divisor is ____, the dividend is ____, and the quotient is ____.

Chapter 3: Division

Understanding Division

8 △ in all.
4 △ in each group.
How many groups?

8 ÷ 4 = 2

There are **2** groups.

8 △ in all.
2 groups of △.
How many △ in each group?

8 ÷ 2 = 4

There are **4** in each group.

Check by multiplication: quotient × divisor = dividend.

2 × 4 = 8 **4 × 2 = 8**

Complete the following.

1. 12 □ in all.
   3 □ in each group.
   How many groups?
   12 ÷ 3 = 4
   There are 4 groups.
   Check: 4 × 3 = 12

2. 12 □ in all.
   4 groups of □.
   How many in each group?
   12 ÷ 4 = ______
   There are ______ □ in each group.
   Check: ______________

3. 20 As in all.
   ______ As in each group.
   How many groups?
   20 ÷ 4 = ______
   There are ______ groups.
   Check: ______________

   AAAA AAAA AAAA AAAA AAAA

4. 20 As in all.
   ______ groups of As.
   How many in each group?
   20 ÷ 5 = ______
   There are ______ As in each group.
   Check: ______________

5. ______ Fs in all.
   ______ Fs in each group.
   How many groups?
   12 ÷ 2 = ______
   There are ______ groups.
   Check: ______________

   FF FF FF FF FF FF

6. ______ Fs in all.
   ______ groups of Fs.
   How many in each group?
   12 ÷ 6 = ______
   There are ______ Fs in each group.
   Check: ______________

Chapter 3: Division

Dividing through 27 ÷ 3

$$\begin{array}{r} 5 \\ \times\ 3 \\ \hline 15 \end{array} \quad \rightarrow \quad 3\overline{)15}^{\,5}$$

If **3 × 5 = 15**, then **15 ÷ 3 = 5**.

$$\begin{array}{r} 6 \\ \times\ 2 \\ \hline 12 \end{array} \quad \rightarrow \quad 2\overline{)12}^{\,6}$$

If **2 × 6 = 12**, then **12 ÷ 2 = 6**.

Divide. Under each division problem, write the corresponding multiplication problem.

1. $3\overline{)6}$ (answer: 2; $3 \times 2 = 6$) **2.** $2\overline{)14}$ **3.** $1\overline{)5}$ **4.** $2\overline{)4}$ **5.** $1\overline{)4}$

6. $3\overline{)27}$ **7.** $1\overline{)3}$ **8.** $2\overline{)18}$ **9.** $1\overline{)7}$ **10.** $3\overline{)21}$

11. $3\overline{)12}$ **12.** $2\overline{)16}$ **13.** $1\overline{)5}$ **14.** $3\overline{)18}$ **15.** $2\overline{)10}$

16. $1\overline{)6}$ **17.** $1\overline{)8}$ **18.** $2\overline{)8}$ **19.** $1\overline{)2}$ **20.** $1\overline{)1}$

Chapter 3: Division

Dividing through 54 ÷ 6

$$\begin{array}{r} 5 \\ \times\ 4 \\ \hline 20 \end{array} \quad \rightarrow \quad 4\overline{)20} = 5$$

If **4 × 5 = 20**, then **20 ÷ 4 = 5**.

$$\begin{array}{r} 8 \\ \times\ 6 \\ \hline 48 \end{array} \quad \rightarrow \quad 6\overline{)48} = 8$$

If **6 × 8 = 48**, then **48 ÷ 6 = 8**.

Divide. Under each division problem write the corresponding multiplication problem.

1. $6\overline{)54}$ 9
6 × 9 = 54

2. $3\overline{)27}$

3. $6\overline{)48}$

4. $5\overline{)25}$

5. $4\overline{)36}$

6. $5\overline{)30}$

7. $4\overline{)24}$

8. $4\overline{)32}$

Divide.

9. $6\overline{)36}$

10. $4\overline{)28}$

11. $5\overline{)35}$

12. $6\overline{)24}$

13. $3\overline{)21}$

14. $5\overline{)45}$

15. $6\overline{)12}$

16. $5\overline{)40}$

17. $3\overline{)24}$

18. $6\overline{)18}$

19. $3\overline{)12}$

20. $2\overline{)16}$

21. $4\overline{)12}$

22. $2\overline{)18}$

23. $3\overline{)9}$

Chapter 3: Division

Problem Solving

Solve each problem.

1. There are 24 hours in a day. If the day is divided into 6 equal time segments, how many hours will be in each time segment?

   There are ________ hours.

   There are ________ time segments.

   There are ________ hours in each time segment.

2. There are 30 desks in the classroom. There are 6 desks in each row. How many rows of desks are there?

   There are ________ desks.

   There are ________ desks in each row.

   There are ________ rows of desks.

3. Mr. Villa handed out 42 papers to 6 students. Each student received the same number of papers. How many papers did each student receive?

   Mr. Villa handed out ________ papers.

   There are ________ students.

   Each student received ________ papers.

4. There are 12 months in a year. There are 4 seasons in a year. If each season has an equal number of months, how many months are in each season?

   There are ________ months in each season.

SHOW YOUR WORK

1.

2.

3.

4.

Chapter 3: Division

Dividing through 81 ÷ 9

$$\begin{array}{r} 6 \\ \times\ 9 \\ \hline 54 \end{array} \quad 9\overline{)54}\ \text{with quotient } 6$$

If **9 × 6 = 54**, then **54 ÷ 9 = 6**.

$$\begin{array}{r} 9 \\ \times\ 7 \\ \hline 63 \end{array} \quad 7\overline{)63}\ \text{with quotient } 9$$

If **7 × 9 = 63**, then **63 ÷ 7 = 9**.

Divide. Under each division problem write the corresponding multiplication problem.

1. $7\overline{)7}$ (answer: 1)
7 × 1 = 7

2. $6\overline{)24}$

3. $8\overline{)56}$

4. $6\overline{)30}$

5. $8\overline{)64}$

6. $6\overline{)12}$

7. $7\overline{)35}$

8. $8\overline{)24}$

Divide.

9. $9\overline{)63}$

10. $9\overline{)81}$

11. $7\overline{)56}$

12. $5\overline{)35}$

13. $8\overline{)24}$

14. $9\overline{)18}$

15. $7\overline{)14}$

16. $7\overline{)21}$

17. $8\overline{)48}$

18. $9\overline{)45}$

19. $7\overline{)49}$

20. $8\overline{)16}$

21. $9\overline{)27}$

22. $9\overline{)9}$

23. $7\overline{)42}$

Chapter 3: Division

Problem Solving

Solve each problem.

1. Spencer wants to save 72 dollars. How many weeks will it take Spencer to save 72 dollars if he saves 9 dollars each week?

Spencer wants to save ________ dollars.

He saves ________ dollars each week.

It will take Spencer ________ weeks to save 72 dollars.

2. Ms. Jefferson worked 40 hours this week. She worked 8 hours each day. How many days did she work this week?

Ms. Jefferson worked ________ hours this week.

She worked ________ hours each day.

She worked ________ days this week.

3. There are 16 football players on the field. If there are 8 players on each team, how many teams are on the field?

There are ________ football players on the field.

There are ________ players on each team.

There are ________ teams on the field.

4. Mrs. Daniels ordered 7 tables and 63 chairs for a banquet. Each table will have the same number of chairs. How many chairs will be at each table?

There will be ________ chairs at each table.

SHOW YOUR WORK

1.

2.

3.

4.

Chapter 3: Division

Division Practice

Divide.

1. $5\overline{)25}$	**2.** $4\overline{)16}$	**3.** $7\overline{)21}$	**4.** $9\overline{)81}$	**5.** $6\overline{)18}$
6. $6\overline{)54}$	**7.** $3\overline{)27}$	**8.** $9\overline{)72}$	**9.** $7\overline{)49}$	**10.** $5\overline{)5}$
11. $3\overline{)24}$	**12.** $4\overline{)28}$	**13.** $9\overline{)36}$	**14.** $2\overline{)14}$	**15.** $1\overline{)9}$
16. $3\overline{)6}$	**17.** $8\overline{)16}$	**18.** $7\overline{)35}$	**19.** $5\overline{)15}$	**20.** $3\overline{)9}$
21. $7\overline{)42}$	**22.** $9\overline{)45}$	**23.** $2\overline{)2}$	**24.** $7\overline{)63}$	**25.** $2\overline{)6}$
26. $5\overline{)20}$	**27.** $2\overline{)18}$	**28.** $8\overline{)32}$	**29.** $4\overline{)24}$	**30.** $8\overline{)72}$
31. $1\overline{)1}$	**32.** $8\overline{)64}$	**33.** $6\overline{)36}$	**34.** $5\overline{)45}$	**35.** $2\overline{)16}$

Chapter 3: Division

Division and Multiplication Practice

Divide or multiply.

1. $3\overline{)6}$ **2.** $9\overline{)18}$ **3.** $4\overline{)36}$ **4.** $6\overline{)54}$ **5.** $3\overline{)27}$ **6.** $2\overline{)4}$

7. $8\overline{)40}$ **8.** $3\overline{)18}$ **9.** $2\overline{)6}$ **10.** $3\overline{)9}$ **11.** $2\overline{)16}$ **12.** $5\overline{)20}$

13. $4\overline{)32}$ **14.** $9\overline{)27}$ **15.** $2\overline{)8}$ **16.** $1\overline{)7}$ **17.** $5\overline{)5}$ **18.** $9\overline{)54}$

19. 50×2 **20.** 30×2 **21.** 40×8 **22.** 20×1 **23.** 10×5 **24.** 90×3

25. 7×6 **26.** 60×5 **27.** 80×5 **28.** 30×3 **29.** 70×4 **30.** 40×2

31. 10×6 **32.** 10×7 **33.** 70×5 **34.** 60×8 **35.** 90×2 **36.** 9×2

Chapter 3: Division

Problem Solving

Make a mental computation first. Then, solve the problem.

In 4 days, Paige saw a total of 32 skydivers. In 4 more days she saw another total of 32 skydivers. If she saw the same number of skydivers each day, how many skydivers did Paige see in one day?

I know 30 plus 30 is 60, and 2 plus 2 is 4, so 32 plus 32 is 64. There are 8 total days, so I need to divide 64 by 8. I know 8 times 8 is 64, so 64 divided by 8 is 8.

$$\begin{array}{r} 32 \\ +32 \\ \hline 64 \end{array} \qquad \begin{array}{r} 4 \\ +4 \\ \hline 8 \end{array} \qquad 8\overline{)64}\ \text{= } 8$$

Mental Computation: 8

Solve each problem.

1. Emma has 50 photos in one box and 10 photos in another. She wants to put an equal number of photos on each of the 10 pages of her album. How many photos should Emma put on each page?

   Mental Computation: ________

   Emma should put ________ pictures on each page.

2. A group of 10 third graders are making cardboard penguins. Each student needs 1 cardboard tube, 2 wiggle eyes, and 1 piece of construction paper. How many items do all 10 third graders need?

   Mental Computation: ________

   All 10 third graders need ________ items for the penguin project.

SHOW YOUR WORK

1.

2.

Chapter 4: Fractions

Understanding Fractions

Fractions are a part of our daily lives. They can be used when your child shares half of their toys with a friend or gives their sibling an equal share of their stickers. Your child just may not yet realize they are working with fractions.

Fractions can be written to show part of a whole item, such as a graham cracker, or part of a set of items, such as a group of toys.

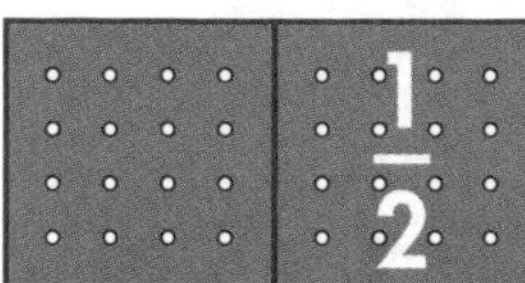

This piece is $\frac{1}{2}$ of the whole graham cracker.

This bear is $\frac{1}{4}$ of the set of bears.

Your child will use their knowledge of fractions to compare fractions. This means they will determine which fraction is greater or less than another fraction. They will also find equivalent, or equal, fractions. These fractions represent the same size but have different numerators and denominators.

Skill Checklist

- ☐ **Write fractions for parts of a whole and parts of a set**
- ☐ **Compare fractions using >, <, or =**
- ☐ **Use a number line to label fractions and find equivalent fractions**
- ☐ **Write fractions for whole numbers**

Chapter 4: Fractions

Helpful Definitions

numerator and denominator:

$\frac{1}{3}$ ⟵ numerator (part of the whole)
⟵ denominator (parts in all)

parts of a whole:

$\frac{3}{4}$ ⟵ parts shaded
⟵ parts in all

$\frac{3}{4}$ of the square is shaded.

parts of a set:

$\frac{1}{3}$ ⟵ part shaded
⟵ parts in all the set

equivalent fractions: fractions that have the same value but different numerators and denominators

$\frac{2}{4} = \frac{1}{2}$

Talk about why these fractions are equivalent. Explain that both fractions are the same size, even though the rectangle on the left is divided into four parts and the rectangle on the right is divided into two parts.

Help your child find equivalent fractions by drawing simple pictures like the models above, making sure the two shapes are the same size.

You can also use number lines to find equivalent fractions.

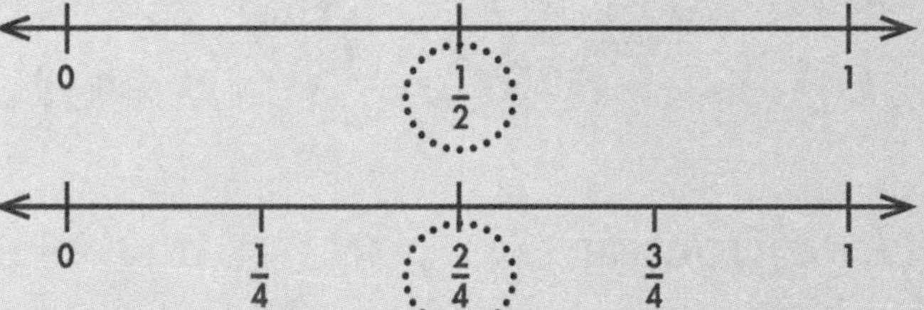

compare fractions:

>	<	=
greater than	less than	equal to

When using these symbols to compare fractions, remind your child that the bigger side of the symbol always points to the fraction with the greater value. The smaller side always points to the fraction that has less value.

Video

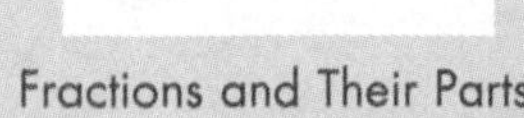

Fractions and Their Parts

Fractions on a Number Line

Chapter 4: Fractions

Parts of a Whole

A fraction is a number for part of a whole.

1 ⟵ **numerator** **(part of the whole)**
4 ⟵ **denominator** **(parts in all)**

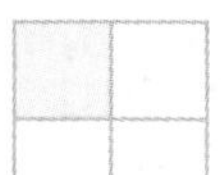

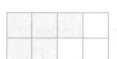

$\frac{1}{4}$ ⟵ **part shaded**, **parts in all**

$\frac{5}{8}$ ⟵ **parts shaded**, **parts in all**

$\frac{1}{4}$ of the square is shaded.

$\frac{5}{8}$ of the rectangle is shaded.

What fraction of each figure is shaded?

1. 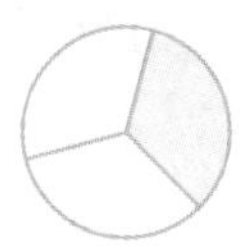 $\frac{1}{3}$

2.  ______

3. 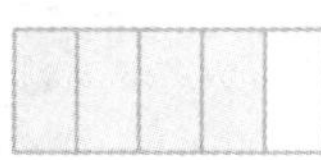 ______

4. 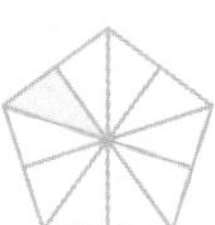 ______

5. 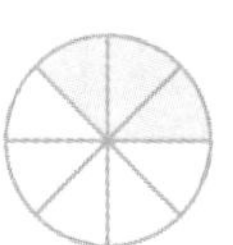 ______

6.  ______

7. 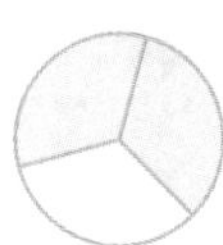 ______

8. 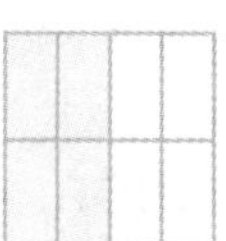 ______

9. 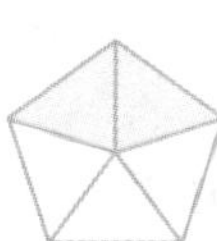 ______

10. 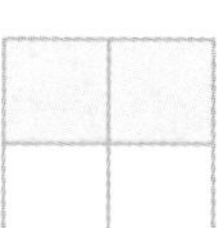 ______

11. 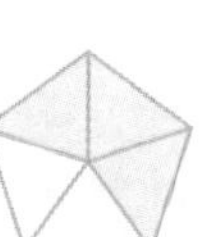 ______

12. 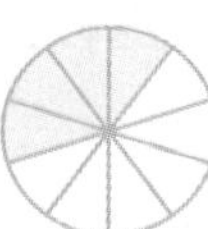 ______

Chapter 4: Fractions

Parts of a Set

A fraction is a number for part of a set.

1 ← **numerator** **(part of the set)**
2 ← **denominator** **(parts in all the set)**

$\frac{1}{2}$ ← **part shaded** / **parts in all the set**

$\frac{2}{3}$ ← **parts shaded** / **parts in all the set**

What fraction of each set is shaded?

1. $\frac{4}{5}$ ____________

2. ____________

3. ____________

4. ____________

5. ____________

6. ____________

Shade the number indicated by the fraction.

7. $\frac{4}{8}$

8. $\frac{3}{4}$

9. $\frac{3}{10}$

10. $\frac{1}{5}$

Chapter 4: Fractions

Comparing Fractions

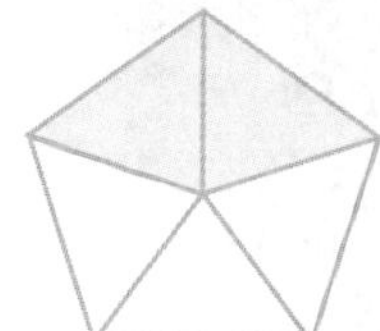 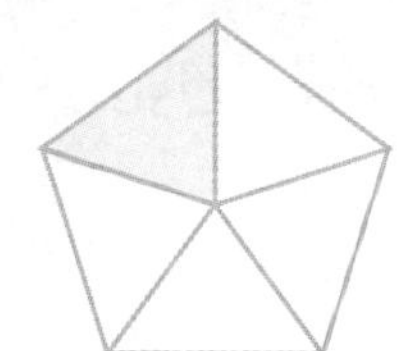

$\frac{2}{5} > \frac{1}{5}$

$\frac{2}{5}$ **is greater than** $\frac{1}{5}$**.**

$\frac{1}{3} < \frac{1}{2}$

$\frac{1}{3}$ **is less than** $\frac{1}{2}$**.**

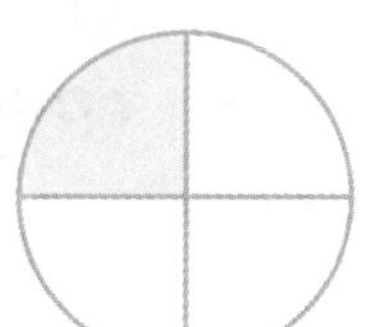 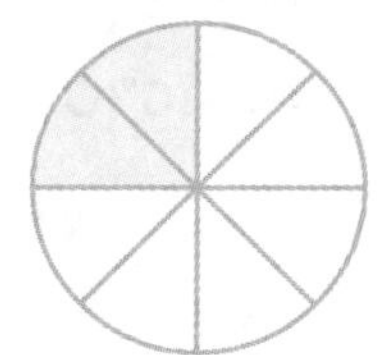

$\frac{1}{4} = \frac{2}{8}$

$\frac{1}{4}$ **is equal to** $\frac{2}{8}$**.**

Use >, <, or = to compare the fractions.

1. 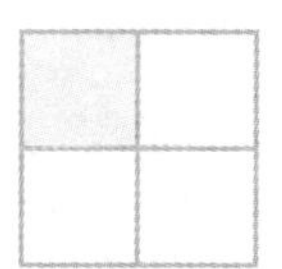 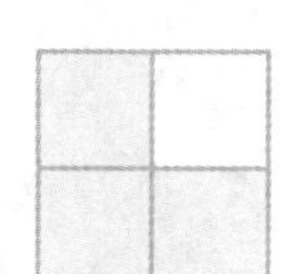

$\frac{1}{4}$ ($<$) $\frac{3}{4}$

2. 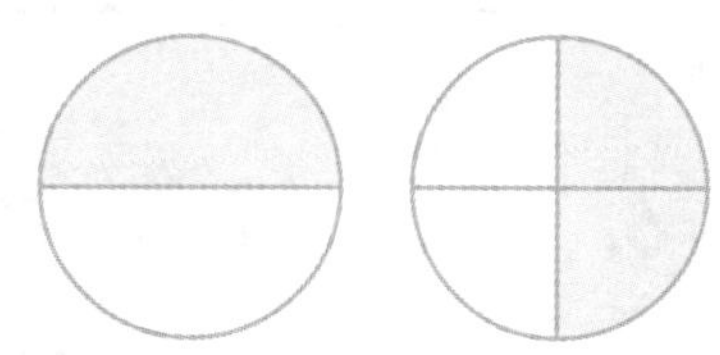

$\frac{1}{2}$ ◯ $\frac{2}{4}$

3.  

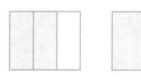

$\frac{2}{3}$ ◯ $\frac{1}{2}$

4. 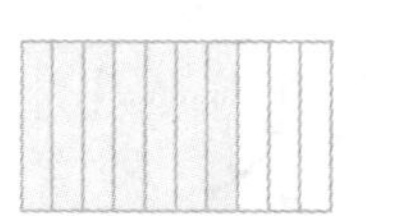 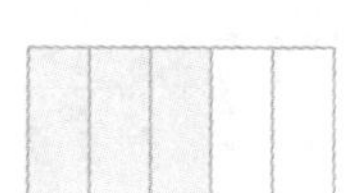

$\frac{7}{10}$ ◯ $\frac{3}{5}$

5. 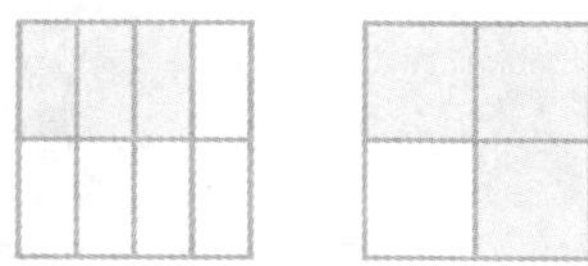

$\frac{3}{8}$ ◯ $\frac{3}{4}$

6. 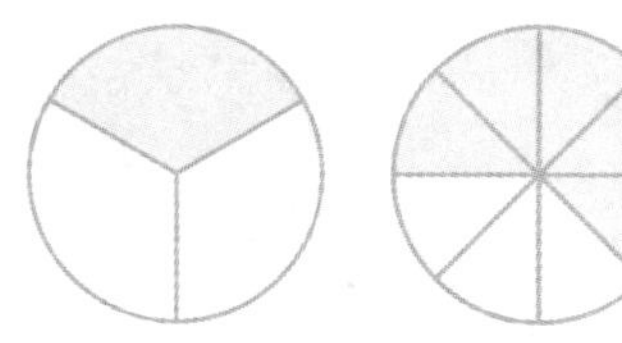

$\frac{1}{3}$ ◯ $\frac{5}{8}$

7. 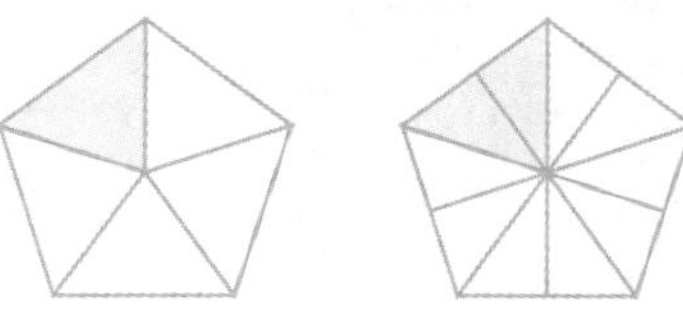

$\frac{1}{5}$ ◯ $\frac{2}{10}$

8. 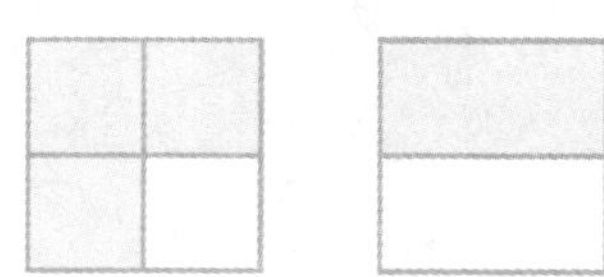

$\frac{3}{4}$ ◯ $\frac{1}{2}$

9. 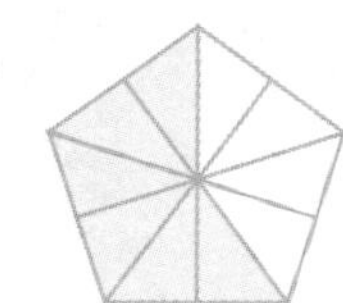 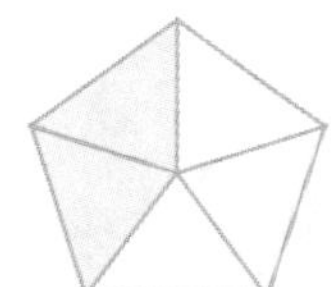

$\frac{6}{10}$ ◯ $\frac{2}{5}$

Chapter 4: Fractions

Comparing Fractions

What fraction of each figure is shaded? Compare the fractions. Use >, <, or =.

1.

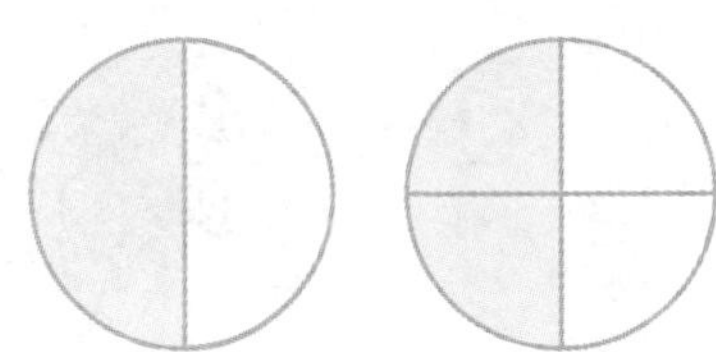

$\frac{1}{2}$ = $\frac{2}{4}$

2.

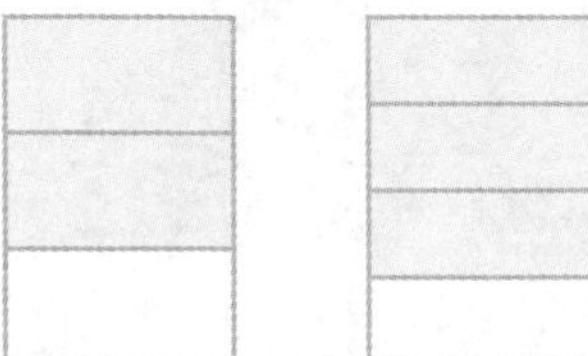

3.

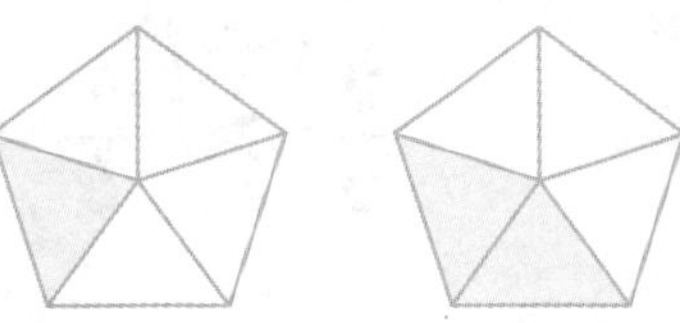

4.

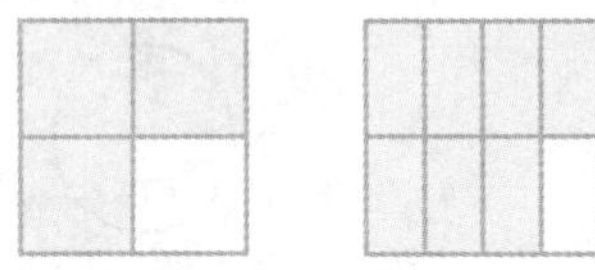

5.

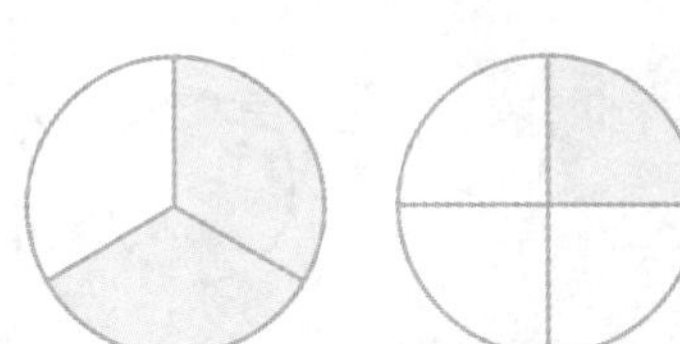

6.

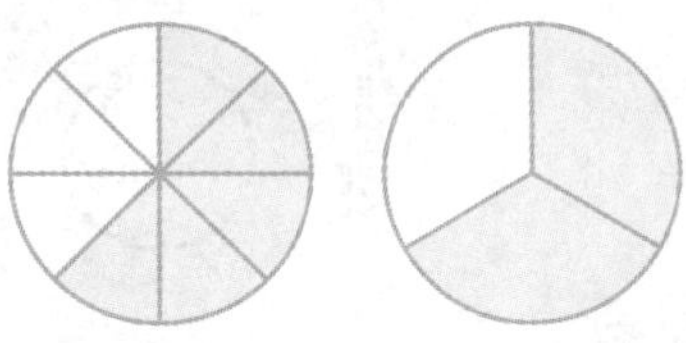

7.

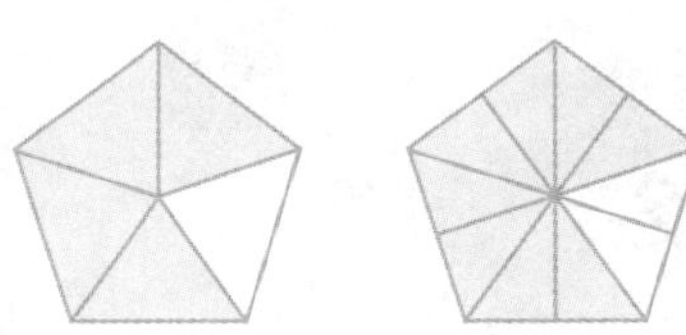

8.

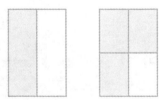

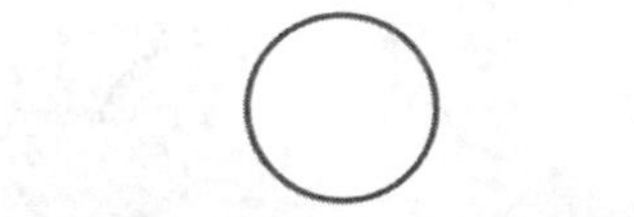

9.

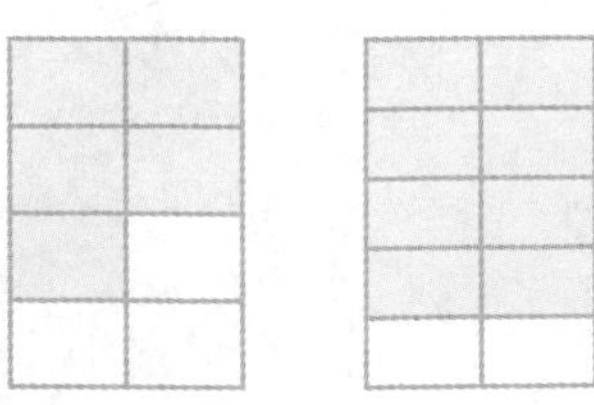

Chapter 4: Fractions

Fractions on a Number Line

Label $\frac{1}{8}$.

0 1

Steps
1. First, divide the number line into 8 equal parts (the denominator).
2. Next, count from zero the parts you need (the numerator).
3. Label the fraction.

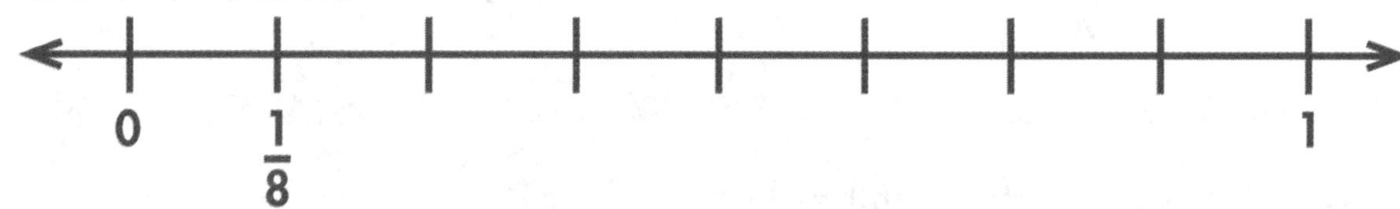

Label the fractions given.

1. $\frac{1}{4}$

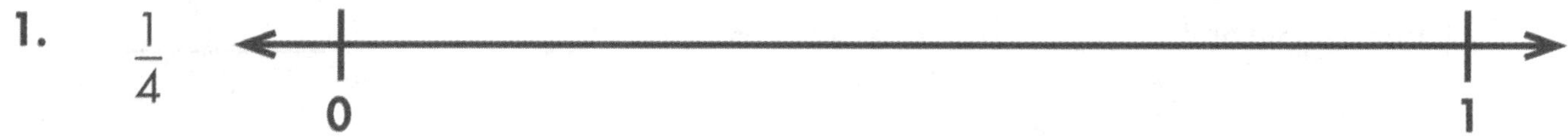

2. $\frac{1}{3}$

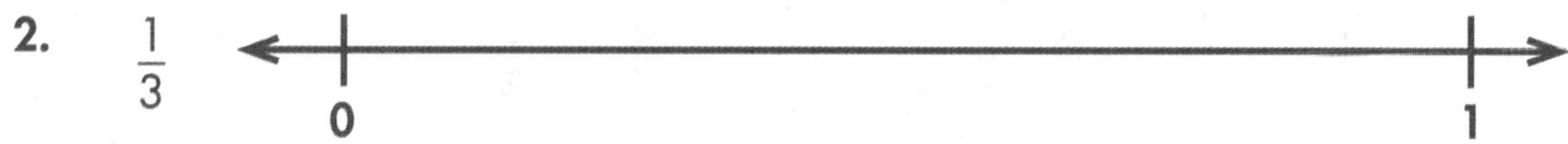

3. $\frac{2}{3}$

0 1

4. $\frac{4}{4}$

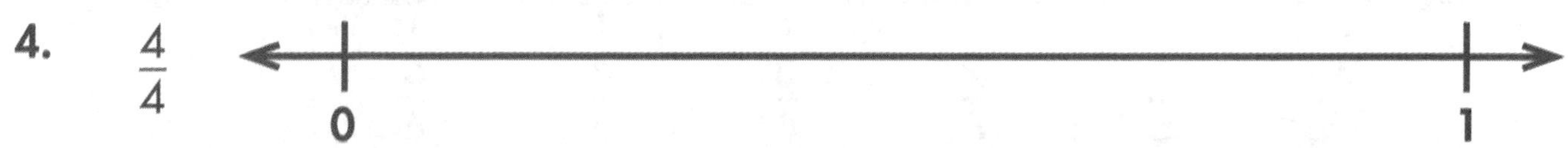

Chapter 4: Fractions

Equivalent Fractions on a Number Line

The fractions $\frac{2}{4}$ and $\frac{1}{2}$ are equivalent because they are at the same spot on the number line.

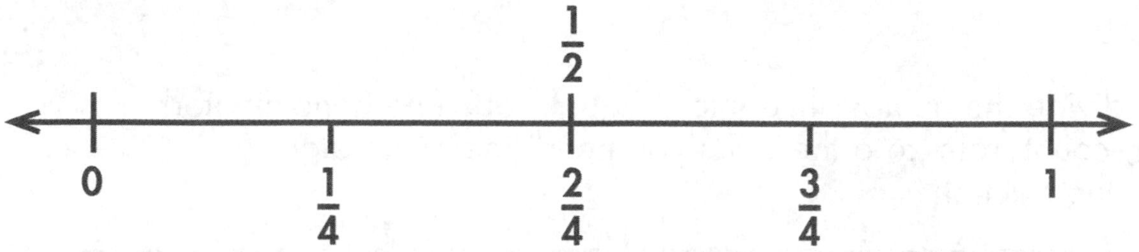

Answer the questions based on the number lines.

1. Are the fractions $\frac{1}{8}$ and $\frac{1}{4}$ equivalent? ________

Name 2 other fractions that are equivalent. ________ ________

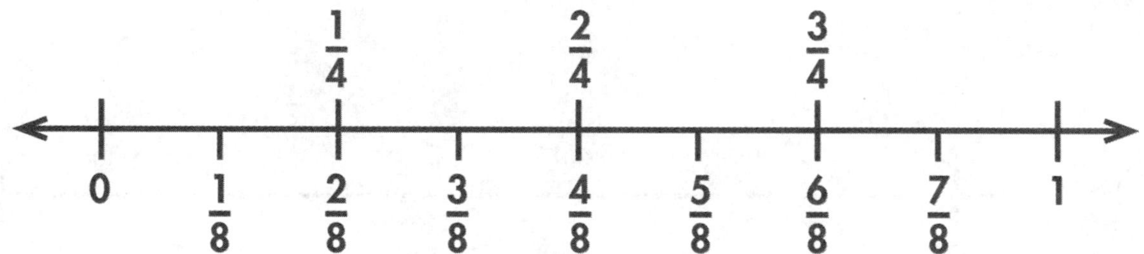

2. Are the fractions $\frac{1}{6}$ and $\frac{2}{3}$ equivalent? ________

Name 2 other fractions that are equivalent. ________ ________

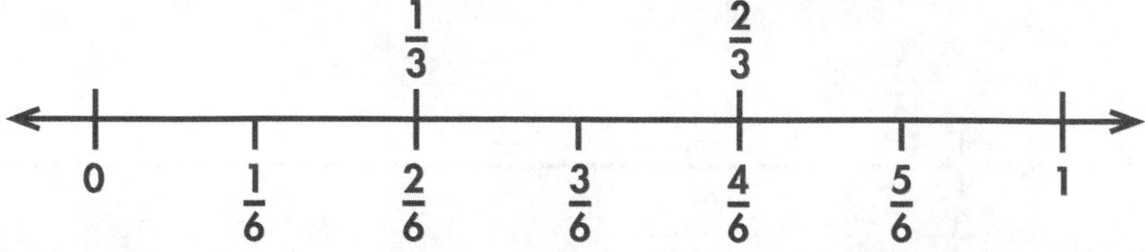

Chapter 4: Fractions

Whole Numbers as Fractions

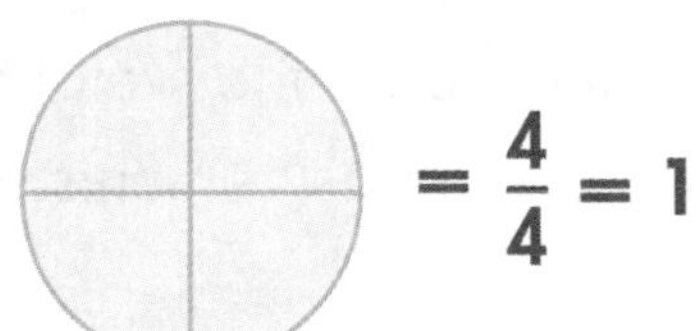

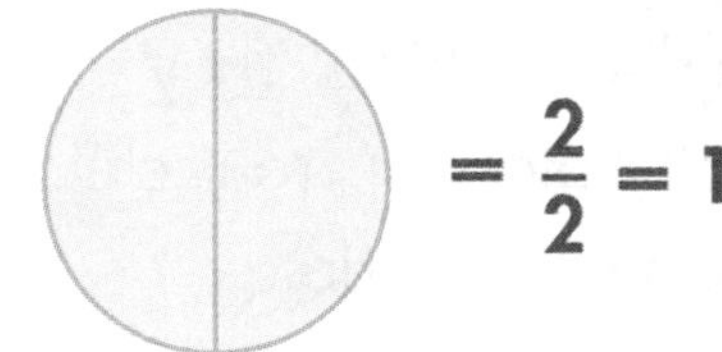

Complete the fractions.

1.  $= \frac{4}{4}$

2.  = ____

3.  = ____

4. 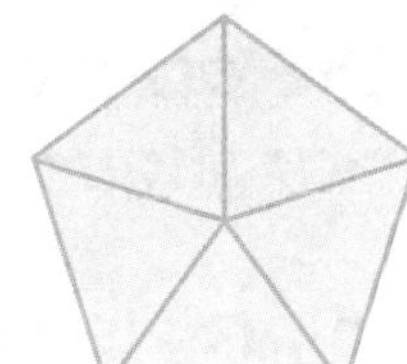 = ____

5.  = ____

6.  = ____

Chapter 5: Measurement

Measuring Objects and Organizing the Data

People measure items every day. Encourage your child to talk about times they have measured something. They may have measured the weight of their pet or the height of a flower they planted. Your child can record measurements over a period of time and create a graph to show the data.

Help your child measure an item and record the data. For example, they can track the height of a plant over the course of a week or more. They can use tally marks to record the height. Organizing the data will not only help your child clearly see the data, but it will also prepare them to create graphs to show the data. For example, they can create a line plot or bar graph to show how much the plant has grown.

Skill Checklist

- ☐ **Measure volume and mass of objects**
- ☐ **Use picture graphs, bar graphs, and line plots to record data**
- ☐ **Measure the area and perimeter of squares, rectangles, and irregular shapes**
- ☐ **Solve word problems related to measurement**

Helpful Definitions

volume: measurement of how much space an object or liquid takes up; liquid volume can be measured using quarts, gallons, and liters

mass: measurement of the weight of an object, in quantities such as ounces, pounds, grams, and kilograms

Chapter 5: Measurement

Helpful Definitions

Gram	Kilogram	Liter
A paper clip weighs about 1 gram.	A tablet weighs about 1 kilogram. 1 kilogram = 1,000 grams	A small jug of milk is about 1 liter.

Have your child measure two similar objects around your home. For example, have them measure the length of two pencils. Ask: "Which pencil is longer? How long is it?"

Then have your child measure a group of items and record the length of each item. They can use the data to make a line plot or graph.

Sample data:

Length of Objects				
5 in.	$5\frac{1}{2}$ in.	6 in.	$6\frac{1}{2}$ in.	7 in.
||	|||	||	|	||

line plot: a graph that shows data on a number line

Length of Objects

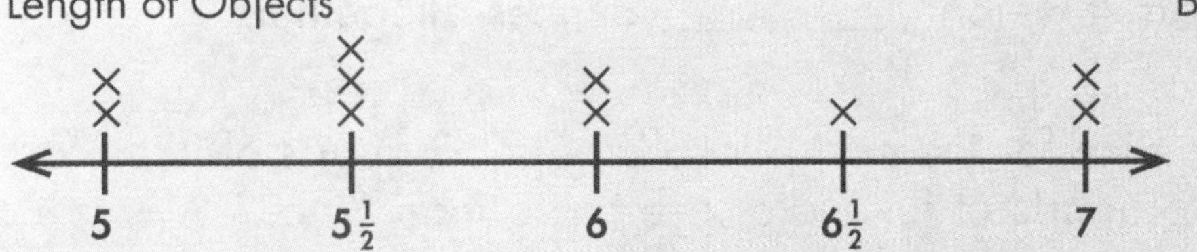

Bar Graph

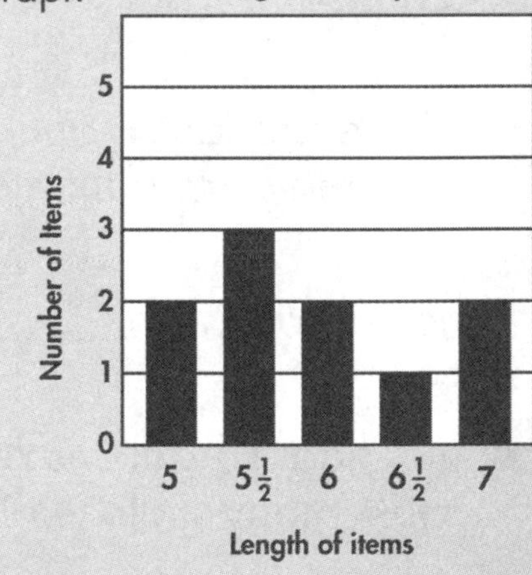

Help your child understand the data by asking questions. For example, "Which measurement was the most common? Which was the least common? How many [category on graph] are there in all?"

square unit: a unit used to measure the area of a shape

area: the amount of space a shape covers

To find the area of the rectangle, multiply the length by the width. This area is 6 inches times 3 inches. The area is 18 square inches.

Finding Area

Chapter 5: Measurement

Measuring Volume and Mass

Answer each question.

1. A refrigerator weighs about:	90 grams	90 kilograms	9 kilograms
2. A wading pool holds about:	500 grams	500 liters	5,000 liters
3. A small dog weighs about:	15 grams	50 grams	5,000 grams
4. A nail weighs about:	1 gram	10 grams	100 grams

Solve.

5. Emily's bag of fruit weighs 32 ounces. Jason's bag of fruit weighs 14 ounces. How many ounces do Emily and Jason's bags weigh altogether?

Emily and Jason's bags of fruit weigh __________ ounces altogether.

6. Vince brought 4 quarts of juice for the party. Jose brought 6 quarts of juice for the party. How many more quarts of juice did Jose bring than Vince?

Jose brought __________ more quarts of juice than Vince.

7. Jim had 18 gallons of paint to paint his entire house. He only used 11 gallons. How many gallons of paint does Jim have left?

Jim has __________ gallons of paint left.

8. Inez weighed 3 kilograms when she was born. Now she weighs 13 kilograms. How much weight did Inez gain since she was born?

Inez gained __________ kilograms since she was born.

Chapter 5: Measurement

Measuring Volume and Mass

Answer each question.

1. A bathtub can hold about:	6 liters	600 liters	6,000 liters
2. A butterfly weighs about:	100 grams	1 gram	10 grams
3. A water bottle can hold about:	1 liter	100 liters	1,000 liters
4. A chicken can weigh:	3 grams	30 grams	3,000 grams

Solve.

5. A carton contains 2 liters of juice. If there are 18 cartons of juice, how many liters of juice are there?

There are __________ liters of juice.

6. A saltshaker holds 5 grams of salt. If there are 20 saltshakers in the restaurant, how many grams of salt are in the restaurant?

There are __________ grams of salt in the restaurant.

7. Clarissa has 6 plants in her house. Each plant weighs 4 kilograms. How many kilograms do the plants weigh altogether?

Clarissa's plants weigh __________ kilograms altogether.

8. Danny caught a fish that was 15 pounds. Ashley caught a fish that was 20 pounds. How many more pounds does Ashley's fish weigh than Danny's fish?

Ashley's fish weighs __________ pounds more than Danny's fish.

Chapter 5: Measurement

Drawing Picture Graphs

A **picture graph** uses symbols to represent data.

The key tells you the value of each symbol on the picture graph.

Use the frequency table to complete the graph.

Students' Hair Color

Brown	웃 웃 웃 웃 웃 웃 웃
Black	웃 웃 웃 웃 웃
Blonde	웃 웃 웃 웃 웃 (half)
Red	웃 (half)

Key: 웃 = 2 students

Frequency Table

Brown	𝍸 𝍸 IIII
Black	𝍸 𝍸
Blonde	𝍸 𝍸 I
Red	III

How many students have red hair?

Each stick figure represents two students.

Count by twos when counting the stick figures in the row labeled "red." Add 1 to the sum for the half stick figure.

3 students have red hair.

Complete the picture graph. Answer the question.

Flowers In My Garden

Key: ✿ = 2 flowers

Frequency Table

Daisies	𝍸 III
Roses	𝍸
Sunflowers	II

How many total flowers are in the garden? ______

Chapter 5: Measurement

Drawing Bar Graphs

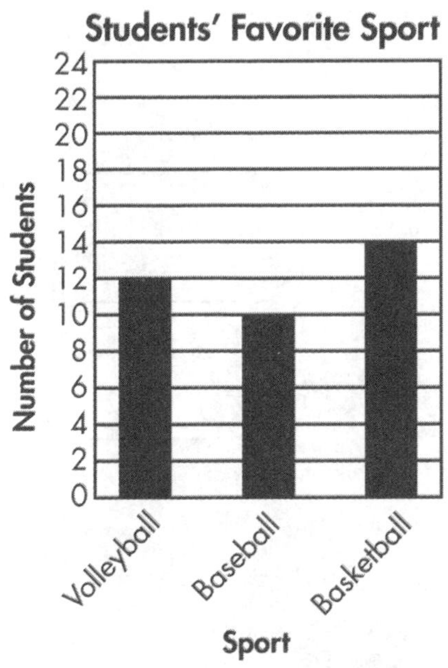

A **bar graph** uses rectangular bars to represent data.

Use the frequency table to complete the graph.

Frequency Table

Volleyball	12
Baseball	10
Basketball	14

How many students chose baseball as their favorite sport?

Find the bar labeled baseball.

Follow the top of the bar to the scale at the left.

This value represents the number of students whose favorite sport is baseball.

__10__ students chose baseball as their favorite sport.

Complete the bar graph. Answer the question.

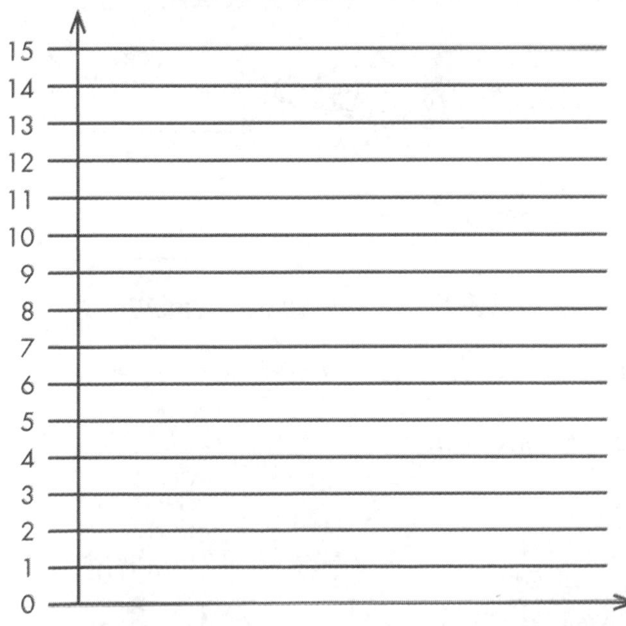

Frequency Table

Abbie	10
Brady	15
Denise	6

How many more candles did Brady sell than Denise? ________

Chapter 5: Measurement

Gathering Data to Draw a Line Plot

Use a ruler to measure the length of each object.

1. 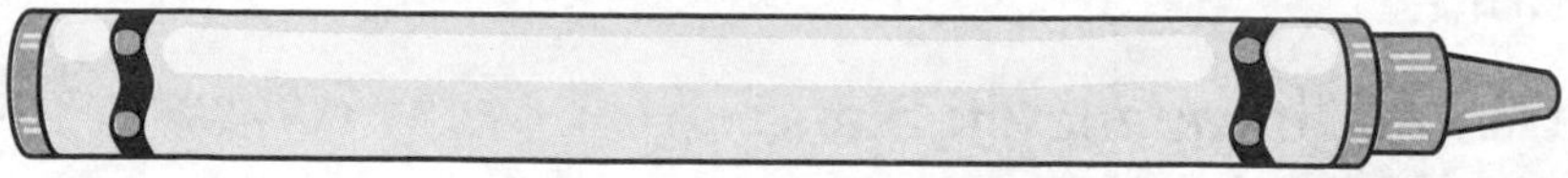 $4\frac{1}{4}$ in.
2. 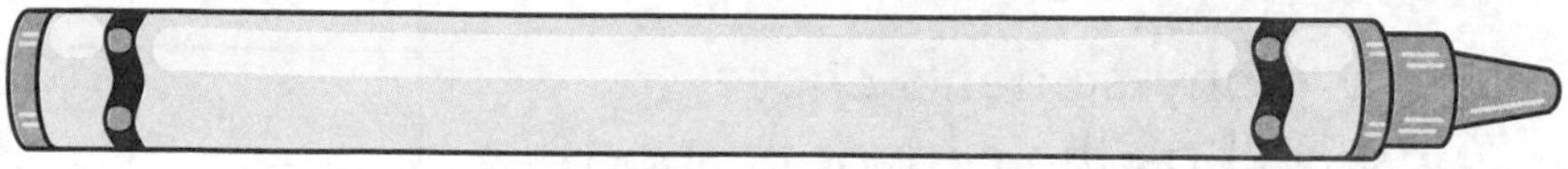 ______ in.
3. 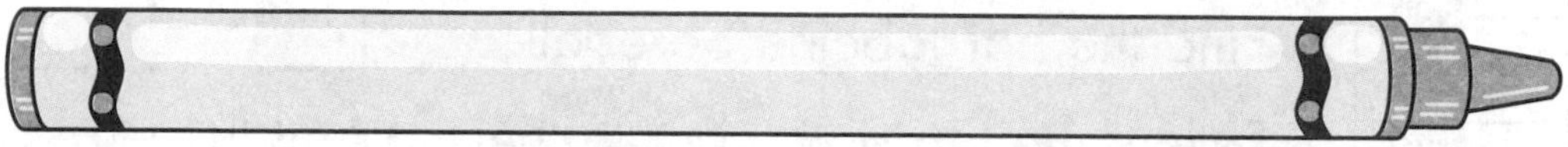 ______ in.
4. 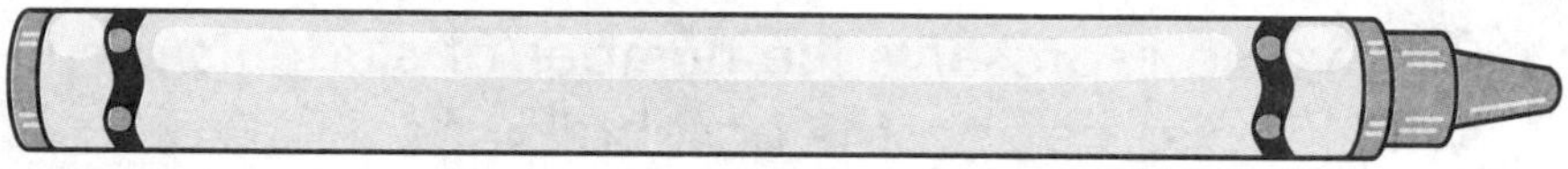 ______ in.
5. 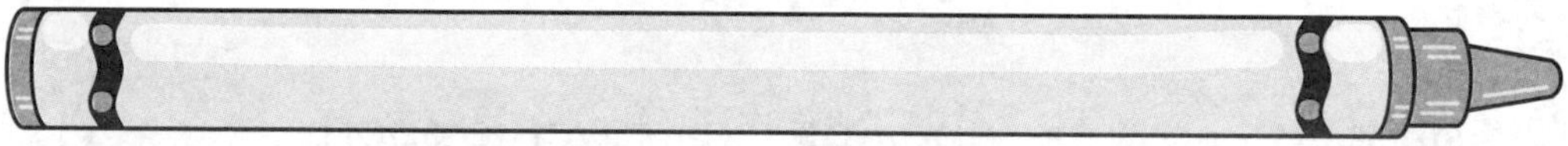 ______ in.
6. 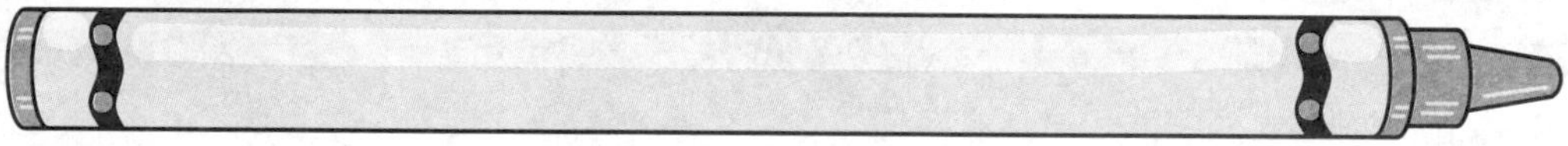 ______ in.
7. 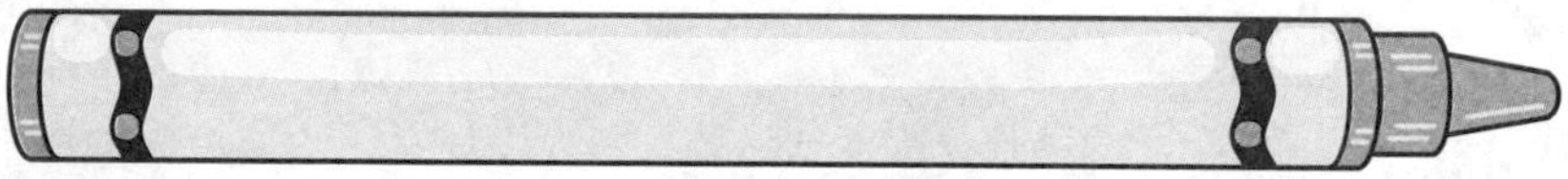 ______ in.
8. 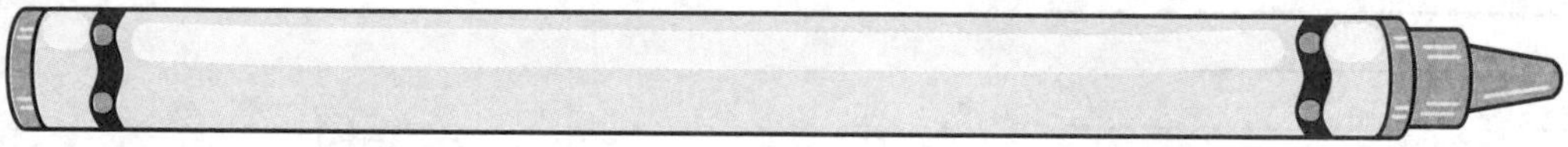 ______ in.
9. 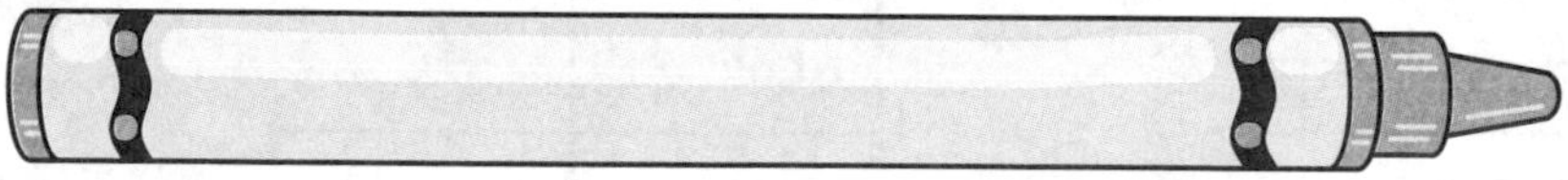 ______ in.

Use the information above to fill in the line plot.

10. **Crayons Used in the Classroom**

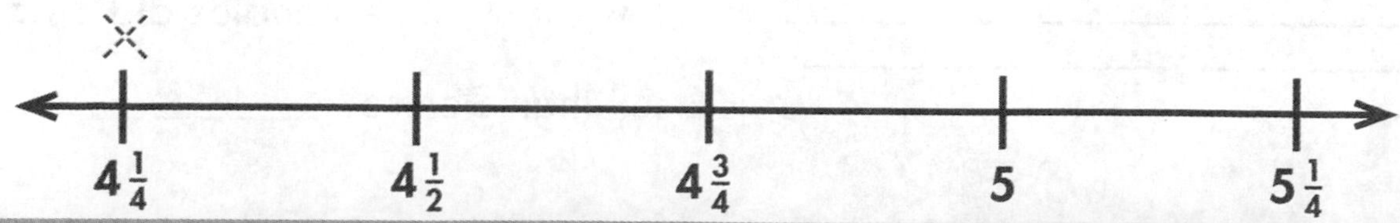

Chapter 5: Measurement

Gathering Data to Draw a Line Plot

Use a ruler to measure the length of each object.

1. $2\frac{1}{2}$ in.

2. ________ in.

4.

________ in.

3.

________ in.

5. ________ in.

6. ________ in.

7.

________ in.

Use the information above to fill in the line plot.

8. **Fish in the Pond**

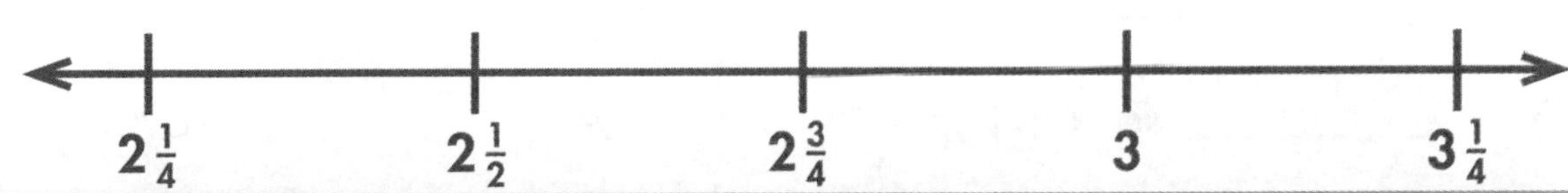

Chapter 5: Measurement

Finding Area with Unit Squares

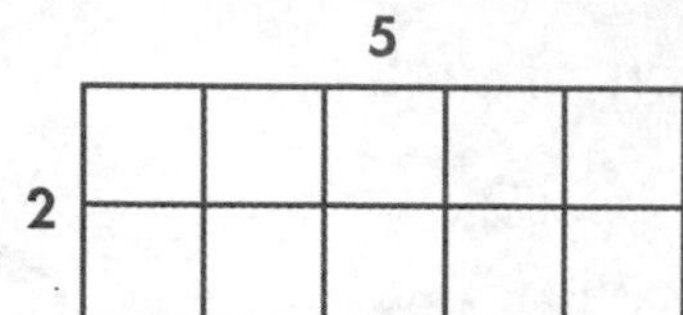

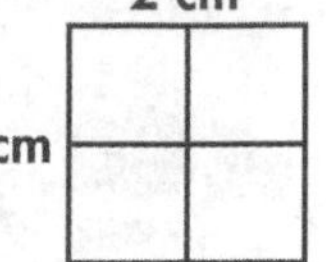

A = 1 square unit **A =** 10 **sq. units** **A =** 4 **sq. cm**

Find the area.

1.

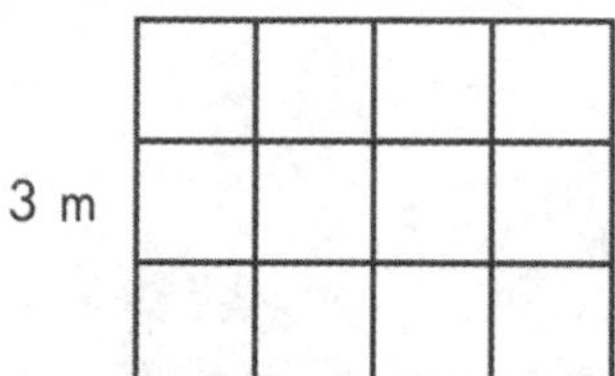

A = __________ sq. m

2.

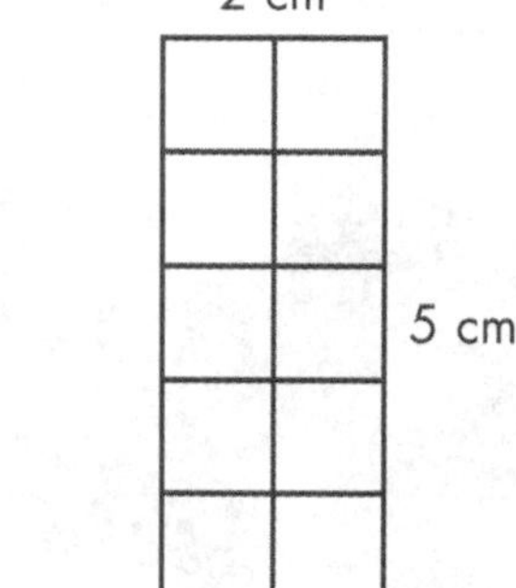

A = __________ sq. cm

3.

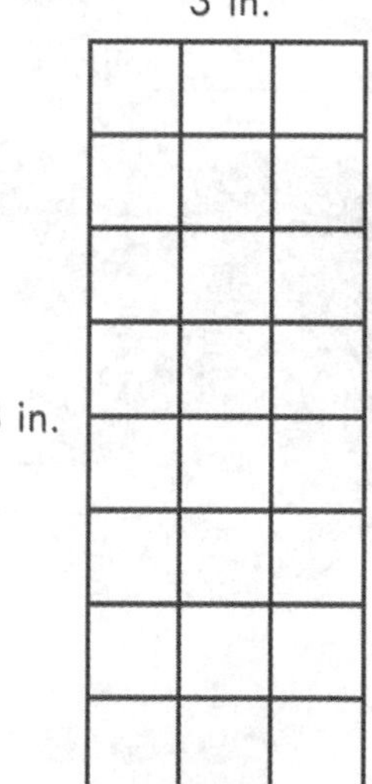

A = __________ sq. in.

4.

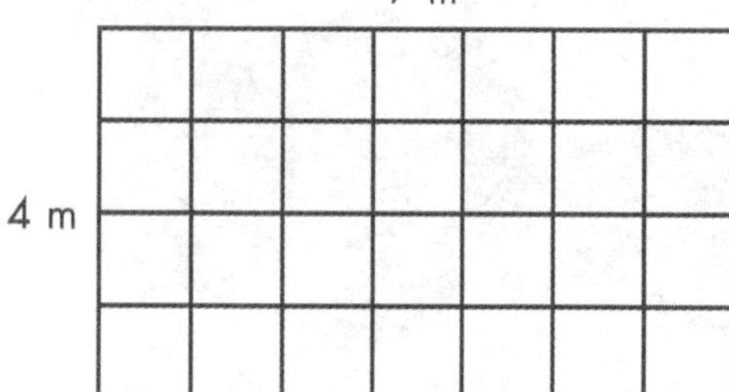

A = __________ sq. m

5.

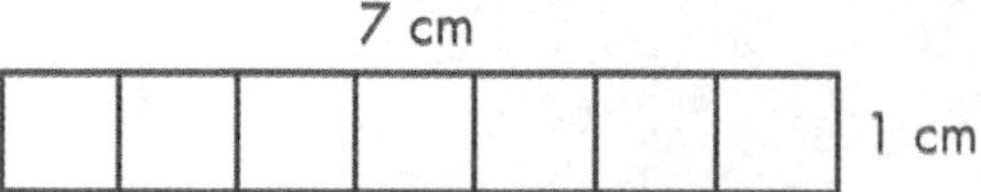

A = __________ sq. cm

6.

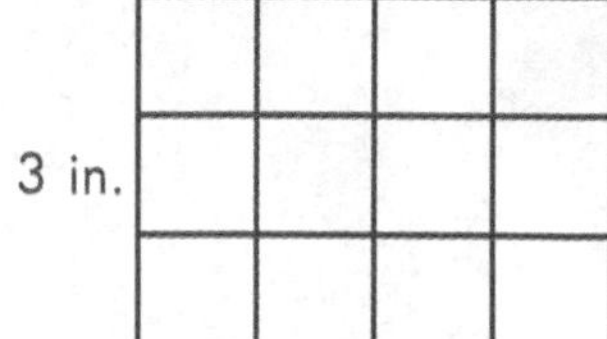

A = __________ sq. in.

Chapter 5: Measurement

Finding Area with Unit Squares

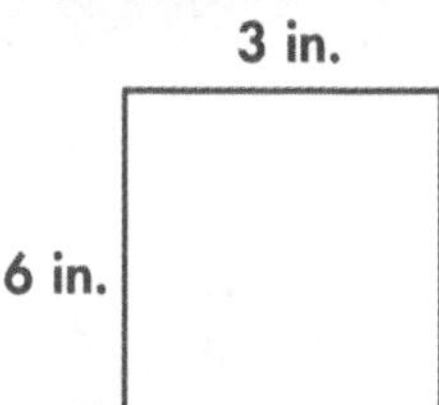

Find the area by drawing the square units.

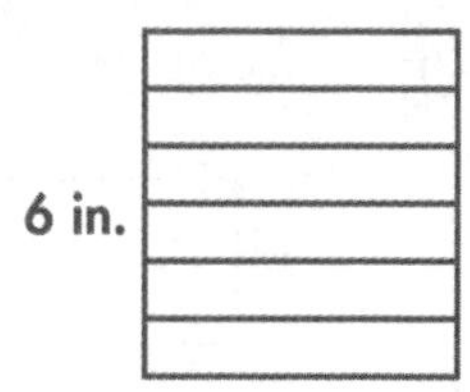

Draw **5** lines across to make **6** rows.

3 in.

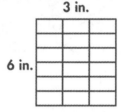

6 in.

Draw **2** lines down to make **3** columns.

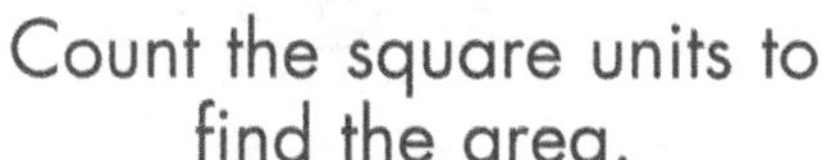

Count the square units to find the area.

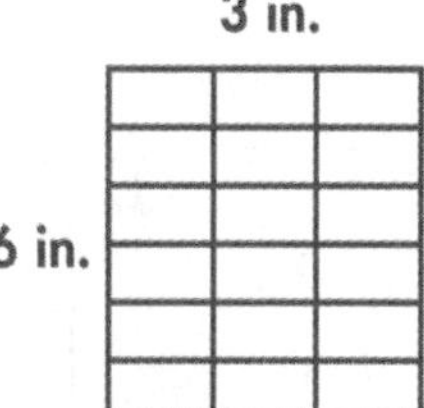

A = ___18___ **sq. in.**

Draw the square units to find the area.

1. 4 cm, 2 cm

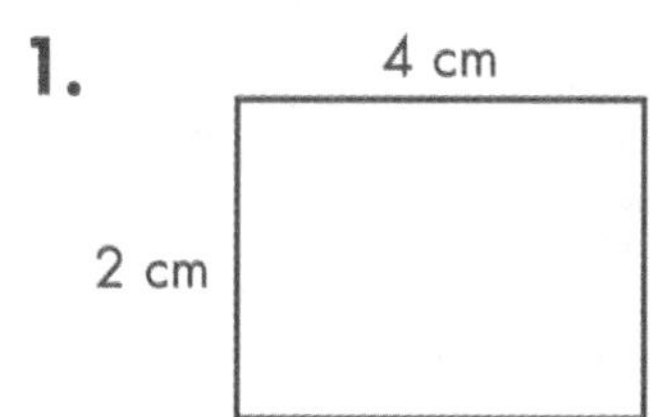

A = ________ sq. cm

2. 4 cm, 7 cm

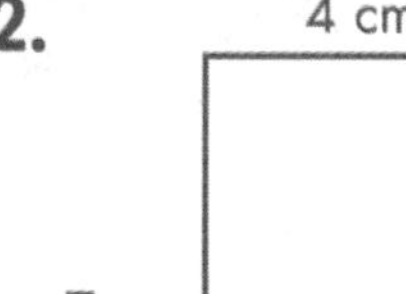

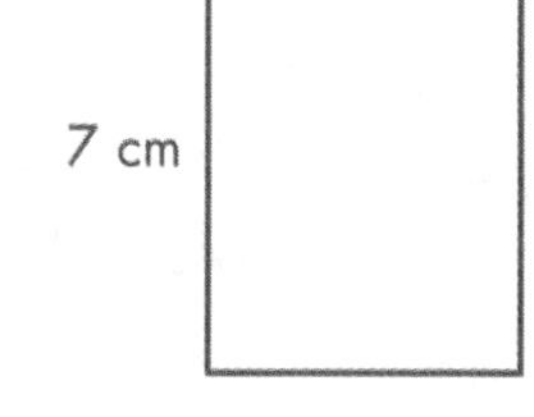

A = ________ sq. cm

3. 3 in., 3 in.

A = ________ sq. in.

4. 3 m, 1 m

A = ________ sq. m

5. 2 cm, 2 cm

A = ________ sq. cm

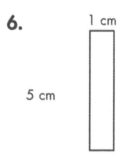

6. 1 cm, 5 cm

A = ________ sq. cm

Chapter 5: Measurement

Measuring Area

To find the area of a square or rectangle, multiply length by width.

10 ft. × 2 ft. = 20 sq. ft.

The product is written as **20** square feet.

10 ft. (length)

2 ft. (width)

Find the area of each shape.

1. 15 in. / 5 in.

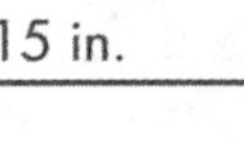

75 sq. in.

2. 8 ft. / 7 ft.

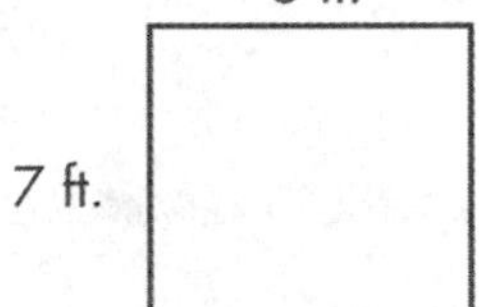

____ sq. ft.

3. 10 ft. / 4 ft.

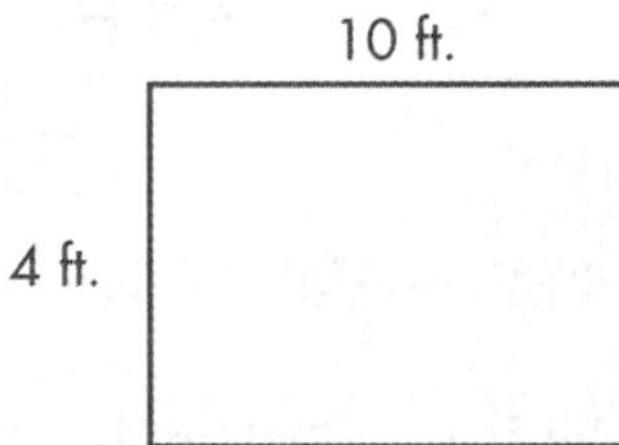

____ sq. ft.

4. 6 in. / 50 in.

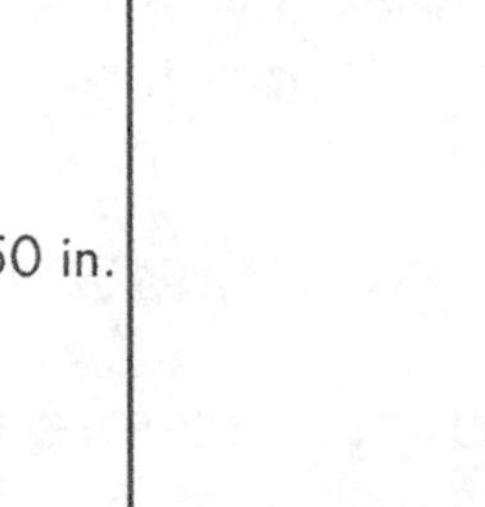

____ sq. in.

5. 7 yd. / 25 yd.

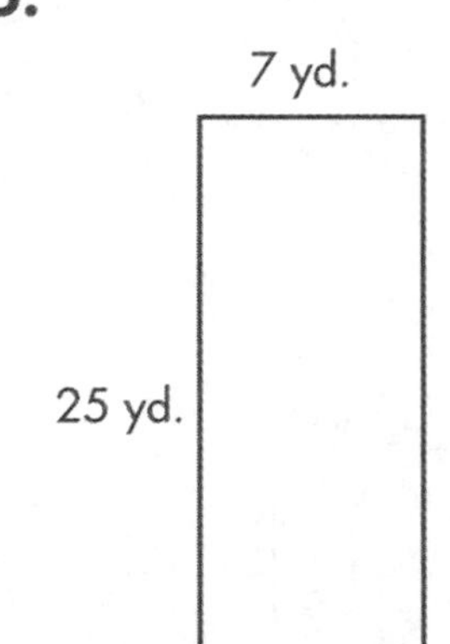

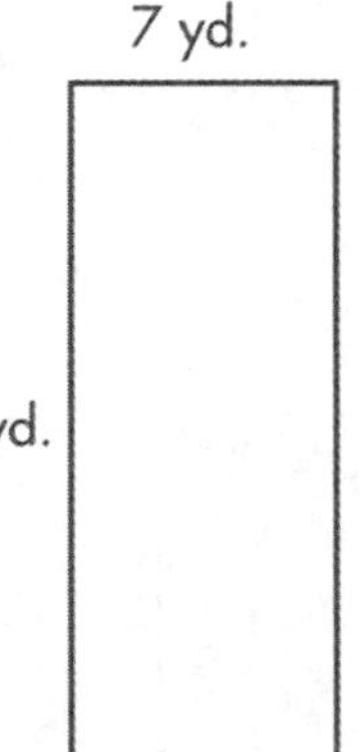

____ sq. yd.

6. 5 in. / 8 in.

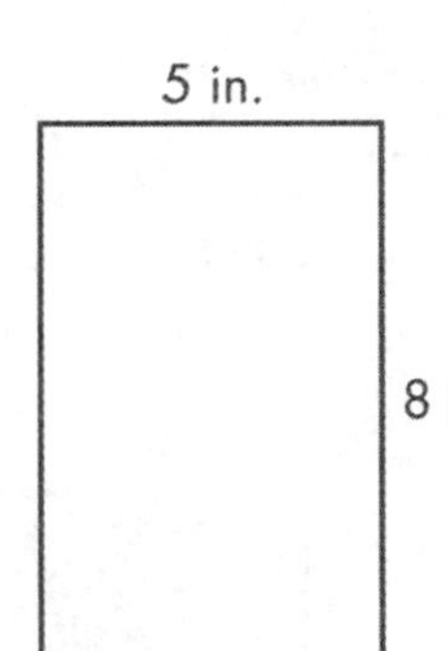

____ sq. in.

7. 4 yd. / 40 yd.

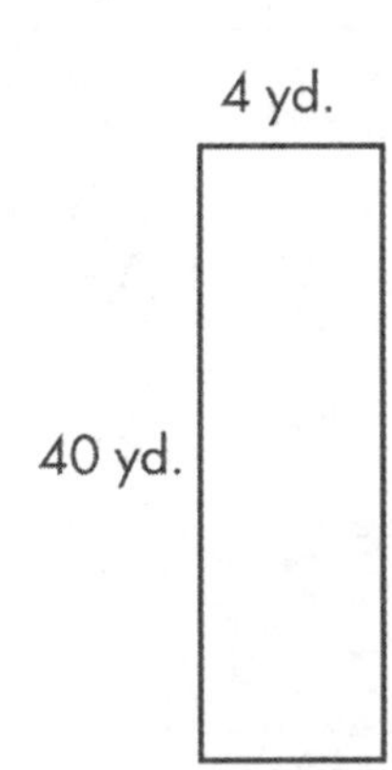

____ sq. yd.

8. 8 yd. / 20 yd.

____ sq. yd.

Chapter 5: Measurement

Measuring Area

Draw the square units.

3 cm

5 cm

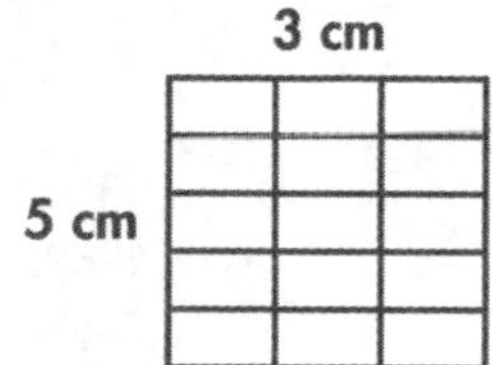

A = 15 **sq. cm**

Multiply to check your answer.

5 × 3 = 15

A = 15 **sq. cm**

Draw the square units. Then, multiply to check your answer.

1.

3 cm

8 cm

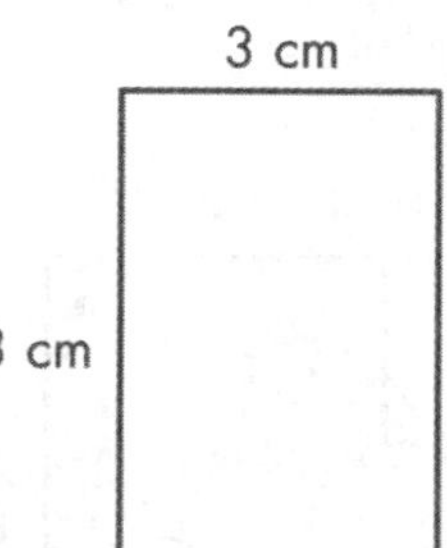

____ × ____ = ____

A = ________ sq. cm

2.

2 in.

2 in.

____ × ____ = ____

A = ________ sq. in.

3.

4 cm

1 cm

____ × ____ = ____

A = ________ sq. cm

4.

9 in.

3 in.

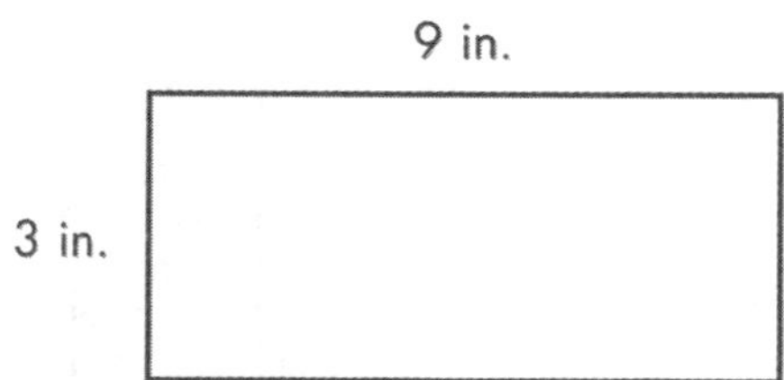

____ × ____ = ____

A = ________ sq. in.

Chapter 5: Measurement

Finding Area of Irregular Shapes

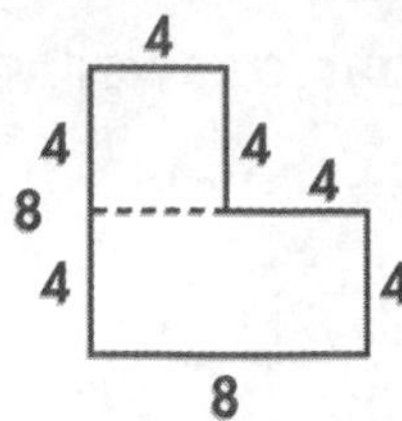

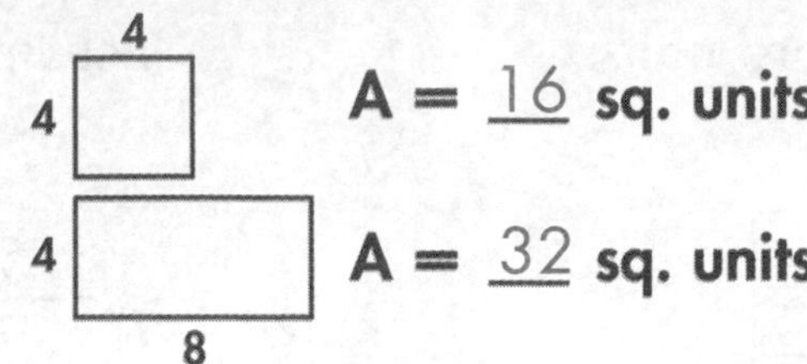

A = 16 sq. units

A = 32 sq. units

Divide the shape into recognizable shapes.

Find the area of each individual shape.

Add the area of each shape together.

16 + 32 = 48 sq. units

Find the area of each shape.

1.

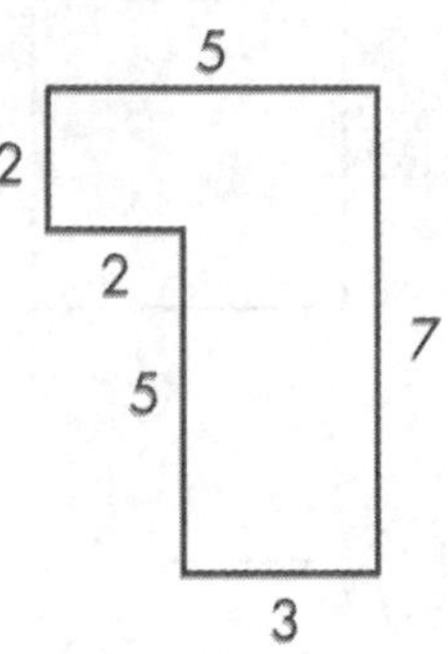

A = __________ sq. units

2.

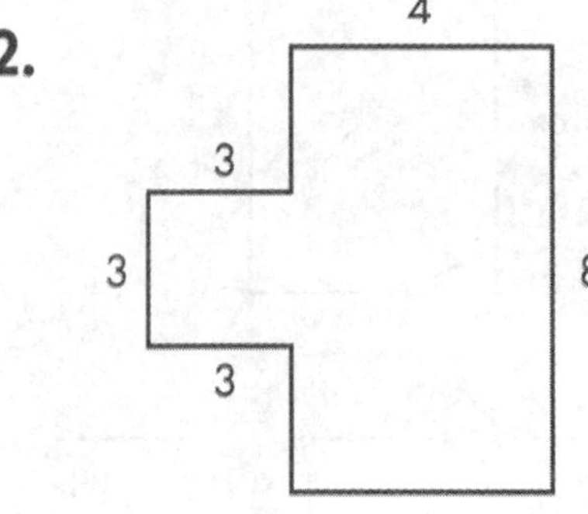

A = __________ sq. units

3.

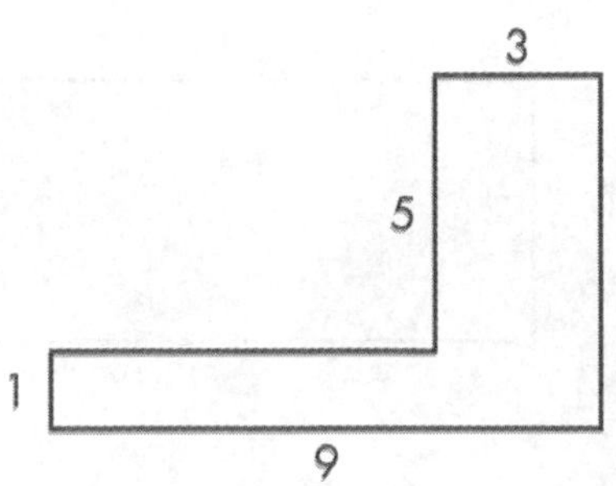

A = __________ sq. units

4.

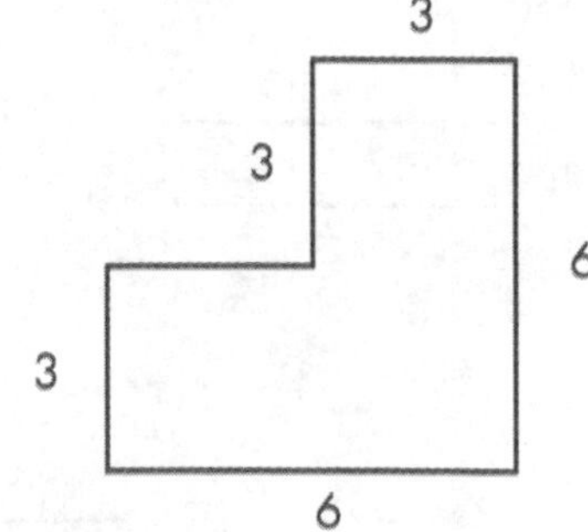

A = __________ sq. units

Chapter 5: Measurement

Problem Solving

Solve each problem.

1. The Garcia brothers are painting a wall in their living room. The wall measures 8 feet by 10 feet. What is the area of the wall?

   The area of the wall is ________ square feet.

2. Freda is putting carpet down in a room that measures 9 feet long by 10 feet wide. What is the area of the room?

   The area is ________ square feet.

3. The zoo is building a new hippo pool that will measure 50 feet by 9 feet. What is the area of the pool?

   The area is ________ square feet.

4. The Fosters' deck was almost finished. Each side of the square deck was 9 feet long. What was the area of the deck?

   The area was ________ square feet.

SHOW YOUR WORK

1.

2.

3.

4.

Chapter 5: Measurement

Measuring Perimeter

Perimeter is the distance around a shape.

To calculate perimeter, add together the lengths of all the sides.

Perimeter = 17 in. + 10 in. + 17 in. + 10 in.

Perimeter = 54 in.

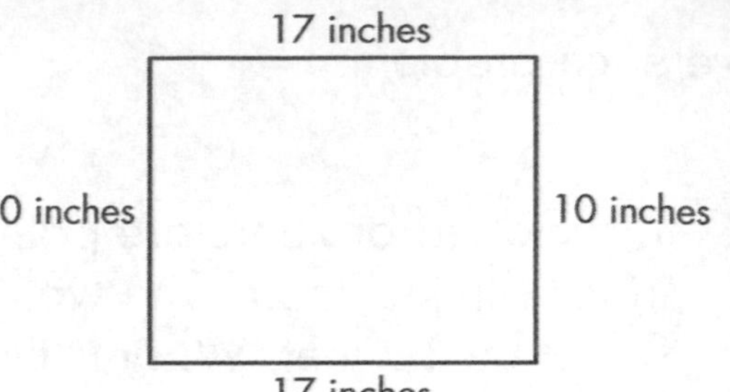

Find the perimeter of each shape.

1.

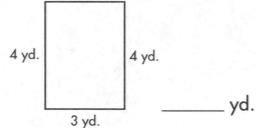

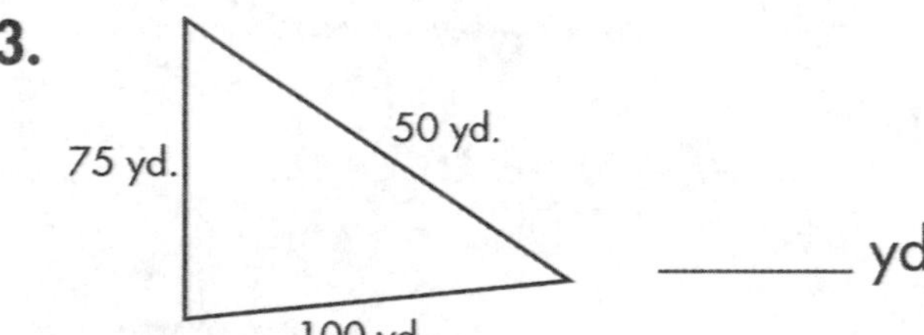

_______ yd.

2.

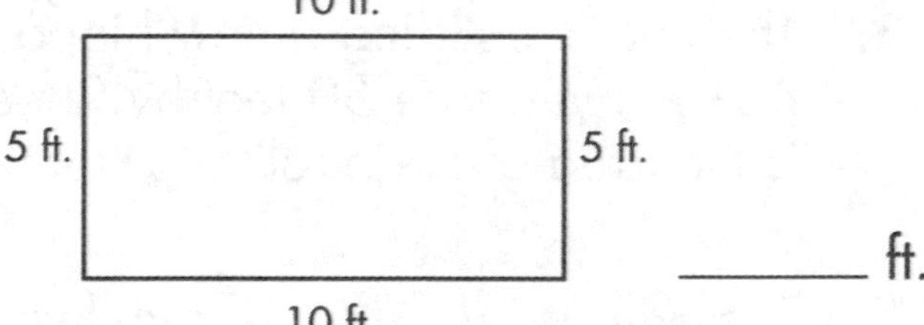

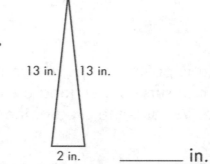

_______ in.

3.

75 yd. / 50 yd. / 100 yd.

_______ yd.

4.

10 ft. / 5 ft. / 5 ft. / 10 ft.

_______ ft.

Find the unknown side.

5.

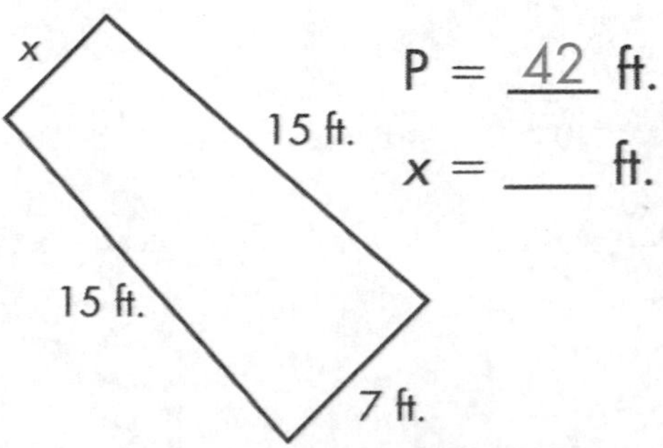

P = 42 ft.

x = ____ ft.

6.

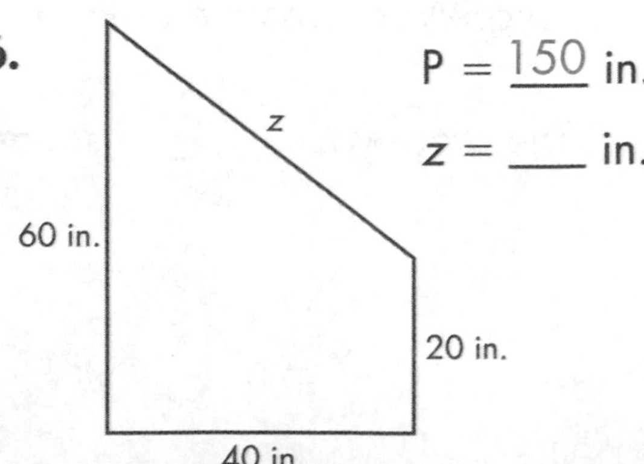

P = 150 in.

z = ____ in.

Chapter 5: Measurement

Problem Solving

Solve each problem.

1. The town of Yarmouth is planning a skateboard park and needs to know the perimeter of the park. The property measures 7 yards by 3 yards by 10 yards by 5 yards. What is the perimeter?

   The park's perimeter is ________ yards.

2. John cleared a vacant lot to plant a garden. The lot measured 35 by 15 feet. What is the perimeter of the garden lot?

   The perimeter of the lot is ________ feet.

3. Gabriel built a cage for his tropical birds. The cage measures 14 feet by 12 feet. What is the perimeter of the cage?

   The perimeter of the cage

   is ________ feet.

4. The length of the walking track is 103 feet and the width is 50 feet. What is the perimeter of the track?

   The perimeter is ________ feet.

SHOW YOUR WORK

1.

2.

3.

4.

Chapter 6: Time

Telling Time Using Analog and Digital Clocks

For years, your child has been relying on adults to keep track of the time. Ask your child to think about why it is important for them to learn to tell time. Why do they need to know how to tell time now? Why will they need to know how to tell time as they get older? Help them recognize the many situations now and later that will require them to know how to tell time.

Help your child understand how to read analog and digital clocks by giving them many opportunities to practice. Encourage your child to be the timekeeper in your home. Have them periodically report the time to household members. Then ask: "What is another way to say the current time?" Help your child understand that the time can be said more than one way. For example, 12:15 is also "15 minutes after 12."

Skill Checklist

- ☐ **Tell time on digital and analog clocks**
- ☐ **Read, write, and tell time in a variety of ways, in both numbers and words**
- ☐ **Use a number line to calculate how much time has passed**

Chapter 6: Time

Helpful Definitions

analog clock:

This analog clock shows the time 4:50. It can also be read as "10 minutes to 5" or "50 minutes after 4."

digital clock:

This digital clock shows the time 1:30. It can also be read as "half past 1" or 30 minutes to 2."

time on a number line:

A number line can be used to find how much time has passed or at what time an event begins. Help your child use a number line to find out how much time passes between events in your home, such as the time between dinner and bedtime. For example, if you eat dinner at 5:30, how long is it until 8:15?

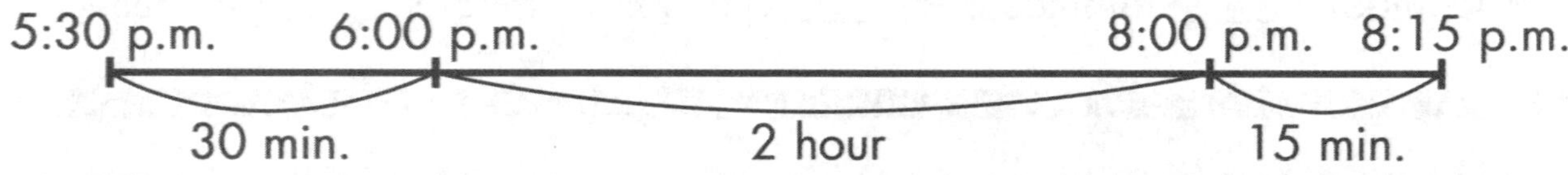

First, find out how much time passes between the start time and the next hour.
Second, find out how much time passes between 6:00 and 8:00.
Then, find out how much time passes between 8:00 and 8:15.
Add the minutes and hours to find the total time that has passed.
30 min. + 2 hours + 15 minutes = 2 hours 45 minutes

Elapsed Time

Chapter 6: Time

Telling Time

5:15 is read "five fifteen" and means "15 minutes after 5."

12:50 is read "twelve fifty" and means "50 minutes after 12" or "10 minutes to 1."

4:45 is read "four forty-five" and means "45 minutes after 4" or "15 minutes to 5."

Complete the following.

1. 6:15 means 15 minutes after 6.

2. 11:50 means ____ minutes to ____.

3. 7:50 means ____ minutes after ____.

4. 7:50 means ____ minutes to ____.

5. 12:45 means ____ minutes after ____.

6. 12:45 means ____ minutes to ____.

For each analog clock face, write the numerals that name the time.

7.

____ : ____

8.

____ : ____

9.

____ : ____

10.

____ : ____

11.

____ : ____

12.

____ : ____

Chapter 6: Time

Telling Time

6:41

The closest hour on an analog clock is determined by the hour hand (the short hand).

The closest half hour, quarter hour, and minute are determined by the minute hand (the long hand).

A half hour is at 30 minutes or 1 hour.

A quarter hour is at 15, 30, 45 minutes, or 1 hour.

What time is it to the nearest hour? 7:00, half hour? 6:30, quarter hour? 6:45, minute? 6:41

Write the time to the nearest hour, half hour, quarter hour, or minute as indicated.

1. 

hour	half hour	quarter hour	minute
___ : ___	___ : ___	___ : ___	___ : ___

2. 

hour	half hour	quarter hour	minute
___ : ___	___ : ___	___ : ___	___ : ___

Draw the hands on the analog clock to express the time presented on the digital clock.

3. 

4. 

5. 

6. 

Chapter 6: Time

Time on a Number Line

Quinn gets up at 7:30 a.m. She leaves the house at 9:20 a.m. How much time passed between when she got up and left the house?

7:30 a.m. 8:00 a.m. 9:00 a.m. 9:20 a.m.

30 min. 1 hour 20 min.

First, find out how much time until the next hour.
Second, find out how much time passed between this hour and the last hour.
Then, find out how much time passed between the last hour and the final time.
Last, add up the minutes and hours to find out the total time that has passed.

1 hour 50 minutes

Solve.

1. Alexa went to the bookstore at 5:45 p.m. She left the bookstore at 9:10 p.m. How long was Alexa at the bookstore?

____

5:45 p.m. 9:10 p.m.

2. Hugo leaves for work at 7:45 a.m. He leaves work to go home at 4:15 p.m. How much time does Hugo spend at work?

____

7:45 a.m. 4:15 p.m.

Chapter 7: Geometry

Plane and Solid Figures

Plane and solid figures are everywhere! Plane figures are flat and range from building windows to the sheet of paper your child uses to do their homework. Have your child draw pictures of some of the plane figures they see around your home.

Solid figures are three-dimensional. Examples include toy blocks, cans of soup, shoeboxes, and basketballs. Help your child find solid figures around them. When they see a cube, for example, ask your child to name the parts of the cube and tell how many faces it has. Or have your child find objects around them that are made up of various solid figures. Have them name the solid figures.

Skill Checklist

- ☐ **Identify and draw plane figures and solid figures, recognize characteristics of each**
- ☐ **Identify different types of quadrilaterals**
- ☐ **Divide shapes into equal parts and write a fraction for each part**

Chapter 7: Geometry

Helpful Definitions

plane figure: a flat shape

circle triangle square rectangle

line segment, corner, square corner

A line segment is any side of a triangle, square, or rectangle. A corner is where two line segments meet. A square corner is where two line segments meet at a 90° angle.

corner
line segment
square corner
corner

solid figure: a three-dimensional object

cube rectangular prism square pyramid sphere cylinder cone

Help your child recognize plane and solid figures in the world around them. For example, point out that the windows on your home are rectangles or squares. When cooking, point out that a can of food is a cylinder. Then show objects from around your home and have your child tell whether each is a plane figure or solid figure. Ask them to name the specific plane or solid figure.

edge, face, vertex, and corner:

A face is a flat surface on a solid figure. An edge is where two faces on a solid figure meet.
A vertex, or corner, is the point where 3 or more edges come together.

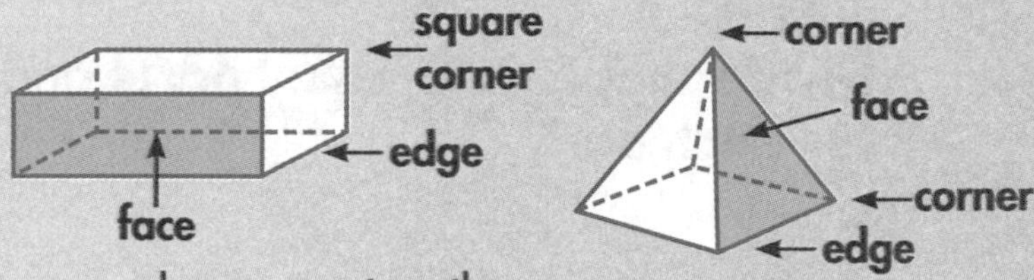

quadrilateral: a shape with four sides that are connected

Ask your child to draw a quadrilateral. Then ask them how many equal parts the shape can be divided into. Have them draw lines to divide the shape into equal parts. Then have them write a fraction for each part.

Video

Plane Figures

Types of Quadrilaterals

Chapter 7: Geometry

Plane Figures

A **plane figure** is a flat surface.

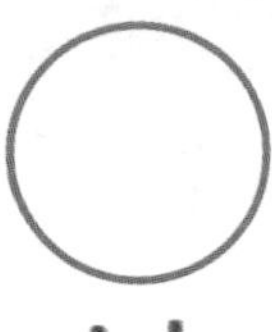

circle **triangle** **square** **rectangle**

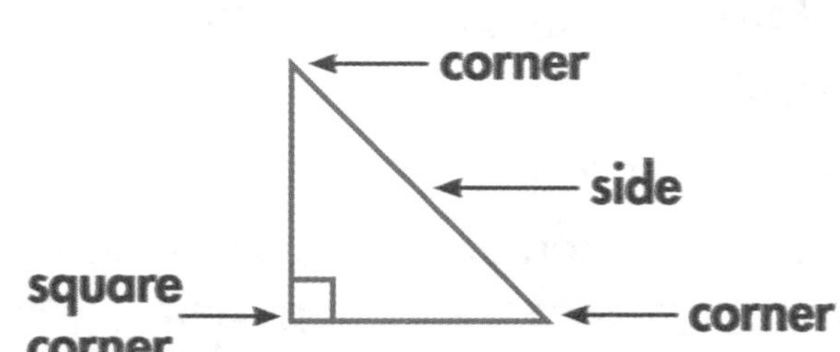

Each side of a triangle, square, and rectangle is a **line segment**.

The point where two line segments meet is a **corner** or a **square corner**.

A square corner is a right angle. A right angle has a measure of 90°.

Draw the following plane figures.

1. triangle **2.** rectangle **3.** square **4.** circle

Complete the following.

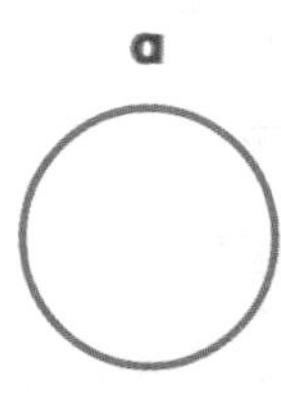

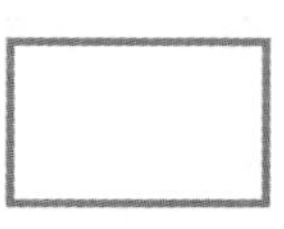

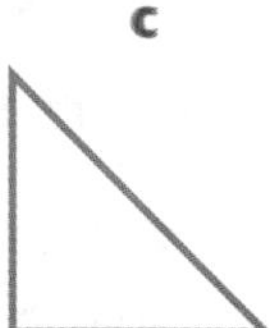

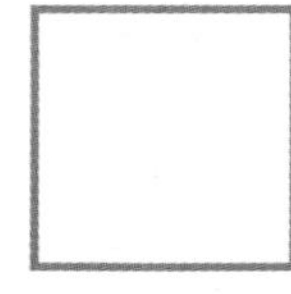

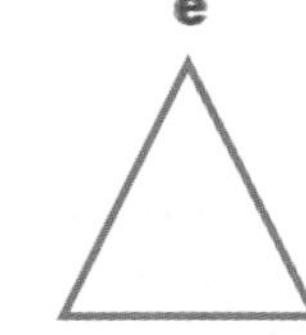

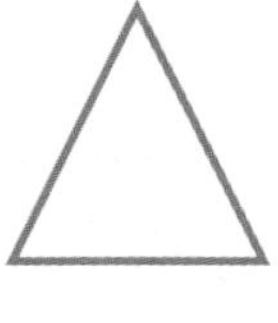

	a	b	c	d	e
5. number of sides	0				
6. number of square corners			1		0
7. number of other corners					

Chapter 7: Geometry

Solid Figures

A **solid figure** is a three-dimensional object. Solid figures may be hollow or solid.

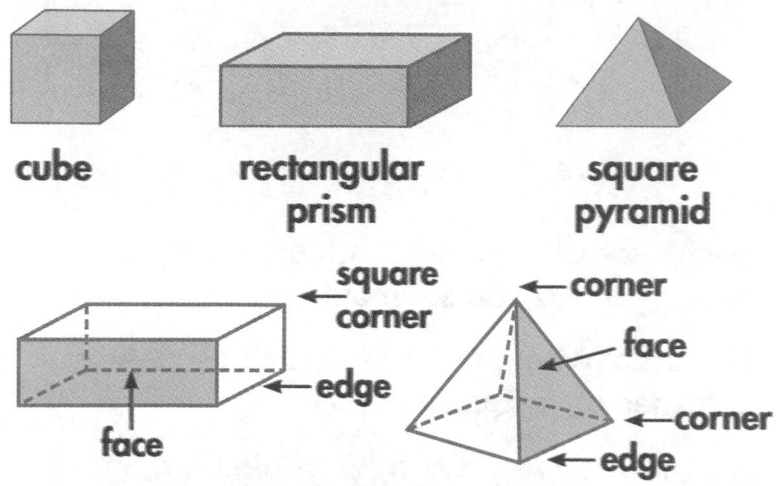

sphere

cylinder

cone

A **face** is the shape formed by the edges of a solid figure.

An **edge** is where 2 faces intersect.

A **vertex** or **corner** is the point where 3 or more edges come together.

Complete the table.

	Solid Figure	Number of Square Faces	Number of Rectangle Faces	Number of Triangle Faces
1.	cube			0
2.	rectangular prism			
3.	square pyramid	1		

4. How many edges does a sphere have? _____ edges

5. How many edges does a square pyramid have? _____ edges

6. How many edges does a cube have? _____ edges

7. How many edges does a rectangular prism have? _____ edges

8. How many corners does a square pyramid have? _____ corners

Give a physical example of each of the following plane figures.

9. cube
building block
____

10. rectangular prism
____

11. square pyramid
____

12. sphere
____

13. cylinder
____

14. cone
____

Chapter 7: Geometry

Classifying Quadrilaterals

Quadrilaterals are four-sided shapes. To be a quadrilateral, all four sides must be connected.

Parallelograms are quadrilaterals with two sets of parallel sides.

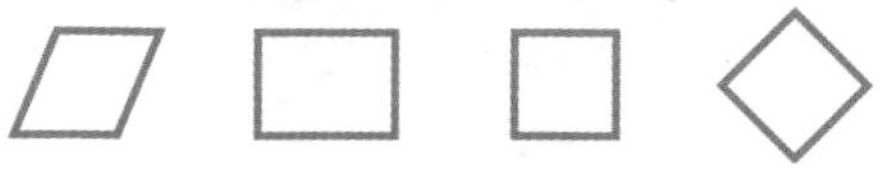

Rectangles are parallelograms with four right angles.

Rhombuses are parallelograms with four sides of equal length.

Squares are rectangles with four equal sides. They are also rhombuses with four right angles.

Circle the shapes named. Then, answer the question.

1. Circle the quadrilaterals. 
2. Circle the parallelograms. 
3. Circle the rectangles. 
4. Circle the rhombuses. 
5. Circle the squares. 
6. Which of the shapes defined above fits into all five categories?

____

Chapter 7: Geometry

Dividing Shapes

Halves = **2** equal pieces

Thirds = **3** equal pieces

Fourths = **4** equal pieces

Fifths = **5** equal pieces

and so on . . .

Divide this shape into thirds.

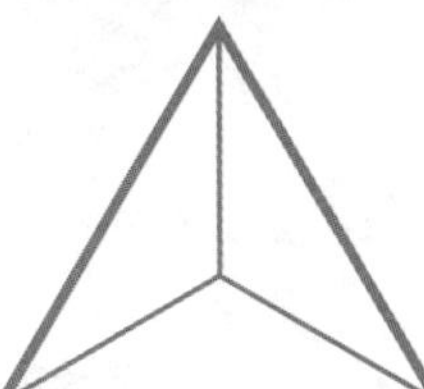

Label each third.

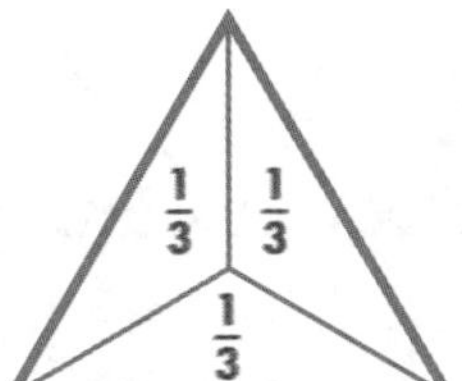

Divide each shape into the given amount of equal parts. Then, label each piece with the appropriate fraction.

1. halves

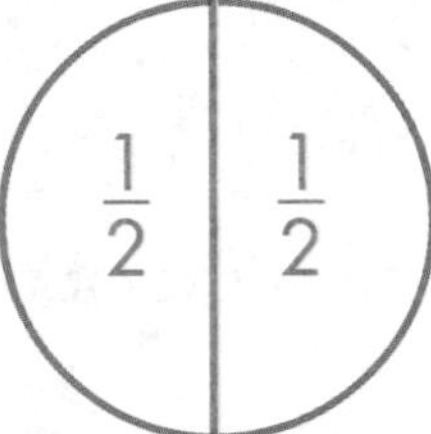

2. thirds

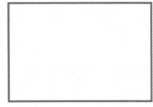

3. thirds

4. halves

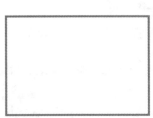

5. fourths

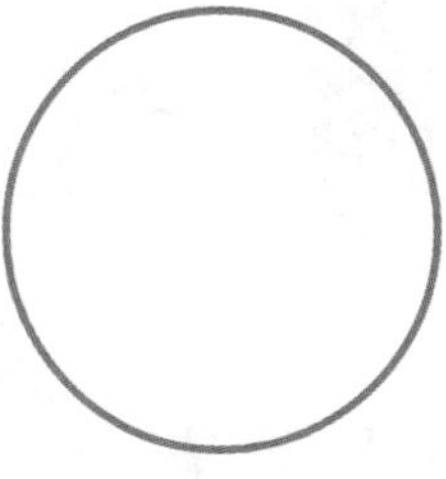

6. fifths

7. halves

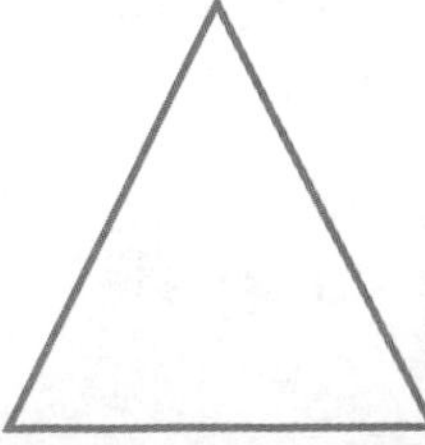

8. fourths

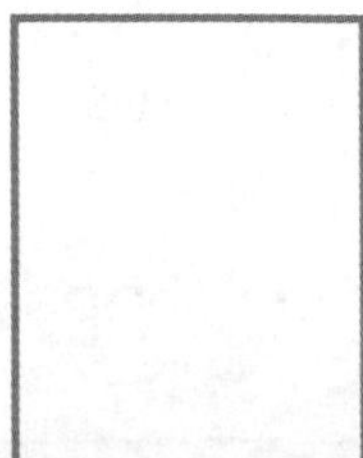

Chapter 8: Preparing for Algebra

Understanding Properties of Numbers

Mathematics follows rules for how numbers are added and multiplied. Understanding these rules can help your child consistently solve problems.

The identity, commutative, associative, and distributive properties are like laws for equations. Following the rules of these properties enables your child to get the correct answer when solving an equation. Now that your child has mastered basic addition and multiplication facts, they will be asked to compute equations by multiplying a few numbers together or by adding and multiplying a series of numbers.

The best way to help your child is to ensure they understand these rules and have many opportunities to practice using them.

Skill Checklist

- ☐ **Complete number patterns**
- ☐ **Understand and use the identity and commutative properties of addition and multiplication**
- ☐ **Understand and use the associative and distributive properties in number sentences**

Chapter 8: Preparing for Algebra

Helpful Definitions

number sentence: a math sentence with numbers and symbols $2 + 9 = 11$ $3 \times 4 = 12$

identity property: related to the properties of 0 and 1 in addition and multiplication

In addition, adding 0 to a number does not change the identity of that number.
For example, $7 + 0 = 7$.

In multiplication, multiplying 1 times any number does not change the identity of that number. For example, $4 \times 1 = 4$.

Help your child understand these properties by drawing pictures to model equations.

$7 + 0 = 7$

Show your child that adding zero items to the picture does not change the number of items.

Then repeat the same process for the multiplication equation. $4 \times 1 = 4$

commutative property: the order in which you multiply or add does not change the answer of the equation; for example, $8 + 2 = 10$ and $2 + 8 = 10$; it does not matter which number is added first

The same is true for multiplication equations. $4 \times 5 = 20$ and $5 \times 4 = 20$. This is very important for your child to understand when memorizing multiplication facts. Once they know one fact, they also know the fact with the numbers reversed.

Help your child with this property by writing an equation on paper. Then have your child write the equation with the placement of the numbers reversed. Help them understand that both equations have the same answer.

associative property: the order in which the numbers are added or multiplied does not change the answer

$6 + 2 + 5 = a$

$8 + 5 = a$ or $6 + 7 = a$

$a = 13$

$3 \times 4 \times 4 = n$

$12 \times 4 = n$ or $3 \times 16 = n$

$n = 48$

distributive property: multiplying the sum of two or more addends by a number will give the same result as multiplying each addend individually by the number and then adding the products together

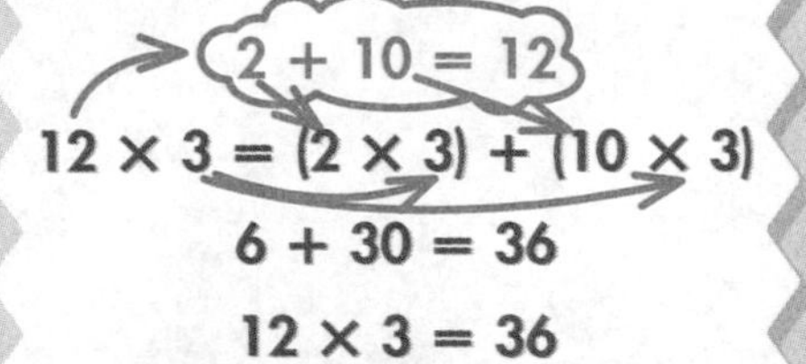

Properties of Addition and Multiplication

The Distributive Property

Chapter 8: Preparing for Algebra

Number Patterns

A number pattern can be developed by addition or subtraction.

Complete this pattern by subtraction.

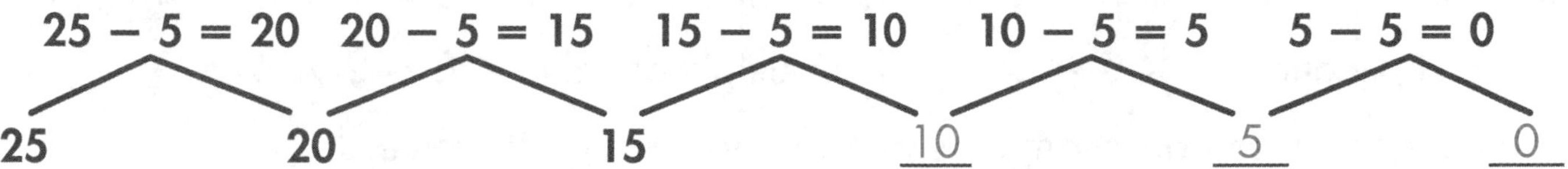

Complete the pattern by using addition or subtraction.

				a	b	c
1.	2	4	6	8	10	12
2.	1	3	5	____	____	____
3.	20	18	16	____	____	____
4.	21	15	10	____	____	____
5.	13	12	11	____	____	____
6.	5	10	15	____	____	____
7.	3	6	9	____	____	____
8.	10	20	40	____	____	____
9.	16	13	10	____	____	____
10.	10	9	8	____	____	____

Chapter 8: Preparing for Algebra

Number Sentences

A **number sentence** is an equation with numbers.

Identity Property		**Commutative Property**	
for addition:	**0 + 3 = 3**	for addition:	**3 + 2 = 2 + 3**
for multiplication:	**1 × 3 = 3**	for multiplication:	**4 × 2 = 2 × 4**

A number sentence can change its look but not change its value.

3 + 5 = 8 or **3 + 5 = 4 + 4** **3 × 8 = 24** or **3 × 8 = 6 × 4**

Complete each number sentence.

1. 0 + 4 = [4] **2.** 0 + 6 = ☐ **3.** ☐ + 2 = 2

4. 1 × 2 = ☐ **5.** 1 × 5 = ☐ **6.** ☐ × 4 = 4

7. 7 + 2 = ☐ + 7 **8.** 3 + 4 = ☐ + 3 **9.** 1 + 2 = 2 + ☐

10. 5 × 7 = 7 × ☐ **11.** 4 × ☐ = 3 × 4 **12.** ☐ × 3 = 3 × 5

Complete the following.

13. 2 + 7 = 9 or
2 + 7 = 5 + [4]

14. 5 + 7 = 12 or
5 + 7 = 6 + ☐

15. 4 + 3 = 7 or
4 + 3 = 5 + ☐

16. 6 + 4 = 10 or
6 + 4 = 5 + ☐

17. 6 + 7 = 13 or
6 + 7 = 8 + ☐

18. 5 + 3 = 8 or
5 + 3 = 6 + ☐

19. 5 × 6 = 30 or
5 × 6 = 10 × ☐

20. 4 × 3 = 12 or
4 × 3 = 2 × ☐

21. 6 × 3 = 18 or
6 × 3 = 9 × ☐

Chapter 8: Preparing for Algebra

Number Sentences

Associative Property

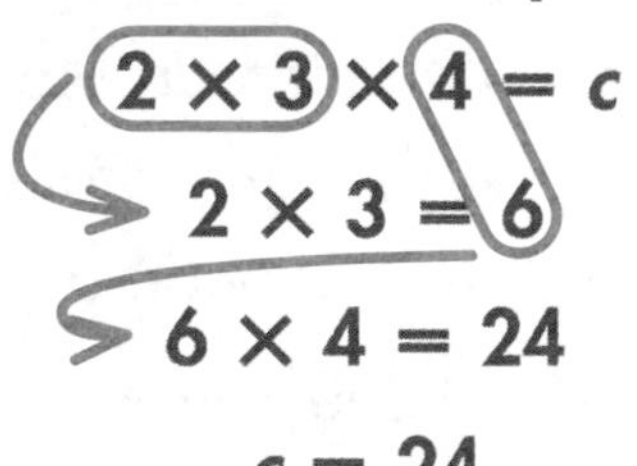

$c = 24$

Distributive Property

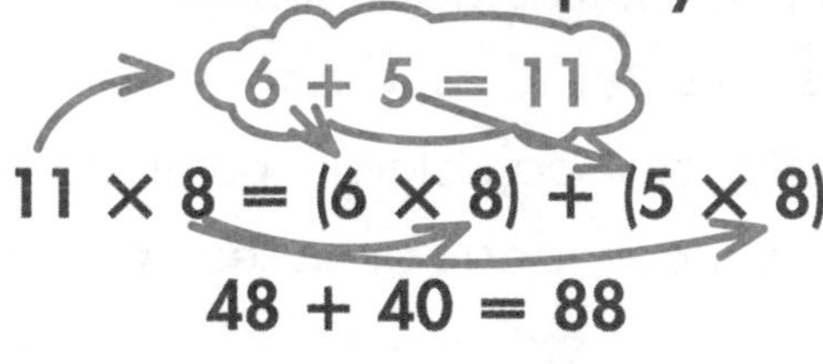

$48 + 40 = 88$

$11 \times 8 = 88$

Solve using the associative property.

1. $3 \times 5 \times 2 = d$

_____ × _____ = _____

_____ × _____ = _____

d = _____

2. $2 \times 9 \times 1 = h$

_____ × _____ = _____

_____ × _____ = _____

h = _____

3. $4 \times 6 \times 2 = e$

_____ × _____ = _____

_____ × _____ = _____

e = _____

4. $7 \times 4 \times 2 = g$

_____ × _____ = _____

_____ × _____ = _____

g = _____

Solve using the distributive property.

5. $12 \times 4 = (6 \times 4) +$ (_____ × 4)

_____ + _____

$12 \times 4 =$ _____

6. $14 \times 3 = (8 \times 3) +$ (_____ × 3)

_____ + _____

$14 \times 3 =$ _____

7. $19 \times 2 = (9 \times 2) +$ (_____ × 2)

_____ + _____

$19 \times 2 =$ _____

8. $16 \times 5 = (7 \times 5) +$ (_____ × 5)

_____ + _____

$16 \times 5 =$ _____

Chapter 1: Grammar

Parts of Speech and Types of Sentences

Parts of speech are the building blocks of English. Understanding grammar rules and parts of speech makes it easier to read and write sentences. When your child can use parts of speech correctly, they can clearly communicate their ideas and thoughts orally and in writing. Knowing basic parts of speech and types of sentences will provide a solid foundation for the more complex sentences your child will write in upcoming years.

Grammar and sentence rules in English can be tricky to learn. Help your child learn about parts of speech and types of sentences as you read books together. For example, ask: "Which word in this sentence is a common noun? Which word is the verb in the sentence?" or "Find a command in this story. Find a question."

Skill Checklist

- ☐ **Identify and use common, proper, and abstract nouns**
- ☐ **Identify and use pronouns**
- ☐ **Identify and use verbs and linking verbs**
- ☐ **Identify and use adjectives, adverbs, and articles**
- ☐ **Identify and use conjunctions**
- ☐ **Identify and use statements, commands, questions, and exclamations**
- ☐ **Identify subject and predicate in sentences**
- ☐ **Identify sentence fragments and run-on sentences**
- ☐ **Use subjects and direct objects, verbs, and adjectives to combine sentences**

Chapter 1: Grammar

Helpful Definitions

Part of Speech	Definition	Examples
common noun	a word that names a person, place, thing, or idea	sister, city, pond
proper noun	a word that names a specific person, place, thing, or idea	Lavonda, Valley Elementary School, California, Friday
abstract noun	a noun that a person cannot experience with their five senses; feelings, concepts, and ideas	pride, excitement, kindness, truth
pronoun	a word that takes the place of a noun	they, him, we, it
verb	an action word that tells what happens in a sentence	laugh, skipped, plays
linking verb	a verb that connects the subject to the rest of the sentence but does not show action	Mary **is** my friend. Tim and Pedro **are** cousins.
adjective	a word that describes nouns or pronouns	**furry** dog, **blue** car, **funny** movie
article	a word that comes before a noun and describes if the noun is specific or nonspecific	the, a, an
adverb	a word that describes verbs, adjectives, and other adverbs	I **quickly** did my chores. Thien **happily** helped his teacher sharpen the pencils.
conjunction	a connecting word that joins words, sentences, or parts of sentences	and, but, or

subject and predicate:

Every sentence has a subject and a predicate. The subject tells who or what the sentence is about. The predicate includes the verb and tells what the subject is doing.

subject / predicate

Mia and Marco ate hamburgers for dinner.

run-on sentence: when two or more sentences are merged together without correct punctuation or a conjunction

The flowers in the vase smell great I really like flowers.

This can either be divided into two separate sentences, or a comma and conjunction can be used to correct the sentence.

The flowers in the vase smell great. I really like flowers.
OR The flowers in the vase smell great, and I really like flowers.

Chapter 1: Grammar

Common and Proper Nouns

A **common noun** can be a person, place, or thing.

teacher (person) *museum* (place)
notebook (thing)

A **proper noun** is a noun that names a specific person, place, or thing. Proper nouns are capitalized to show that they are important.

Here are some examples of common and proper nouns:

Common nouns	Proper nouns
school	Hickory Hills Elementary School
zoo	Memphis Zoo
brother	Alexander
city	Tallahassee
day	Sunday
cat	Sasha

Complete It

Complete the sentences below with a noun from the box. If there is a **P** after the space, use a proper noun. If there is a **C** after the space, use a common noun.

Walnut High School	**Saturday**	**town**
dog	**Jordan Lake**	**brother**

1. Uncle Dale is taking me fishing at ____________________ (P).
2. We will leave early on ____________________ (P) morning.
3. My ________________ (C), Kris, is coming with us.
4. Uncle Dale lives an hour away in a __________(C) called Rockvale.
5. He is a math teacher at ________________________ (P).
6. Uncle Dale's __________ (C), Patches, always comes fishing with us.

Chapter 1: Grammar

Common and Proper Nouns

Identify It

Underline the nouns in the sentences below. The number in parentheses will tell you how many nouns there are. Above each noun, write **P** for *proper* or **C** for *common*.

1. Patches jumped into the rowboat. (2)
2. Kris and I put on our life jackets. (2)
3. Last August, we went to Griggs Lake. (2)
4. We stopped at Elmwood Historic Car Museum on the way home. (2)
5. We caught six fish on our trip. (2)
6. Uncle Dale cooked them on the grill. (2)
7. Mom made some coleslaw and potatoes. (3)

Try It

1. Write a sentence using at least two common nouns. Circle the nouns.

____

____

2. Write a sentence using two proper nouns and one common noun. Circle the common noun. Underline the proper nouns.

____

____

Chapter 1: Grammar

Abstract Nouns

Abstract nouns are nouns that you can't experience with your five senses. They are feelings, concepts, and ideas. Some examples are *friendship, childhood, bravery, hope,* and *pride.*

Identify It

Underline the abstract noun or nouns in each sentence below.

1. Maya's honesty is one of the reasons we are best friends.
2. Martin Luther King, Jr., wanted to change hate and injustice in the world.
3. Darius's patriotism is the reason he joined the army.
4. I love the delight on my sister's face on her birthday.
5. Your kindness will not be forgotten.
6. Benji felt great pride when his team won the championship.
7. What are your parents' best stories about their childhood?
8. It is important to me that you always tell the truth.

Chapter 1: Grammar

Abstract Nouns

Complete It

Fill in each blank below with an abstract noun from the box.

wisdom	liberty	freedom	knowledge
courage	joy	kindness	

1. Our country was founded on the ideas of ____________________ and ____________________ for all.
2. It took great ____________________ to rebuild after the hurricane.
3. Uncle Zane's ____________________ of birds amazes me.
4. The room was filled with ____________________ when Will found his lost puppy.
5. Neighbors showed us much ____________________ when my baby sister was born.
6. Grandpa has the ____________________ that comes with a long life.

Try It

Write three sentences that use abstract nouns. You may use abstract nouns from the exercises or think of your own.

1. ____
2. ____
3. ____

Chapter 1: Grammar

Pronouns

A **pronoun** is a word that takes the place of a noun. Pronouns keep you from using the same noun or nouns over and over again.

Some pronouns take the place of a single person or thing: *I, me, you, he, she, him, her*, and *it*. Other pronouns take the place of plural nouns: *we, us, they*, and *them*.

In the examples below, pronouns take the place of the underlined nouns.

> The <u>grizzly bears</u> waded into the stream.
> *They* waded into the stream.
> <u>Molly</u> finished her report at noon.
> *She* finished her report at noon.
> Put <u>the bowl</u> on the table.
> Put *it* on the table.

Identify It

Read the paragraphs below. Circle each pronoun. You should find 15 pronouns.

Sonja Henie was an amazing figure skater. She was born in Oslo, Norway, in 1912. When Sonja was only five years old, she won her first skating contest. It was the start of a great career. She was a world champion for ten years. People around the world became interested in skating. They followed the career of the talented young girl.

Sonja also wanted to be a movie star. She moved to Hollywood and began acting. She also performed in a traveling ice show. It was very popular. Huge crowds came to watch Sonja perform. They could not get enough of her. Sonja enjoyed her fame and the money it brought her. But her first and greatest love was always skating.

Chapter 1: Grammar

Pronouns

Rewrite It

Read the sentences below. Rewrite each sentence using a pronoun in place of the underlined noun or nouns.

Example: David kicked the ball toward the goal.
He kicked the ball toward the goal.

1. Bryan and Anna had their first skating lesson on Tuesday.

___

2. Bryan had never skated before.

___

3. The ice was slick and shiny.

___

4. The teacher helped Anna tighten her skates.

___

5. The teacher told Bryan and Anna that they did a great job.

___

Try It

1. Think about the first time you tried something new. Write a sentence about your experience. Circle the pronoun.

___

2. Write a sentence using the pronoun *he*, *she*, or *it*.

___

Chapter 1: Grammar

Verbs

Verbs are often action words. They tell what happens in a sentence. Every sentence has a verb.

Ramon *put* on his running shoes. He *grabbed* his headphones. He *opened* the door and *took* a deep breath. Ramon *stretched* for a few minutes. Then, he *ran* down the street toward the park.

Complete It

A verb is missing from each sentence below. Complete the sentences with verbs from the box.

breathed	**moved**	**attached**	**invented**
gave	**kept**	**carried**	**helped**

1. In 1819, August Siebe ________________ the first diving suit.
2. The large helmet ________________ to a leather and canvas suit.
3. Weights ________________ divers stay underwater.
4. The divers underwater ________________ air through hoses.
5. Later on, rubber suits ________________ divers dry.
6. The invention of scuba gear ________________ divers more freedom.
7. Divers ________________ from place to place on their own.
8. They ________________ their air with them.

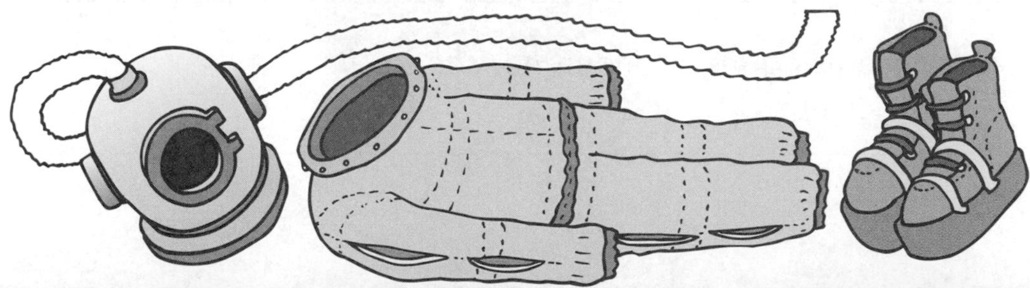

Chapter 1: Grammar

Verbs

Identify It

Circle the 10 action verbs in the paragraphs below.

Jacques Cousteau explored many of Earth's oceans. In 1950, he bought a ship called *Calypso*. On the *Calypso*, Jacques traveled to bodies of water around the world. He wrote many books and made many movies about his travels. He won prizes for some of his work. Jacques also invented things, like an underwater camera and the first scuba equipment.

Jacques Cousteau believed it was important to protect ocean life. He created a group called the *Cousteau Society*. More than 300,000 people belong to the Cousteau Society today.

Try It

1. Write a sentence about a place you would like to visit one day. Circle the verb.

____

____

____

2. Write a sentence about your favorite thing to do during the weekend. Circle the verb.

____

____

____

Chapter 1: Grammar

Linking Verbs

A **linking verb** links the subject to the rest of the sentence. Linking verbs are not action words.

The verb *to be* is a linking verb. Some different forms of the verb *to be* are *is*, *am*, *are*, *was*, and *were*. Some other linking verbs are *become*, *feel*, and *seem*.

Identify It

Read the sentences below. Underline the linking verbs. Circle the action verbs. Some sentences may have more than one verb.

1. My grandmother is a marine biologist.
2. She studies undersea life.
3. She was always a good student.
4. She loved the ocean and animals as a child.
5. It was hard for her to become a scientist.
6. When she was young, some people felt women could not be good at science.
7. My grandma proved she was smart and hardworking.
8. One day, I might become a marine biologist myself.

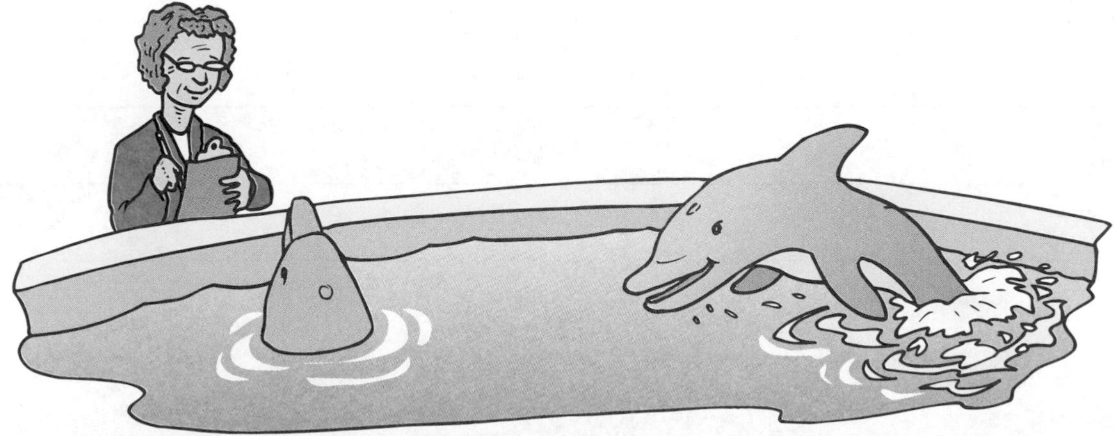

Chapter 1: Grammar

Linking Verbs

Solve It

Use the linking verbs from the box to complete each sentence. Some may work for more than one sentence. Then, look for the linking verbs in the word search puzzle. Circle each word you find.

1. Today, my grandfather ________________ a stage actor.
2. He first ________________ a movie star at the age of 22.
3. He ________________ lucky to have had such an amazing career.
4. I ________________ going to see him in a Broadway play next week.
5. When my dad ________________ little, he was in one of Grandpa's movies.

feels	**am**	**became**
was	**is**	

a	d	r	j	k	f	p
b	e	c	a	m	e	i
d	w	a	s	b	e	y
a	f	v	c	u	l	p
m	u	f	q	i	s	g

Try It

1. Write a sentence using a linking verb.

____

____

2. Write a sentence using a linking verb and an action verb.

____

____

Chapter 1: Grammar

Adjectives and Articles

Adjectives are words that describe. They give more information about nouns. Adjectives answer the questions *What kind?* and *How many?* They often come before the nouns they describe.

Fat raindrops bounced off the umbrella. (what kind of raindrops?)

Adjectives can also appear other places in the sentence. If you are not sure a word is an adjective, look for the noun you think it describes.

The robot was *helpful*. The package is *huge*!

An **article** is a word that comes before a noun. *A*, *an*, and *the* are articles.

Use *the* to talk about a specific person, place, or thing.

the computer *the* jacket *the* bicycle *the* starfish

Use *a* or *an* to talk about any person, place, or thing. If the noun begins with a consonant sound, use *a*. If it begins with a vowel sound, use *an*.

a wig *a* bed *an* apple *an* envelope

Complete It

Complete each item below with an adjective from the box.

shy	**electric**	**prickly**	**warty**	**smelly**
seven	**skinny**	**tiny**	**howling**	**wrinkled**

1. the ________________ porcupine

2. the ________________ toad

3. the ________________ eel

4. the gray, ________________ elephant

5. the ________________ hummingbird

6. the tall, ________________ giraffe

7. the ________________ skunk

8. the ________________ deer

9. the ________________ wolf

10. ________________ flamingos

Chapter 1: Grammar

Adjectives and Articles

Rewrite It

The sentences below do not give the reader much information. Rewrite the sentences. Add at least two adjectives to each sentence.

1. The dog barked at the squirrel as it ran up the tree.

____

____

2. The dolphin dove into the waves and swam toward the sunset.

____

____

Proof It

Read the paragraph below. Circle the 20 articles you find. Six of the articles are incorrect. Cross them out, and write the correct articles above them.

A time capsule is a interesting way to communicate with people in a future. A time capsule is a group of items from the present time. An items tell something about a person, a place, or a moment in time. They are sealed in a container. A glass jar or the plastic box with a tight lid works well. Then, the capsule is buried or put in an safe place. An attached note should say when the capsule will be opened. Some capsules are opened in the year or in ten years. Others will stay buried or hidden for a thousand or even five thousand years!

Chapter 1: Grammar

Adverbs

Adverbs are words that describe verbs. Adverbs often answer the questions *When? Where?* or *How?*

She *joyfully* cheered for them.	*Joyfully* tells *how* she cheered.
Yesterday, I had a picnic.	*Yesterday* tells *when* I had a picnic.
Brady put the box *downstairs*.	*Downstairs* tells *where* Brady put the box.

Adverbs can also describe adjectives. They usually answer the question *How?*

Sierra was ***too*** *late*. The sunset was ***really*** *beautiful.*

Adverbs can describe other adverbs, too.

Luke spoke ***extremely*** *quietly*. Shawn ***very*** *sadly* said good-bye.

Complete It

An adverb is missing from each sentence below. Choose the adverb from the box that best completes each sentence. Write it on the line. Then, circle the word the adverb describes.

loudly	**brightly**	**often**
beside	**suddenly**	**completely**

1. Dylan sat ________________ Amina at the school play.
2. The two friends ________________ went to plays together.
3. The room was ________________ dark.
4. ________________, the curtain opened.
5. The scenery onstage was ________________ painted.
6. The children said their lines ________________ so that everyone could hear them.

Chapter 1: Grammar

Adverbs

Solve It

Read the sentences below. Find the adverb in each sentence. Write it on the lines after the sentence.

1. The prince slowly climbed Rapunzel's long hair.
   ___ ___ ___ (___) ___ ___
2. Little Red Riding Hood safely returned home.
   (___) ___ ___ ___ ___ ___
3. The wolf hid outside. (___) ___ ___ ___ ___ ___ ___
4. Jack climbed down the beanstalk to escape the giant.
   (___) ___ ___ ___
5. The cast proudly bowed at the end of the play.
   ___ ___ (___) ___ ___ ___ ___

Write the circled letters from your answers on the lines below.

___ ___ ___ ___ ___

Unscramble the letters to find the missing word in the title of the play.

Into the ________________

Try It

Write two sentences about a fairy tale. Use an adverb from the box in each sentence. Circle the adverb. Then, underline the word the adverb describes.

quickly	carefully	softly	completely
suddenly	gently	sadly	

1. ____

2. ____

Chapter 1: Grammar

Conjunctions

A **conjunction** joins together words, phrases, and parts of sentences. The most common conjunctions are *and*, *or*, and *but*. Other conjunctions are *since*, *because*, *although*, *if*, *while*, *unless*, and *however*.

Chloe loves Brussels sprouts, *but* Haley won't eat them.

Since you play soccer, can you give me some tips?

Complete It

Choose a conjunction to complete each sentence. Write it on the line.

1. Do you want to play the violin ________________ the piano? (or, but)
2. Mr. Randall canceled Lucy's lesson ________________ he had a cold. (unless, because)
3. Let's play a duet at the recital ________________ we can learn it in time. (while, if)
4. Owen plays the drums, ________________ Marcus plays the trombone. (and, or)
5. Mrs. Klein likes to knit ________________ Ezra practices singing. (however, while)
6. Liam always practices his scales, ________________ Alla never does. (but, if)
7. Jade can buy a drum set, ________________ her parents want her to help pay for it. (however, or)
8. ________________ Vikram's lesson is at 11:00, he often arrives at 10:30. (While, Although)

Chapter 1: Grammar

Conjunctions

Rewrite It

Combine each pair of sentences using a conjunction. There may be more than one correct answer for each item.

1. Jack wants to take violin lessons. His sister has been taking them for years.

____

____

2. Nora plays piano by ear. She can't read notes at all.

____

____

3. Dion enjoys listening to music. He doesn't play any instruments yet.

____

____

4. Mr. Santiago hums. He practices every afternoon.

____

____

Try It

Write a short paragraph about music. Use at least four conjunctions, and circle them.

____

____

____

____

Chapter 1: Grammar

Statements and Commands

A **statement** is a sentence that begins with a capital letter and ends with a period. A statement gives information.

Diego will be 13 in April. **S**udan is a country in Africa.

Commands are sentences that tell you to do something. Commands also begin with a capital letter and end with a period.

Use the bright blue marker. **C**hop the onions.

Tip	Statements usually begin with a noun or a pronoun. Commands often begin with a verb.

Complete It

The statements below are missing periods. Add periods where they are needed. Circle each period you add so that it is easy to see.

Monday, July 16

Dear Diary,

On Saturday, Shi-Ann and I set up a lemonade stand We made colorful signs to hang around the neighborhood Dad helped us make cookies and chocolate pretzels We wanted to make sure our customers would be thirsty

At the store, we bought a tablecloth, cups, and napkins Dad let us borrow some money to use in our change box Once we opened for business, we had tons of customers Shi-Ann and I had to keep making fresh lemonade all day

We each made ten dollars from our lemonade stand I had fun, but now I know that owning a business is a lot of work

Chapter 1: Grammar

Statements and Commands

Identify It

Read the sentences below. If a sentence is a statement, write **S** in the space. If it is a command, write **C** in the space.

1. It is simple and fun to make your own lemonade. _____
2. Ask an adult to cut ten lemons in half. _____
3. Use a juicer to squeeze the juice from the lemons. _____
4. Mix the lemon juice with six cups of water. _____
5. The amount of sugar you add depends on how sweet you like your lemonade. _____
6. I use one cup of sugar. _____
7. Stir in the sugar until it dissolves. _____
8. Add some ice, and enjoy a glass of cool, refreshing lemonade. _____

Try It

1. Write a command you might use to advertise a lemonade stand. Remember, a command usually begins with a verb.

   Example: Buy some cold, sweet lemonade today.

   ____

2. Write a statement about a business that you could start on your own.

   ____

Chapter 1: Grammar

Questions

Questions are sentences that ask something. When a person asks a question, he or she is looking for information. A question begins with a capital letter and ends with a question mark.

Will you go to the party with me**?**

What is the weather like in Phoenix**?**

Rewrite It

Read each statement below. Then, rewrite it as a question.

Example: It was cold and rainy on Saturday.

What was the weather like on Saturday?

1. The largest frog in the world is called the Goliath frog.

____

2. The skin of a toad feels dry and bumpy.

____

3. Gliding leaf tree frogs can glide almost 50 feet in the air.

____

4. The poison-dart frog lives in Colombia, South America.

____

5. There are more than 4,000 species of frogs in the world.

____

Tip Questions often begin with the words *who, what, where, when, how,* or *why.*

Chapter 1: Grammar

Questions

Proof It

Read the following paragraphs. There are seven incorrect end marks. Cross out the mistakes. Then, write the correct end marks above them.

Have you ever heard someone say it was "raining frogs". You might have thought that it was just a figure of speech. But in rare cases, it has actually rained frogs? How could this happen. It sounds impossible. During a tornado or a powerful thunderstorm, water from a pond or lake can be sucked into the air. This includes anything that is in the water.

The storm continues to move? As it travels, it releases the water into the air. Does this mean that frogs and fish come raining down from the sky. Yes, this is exactly what happens.

Cases of strange things falling from the sky have been reported for many years? People have seen small frogs, fish, grasshoppers, and snails drop from the sky in places like France, India, Louisiana, and Kansas. Are animals the only things that get swept up by storms. No. In fact, in 1995, it rained soda cans in the Midwest.

Try It

1. Write a question you would like to ask a frog expert.

____

2. Write a question you would like to ask a weather expert.

____

Chapter 1: Grammar

Exclamations

Exclamations are sentences that show excitement or surprise. Exclamations begin with a capital letter and end with an exclamation point.

The Gold Nuggets won the championship**!**

We missed the bus**!**

Sometimes an exclamation can be a single word. Sometimes it can contain a command.

Oops!   Uh-oh!   Watch out!   Come back!

Complete It

Read the advertisement below. Some of the end marks are missing. Write the correct end marks on the lines.

Kirby's Toy Store
is closing.
Get new toys while they last___
Our store is open every night until 9:00___
We are located at the corner of Nelson Road and Ash Street___
Tell your friends___ Tell your neighbors___
Don't miss out on the
best toy sale of the year___
Prices are being
slashed every day!
Toys are
50%-75% off___

Chapter 1: Grammar

Exclamations

Proof It

Read the sentences below. If the end mark is correct, make a check mark (✓) on the line. If the end mark is not correct, cross it out and write the correct end mark in the space.

1. Watch out. _____
2. Did you take the dog for a walk! _____
3. Luis is going to learn how to play the trumpet? _____
4. We won the game. _____
5. I lost my wallet? _____
6. How old is Ella. _____
7. My grandma had 16 brothers and sisters! _____
8. Harry wore a new suit to the wedding. _____

Try It

Imagine that you were going on a jungle animal safari. Think of two exclamations you might make. Write them on the lines below.

Examples: Watch out for that big snake!
That leopard runs really fast!

____

____

Chapter 1: Grammar

Parts of a Sentence: Subject

The **subject** of a sentence is what a sentence is about. In a statement, the subject is usually found at the beginning of the sentence before the verb. A subject can be a single word or it can be several words.

The entire team cheered when the winning goal was scored.
Irina loves to eat oatmeal for breakfast.
Brian Adams and Brian Rowley are in the same class.
Four raccoons, three chipmunks, and an opossum live in my backyard.

Identify It

Underline the subject in each sentence below.

1. The Golden Gate Bridge is located in San Francisco, California.
2. The bridge was built in 1937.
3. It was the longest suspension bridge in the world until 1964.
4. A suspension bridge is a bridge that hangs from cables.
5. Joseph Strauss was the engineer who designed the amazing bridge.
6. The Verrazano Narrows Bridge and the Mackinac Bridge are two other famous bridges.
7. The bridge's orange color was chosen so that it would be easy to see on foggy days.
8. Many movies and TV shows have included views of the bridge.
9. You can walk or bike across the Golden Gate Bridge during the day.

Chapter 1: Grammar

Parts of a Sentence: Subject

Complete It

Each sentence below is missing a subject. Find the subject in the box that best fits each sentence. Write the subject on the line.

The Golden Gate Bridge	**A statue of Joseph B. Strauss**
People and cars	**Maria**
The cost to build the bridge	**About nine million people**

1. ______________________ learned all about different kinds of bridges from her teacher.
2. ______________________ is 1.7 miles long.
3. ______________________ celebrates the famous engineer.
4. ______________________ visit the bridge every year.
5. ______________________ that travel north on the bridge do not have to pay a toll.
6. ______________________ was 27 million dollars.

Try It

1. Write a sentence in which the subject is a person's name. Underline the subject.

   ____

2. Write a sentence in which the subject is more than one word. Underline the subject.

   ____

Chapter 1: Grammar

Parts of a Sentence: Predicate

A **predicate** tells what happens in a sentence. It tells what the subject is or does. The predicate always includes the verb. Finding the verb in a sentence can help you identify the predicate.

In the sentences below, the verbs are in bold type. The predicates are in italics.

Evelina ***recycles*** *all her cans and bottles.*
The seagull ***soared*** *above the stormy waters.*
Jermaine ***took*** *a picture of the dog with his camera.*

Identify It
Read the paragraph below. Underline the predicate in each sentence.

In the United States, April 22 is Earth Day. On Earth Day, people celebrate the planet Earth. They take the time to remember that the environment is fragile. The first Earth Day was held in 1970. About 20 million Americans celebrated that year. Today, more than 500 million people around the world take part in Earth Day activities.

On Earth Day, people learn about different types of pollution. They also learn what they can do to help save the planet. Many people recycle things. Paper, glass, and aluminum can be reused in new ways. Some groups plant trees to help keep the air clean. Others pick up litter in their parks and neighborhoods. For some caring people, every day is Earth Day!

Chapter 1: Grammar

Parts of a Sentence: Predicate

Rewrite It

One box below is filled with subjects. One box is filled with predicates. Draw a line to match each subject to a predicate. Then, write the complete sentences on the lines below. (There is more than one correct way to match the subjects and predicates.)

Subjects	Predicates
Roma and Patrick	held an Earth Day 5K Run.
Alexis	cleaned up litter at McCoy Park.
Ms. Piazza's class	learned many ways to reuse newspapers.
My sister and I	donated ten dollars to a fund for endangered animals.
The students at Waxhill Elementary	planted eight small trees on Earth Day.

1. ______________________________
2. ______________________________
3. ______________________________
4. ______________________________
5. ______________________________

Try It

Write two sentences about something you can do every day to protect the planet. Underline the predicate in each sentence.

____

____

Chapter 1: Grammar

Sentence Fragments and Run-On Sentences

A sentence is a group of words that contains a complete thought or idea. All sentences have a subject and a predicate. Part of a sentence, or an incomplete sentence, is called a **sentence fragment**. Sentence fragments cannot stand alone.

Examples: *Drove to the store.* (no subject)
Because the sun. (group of words)
The girls on the porch. (no predicate)

Run-on sentences are sentences that are too long. They are hard to follow, so they need to be split into two separate sentences. If the two sentences are about the same idea, they can be joined with a comma and a conjunction like *and* or *but*.

Clare likes cheese her brother Miles does not. (run-on)
Clare likes cheese. *Her* brother Miles does not. (split into two sentences)
Clare likes cheese, *but* her brother Miles does not. (combined with a comma and conjunction)

Identify It

Read each item below. If it is a complete sentence, write **C** on the line. If it is a sentence fragment, write **F** on the line.

1. ______ Threw the ball.

2. ______ After Madeline made a basket.

3. ______ James scored a goal.

4. ______ Cheered, clapped, and yelled.

5. ______ The volleyball bounced off the net.

Chapter 1: Grammar

Sentence Fragments and Run-On Sentences

Proof It

Read the paragraphs below. There are four run-on sentences. Make a slash (/) where you would break the run-on sentences into two sentences.

Example: The clown wore enormous shoes / he had a large, red nose.

There are many different breeds of dogs each one has a special personality. Basset hounds are often thought of as hunting dogs. They have long, floppy ears and wrinkly skin they can be loyal, friendly, and stubborn. Some people think their droopy eyes are sweet others think these hounds always look sad.

Cocker spaniels are good dogs for families. They are friendly and good with children they have beautiful, long silky ears. Cocker spaniels are usually tan or black in color.

Try It

On a separate piece of paper, write two sentence fragments. Trade papers with a classmate. On the lines below, turn your classmate's fragments into complete sentences.

1. ______________________________

2. ______________________________

Chapter 1: Grammar

Combining Sentences: Subjects and Objects

Sometimes sentences that tell about the same thing can be combined. Then, the writer does not have to repeat words. Instead, the writer can combine two sentences into one by using the word *and*.

Terrence likes popcorn. Peter likes popcorn.

Terrence *and* Peter like popcorn.

Because the subject (Terrence and Peter) is plural, the verb form has to change from *likes* to *like*.

In the example below, both sentences tell about what Jill read, so they can be combined.

Jill read a new book. Jill read a magazine.

Jill read a new book *and* a magazine.

Identify It

Read each pair of sentences below. If the sentences tell about the same thing and can be combined with the word *and*, make a check mark (✓) on the line. If they tell about different things and cannot be combined, make an **X** on the line.

1. _____ Snakes are reptiles. Lizards are reptiles.

2. _____ Cheetahs are mammals. Toads are amphibians.

3. _____ The robin ate some berries. The robin ate a worm.

4. _____ Tarantulas are spiders. Black widows are spiders.

5. _____ The dolphin swam beside its baby. The whale headed for deeper waters.

Chapter 1: Grammar

Combining Sentences: Subjects and Objects

Rewrite It

Combine each pair of sentences below into one sentence. Write the new sentence on the line.

1. Bobcats live in the mountains of Virginia. Bears live in the mountains of Virginia.

____

2. The deer drinks from the stream. The coyote drinks from the stream.

____

3. The airplane startled the rabbit. The airplane startled the owl.

____

4. It is rare to spot mountain lions. It is rare to spot bald eagles.

____

5. Andy saw a deer at dusk. Andy saw a raccoon at dusk.

____

Try It

Write two sentences about wild animals you have seen. Then, combine your sentences into a single sentence.

Example: I saw a wild turkey. I saw a woodpecker.
I saw a wild turkey and a woodpecker.

____

____

Chapter 1: Grammar

Combining Sentences: Verbs

When two sentences tell about the same thing, they can sometimes be combined using the word *and*. The first two sentences below are about what Veronica did at breakfast, so they can be combined.

Veronica ate some cereal. Veronica drank a glass of orange juice.

Veronica ate some cereal *and* drank a glass of orange juice.

Some sentences can be combined using the word *or*. Use *or* if there are several choices about what might happen. In the example below, we do not know which choice Habib will make, so the word *or* is used.

Habib might walk home. Habib might ride his bike home. Habib might run home.

Habib might walk, ride his bike, *or* run home.

If you list several things in a row, place a comma after each one except the last.

Complete It

Read the sentences below. Fill in each blank with the missing word.

1. Grandpa spread out the tent. Grandpa hammered the stakes.

   Grandpa spread out the tent ________ hammered the stakes.

2. Will might look for sticks. Will might cook dinner.

   Will might look for sticks ________ cook dinner.

3. Will put the pillows in the tent. Will unrolled the sleeping bags.

   Will put the pillows in the tent ________ unrolled the sleeping bags.

4. Grandpa and Will might make sandwiches. Grandpa and Will might grill hamburgers.

   Grandpa and Will might make sandwiches ________ grill hamburgers.

Chapter 1: Grammar

Combining Sentences: Verbs

Rewrite It

Combine each set of sentences below into one sentence. Write the new sentence on the line.

1. Grandpa stacked the wood. Grandpa found the matches. Grandpa lit the fire.

   ____

2. Grandpa toasted a marshmallow. Grandpa placed it between two graham crackers.

   ____

3. Will read in the tent with a flashlight. Will finished his book.

   ____

4. Grandpa and Will looked at the night sky. Grandpa and Will found the Big Dipper.

   ____

5. Next summer, they might sail down the coast. Next summer, they might go fishing.

   ____

Try It

1. Write two sentences that tell about things you do in the morning. Use a different verb in each sentence.

   ____

   ____

2. Now, combine the two sentences you wrote using the word *and*.

   ____

Chapter 1: Grammar

Combining Sentences: Adjectives

Sometimes, sentences can be combined.

The leaves are green. They are shiny. They are large.

The adjectives *green*, *shiny*, and *large* all describe *leaves*. The sentences can be combined into one by using the word *and*. Remember to use a comma after each adjective except the last.

The leaves are green, shiny, *and* large.

In the example below, only a comma is needed to combine the two sentences. Both sentences describe the jacket.

The red jacket is Amelia's favorite. The jacket is warm.

The warm, red jacket is Amelia's favorite.

Identify It

Read each set of sentences below. If the adjectives describe the same thing, the sentences can be combined. Make a check mark (✓) on the line. If they describe different things, the sentences cannot be combined. Make an **X** on the line.

1. ______ The strawberries are red. They are juicy.
2. ______ The lemons are tart. The lemonade is sweet.
3. ______ I like wild blueberries. I like fresh blueberries.
4. ______ The grapes are ripe. They are dark purple. They are plump.
5. ______ The fuzzy kiwi is on the table. It is round.
6. ______ Oranges are tropical. Apples can be red, green, or yellow.

Chapter 1: Grammar

Combining Sentences: Adjectives

Rewrite It

Combine each set of sentences below into one sentence. Write the new sentence on the line.

1. Cucumbers are long. They are thin. They are green.

____

2. Sam grew some huge tomatoes in his garden. They were juicy.

____

3. The rabbits seem to love Mom's lettuce. It is leafy.

____

4. The seedlings are tiny. The seedlings are pale green.

____

5. Rohan's peppers were small. They were spicy.

____

Try It

1. Write two sentences that describe a piece of clothing you are wearing. Use a different adjective in each sentence.

   Example: I am wearing a new shirt. My shirt is striped.

____

____

2. Now, write a sentence that combines the two sentences you wrote.

   Example: I am wearing a new, striped shirt.

____

Chapter 2: Mechanics

Capitalization and Punctuation

Mechanics refers to the rules of a written language. These rules include knowing when to capitalize words and when to use specific punctuation. Your child probably already knows to capitalize proper nouns and the first word in a sentence. But there are other rules for when to capitalize words, such as in the title of a book or song. Dates and holidays are also capitalized.

One of the best ways for children to learn about the rules of language is through reading a variety of materials. Help your child pay attention to capitalization and punctuation when reading. For example, point out the quotation marks used to show dialogue in a story. Have your child read the dialogue in the story while you read any text that is not part of the dialogue. Doing this will help your child pay better attention to the story and to punctuation throughout the text.

Skill Checklist

- ☐ **Capitalize the first word in a sentence and in names, titles, place names, dates, holidays, books, movies, and songs**
- ☐ **Use periods in statements, commands, and abbreviations**
- ☐ **Use question marks and exclamation points**
- ☐ **Use commas with dates, cities, states, and addresses**
- ☐ **Use commas in a series and compound sentences**
- ☐ **Use punctuation in dialogue**
- ☐ **Use punctuation in titles, such as books, movies, and stories**

Chapter 2: Mechanics

Helpful Definitions

abbreviation: a shortened version of a word that is usually followed by a period

Dr. = Doctor

Dec. = December

St. = Street

Ave. = Avenue

Help your child find abbreviations in the world around them. For example, point out abbreviations on pieces of mail. Ask your child to name the word the abbreviation stands for.

compound sentence: two or more complete sentences joined together with a comma and a conjunction

The library is closed today, **so** we are going to the park.

Tatum was tired, **but** she still wanted to swim.

Mark brought his bike to school, **and** Tim brought his scooter.

dialogue: the exact words a person says, shown with quotation marks

Beckett asked his sister, **"Can I use the tablet?"**

"Sure! Give me a couple minutes to finish this game," she responded. His sister was just about to earn her highest score ever in Zombie Crush. She did it!

"Yes!" she exclaimed. **"I earned five stars on this level. I'll take a break so you can play."**

"Good job! Thank you!" Beckett told his sister.

Video

Using Capital Letters

Using Commas in a Series

Chapter 2: Mechanics

Capitalizing the First Word in a Sentence

The first word of a sentence always begins with a **capital letter**. A capital letter is a sign to the reader that a new sentence is starting.

I live on the third floor of the apartment building.
Do you like green beans?
Here comes the parade!
Maya grinned at Jeff.

Proof It

Read the paragraphs below. The first word of every sentence should be capitalized. To capitalize a letter, underline it three times (≡). Then, write the capital letter above it.

Example: (M) my sister taught me a new computer game.

have you ever played golf? if you have, you know that it can be harder than it looks. golfer Michelle Wie West makes it look pretty easy. that's because she can hit a golf ball more than 300 yards! at the age of 13, Michelle became the youngest winner ever of the Women's Amateur Public Links. she has even played on the famous men's golf tour, the PGA Tour. some people think that this amazing six-foot-tall golfer will be the next Tiger Woods.

Chapter 2: Mechanics

Capitalizing the First Word in a Sentence

Rewrite It

Rewrite each sentence below. Make sure your sentences begin with a capital letter.

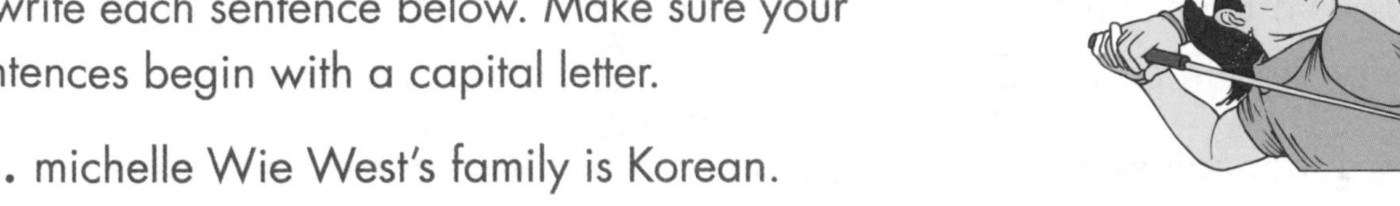

1. michelle Wie West's family is Korean.

   ____

2. she started beating her parents at golf when she was about eight.

   ____

3. today, Michelle plays regularly on the LPGA Tour.

   ____

4. *competitive* and *determined* are two words that describe Michelle.

   ____

5. david Leadbetter was Michelle's coach for years.

   ____

6. what kind of golfing records will Michelle set in the future?

   ____

Try It

1. What sports do you like to play or watch? Begin your sentence with a capital letter.

   ____

2. What sports figure do you most admire? Begin your sentence with a capital letter.

   ____

Chapter 2: Mechanics

Capitalizing Names and Titles

Capitalize the **specific names of people and pets**.

My cousin *Umeko* moved here from Japan.
We named the puppy *George*.

A **title** is a word that comes before a person's name. A title gives more information about who a person is. Titles that come before a name are capitalized.

Grandpa Bruce
Captain Albrecht
Senator Barbara Boxer
Aunt Juliet
President Abraham Lincoln
Judge Naser

Titles of respect are also capitalized.

Mr. Watterson
Miss Newton
Mrs. Cohen
Dr. Gupta
Ms. Liang

Tip	If a title is not used with a name, it is not capitalized. My *aunt* is funny. The *judge* was here. But, if a title is used as a name, it is capitalized. Tell *Mom* I am going to the park. *Grandpa* will fix the computer.

Complete It

Complete each sentence below with the words in parentheses ( ). Some of the words will need to be capitalized. Others will not.

1. Kelly took her dog, ___________________, for a walk to the park. (abby)
2. My school has a new ___________________. (principal)
3. On Tuesday, ___________________ is coming to visit. (grandma)
4. The best teacher I ever had was ___________________. (mr. butler)
5. The baby dolphin at the zoo is named ___________________. (michi)

Chapter 2: Mechanics

Capitalizing Names and Titles

Proof It

Read the letter below. There are ten mistakes. To capitalize a letter, underline it three times, and write the capital letter above it. To lowercase a letter (or change it from a capital letter to a small letter), make a slash through it. Then, write the small letter above it.

Example: Olivia and matt asked their Grandma if she knew mr. Buckman.

April 12

Dear mayor Hendricks,

My name is annie Chun. My aunt and Uncle live near Pebblebrook Creek. When I visited them last week, we went wading. We were looking for rocks for a science project I am doing in mrs. sutton's class. We found the rocks, but we found many other things, too. For example, aunt Rose found several soda cans. Uncle Richard found some candy wrappers. Their dog, louie, discovered an old bottle. He thought it was a bone.

I would like to organize a cleanup of Pebblebrook Creek. I know the environment is important to you as the town Mayor. Can you help me organize this event? Maybe the next time my Aunt, uncle, Louie, and I go wading, we won't find anything but rocks.

Sincerely,

Annie chun

Chapter 2: Mechanics

Capitalizing Place Names

The **names of specific places** always begin with a capital letter.

Madison, Wisconsin | *Rocky Mountains*
Italy | *Liberty Avenue*
Science Museum of Minnesota | *Jupiter*
Jones Middle School | *Los Angeles Public Library*

Complete It

Complete each sentence below with the word or words in parentheses ( ). Remember to capitalize the names of specific places.

1. There are many _________________ (towns) across _________________ (america) that have interesting names.
2. Have you ever heard of Okay, _________________ (arkansas)?
3. Some towns are named after foods, like Avocado, California, and _________________ (two egg), Florida.
4. Some names, like Chickasawhatchee and _________________ (goochland) are fun to say.
5. A person from _________________ (russia) might be surprised to find a town named Moscow in Vermont.
6. If you're on your way to visit _________________ (mount rushmore), look for Igloo, South Dakota.
7. Would you like to go to ___________________________________ (boring elementary school) in Boring, Oregon?

Tip

In the names of specific places, some words are not capitalized. All the important words begin with a capital letter. Small words, like *of*, *the*, *and*, and *a*, do not begin with a capital letter unless they are at the beginning of a sentence.

Chapter 2: Mechanics

Capitalizing Place Names

Proof It

Read the directions below. Capitalize the names of specific places. To capitalize a letter, underline it three times (≡), and write the capital letter above it.

- Take wilbur street to preston parkway, and turn left.
- Travel about two miles on preston parkway.
- You will pass montgomery library and the talbot recreation center.
- At the light, turn right onto solomon road.
- You will drive over haystack bridge and pass a gas station.
- children's playhouse is located on the west side of the street.
- The address is 1548 solomon road.

Try It

On the lines below, write your own set of directions from your home to a friend's house. Be sure to include street names and any landmarks like schools, libraries, parks, and so on.

___

___

___

Chapter 2: Mechanics

Capitalizing Dates and Holidays

The **days of the week** each begin with a capital letter.

Monday, Tuesday, Wednesday, Thursday, Friday, Saturday, Sunday

The **months of the year** are capitalized.

January, February, March, April, May, June, July, August, September, October, November, December

The **names of holidays** are capitalized.

Memorial Day, Mother's Day, Thanksgiving, Kwanzaa

Complete It

Complete the sentences below with the name of a day, month, or holiday. Remember to use capital letters where needed.

1. I was born in the month of ____________________.
2. On ____________________, many people stay up until midnight to welcome the new year.
3. My favorite day of the week is ____________________.
4. On ____________________, Austin made a card for his dad and washed his dad's car.
5. ____________________ is the middle of the week.
6. In northern states, it often snows in ____________________.
7. The groundhog did not see his shadow on ____________________ this year.
8. Independence Day is on ____________________ 4th every year.

Tip	The names of the seasons (*spring*, *summer*, *autumn*, and *winter*) are not capitalized unless they appear at the beginning of a sentence.

Chapter 2: Mechanics

Capitalizing Dates and Holidays

Rewrite It

Rewrite the sentences below. Capitalize the names of days, months, and holidays.

1. presidents' day is on monday, february 21.

   ____

2. If the weather is nice, we will have a cookout on labor day.

   ____

3. thanksgiving day always falls on a thursday.

   ____

4. Ty gave a valentine to every person in his class on valentine's day.

   ____

5. Jessy is having a pool party on saturday, june 20.

   ____

Try It

1. What is your favorite holiday? Why?

   ____

   ____

2. What is the coldest month of the year where you live? What is the warmest month?

   ____

   ____

Chapter 2: Mechanics

Capitalizing Book, Movie, and Song Titles

The titles of books, movies, and songs are capitalized. Small words, like *of, the, and, in, to, a, an,* and *from,* do not begin with a capital letter unless they are the first or last word of a title.

Books	Movies	Songs
Stuart Little	Epic	"Down by the Bay"
Ramona the Brave	The Secret Garden	"Pop Goes the Weasel"
A Light in the Attic	Jumanji	"When You Wish Upon a Star"

Rewrite It

Rewrite the sentences below. Capitalize the names of books, movies, and song titles.

1. It took Shakhil only two days to read the book how to eat fried worms.

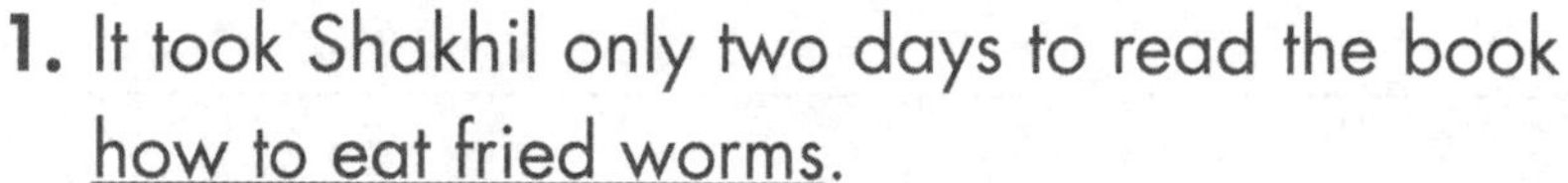

____

2. Sara is sleeping over tonight, and we are going to watch toy story 2.

____

3. The song "let it go" is from the movie frozen.

____

4. I love the poems in Bruce Lansky's book no more homework, no more tests.

____

5. Devon listened to the song "yellow submarine" on his mom's music playlist.

____

Chapter 2: Mechanics

Capitalizing Book, Movie, and Song Titles

Proof It

Read the sentences below. There are 24 words that should begin with a capital letter but do not. To capitalize a letter, underline it three times. Then, write the capital letter above it.

1. I love to sing "hakuna matata" from the Lion King because the words are fun to say.
2. Have you seen the old version or the new version of The parent trap?
3. Felipe borrowed the way things work by David Macaulay from the library.
4. If you watch Schoolhouse Rock, you can learn the song "conjunction junction."
5. Last week, Lottie read Freckle juice and Chocolate fever.
6. madeline is the name of a book and a movie.
7. Reading the great kapok tree by Lynne Cherry is a good way to learn about rain forests.
8. My little sister sings "shake your sillies out" every morning.
9. Paul and Tyler saw walking with dinosaurs three times in the movie theater!

Try It

1. Imagine that you were shipwrecked on a desert island. If you could bring only one book with you, what would it be?

   ___

2. What is the funniest movie you have seen in the last year?

   ___

Chapter 2: Mechanics

Periods

A **period** is an end mark that follows a statement or a command.

Put your bike in the garage. Natalie has four brothers.

Periods are also used after initials. An **initial** is a letter that stands for a name.

Darren *B.* Johnson *P. L.* Travers *J. P.* O'Bryan

The **days of the week** are often written as abbreviations, or in a shorter form. A period follows the abbreviation.

Mon. Tues. Wed. Thurs. Fri. Sat. Sun.

The **months of the year** can also be abbreviated. May, June, and July are not abbreviated because their names are short.

Jan. Feb. Mar. Apr. Aug. Sept. Oct. Nov. Dec.

People's titles are usually abbreviated when they come before a name.

Mrs. = mistress *Mr.* = mister *Dr.* = doctor

Types of streets are written as abbreviations in addresses.

St. = street	*Ave.* = avenue	*Dr.* = drive	*Ln.* = lane
Rd. = road	*Blvd.* = boulevard	*Ct.* = court	*Cir.* = circle

Match It

Write the letter of the correct abbreviation on the line.

1. ______ October 2 **a.** Oct. 2 **b.** Octob. 2

2. ______ John Fitzgerald Kennedy **a.** John F Kennedy **b.** John F. Kennedy

3. ______ Tuesday **a.** Tu. **b.** Tues.

4. ______ Chester Avenue **a.** Chester Avn. **b.** Chester Ave.

5. ______ December 19 **a.** Dec. 19 **b.** Dcmbr. 19

6. ______ Madison Anne Hall **a.** Madison A Hall **b.** Madison A. Hall

Chapter 2: Mechanics

Periods

Proof It

Read the schedule below. Cross out words that can be written as abbreviations. Write the correct abbreviations above them.

Monday, March 7	Hot Potatoes concert at 422 Lakeshore Drive—7:00
Thursday, April 14	Cassie's dentist appointment with Doctor Phillips—10:00
Friday, April 29	Meeting with Mister Haddad—noon
Saturday, May 21	Drop-off costumes at Mistress Jensen's house—1668 Dublin Lane
Tuesday, August 30	Jimmy Ortega's birthday party—46 Brentwood Boulevard
Sunday, September 18	Brunch with Mister Sato—11:00

Try It

1. Write a sentence about what you would do if someone gave you a hundred-dollar bill. End your sentence with a period.

____

2. Ask three friends when their birthdays are. Write the dates on the line using abbreviations for the names of the months.

____

Tip	Abbreviations for days, months, and types of streets are used only in addresses and casual writing. For example, you might abbreviate the name of a day or month in a calendar or a note. Do not use these abbreviations in the body of a letter, a report, or a story.

Chapter 2: Mechanics

Question Marks

Use a **question mark** to end a sentence that asks a question.

Would you like some fruit punch**?**
Where is Connor going**?**
How many books did you read**?**
Can all birds fly**?**

Complete It

Read each answer below. Then, write the question that goes with the answer.

Example: **Q:** How tall is Mr. Stein?

A: Mr. Stein is six feet tall.

1. Q: ______________________________

A: Jupiter has at least 63 known moons.

2. Q: ______________________________

A: The sun is the largest body in the solar system.

3. Q: ______________________________

A: Mars is closer to the sun than Saturn.

4. Q: ______________________________

A: Galileo made his first telescope in 1608.

5. Q: ______________________________

A: Astronaut Shannon Lucid has spent more than 200 days in space.

6. Q: ______________________________

A: Mercury is the smallest planet.

Chapter 2: Mechanics

Question Marks

Proof It

Read the paragraphs below. Cross out the six incorrect end marks. Add the correct end marks, and circle them.

Have you ever visited the Sleeping Bear Dunes. They are located along the shore of Lake Michigan. The enormous dunes, or sand hills, are more than 400 feet tall in places. Many people travel to Michigan every year to climb the dunes? Most visitors come in the summer, but some people come in the winter, instead. Why would they visit the icy shores of the lake in the winter. Sledding down the steep slopes can be a lot of fun!

Do you know where the dunes got their name. A Native American legend says that a mother bear lay on the beach to watch for her cubs after a fire. Over time, sand covered the bear? Some people still think they can see the shape of a bear sleeping on the beach. This is how the dunes came to be called the Sleeping Bear Dunes?

Try It

On the lines below, write a question you could ask a park ranger at Sleeping Bear Dunes National Lakeshore.

___

___

Chapter 2: Mechanics

Exclamation Points

An **exclamation point** is used to end a sentence that is exciting or expresses strong feeling. Sometimes exclamation points are used to show surprise or fear.

That pan is hot**!**
Lindsay won first prize**!**
I can't believe you broke the chair**!**
There's a snake**!**

Proof It

Read the diary entry below. Five of the periods should be exclamation points. Find the five incorrect periods, and cross them out. Then, add exclamation points where they are needed.

Saturday, May 6

Dear Diary,

Something interesting happened today. I am going to be in a movie. The movie The Time Travelers is being filmed in my town. My mom works at the library. The director was learning about the history of the town at the library. My mom helped the director find what she needed. The director saw my picture on my mom's desk. She asked my mom if I would be interested in a small part in the movie. Would I ever.

I will have only two lines to say. Mom said she will help me memorize them. My scene will last about five minutes. Do you know what the best part is? I get to work with my favorite actor. I can't wait to start filming. Who knows? Maybe I'll be famous one day.

Chapter 2: Mechanics

Exclamation Points

Complete It

The sentences below are missing end marks. Add the correct end mark in the space following each sentence. You should add four periods, two question marks, and three exclamation points.

1. Evan and Tanner have been jumping on the trampoline all morning__
2. Have you read the book A Cricket in Times Square __
3. Kazuki's swimming lesson was cancelled__
4. Watch out__
5. Please clean your room before bedtime__
6. The Bradview Tigers won the championship__
7. Would you like cheese on your sandwich__
8. There's a huge spider in my bed__
9. Tereza traded stickers with her little brother__

Try It

1. Write a sentence that shows excitement. Your sentence should end with an exclamation point.

   ____

2. Write a sentence that shows fear. Your sentence should end with an exclamation point.

   ____

Chapter 2: Mechanics

Commas with Dates, Cities, States, and Addresses

Commas are used in dates. They are used in between the day and the year.

March 4, 2006   September 22, 1750   June 1, 1991

Commas are also used in between the names of cities and states or cities and countries.

Portland, Oregon   Paris, France   Minneapolis, Minnesota

When the names of cities and states (or countries) are in the middle of a sentence, a comma goes after the state or country, too.

Bethany stopped in Burlington, Vermont, on her way home.

In an address, a comma is used between the city name and state abbreviation.

Richmond, VA   Juneau, AK

Proof It

Read the sentences below. Add commas by using this symbol (^).

Example: The Rock and Roll Hall of Fame is in Cleveland^Ohio.

1. Basketball star LeBron James was born on December 30 1984.
2. Sarah Hughes skated in the Winter Olympics in Salt Lake City Utah.
3. Tennis stars Serena and Venus Williams won the doubles event at the Olympics in August 2012.
4. Olympic swimmer Michael Phelps was born in Baltimore Maryland in 1985.

Tip

When only a month and year are given, do not separate them with a comma.

August 1999   February 2014   December 1941

Chapter 2: Mechanics

Commas with Dates, Cities, States, and Addresses

Identify It

There are two choices below for each item. Choose the correct version, and write the letter in the space.

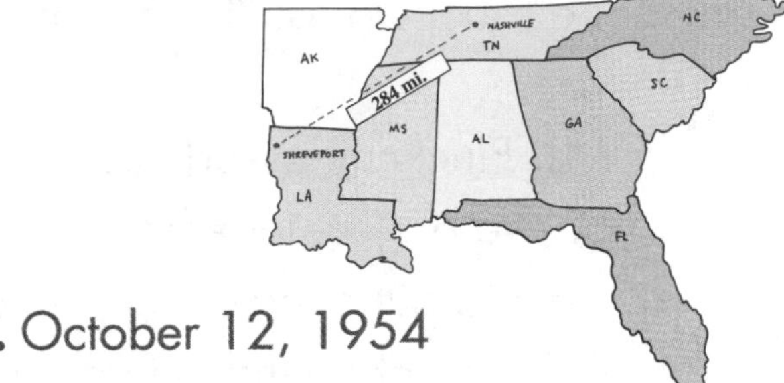

1. _____ **a.** October, 12 1954 **b.** October 12, 1954

2. _____ **a.** Omaha, NE **b.** Omaha NE

3. _____ **a.** August, 2007 **b.** August 2007

4. _____ **a.** January 24, 1936 **b.** January, 24, 1936

5. _____ **a.** Amarillo Texas **b.** Amarillo, Texas

6. _____ **a.** September 30, 2015 **b.** September 30 2015,

7. _____ **a.** Nashville, Tennessee, is 284 miles from Shreveport, Louisiana.
b. Nashville Tennessee, is 284 miles from Shreveport, Louisiana.

8. _____ **a.** The ship traveled from Crete, Greece, to the shores of Turkey.
b. The ship traveled from Crete, Greece to the shores of Turkey.

Try It

Ask two people in your class or your family the questions below. Record their answers on the lines.

1. In what city and state were you born?

____

____

2. What is your birth date?

____

____

Chapter 2: Mechanics

Commas in a Series

A **series** is a list of words. Use a comma after each word in a series except the last word.

Ms. Pinckney asked Alonzo, Erica, and Charley to work on the project together.

Dakota put a sandwich, an apple, and a granola bar in her lunchbox.

Our neighbors have two dogs, three cats, seven chickens, and a goat.

Proof It

Read the note below. Twelve commas are missing. Add commas where they are needed by using this symbol (^).

Dear Dillon,

Please go to the store for me when you get home from school. Tonight we are going to make muffins for Grandad's birthday breakfast. We will need blueberries eggs sugar and lemon juice. I left some money on the kitchen table.

Ellie is going swimming with Rob Aliya Eve and Hunter. She will be home around 4:00. Please remind her to let the dog out hang up her swimsuit and start her homework.

I made a list of the things you said you will need for your science project. I put glue sand newspaper vinegar and baking soda on the list. Is anything missing? We can go shopping tomorrow afternoon.

See you in a couple of hours!

Love,

Mom

Chapter 2: Mechanics

Commas in a Series

Rewrite It

The numbered sentences are missing commas. Rewrite each numbered sentence in the recipe, using commas where needed.

Lemony Blueberry Muffins

$1\frac{1}{2}$ cups flour
$\frac{1}{2}$ cup yellow cornmeal
$\frac{1}{2}$ cup sugar
$1\frac{1}{2}$ teaspoons baking powder
$\frac{1}{2}$ teaspoon baking soda
$\frac{1}{4}$ teaspoon salt

$\frac{1}{2}$ cup milk
$\frac{1}{2}$ cup plain yogurt
3 tablespoons oil
1 tablespoon lemon juice
1 egg
1 cup blueberries

*Always have an adult help you when you are cooking.

- (1) You will also need cooking spray a muffin tin a measuring cup two bowls a teaspoon a tablespoon and a wooden spoon.

  ____

  ____

  ____

- Preheat the oven to 400°F. Spoon the flour into the measuring cup.
- (2) Combine the flour cornmeal sugar baking powder baking soda and salt.

  ____

  ____

- (3) In the other bowl, combine the milk yogurt oil lemon juice and egg.

  ____

  ____

- Add the wet mixture to the flour mixture. Stir until moist. Fold in the blueberries.
- Spoon the batter into the muffin tin. Bake at 400°F for 20 minutes.
- (4) Remove the muffins from the pan place them on a wire rack and let them cool.

  ____

  ____

Chapter 2: Mechanics

Commas in Compound Sentences

A **simple sentence** tells about one complete thought. A **compound sentence** is made of two or more simple sentences. To form a compound sentence, use a comma and the conjunction *and*, *or*, or *but* to join the simple sentences.

In the examples below, the underlined parts of each compound sentence can stand alone as simple sentences. Notice that a comma follows the first simple sentence.

Sadie likes orange juice, *but* her brother prefers apple juice.
Do you want to go to the zoo, *or* would you rather go to the art museum?
Alejandro collects baseball cards, *and* Adam collects coins.

Identify It

Read each sentence below. If it is a simple sentence, write **S** on the line. If it is a compound sentence, write **C** on the line. Then, underline each simple sentence in the compound sentence.

1. _____ Have you noticed birds in your yard or your neighborhood?
2. _____ Feeding birds can be fun, and it can be educational.
3. _____ Some birds like birdseed, but others like suet, a type of fat.
4. _____ In the winter, many birds prefer fatty foods, like peanut butter.
5. _____ Bird food placed on the ground will attract birds, but it will also attract other animals.
6. _____ Squirrels are known for eating bird food and scaring birds away.
7. _____ Once birds notice that you are feeding them, they will come to visit often.
8. _____ Finches love thistle seed, and orioles love oranges.

Chapter 2: Mechanics

Commas in Compound Sentences

Proof It

Read the paragraph below. Three commas are missing from compound sentences. Add each comma by using this symbol (^).

If you have a plastic soda bottle, you can make your own bird feeder. With an adult's help, make two holes on opposite sides of the bottle and push a twig through each hole. Small birds can perch on the twig. Then, make several other holes in the bottle. The birds will be able to eat seeds from these holes. Tie some string around the neck of the bottle and hang it from a sturdy tree branch. Enjoy watching the birds from a window but don't forget to feed them.

Try It

1. Write a simple sentence about birds you have seen at a park or in your neighborhood.

____

____

2. Write a compound sentence about other city wildlife you have seen.

____

____

Chapter 2: Mechanics

Punctuating Dialogue

The exact words a person says are called **dialogue**. One set of quotation marks is used before the first word of dialogue. A second set of quotation marks is used after the last word of dialogue.

"I love to sail**."** "Is the fruit ripe**?"**

If the dialogue does not end the sentence, put a comma (not a period) inside the quotation marks. The period belongs at the very end of the sentence.

"I love to sail**,"** Chloe said**.** "The fruit isn't ripe**,"** said Geoff**.**

If the dialogue is a question and does not end the sentence, keep the question mark inside the quotation marks.

"Do you love sailing**?"** Chloe asked.
"Are the bananas ripe**?"** asked Geoff.

If part of the sentence comes before the dialogue, put a comma after that part of the sentence. The period at the end of the sentence belongs inside the quotation marks.

Chloe said**,** "I love to sail**."** Geoff asked**,** "Is the fruit ripe**?"**

Proof It

Read each sentence below. If the sentence is correct, make a check mark on the line (✓). If it is not correct, make an **X** on the line. Then, use the proofreading marks in the box to show the changes.

^	**= insert comma**
⊙	**= insert period**
^"	**= insert quotation marks**

Example: __X__ "Our suitcases are in the attic," said Dad.

1. _____ This summer, I am going to take Spanish lessons, said Mackenzie.
2. _____ "My family is driving all the way across the country in an RV," Ryan said.
3. _____ Nicolae said "I plan to go swimming at the lake every day

Chapter 2: Mechanics

Punctuating Dialogue

Rewrite It

The sentences below are missing commas, periods, and quotation marks. Rewrite each sentence. Add punctuation marks where needed.

1. I have never been to a farm before replied Audrey

____

2. Neither have I agreed Nicolae

____

3. My grandparents have cows, horses, goats, and barn cats said Van

____

4. He added I stay with them every summer, and there is always something to do

____

5. I would love to learn how to ride a horse or milk a cow said Audrey

____

6. Van grinned at Audrey and said My grandparents can always use an extra hand

____

Try It

Ask two of your classmates what they plan to do next summer. Record their answers on the lines below. Remember to use quotation marks to show the exact words your classmates use.

1. ____

2. ____

Chapter 2: Mechanics

Punctuating Titles

Titles of books, movies, and plays are underlined.

Lucas did a book report on <u>Two Heads Are Better Than One</u>.
The movie <u>Two Brothers</u> is an adventure about twin tiger cubs.
For Dionne's birthday, her family went to see the play <u>Peter Pan</u>.

Titles of songs, poems, and stories are set in quotation marks.

Judith Viorst wrote the poem "If I Were in Charge of the World."
The story "The Emperor's Clothes" is in my book of fairy tales.
My favorite song is "Bright Eyes" by Remy Zero.

Complete It

Read each sentence below. Underline the titles of books, movies, and plays. Put quotation marks around the titles of songs, stories, and poems.

1. Before the first softball game of the season, we always sing Take Me Out to the Ballgame.
2. Scotty Smalls is the main character in the movie The Sandlot.
3. My favorite poem is Eletelephony by Laura E. Richards.
4. In the play Annie, Bridget McCabe had the lead role.
5. Laura Ingalls Wilder wrote Little House in the Big Woods.
6. The movie The Incredibles won an award for Best Animated Film.
7. When it was time for bed, Dad told me a story called Gregory and Grandpa's Wild Balloon Ride.
8. I memorized Edward Lear's poem The Owl and the Pussycat.
9. Singing the song Purple People Eater makes my sister laugh.

Tip	Remember to place periods inside quotation marks if a title comes at the end of a sentence.

Chapter 2: Mechanics

Punctuating Titles

Proof It

Read the diary entry below. Find the titles, and underline them or place them in quotation marks. To add quotation marks, use this symbol (v̋).

Thursday, October 8

Dear Diary,

I had a very busy week. On Monday, I went to the library after school. I worked on the story I am writing. It is called The Mystery of the Golden Toothbrush. I borrowed the books Summer of the Sea Serpent, Stone Fox, and Pink and Say. I am going to write a book report on one of them, but I haven't decided which one.

On Wednesday, I recited two poems for Poetry Week. I chose The Shadow by Robert Louis Stevenson and Jellyfish Stew by Jack Prelutsky. After school, I tried out for the play The Princess and the Pea. I hope I land the role of the princess.

On Friday night, Ankit and Kendra came over to watch some movies. We rented Antz and My Neighbor Totoro. Antz is Kendra's favorite movie. My parents made subs and popcorn for us. We had a lot of fun, but I'm glad this crazy week is over!

Try It

1. What is your favorite song? Write the title on the line.

   ____

2. Think of an idea for a story you could write. Then, write two possible titles for your story on the lines below.

   ____

   ____

Chapter 3: Usage

Correctly Using Words

Most of the time, the English language follows specific grammar rules. For example, when making a verb past tense, you often can add *-ed* to the present form of the verb.

walk	**walked**
jump	**jumped**
help	**helped**

But there are times when verbs do not follow these rules. For example, the past tense of *run* is *ran*, not *runned*. And the past tense of *make* is *made*, not *maked*. Help your child find the exceptions to the rules when speaking or reading.

Reading a variety of books, stories, and other texts together will give you the opportunity to reinforce correct word usage. Point out a sentence and ask questions, such as:

- What is the subject?
- What is the verb? What tense is it?
- What would the verb be in the past (or other) tense?
- Find a contraction. What words are combined to make it?
- Is this noun singular or plural?
- What is a homophone for this word? How is it spelled?
- What does this word mean? Are there any other meanings of the word?

Skill Checklist

- ☐ **Use correct subject-verb agreement**
- ☐ **Use regular and irregular past tense verbs and future tense verbs**
- ☐ **Use contractions**
- ☐ **Use negative words and avoid double negatives**
- ☐ **Use regular and irregular plural nouns**
- ☐ **Use singular and plural possessive nouns**
- ☐ **Use subject and object pronouns**
- ☐ **Use comparative adjectives and adverbs**
- ☐ **Use synonyms and antonyms, homophones, and multiple-meaning words**

Chapter 3: Usage

Helpful Definitions

irregular past tense verbs: verbs that cannot be made past tense by adding *ed* or *d*

Present	Past
sing	sang
begin	began
swim	swam
take	took

contraction: a combination of two words where an apostrophe (') takes the place of the missing letters

she is	she's
they will	they'll
I would	I'd
is not	isn't
can not	can't

irregular plural: a plural noun that does not follow the rule of adding *s* or *es*

Singular Noun	Plural Noun
foot	feet
mouse	mice
sheep	sheep
ox	oxen

homophones: words that sound alike but have different spellings and meanings

two	too	to
their	there	they're
new	knew	
here	hear	

singular and plural possessive nouns:

Singular Possessive Noun
my child's cat
the lady's team
the family's picnic
my brother's books

Plural Possessive Noun
my children's cat
the ladies' team
the families' picnic
my brothers' books

multiple-meaning words: words that are spelled the same but have different meanings

Example: change

The word *change* can be used to tell that something was made different, as in when you **change your clothes**. It can also mean the **money that you get back** when you give a cashier more than the total amount of the sale.

Video

Subject-Verb Agreement

Past Tense Verbs

Possessive Nouns

Chapter 3: Usage

Subject-Verb Agreement: Adding s and es

The **subject** of a sentence tells who or what the sentence is about. When the subject is **singular**, it is only one person, place, or thing. When there is a singular subject, the verb ends with **s** or **es**.

Add **s** to most regular verbs that have a single subject.

The boat sail**s** close to shore. *The woman* water**s** the flower.

Add **es** to regular verbs that have a single subject and end in **sh**, **ch**, **s**, **x**, and **z**.

Gran kiss**es** us good-bye. *Jake* crunch**es** his cereal loudly.

When the subject is **plural**, it is more than one person, place, or thing. When the subject is plural, the verb does not end with **s** or **es**.

The kittens sleep on the sofa. *Zared and Nina* latch the gate.

Proof It

Read the paragraph below. Underline the subjects. Find the verbs that do not agree with their subjects. Add or delete **s** or **es** from the verbs so that they agree with their subjects. Use this symbol (^) to add a letter or letters. Cross out letters that don't belong.

Mr. Ruskin wash his historic car on Saturdays. Aaron and Ali helps him. Mr. Ruskin sprays the old car with warm water. He scrub every inch of the car with a big sponge. The children polishes the windshield and the mirrors. They use clean, soft rags. Aaron wax the beautiful red car. It shine in the sunlight. He wishes to have a car just like his dad's one day. Mr. Ruskin take Aaron and Ali for a drive in the shiny car every Saturday afternoon. They buy ice-cream cones. Then, they walks in the park.

Chapter 3: Usage

Subject-Verb Agreement: Adding s and es

Complete It

Read each sentence below. Then, read the pair of verbs in parentheses ( ). Choose the correct verb form. Write it on the line.

1. Emily and Mateo ________________ a ball in the backyard. (toss, tosses)
2. The Jorgensons ________________ their pumpkins every autumn. (harvest, harvests)
3. My little brother ________________ his teeth with an electric toothbrush. (brush, brushes)
4. Britta ________________ ten miles a day when she is in training for the race. (bike, bikes)
5. The blender ________________ the ingredients. (mix, mixes)
6. The Guzmans ________________ near a crystal-clear mountain lake every summer. (camp, camps)
7. The shaggy Irish setter ________________ the ball each time I throw it. (catch, catches)
8. Aunt Celeste ________________ about two hours away. (live, lives)

Try It

1. Write a sentence using one of the following verbs: *climb*, *skate*, *twirl*, *travel*, *race*, *point*, or *bake*. Underline the subject in your sentence, and circle the verb. Make sure that the subject and the verb agree.

   ____

2. Write a sentence using one of the following verbs: *push*, *crash*, *finish*, *pitch*, *watch*, *miss*, or *fix*. Underline the subject in your sentence, and circle the verb. Make sure that the subject and the verb agree.

   ____

Chapter 3: Usage

Irregular Verbs: *Am, Is, Are*

Am, is, and *are* are all different forms of the verb *to be.*

Am is used only with the subject *I.*

I **am** sleepy. *I* **am** hungry. *I* **am** under the bed.

Is is used when the subject is singular.

Mickey **is** sixteen. *Annabelle* **is** tall. *The beach* **is** rocky.

Are is used with the subject *you.*

You **are** very funny. *You* **are** correct. *You* **are** first in line.

Are is also used when the subject is plural.

Haley Joel Osment and Dakota Fanning **are** actors.
The boys **are** at home.

Rewrite It

Rewrite each sentence below. If it has a plural subject, rewrite it with a single subject. If it has a single subject, rewrite it with a plural subject. Remember that the form of the verb must agree with the subject and verb.

Example: The salad dressing and the salad are on the table.
The salad dressing is on the table.

1. Nissa and Toby are eight.

____

2. The photograph is in an album.

____

3. The books on the shelf are from the library.

____

4. We are excited about traveling to Mexico.

____

Chapter 3: Usage

Irregular Verbs: *Am, Is, Are*

Proof It

Read the paragraphs below. There are 11 mistakes with the verbs *am*, *is*, and *are*. Cross out each mistake. Then, write the correct form of the verb above it.

A topiary (*toe pee air ee*) are a kind of sculpture made from plants. Topiaries is cut to look like many different things. Some am shaped like animals. For example, a topiary can look like an elephant, a bear, a horse, or even a dinosaur. Other topiaries is trimmed to look like castles, cones, or mazes.

A topiary gardener are an artist. He or she can turn simple shrubs into beautiful sculptures. Boxwood, holly, bay laurel, and yew am some of the best plants to use for topiary. They is easy to train and to trim.

In May, I are going to visit the Green Animals Topiary Garden in Rhode Island. It am one of the oldest topiary gardens in the country. There am 80 pieces of topiary there! It are fun to imagine all the green animals coming to life and roaming the gardens.

Try It

Write three sentences on the lines below. Use the verbs *am*, *is*, or *are* in each sentence.

____

____

____

Chapter 3: Usage

Irregular Verbs: *Has, Have*

Has and *have* are different forms of the verb *to have.*

Have is used when the subject is *I* or *you.*

I **have** a cold. *You* **have** two brothers.

Have is also used with plural subjects.

We **have** a book about dinosaurs.
Roberto and Chiara **have** a baby sister.
They **have** a yellow house. *Both cars* **have** flat tires.

Has is used when there is a single subject like *he, she,* or *it.*

She **has** blonde hair. *The librarian* **has** a cheerful smile.
A male deer **has** antlers.

Complete It

Complete each sentence below with the word *has* or *have.* Write the correct word in the space.

1. Gus and Emily _________ a shell collection.
2. A horse conch _________ a cone shape and can grow to be almost two feet long.
3. Shells _________ value when they are beautiful or rare.
4. The shapes of some shells _________ interesting names, like helmet, basket, lamp, frog, and trumpet.
5. Oysters and clams _________ shells that are hinged at the back.
6. Emily _________ a necklace made from polished pieces of shell.
7. Cowrie shells _________ been used as money on Indian and Pacific islands.
8. If Gus _________ more than one of a certain shell, he will trade it with other collectors.

Chapter 3: Usage

Irregular Verbs: *Has, Have*

Proof It

Read the letter below. There are eight mistakes with the verbs *have* and *has*. Cross out each incorrect verb. Then, write the correct form of the verb above it.

August 6, 2015

Dear Kyra,

How is life at home in Massachusetts? We are having a great time in Florida. Gus and I has 40 new shells to add to our collection! We has been busy searching the beaches here. Gus and I already has labels for our new shells. We don't want to forget their names by the time we get home.

Some shells still has animals living in them. We never collect those shells. Our parents has helped us look in rock crevices and tide pools. That is how we found a true tulip shell. It have a pretty peachy color and an interesting pattern.

I has a surprise to bring home for you. You has never seen a shell like this. I can't wait to see you. Wish you were here!

Your friend,

Emily

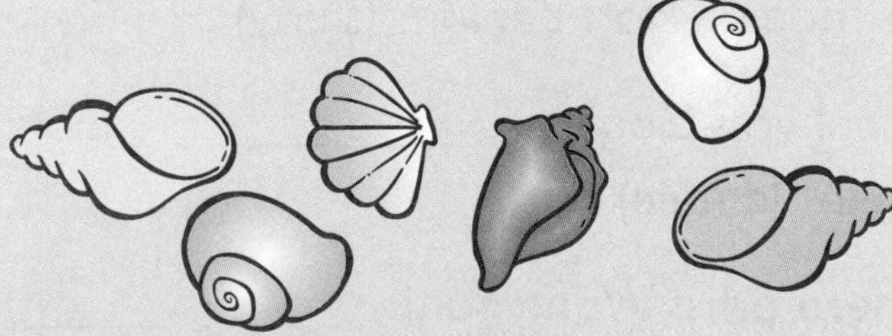

Chapter 3: Usage

Forming the Past Tense by Adding ed

Verbs in the **present tense** tell about things that are happening right now. Verbs in the **past tense** tell about things that have already happened.

Add **ed** to a regular verb to change it to the past tense. If the verb already ends in **e**, just add **d**.

The concert end**ed** at 9:00.
Uncle Donny taste**d** the pudding.
It snow**ed** 16 inches yesterday!
The waitress smile**d** at the girl.

If a verb ends in **y**, change the **y** to **i** and add **ed**.

We hurr**y** to catch the bus. — We hurr**ied** to catch the bus.
I dr**y** the laundry outside. — I dr**ied** the laundry outside.

Complete It

Read the sentences below. Complete each sentence with the past tense of the verb in parentheses ( ).

1. Leonardo da Vinci ______________ the mysterious *Mona Lisa*. (paint)
2. Women and children often ______________ for artist Mary Cassatt. (pose)
3. The Impressionists ______________ the world that not all paintings had to look realistic. (show)
4. Grandma Moses ______________ to paint cheerful pictures of life in the country. (love)
5. Jackson Pollack, who made colorful paint-splattered paintings, ______________ with Thomas Hart Benton. (study)
6. Vincent van Gogh ______________ more than 800 oil paintings during his lifetime! (create)
7. Chinese artist Wang Yani ______________ painting when she was only two. (start)

Chapter 3: Usage

Forming the Past Tense by Adding ed

Rewrite It

Read the sentences below. They are all in the present tense. Underline the verb in each sentence. Then, rewrite the sentences in the past tense.

1. Norman Rockwell lives from 1894 until 1978.

   ___

2. Norman studies at the National Academy of Design in New York.

   ___

3. He illustrates issues of children's magazines, like *Boys' Life*.

   ___

4. Norman paints scenes from everyday small-town life.

   ___

5. Norman calls himself a storyteller.

   ___

6. A fire destroys many of Norman's paintings.

   ___

7. Norman Rockwell receives the Presidential Medal of Freedom in 1976.

   ___

Try It

1. Write a sentence in the present tense that describes a piece of art you have seen or made.

   ___

2. Now, rewrite the same sentence in the past tense.

   ___

Chapter 3: Usage

Irregular Past-Tense Verbs: *Ate, Said, Grew, Made, Rode*

Some verbs do not follow the pattern of regular verbs. The past tenses of these verbs are different. To form the past tense, do not add **ed** or **d** to these verbs. Instead, you must change the entire word.

Present tense	Past tense
She *eats* a snack every day.	She *ate* a snack every day.
Mario *says* it will rain tonight.	Mario *said* it will rain tonight.
The tiny pine tree *grows* quickly.	The tiny pine tree *grew* quickly.
Catalina *makes* bracelets.	Catalina *made* bracelets.
I *ride* the bus downtown.	I *rode* the bus downtown.

Proof It

Some of the verbs below are in the wrong tense. Cross out the verbs in bold type. Use this symbol (^), and write the correct word above it.

When my mom was a little girl, her family owned a bakery. Mom **says** that she loved the sweet smell of bread and pastries baking in the ovens. Every morning, Mom **eats** a cinnamon roll for breakfast. She **rides** her bike to school when the weather was nice. In her bag, she carried fresh muffins for her teachers and her friends.

In the afternoon, she and her dad **make** crusty rolls and chewy bagels. Grandpa put all the ingredients in a big bowl. He and Mom took turns kneading the dough. Then, he covered it with a clean towel. The dough **grows** and **grows**. Mom **says** she loved to punch it down. Finally, she and Grandpa shaped the dough and popped it into the ovens. Mom's family **eats** fresh bread with dinner every night!

Chapter 3: Usage

Irregular Past-Tense Verbs: *Ate, Said, Grew, Made, Rode*

Solve It

Read each sentence below. On the line, write the past tense of the underlined verb.

1. Grandma always <u>eats</u> a blueberry bagel with cream cheese for breakfast.

   ____

2. The Larsons <u>say</u> that Hot Cross Buns was the best bakery in town.

   ____

3. Mom's cousin, Eddie, <u>rides</u> his bike around town and delivered bread. ______________

4. Mom <u>grows</u> up helping her parents at the bakery. ______________

5. Every Saturday, Mom and Grandpa <u>make</u> 12 loaves of wheat bread, 15 loaves of French bread, and 100 dinner rolls.

   ____

h	q	s	a	i	d	r
m	p	n	t	m	a	l
z	g	r	e	w	g	k
u	d	k	y	f	l	g
j	h	v	r	u	a	e
i	b	b	o	w	d	y
t	m	a	d	e	x	c
j	s	f	e	p	p	e

Now, find each past-tense verb in the word search puzzle. Circle the words you find. Words are written across and down.

Try It

1. What did you eat for dinner last night? Use a complete sentence to answer the question.

   ____

2. Write a sentence that uses the past tense of one of these words: *say, grow, make,* or *ride.*

   ____

Chapter 3: Usage

Irregular Past-Tense Verbs: *Gave, Flew, Brought, Thought, Wrote*

The past tenses of some verbs do not follow the patterns of regular verbs. To form the past tense, do not add **ed** or **d**. Instead, you must change the entire word.

Present tense	Past tense
Franklin *gives* her an orange.	Franklin *gave* her an orange.
The goose *flies* over the pond.	The goose *flew* over the pond.
Marisa *brings* some games.	Marisa *brought* some games.
Beth *thinks* she got an A.	Beth *thought* she got an A.
I *write* a letter to my grandma.	I *wrote* a letter to my grandma.

Rewrite It

The sentences below are all in the present tense. Rewrite them in the past tense.

1. Ms. Lucetta gives the class an assignment.

____

2. Nicholas and Liv write a play about a giant who lives in the forest.

____

3. They think the giant should be kind, not scary.

____

4. A small bluebird flies many miles to save the kind giant.

____

5. The bluebird brings him an important message.

____

6. The giant gives the bluebird shelter in his cave.

____

Chapter 3: Usage

Irregular Past-Tense Verbs: *Gave, Flew, Brought, Thought, Wrote*

Proof It

Some of the verbs below are in the wrong tense. Cross out the underlined verbs. Use this symbol (^), and write the correct past-tense verbs above them.

Pradeep and Kent <u>write</u> a play for Ms. Lucetta's class. Their play was about a brother and sister who <u>think</u> that an alien spaceship landed near their house. They named the brother and sister Harry and Carrie. In the play, something very large <u>flies</u> over Harry and Carrie's house one night. It made a loud whirring noise. Its lights flashed on and off.

Carrie ran to the window. She <u>thinks</u> it was a helicopter until she saw how big it was. Harry ran into the backyard. He <u>brings</u> his camera with him. Harry took as many photos as he could. Then, the ship grew silent and quickly <u>flies</u> away.

Pradeep and Kent <u>think</u> the play they <u>write</u> was fun and exciting. They were not sure how to end it though. Did aliens actually visit Harry and Carrie's house? Was it all a dream? They knew they would have to decide before they <u>give</u> their play to Ms. Lucetta.

Try It

In the selection above, why did the spaceship fly away? Use the past tense of the verb *fly* in your answer.

____

____

Chapter 3: Usage

Forming the Future Tense

To write or speak about something that is happening right now, use the **present tense**. When something has already happened, use the **past tense**. When something has not happened yet, use the **future tense**.

Past: I *used* all the shampoo.
Present: I *use* all the shampoo.
Future: I *will use* all the shampoo.

The future tense is formed by using the word *will* with a verb. The word *will* means that something has not taken place yet, but it will happen in the future.

Seamus *will come* home in three days.
The plumber *will fix* the leaky pipe.
The water *will boil* in a minute or two.
Ms. Webster *will make* lasagna for dinner.

Complete It

Complete each sentence with the future tense of the verb in parentheses ( ).

1. Charlotte ________________ a doctor when she grows up. (be)
2. Fernando ________________ to speak eight languages. (learn)
3. Maddy ________________ for the Olympics. (train)
4. Travis ________________ a cure for a serious disease. (find)
5. Akio ________________ wild animals. (photograph)
6. Elena ________________ all around the world. (travel)

Chapter 3: Usage

Forming the Future Tense

Rewrite It

On the line, write **PA** if a sentence takes place in the past. Write **PR** if it takes place in the present. Then, rewrite each sentence in the future tense.

Example: PA The movie ended at 8:00.

The movie will end at 8:00.

1. _____ The sheepdog barked at the mail carrier.

____

2. _____ The gardener picks flowers from her wildflower garden.

____

3. _____ The robin pulls a fat earthworm from the soil.

____

4. _____ A ladybug landed on Layla's shoulder.

____

Try It

1. Write a sentence about someplace you have been in the past. Underline the verb.

____

2. Write a sentence about where you are right now. Underline the verb.

____

3. Write a sentence about somewhere you will go or something you will do in the future. Underline the verb.

____

Chapter 3: Usage

Contractions with *Not, Will,* and *Have*

A **contraction** is a short way of saying something by combining two words into one. An apostrophe (') takes the place of the missing letters.

Many contractions are formed when a verb and the word *not* are combined. The apostrophe takes the place of the letter **o** in *not*.

is not = isn't	are not = aren't	was not = wasn't
were not = weren't	does not = doesn't	did not = didn't
do not = don't	can not = can't	

Some contractions can be formed with pronouns and the verb *will*. An apostrophe takes the place of the letters **wi** in *will*.

I will = I'll	it will = it'll	you will = you'll
we will = we'll	she will = she'll	they will = they'll
he will = he'll		

Contractions can also be made with the verb *have*. An apostrophe takes the place of the letters **ha** in *have*.

I have = I've	we have = we've
you have = you've	they have = they've

Proof It

Cross out the five incorrect contractions below. Use this proofreading mark (^), and write the correct contraction above it.

My neighborhood is having a giant yard sale on Saturday. Wel'l post signs all around town. This week, I'ill go through the boxes under my bed and in the attic. There are many things I know we do'nt need. At first, my little brother did'nt want to help. Then, I told him all the money would go to the animal shelter where we got our dog Maisy. I think he'ill be happy to help now.

Contractions with *Not, Will,* and *Have*

Rewrite It

Circle the two words in each sentence that could be combined to make a contraction. Then, rewrite the sentences using contractions.

1. We were not even open for business yet when the first customers arrived.

____

2. "I will give you 15 dollars for the tricycle," said Mrs. Smythe.

____

3. "You will find many great bargains," Justin told our customers.

____

4. Our free lemonade did not last long.

____

5. We have raised hundreds of dollars for the animal shelter!

____

6. Maisy and I can not wait to give the check to the shelter's director.

____

Try It

1. Write a sentence about something you do not like doing. Use a contraction with *not* in your sentence. Circle the contraction.

____

2. Write a sentence about something you will do in the future. Use a contraction with *will* in your sentence. Circle the contraction.

____

Chapter 3: Usage

Contractions with *Am, Is, Are,* and *Would*

Contractions can be made with different forms of the verb *to be*. The apostrophe takes the place of the first vowel in *am, is,* and *are*.

I am = I'm	it is = it's
you are = you're	we are = we're
he is = he's	they are = they're
she is = she's	

Contractions formed with the word *would* are a little different. The apostrophe takes the place of the entire word, except for the **d**.

I would = I'd	it would = it'd
you would = you'd	we would = we'd
he would = he'd	they would = they'd
she would = she'd	

Match It

Match each pair of underlined words with its contraction. Write the letter of the contraction in the space.

1. _____ I am going to take gymnastics lessons with my friend, Elise.
2. _____ She is a year older than I am.
3. _____ Elise said she would show me some warm-up stretches.
4. _____ Our class meets on Wednesdays. It is in an old building on Fourth Street.
5. _____ We are going to carpool to class.
6. _____ Elise's dad teaches gymnastics. He is also the high school coach.
7. _____ I would like to be on his team when I am in high school.

a. We're
b. she'd
c. He's
d. I'm
e. I'd
f. It's
g. She's

Chapter 3: Usage

Contractions with *Am, Is, Are,* and *Would*

Complete It

Fill in each blank below with a contraction from the box.

I'm	It's	He's	It'd
We're	she'd	I'd	She's

1. __________ like to meet Olympic gymnast Simone Biles one day.
2. __________ from my hometown of Spring, Texas.
3. I think __________ be a great gymnastics coach one day.
4. Elise's favorite gymnast is Sam Mikulak. __________ a three-time Olympic gymnast.
5. __________ each going to write a letter to Simone and Sam.
6. __________ sure they will write back to us when they hear what big fans we are.
7. __________ be an amazing experience to see the Olympic Games live.
8. __________ my dream to travel to the Olympics.

Try It

1. Write a sentence about a famous person you would like to meet. Use a contraction in your sentence. Underline the contraction.

   ____

2. Write a sentence that includes a contraction with the word *am*, *is*, or *are*. Underline the contraction.

   ____

Chapter 3: Usage

Negative Words and Double Negatives

Negative words are words like *no, none, never, nothing, nobody, nowhere,* and *no one*. The word *not* and contractions that use *not* are also negative words. A sentence needs only one negative word. It is incorrect to use a **double negative**, or more than one negative word, in a sentence.

Correct: There were *not* any oranges in the refrigerator.
There were *no* oranges in the refrigerator.
Incorrect: There were *not no* oranges in the refrigerator.

Correct: Kevin *never* saw anyone he knew at the store.
Kevin saw *no one* he knew at the store.
Incorrect: Kevin *never* saw *no one* he knew at the store.

Correct: *None* of the students were born in another country.
Incorrect: *None* of the students *weren't* born in another country.

Proof It

Read the paragraphs below. There are five double negatives. Cross out one negative word or phrase in the incorrect sentences to correct them.

If you haven't never heard of Jellyfish Lake, you should learn more about it. This amazing saltwater lake is in Palau, an island in the Philippines. You do not never want to get too close to a jellyfish in the ocean. Ocean jellyfish sting their prey. The jellyfish of Jellyfish Lake do not have no stingers. Instead, they use algae and sunlight to get the nutrients they need.

These jellyfish have only one predator—the sea anemone. This is why there are so many of them. No one can never swim in the lake without seeing millions of these jellyfish. It is a special experience for humans. Not nowhere else in the world can people swim surrounded by more than 25 million harmless jellyfish.

Chapter 3: Usage

Negative Words and Double Negatives

Complete It

Read each sentence below. Circle the word or words from the pair in parentheses ( ) that correctly complete each sentence.

1. The jellyfish don't (never, ever) stop moving.
2. They don't do (anything, nothing) but follow the sun across the lake all day long.
3. My aunt said there (is, is not) nowhere on Earth she would rather go snorkeling.
4. People who swim with the jellyfish shouldn't (ever, never) lift or throw the delicate animals.
5. There aren't (no, any) jellyfish without stingers in the oceans of the world.
6. Because the jellyfish don't have to hunt for their food, there (was, was not) no need for stingers.
7. The beautiful jellyfish don't (never, ever) seem to be too bothered by human visitors.
8. El Niño brought high temperatures to Palau in the late 1990s. Suddenly, there weren't (any, no) jellyfish in the lake.

Try It

1. Write a sentence using one of these negative words: *no, none, never, nothing, nobody, nowhere, no one,* or *not.*

   ____

2. On another piece of paper, write a sentence using a double negative. Trade papers with a classmate. On the line below, write your classmate's sentence correctly.

   ____

Chapter 3: Usage

Forming Plurals with s and es

The word **plural** means *more than one*. To make many nouns plural, add **s**.

one egg → two egg**s**
one pencil → many pencil**s**
one dog → six dog**s**
one photo → nine photo**s**

If a noun ends in **sh**, **ch**, **s**, or **x**, form the plural by adding **es**.

one bu**sh** → three bush**es**
one fo**x** → two fox**es**
one pea**ch** → five peach**es**
one bu**s** → several bus**es**

If a noun ends with a consonant and a **y**, drop the **y** and add **ies** to form the plural.

one bab**y** → all the bab**ies**
one cit**y** → many cit**ies**

Complete It

Read each sentence below. Complete it with the plural form of the word in parentheses ( ).

1. Ethan made two ________________ as he blew out his birthday candles. (wish)
2. All the ________________ in the yard came down during the huge thunderstorm last week. (branch)
3. Jacob takes care of the ________________ next door when our neighbors go out of town. (cat)
4. We need about six ripe ________________ to make apple pie. (apple)
5. Hallie left her ________________ at a friend's house. (glass)
6. Claudia and Crista picked sour ________________ from the tree in the yard. (cherry)
7. Please recycle the ________________ in the garage. (box)
8. Four ________________ have volunteered to organize the book sale. (family)

Forming Plurals with s and es

Solve It

Read the clues below. Find the word in the box that matches each clue. Then, make the word plural, and write it in the numbered space in the crossword puzzle.

airplane	**dress**
bed	**beach**
giraffe	**fox**
dish	**baby**

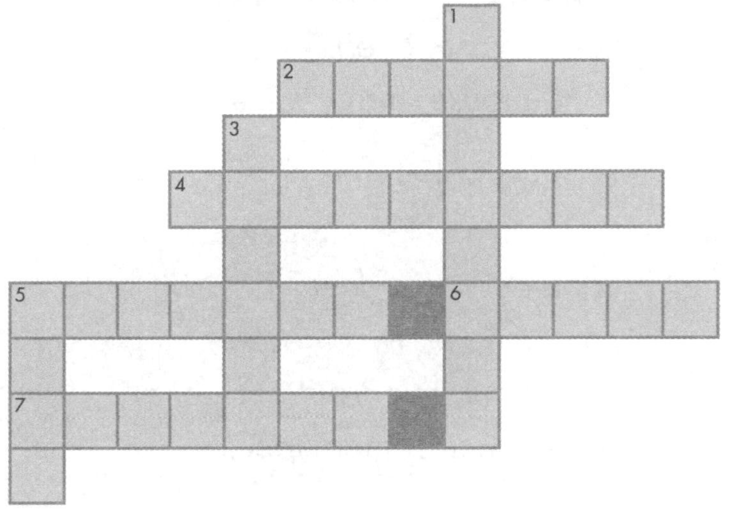

Across

2 very young people

4 machines that let people fly in the sky

5 sandy places near lakes or oceans

6 red animals with pointy ears and fluffy tails

7 pieces of clothing worn by girls

Down

1 tall animals with long, skinny necks

3 cups, plates, and bowls

5 soft pieces of furniture that you sleep in

Try It

1. Write a sentence using the plural form of one of these words: *peach*, *watch*, *wish*, *bush*, *dress*, *class*, or *box*.

 ____

2. Write a sentence using the plural form of any word. Circle the plural word.

 ____

Chapter 3: Usage

Irregular Plurals

Some plural words do not follow the rules. Instead of adding an ending to these words, you need to remember their plural forms.

one *man*, seven *men*
one *woman*, five *women*
one *ox*, six *oxen*
one *mouse*, many *mice*
one *foot*, two *feet*
one *goose*, ten *geese*
one *child*, a lot of *children*
one *die*, two *dice*

Some words do not change at all. The singular and plural forms are the same.

one *deer*, six *deer*
one *moose*, two *moose*
one *trout*, five *trout*
one *species*, nine *species*
one *fish*, forty *fish*
one *sheep*, a dozen *sheep*
one *series*, three *series*

Match It

Match each phrase below to the correct plural form. Write the letter on the line.

1. _____ one woman **a.** fifty womans **b.** fifty women

2. _____ one die **a.** six dice **b.** six dies

3. _____ a moose **a.** many moose **b.** many mooses

4. _____ the trout **a.** hundreds of trout **b.** hundreds of trouts

5. _____ one species **a.** eight species **b.** eight specieses

6. _____ the goose **a.** four gooses **b.** four geese

7. _____ one ox **a.** a herd of oxes **b.** a herd of oxen

8. _____ a child **a.** most childs **b.** most children

Chapter 3: Usage

Irregular Plurals

Solve It

On the lines below, write the plural form of each word in the box.

foot ___________	**ox** ___________	**deer** ___________
man ___________	**mouse** ___________	**sheep** ___________

Use the words in the box to complete the rhymes below.

1. The room was filled with 25 _______________, and every single man's name was Ken.
2. "Hurry, hurry, hurry!" said all of the _______________. "Walking's too slow, let's take the jeep!"
3. I am only one tiny gray _______________, and yet there are dozens of cats in this house.
4. Please do me a favor and move your _______________. I do not want footprints all over my seat!
5. In the garden I see dozens of _______________, and they've eaten all of my lettuce, I fear.
6. The man scratched his head and looked at the _______________. "Was it you who ate my bagel and lox?"
7. If I've told you once, I've told you twice. There's no room in this house for any more _______________!

Try It

On the lines below, make up two of your own rhymes using one of the plurals from the exercise above.

1. ____
2. ____

Chapter 3: Usage

Singular Possessives

When something belongs to a person or thing, they *possess* it. An apostrophe (') and the letter **s** at the end of a word show that the person or thing is the owner in a **possessive**.

Julianne**'s** violin
Ichiro**'s** basketball
the park**'s** gates
the school**'s** gym
the tiger**'s** stripes
Trent**'s** sister

Proof It

The possessives below are missing apostrophes. To add an apostrophe, use this symbol (v̓).

1. The White Houses address is 1600 Pennsylvania Avenue.
2. Two fires almost destroyed the home of the nations president.
3. The Presidents House, the Presidents Palace, and the Executive Mansion were early names for the White House.
4. The Oval Offices shape was chosen by President Taft.
5. Some of the worlds best artists have work displayed in the White House.
6. President Bushs dogs, Barney and Miss Beazley, were Scottish terriers.

Chapter 3: Usage

Singular Possessives

Rewrite It

Rewrite the sentences below. Replace the underlined words in each sentence with a possessive.

Example: The capital of Hawaii is Honolulu.

Hawaii's capital is Honolulu.

1. The hometown of Ronald Reagan was Tampico, Illinois.

2. The nickname of Benjamin Harrison was "Little Ben."

3. Theodore Roosevelt was the youngest president of the nation.

4. Michelle Obama, the wife of President Obama, is an advocate for healthy eating.

5. The 39th president of America was Jimmy Carter.

6. Before he became president, one of the jobs of Harry Truman was farming.

Try It

Write a sentence about a well-known figure from history. Use a possessive in your sentence.

Chapter 3: Usage

Plural Possessives

To form the **possessive of a plural** word that ends in **s**, add an apostrophe after the **s**.

the girls' room | the monkeys' food
the berries' juice | the teachers' decision

For plural words that do not end in **s**, add an apostrophe and an **s** to form the possessive.

the people**'s** goals | the men**'s** clothes

Complete It

Read each sentence below. Replace the words in parentheses ( ) with a possessive. Write the possessive in the space.

1. (The thick white fur of polar bears) ______________________________ keeps them warm during Arctic winters.
2. (The mother of the bear cubs) ______________________________ protects her babies from wolves and other predators.
3. (The coats of caribous) ______________________________ change colors, depending on the seasons.
4. (The flippers of seals) ______________________________ make them strong, speedy swimmers.
5. When the young girl listened quietly, she could hear (the songs of walruses) ______________________________.

Tip

Apostrophes are the key to telling the difference between a plural and a possessive.

Plural	Possessive
thousands of bugs	a bug's wings
several boys	the boys' clubhouse
four watermelons	the watermelon's seeds

Chapter 3: Usage

Plural Possessives

Identify It

Read each phrase below. If it is plural, write **PL** on the line. If it is plural possessive, write **PP**.

1. _____ the playful baby seals

2. _____ the igloos' walls

3. _____ the floating icebergs

4. _____ the Arctic rivers

5. _____ hundreds of salmon

6. _____ the puffins' brightly-colored beaks

7. _____ the explorers' route

8. _____ the people's warm clothing

Try It

Write two sentences that include plural words.

1. ____

2. ____

Now, write two sentences that use the possessive form of the plural words from above.

3. ____

4. ____

Chapter 3: Usage

Subject and Object Pronouns

Pronouns are words that take the places of nouns and proper nouns. **Subject pronouns** take the place of subjects in sentences. Some subject pronouns are *I*, *you*, *he*, *she*, *it*, *we*, and *they*.

Eduardo likes to rollerblade. — *He* likes to rollerblade.
The mall was crowded. — *It* was crowded.
Serena and Libby were in the newspaper. — *They* were in the newspaper.

Object pronouns often follow action words or words like *to*, *at*, *from*, *with*, and *of*. Some object pronouns are *me*, *you*, *him*, *her*, *it*, *us*, and *them*.

The horse ***jumped*** *the fence*. — The horse ***jumped*** *it*.
Joey went ***with*** *Mr. Simms*. — Joey went ***with*** *him*.
I put the letter on top ***of*** *the dresser*.
I put the letter on top ***of*** *it*.

Identify It

Read the sentences below. Underline each pronoun. Write **SP** above it if it is a subject pronoun. Write **OP** above it if it is an object pronoun.

1. The librarian gave him the book.

2. Heather and Chase took the puppy with them.

3. It will be sunny and 65 degrees today.

4. The children sang the song to her.

5. I will ask the owner tomorrow.

6. Ngozi received all the information from you.

Tip

When you are talking about yourself and another person, always put the other person before you.

Jaya and I   Lee and me   He and I

Chapter 3: Usage

Subject and Object Pronouns

Proof It

Read the sentences below. Cross out the incorrect pronouns. Then, use this symbol (^), and write the correct pronouns above them.

1. The students in Ms. Curry's class are going on a field trip. Them are going to the museum.
2. Ms. Curry told we that the museum is her favorite field trip.
3. The bus will leave at 8:30 in the morning. She will be parked in the school's west lot.
4. Casey and Allison will sit together. Them are best friends.
5. Ibrahim or Peter might sit with I.
6. The Goose Creek museum is not far away. It did not take we long to drive to him.
7. Michael forgot to bring his lunch. Ms. Curry gave he half of her sandwich and an apple.
8. Me loved seeing all the fossils.

Try It

1. Write a sentence using a subject pronoun. Circle the pronoun.

   ____

2. Write a sentence using an object pronoun. Circle the pronoun.

   ____

Chapter 3: Usage

Comparative Adjectives

Adjectives can be used to compare people or things that are similar. Add **er** to an adjective to compare two things.

"The medium chair is hard**er** than the small chair," said Little Red Riding Hood.

Add **est** to compare three or more things.

Papa Bear's bed is soft. Mama Bear's bed is soft**er**. Baby Bear's bed is soft**est**.

For adjectives that end in **e**, just add **r** or **st**.

nic**e**, nice**r**, nice**st**   clos**e**, close**r**, close**st**   gentl**e**, gentle**r**, gentle**st**

For adjectives that end in a consonant and a **y**, drop the **y** and add **ier** or **iest**.

tin**y**, tin**ier**, tin**iest**   spic**y**, spic**ier**, spic**iest**   bus**y**, bus**ier**, bus**iest**

Identify It

Read the sentences below. Choose the correct adjective from the pair in parentheses, and circle it.

4th Annual Fitness Challenge a Success!

Here are the results from last week's Fitness Challenge.

- Brad Dexter and Ariela Vega were the (faster, fastest) sprinters.
- The (youngest, young) student to participate was six-year-old Emily Yu.
- Most students said the obstacle course this year was (hardest, harder) than the one last year.
- Everyone agreed that the (easyest, easiest) event was the beanbag toss.
- The weather was both (sunnyer, sunnier) and (coldest, colder) than last year.
- The (stranger, strangest) thing that happened all week was when the clown made a homerun at the kickball game. No one knows who was wearing the clown costume!
- The cafeteria was (busiest, busier) after the challenges than it usually is at lunchtime.
- Morgan Bonaventure won the award for (Greatest, Greater) Overall Performance.

Chapter 3: Usage

Comparative Adjectives

Complete It

Read each sentence below. Complete it with the correct comparative form of the adjective in parentheses ( ).

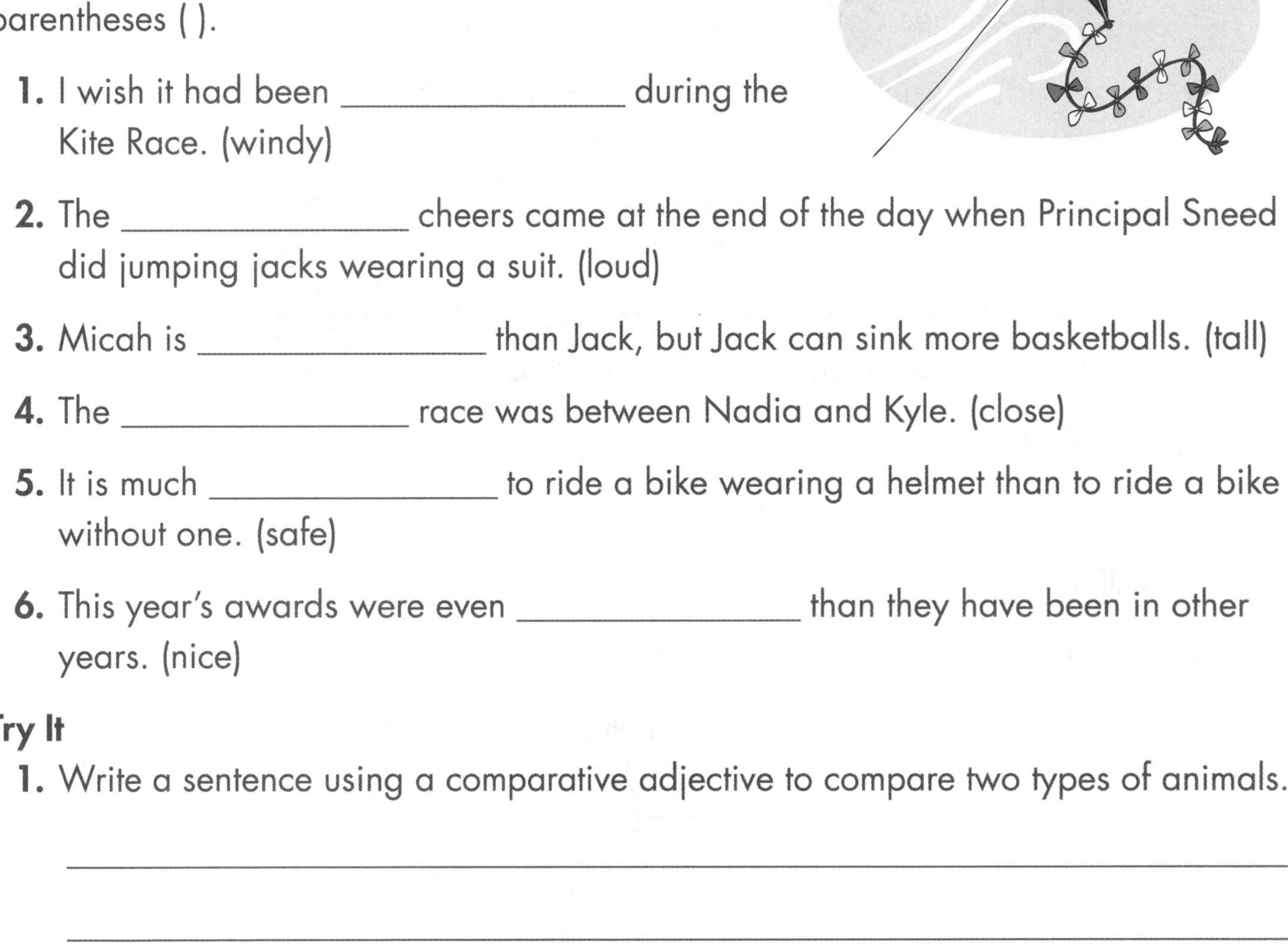

1. I wish it had been ________________ during the Kite Race. (windy)

2. The ________________ cheers came at the end of the day when Principal Sneed did jumping jacks wearing a suit. (loud)

3. Micah is ________________ than Jack, but Jack can sink more basketballs. (tall)

4. The ________________ race was between Nadia and Kyle. (close)

5. It is much ________________ to ride a bike wearing a helmet than to ride a bike without one. (safe)

6. This year's awards were even ________________ than they have been in other years. (nice)

Try It

1. Write a sentence using a comparative adjective to compare two types of animals.

____

____

2. Write a sentence using a comparative adjective to compare two things that you can see from where you are sitting.

____

____

Chapter 3: Usage

Comparative Adverbs

Adverbs can be used to make comparisons. Some adverbs follow the same rules that adjectives do. For most one-syllable adverbs, add **er** or **est** to make a comparison.

The boy in the blue shorts ran *faster* than I did.

Over the summer, Katherine grew *taller* than Jane.

To make a comparison using adverbs that end in **ly**, use the words *more* or *most*.

Aunt Peg read the book *more slowly* than Uncle Calvin.

My sister sang *most beautifully* of all the girls in her class.

Complete It

Fill in the spaces in the chart with the correct adverbs. Remember that some comparative adverbs need to be used with the words *more* or *most*.

slowly	__________	most slowly
fast	faster	__________
skillfully	__________	__________
happily	more happily	__________
__________	more patiently	most patiently
__________	__________	latest
safely	__________	most safely
playfully	__________	__________

Chapter 3: Usage

Comparative Adverbs

Proof It

Read the diary entry below. There are seven comparative adverb mistakes. Cross out each mistake. To add a word, use this symbol (^) and write the correct word above it.

Saturday, September 24

Dear Diary,

Today was the first day of Flannery's obedience class. We got there soonest than most of the other dogs and owners. Flannery sniffed and greeted the dogs as they arrived. She wagged her tail most cheerfully than any other dog.

The class leader helped everyone teach their dogs some basic commands. He laughed more harder than anyone when Flannery stole a treat out of his pocket. I'm sure he will hide them carefullier next time. The little dachshund standing next to us fetched more eagerly of all the dogs. She had short little legs, but she could run more fast than many of the bigger dogs. At the end of the class, Mom and I clapped most loudest of all the owners! Flannery will get her diploma in no time!

Try It

1. Write a sentence comparing two or more people or things. Use some form of the adverb *playfully*.

Chapter 3: Usage

Synonyms and Antonyms

Synonyms are words that have the same, or almost the same, meanings. Using synonyms in your writing can help you avoid using the same words over and over. They can make your writing more interesting.

quick, fast	present, gift	sad, unhappy
close, near	jump, hop	tired, sleepy

Antonyms are words that have opposite meanings.

old, young	wide, narrow	true, false
never, always	funny, serious	smile, frown

Complete It

Read each sentence below. If the sentence is followed by the word *synonym*, write a synonym for the underlined word on the line. If it is followed by the word *antonym*, write an antonym for the underlined word.

1. The rocks in the walls of the Grand Canyon are millions of years <u>old</u>. (antonym)
   ____
2. Limestone is the <u>top</u> layer in the nine layers of rocks. (antonym)
   ____
3. The waters of the Colorado River formed the <u>enormous</u> canyon. (synonym)
   ____
4. Francisco Vásquez de Coronado led the <u>first</u> Europeans to see the canyon. (antonym) ____________________
5. American Indians lived in the canyon <u>before</u> Europeans arrived. (antonym)
   ____
6. If you <u>yell</u> into the canyon, you will hear echoes of your voice. (synonym)
   ____
7. People <u>like</u> taking burro rides through the canyon. (synonym) ____________________

Chapter 3: Usage

Synonyms and Antonyms

Solve It

Write a synonym from the box beside each word in numbers 1–5. Write an antonym from the box beside each word in numbers 6–10.

difficult	wrong	destroy	sleepy	giggle
close	cheap	speak	loose	same

1. laugh ________________
2. wreck ________________
3. talk ________________
4. shut ________________
5. tired ________________
6. right ________________
7. expensive ________________
8. tight ________________
9. easy ________________
10. different ________________

r	t	j	d	e	g	h	o	s	q	d
f	d	i	f	f	i	c	u	l	t	g
j	e	i	b	w	g	h	m	e	y	y
o	s	a	m	e	g	e	d	e	u	r
a	t	w	b	k	l	a	e	p	z	n
w	r	o	n	g	e	p	n	y	u	o
l	o	o	s	e	k	c	l	o	s	e
g	y	c	l	n	s	p	e	a	k	d

Now, find the words from the box in the word search puzzle. Circle each word you find. Words are written across and down.

Try It

1. Write a sentence using a synonym for *terrific*.

____

2. Write a sentence using an antonym for *boring*.

____

Chapter 3: Usage

Homophones

Homophones are words that sound alike but have different spellings and meanings. Here are some examples of homophones.

Did you *hear* that noise?
Connor *knew* it would rain today.
There is only *one* pancake left.
Our family is very large.
Your mom speaks Spanish.

The party is *here*.
I like your *new* haircut.
I *won* the raffle!
Pick Sam up in an *hour*.
You're my best friend.

Identify It

Read each sentence below. If the word in **bold** type is used correctly, make a check mark (✓) on the line. If it is not used correctly, write its homophone on the line.

1. ________ Mei **new** the best way to get from Seattle, Washington, to Portland, Oregon.
2. ________ We are meeting for lunch an **hour** before we go up in the Space Needle.
3. ________ **You're** sister said that it rains a lot in Seattle.
4. ________ The Seattle Mariners **won** the game on Friday night!
5. ________ **Hour** class is going on a field trip to Pike Place Market.
6. ________ Is **your** boat docked in Puget Sound?
7. ________ The 1962 World's Fair was held **hear** in Seattle.
8. ________ The **knew** Seattle Central Library is a beautiful glass and steel building located downtown.

Chapter 3: Usage

Homophones

Complete It

Read the following sentences. Complete each sentence with a word from the pair of homophones in parentheses. Write the word on the line.

1. Jada ________ they would take the Washington State Ferry to Bainbridge Island. (knew, new)
2. ________ family moved to Seattle because Mom works with computers. (Hour, Our)
3. I can see the Cascade Mountains from ________! (hear, here)
4. I am excited that ________ going hiking at Mount Rainier this weekend. (your, you're)
5. ________ of Seattle's most famous residents is computer giant Bill Gates. (Won, One)
6. Brendan did not ________ the guide say that Smith Tower was Seattle's first skyscraper. (hear, here)
7. The Seattle Seahawks moved into their ________ football stadium in 2002. (new, knew)
8. Does ________ uncle still work at the Seattle Children's Museum? (you're, your)

Try It

On the lines below, write two sentences. Use the word *won* in the first sentence. Use the word *one* in the second sentence.

1. ____
2. ____

Chapter 3: Usage

Multiple-Meaning Words

Multiple-meaning words are words that are spelled the same but have different meanings. Look at how the word is used in the sentence to figure out which meaning it has.

In the first sentence below, the word *trunk* means *an elephant's snout*. In the second sentence, it means *a sturdy box used for storage*.

The elephant used its *trunk* to pick up the stick.
Grandpa's old photos are stored in a *trunk* in the attic.

In the first sentence below, the word *fair* means *a carnival*. In the second sentence, it means *equal* or *just*.

Jonah rode on a Ferris wheel at the county *fair*.
It is not *fair* that I have to go to bed an hour earlier than Amanda.

Find It
The dictionary entry below shows two different meanings for the same word. Each meaning is a different part of speech. Use the dictionary entry to answer the questions below.

watch *noun*: a small device that is worn on the wrist and used to keep time
verb: to look at or follow with one's eyes

1. Mikayla's grandparents gave her a watch for her birthday.
Which definition of *watch* is used in this sentence? _____
a. the first definition **b.** the second definition

2. Did you watch the movie you rented?
Which definition of *watch* is used in this sentence? _____
a. the first definition **b.** the second definition

3. What part of speech is *watch* when it is used to mean *a device used to keep time?* _____
a. a noun **b.** a verb

Chapter 3: Usage

Multiple-Meaning Words

Match It

Read each sentence below. Choose the definition that matches the way the word in **bold** type is used in the sentence. Write the letter of the definition on the line.

1. _____ If you don't hurry, you'll miss the **train**!
   a. to teach something by repeating it
   b. a line of cars that move together along a track

2. _____ Mark scored a **goal** in the second half of the game.
   a. something that people work hard to achieve
   b. a score in a game when a puck or ball is shot into a certain area

3. _____ Eloise is the **second** child in a family of four girls.
   a. number two; the one that comes after the first
   b. a moment in time; a small part of a minute

4. _____ We dropped pennies in the **well** and made a wish for each one.
   a. healthy; good
   b. a deep hole in the ground, used to get water or oil

5. _____ Gabrielle's piano teacher is **patient** when she makes mistakes.
   a. not easily irritated or annoyed
   b. someone who is getting medical treatment

Try It

1. Write a sentence using one of the multiple-meaning words from the exercise above (*train, goal, second, well, patient*).

____

2. Now, write a sentence using the other meaning of the word you chose.

____

Chapter 4: Writer's Guide

The Process of Writing

Writing is a process, not a one-hour or one-day event. Writers need to plan what they will write about before they even write a sentence. Then they spend time writing a first draft of their work, knowing they will later want to change many things. The process of revising and proofreading may happen many times during the writing process before a writer is satisfied with their work.

Writing in a clear and concise way is one of the most important skills that your child can learn. Many everyday tasks, such as writing an email to a friend or making a birthday wish list, require the ability to clearly communicate in writing. You can help your child improve their writing by having them write often. After they write, have them read their work to you. Then help your child revise and proofread to improve the passage. Explore fun ways to publish your child's work, such as printing it on special paper and sharing it with a relative.

Skill Checklist

- ☐ **Develop and organize ideas to write about**
- ☐ **Develop a draft that stays on topic, includes details, and uses complete sentences**
- ☐ **Revise, proofread, and edit to strengthen writing**
- ☐ **Publish in a variety of ways, including using technology**
- ☐ **Write paragraphs with a main idea and details**
- ☐ **Write friendly letters**
- ☐ **Write persuasive pieces with reasons to support a point of view**

Chapter 4: Writer's Guide

Helpful Definitions

The Writing Process:

1. **Planning:** brainstorm ideas to write about; plan your writing
2. **Writing:** write a rough draft; in this stage, spell words the best you can, but mostly focus on getting your thoughts on paper
3. **Revising:** change, add, or rewrite words, phrases, and paragraphs to make the writing better
4. **Proofreading:** correct spelling, grammar, and punctuation errors
5. **Publishing:** write or type a final version of your writing; read it to your classmates or members of your household

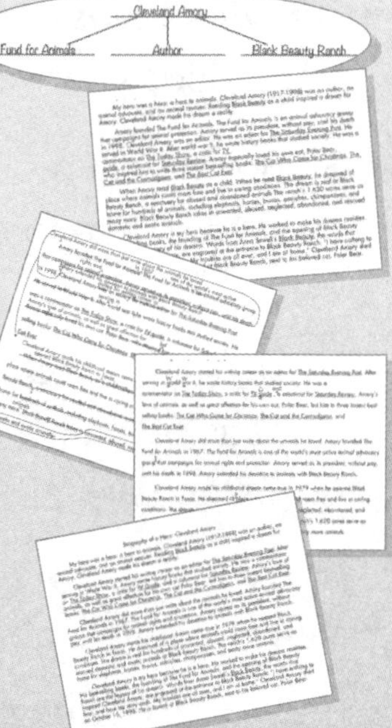

Proofreading Marks:

Proofreading Note	Symbol
Add a word or words	^
Remove a word or words	[circle with delete loop]
Add a period	⊙
Add a comma	[comma under a caret]
Start a new paragraph	¶
Fix the spelling	sp. [circle]
Change to a capital letter	≡

Using Proofreading Marks

Chapter 4: Writer's Guide

Planning

Before you start writing, you need to make a plan. **Brainstorming** is one way to come up with ideas. You may not use all of your ideas. Still, you will find the one or two great ideas you were looking for.

Sit down with a pen and a piece of paper. Make a list of things you know a lot about or would like to learn more about.

life in the Sahara desert	Eiffel Tower
basketball	space travel
islands	being an artist

Which topic is most interesting? Once you choose your topic, you can start learning more about it. You may need to go to the library. You may need to use the Internet. You may even need to interview someone.

Once you have all your information, make an **idea web**. It can help you put your ideas in order before you start writing.

Try It

On a separate piece of paper, brainstorm your own list of ideas. Let your imagination go, and have fun! Choose the most interesting topic. If you need to, look for more information. Then, create an idea web.

Chapter 4: Writer's Guide

Writing

When you first begin writing, do not worry about mistakes. You are just writing a **rough draft**. Look at the idea web you made when you were planning. Turn your ideas into sentences and paragraphs.

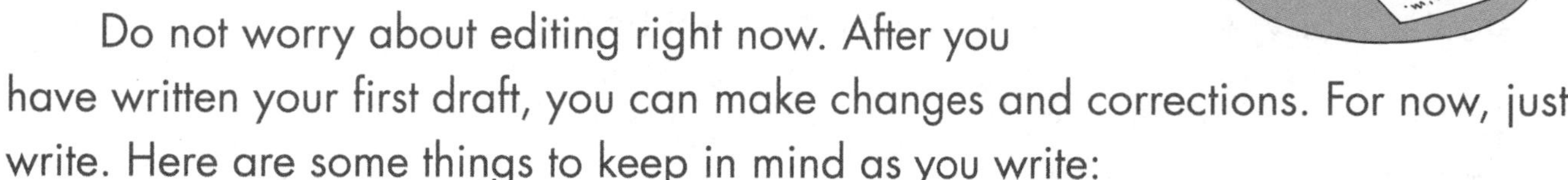

Do not worry about editing right now. After you have written your first draft, you can make changes and corrections. For now, just write. Here are some things to keep in mind as you write:

- Stay on topic.
- Include all the important details.
- Use complete sentences.

Here is an example of a rough draft. Can you see how the writer used the idea web to help write this paragraph?

The Eiffel Tower is an intresting place to visit. It was built in Paris France. It was made for a world's fair The Louvre is a famous museum in Paris. The tower is very tall. It was the tallest building in the world many people did not think it should be built. it looks like they were wrong, though. Millions of people visit it every year! It is one of the most famus landmarks.

Try It

Use the idea web you made to write a rough draft on another piece of paper. Remember, this stage is all about writing, so write! You'll be able to edit your work later.

Chapter 4: Writer's Guide

Revising

Now that you have finished writing, it is time to **revise**. Read what you have written. Sometimes it helps to read your work out loud. Ask yourself these questions:

- Do all of my sentences tell about the main idea?
- Can I add any details that make my writing more interesting?
- Are there any words or sentences that do not belong?

in 1889
The Eiffel tower is an intresting place to visit. It was built^in
Paris France. It was made for a world's fair. ~~The Louvre is a famous~~
986 feet
~~museum in Paris~~. The tower is^~~very~~ tall. It was the tallest building in
for 41 years They thought it would be ugly.
the world^many people did not think it should be built.^it looks like
About 6 the Eiffel tower
they were wrong, though.^Millions people visit ~~it~~^every year! It is
in the world
one of the most famus landmarks.^

In the paragraph above, the writer added some details. For example, explaining that the Eiffel Tower is very tall does not tell the reader much. It is more helpful to know that the Eiffel Tower is 986 feet tall.

The writer also took out a sentence that was not needed. The Louvre is in Paris, but it does not have anything to do with the Eiffel Tower. The writer decided that the sentence about the Louvre was not on topic.

Try It

Look at all the changes the writer made. Can you see why each change was needed? Now, revise your rough draft. Doesn't it sound better already?

Chapter 4: Writer's Guide

Proofreading

Proofreading makes your writing stronger and clearer. Here are some things to ask yourself when you are proofreading:

- Do sentences and proper nouns start with a capital letter?
- Does each sentence end with a punctuation mark?
- Are any words misspelled? Use a dictionary if you are not sure.
- Are commas used in the right places?

Proofreading Marks

Mark	Meaning	Example
^	= add, or insert	The ^black cat sat in the window.
^,	= add a comma	the tiny,^ spotted mushroom
g (G)	= capitalize	meg (M)
⊙	= add a period	We picked the tomatoes⊙
/T	= lowercase	The /Painting is on the wall.

The Eiffel Tower is an in^(e)tresting place to visit. It was built in 1889 in Paris^, France. It was made for a world's fair. The tower is 986 feet tall. It was the tallest building in the world for 41 years⊙ (M)many people did not think it should be built. They thought it would be ugly. (I)it looks like they were wrong, though. About six /Million people visit the Eiffel (T)tower every year! It is one of the most famu^(o)s landmarks in the world.

Try It

Use proofreading marks to edit your writing. Trade papers with a friend. It can be easier to spot mistakes in someone else's work.

Chapter 4: Writer's Guide

Publishing

After all your changes have been made, write or type a final copy of your work. Your paper should look neat and clean. Now, you are ready to publish. **Publishing** is a way of sharing your writing with others. Here are some ways to publish your work:

- Read your writing to your family, your friends, or your classmates.
- Make a copy of your writing. Send it to someone who lives far away.
- Read your writing aloud. Have a teacher or parent record you. You can use a video camera or a tape recorder.
- Make copies, and give them to your friends.
- Ask an adult to help you e-mail your writing to a friend or a family member.
- Get together with some other students. Make copies of everyone's writing. Combine the copies into a booklet that each student can take home.

From: Tucker Boone

Date: May 20

To: auntlouisa@smileyhorse.net; grandpajoe@21stcentury.com

Subject: Eiffel Tower report

The Eiffel Tower is an interesting place to visit. It was built in 1889 in Paris, France. It was made for a world's fair. The tower is 986 feet tall. It was the tallest building in the world for 41 years. Many people did not think it should be built. They thought it would be ugly. It looks like they were wrong, though. About six million people visit the Eiffel Tower every year! It is one of the most famous landmarks in the world.

Try It

Choose one of the ways listed above to share your work. What kinds of comments do your friends and family have? Can you think of any other ways to share your writing?

Chapter 4: Writer's Guide

Writing a Paragraph

A **paragraph** is a group of sentences. Each paragraph is about one main idea. All the sentences tell more about the main idea. When you are ready to write about a new idea, start a new paragraph. When the paragraphs are put together, they make a letter, a story, or a report.

A new paragraph does not start at the left edge of a piece of paper. It starts about five spaces from the edge. Leave an **indent**, or a space, about the size of the word **write**. This space tells the reader a new paragraph is starting.

The first sentence in a paragraph is the **topic sentence**. It tells what the paragraph will be mostly about. The next few sentences give more details about the topic. The last sentence is a **closing sentence**. It sums up the paragraph.

In the paragraph below, each important part is labeled.

indent → **topic sentence**

The Eiffel Tower is an interesting place to visit. It was built in 1889 in Paris, France. It was made for a world's fair. The tower is 986 feet tall. It was the tallest building in the world for 41 years. Many people did not think it should be built. They thought it would be ugly. It looks like they were wrong, though. About six million people visit the Eiffel Tower every year! It is one of the most famous landmarks in the world.

details (bracket beside the paragraph)

closing sentence

Chapter 4: Writer's Guide

Writing a Friendly Letter

Writing a letter can be fun. It is exciting to open the mailbox and see a letter waiting. Writing letters can also be a good way to keep in touch with people who live far away.

Here are some things to keep in mind when you write a letter:

- **Write the date in the top right corner.** Remember to start the name of the month with a capital letter. Use a comma between the day and the year.
- **Begin your letter with a greeting.** Follow it with the person's name and a comma. Most letters begin with the word **Dear**.
- **Share some news in your letter.** What is new in your life? Have you done anything fun? Have you been someplace exciting?
- **Ask questions.** It is polite to ask how others are doing.
- **End your letter with a closing.** Some popular closings are **Sincerely**, **Yours truly**, **Love**, and **Your friend**. Use a capital letter to begin your closing. Use a comma after it.
- **Sign your name below the closing.**

May 20, 2014

Dear Grandma,

How are you? I am doing fine. Last week, I wrote a report about the Eiffel Tower. Mom helped me do some research on the Internet. I learned many interesting facts. For example, did you know that the Eiffel Tower has 1,665 steps? Mr. Strasser said my report was excellent. I told him that I plan to see the Eiffel Tower in person someday.

Please write back to me, and tell me what's new in Park City. I miss you a lot and hope you can visit soon.

Love,
Tucker

Chapter 4: Writer's Guide

Writing to Convince

Have you ever tried to convince someone of something? To **convince** means **to get people to see things your way**. Maybe you have tried to convince your teacher that recess should be longer. Maybe you have tried to convince your parents to give you a later bedtime.

Words can be very powerful. You can change people's ideas with your words. Here are some tips for writing to convince:

- Think of all the reasons you feel a certain way. Make a list of your ideas.
- Now, think about why people might not agree with you. What could you say to change their minds? Add these ideas to your list.
- You are ready to begin writing. First, write a topic sentence about what you want or believe. Next, list your reasons. Finally, write a sentence that sums up your ideas.

Eiffel Tower should be free	**it's a public place**
	more people might visit if free
	people could donate money
	money used to care for tower

People should not have to pay to visit the Eiffel Tower. The tower is like a park or a library. It belongs to everyone. People should be able to enjoy it at any time. Instead of paying to see it, people could donate money if they wanted to. This money could be used to take care of the tower. More people might visit the Eiffel Tower if they did not have to pay. It should be free for everyone to enjoy.

Chapter 5: Reading

Developing Comprehension Skills

One of the most important ways to support your child's education is to make sure they are reading a wide variety of texts and reading often. Encourage your child to read both fiction and nonfiction. Ask them to read signs while riding in the car. Have them read menu options when your family goes to a restaurant. Encourage your child to choose books about topics that interest them. Take them to the local library often to check out books to ensure they always have something to read.

You can read to your child and have them read to you. Both situations help your child strengthen their reading and comprehension skills. When reading, support your child in the following ways:

- Ask your child to tell you the main idea of the text. This is what the text is mostly about. Ask your child to tell you about details in the text that support the main idea. If they are not sure, ask your child to reread sections of the text.
- Ask open-ended questions while reading with your child. These are questions that do not have a yes or no answer. For example, "Why do you think the author says [sentence from text]?"
- Ask your child to tell you about the characters, setting, and plot in a story. Talk about the main character and why he or she does certain things in the story. Ask questions about the character, such as "What is the problem the character has? What does he or she do to solve the problem?"
- After reading a text about a particular topic, have your child read another text about the same topic. Encourage your child to talk about the ways the texts were similar and different.

Skill Checklist

- ☐ **Read a variety of literature and informational texts**
- ☐ **Determine the main idea and details of a text**
- ☐ **Refer to details and examples to explain what a text says**
- ☐ **Determine the meaning of words or phrases in a text**

Chapter 5: Reading

Helpful Definitions

open-ended questions: questions that cannot be answered with *yes* or *no*

Open-Ended Question	Closed Question
What does the character think when he runs into the bully? How does this detail support the main idea?	Is the character scared of the bully? Does this sentence support the main idea?

close reading: when a reader carefully looks at a text to analyze the text's structure, word choice, main ideas and details, author's point of view, and other text features

Encourage your child to read a text more than once. They may even want to take notes, including a list of unknown words. After close reading, discuss the text with your child.

fact and opinion:

A fact is something that can be proven with evidence. An opinion is how someone thinks or feels about a topic.

Fact	Opinion
Elsa's shirt is blue.	Elsa's shirt is prettier than Jasmine's shirt.
The sun is a star.	The sun is too hot today.

dialogue: the exact words a person says to another person, shown with quotation marks

"I am so hungry!" exclaimed Mickey to his father.

"Lunch is almost ready. Why don't you eat an apple while you wait?"

"Good idea, Dad!" Mickey replied.

Video

Realistic Fiction and Fantasy

Chapter 5: Reading

Dad's First Day

Read to see why Dad is upset.

1 I think Dad is nervous. At breakfast, he almost poured milk into his orange juice instead of into his cereal bowl! Mom doesn't seem worried. She knows why Dad is a little upset. Today is his first day at a new job.

2 My dad builds bridges. Some of them look heavy and strong. Others look light, as if they are just hanging in the air. Dad says the light bridges are just as strong as the heavy ones.

3 Dad is an excellent bridge builder, even at home. Once, we almost filled my whole room with bridges. We used boxes, blocks, pots, pans, and even the dog's dish. It was great.

4 I know Dad has tons of great bridge ideas, so he shouldn't be nervous. I guess he just wants to practice making one more bridge before he goes to work.

Chapter 5: Reading

1. What kinds of bridges does Dad build?

2. Why is Dad nervous?

3. How does the boy know that Dad is nervous?

4. What kind of bridge did the boy and Dad make at home?

5. From whose point of view is the story told?

6. The last line of the story says that Dad is going to make one more bridge at home. What does he use to make it?

7. Is the first sentence of the story a fact or an opinion?

Chapter 5: Reading

Bridges

What kinds of bridges are there?

1 Have you ever stepped on a stone to get across a puddle or stream? If you have, you were using a bridge.

2 Bridges are different sizes and shapes. Some bridges have straight "legs," or supports, called beams. Other bridges have curved supports, called arches. Still others actually hang from strong steel ropes, or cables, that are strung above the surface of the bridge. The cables are then attached to the land on either end of the bridge.

3 Most bridges go over water, but some bridges were made to carry water. About 2,000 years ago, the Romans built this kind of bridge. One such bridge, in France, had three levels. Water flowed in the top level, and people and carts traveled on the two lower levels.

Chapter 5: Reading

1. This passage is mostly about

   ______ old bridges.

   ______ kinds of bridges.

   ______ making bridges.

2. The author wrote this selection to

   ______ make you laugh.

   ______ help you learn.

3. Think about what you already know about bridges. What are bridges for?

   ____

4. This passage tells about another use for bridges. What is it?

   ____

5. Are all bridges made by humans? What might a natural bridge be made of?

   ____

   ____

6. How are bridges with arches and beams different?

   ____

   ____

7. *The Golden Gate Bridge is the prettiest bridge in the U.S.* Is this a fact or an opinion?

   ____

Chapter 5: Reading

Bridges to Remember

Read to find out what is special about these bridges.

1 Some people do not like to drive across bridges. They look straight ahead and try to hold their breath until they get to the other side. Good luck if those people are driving in Louisiana. There is a 24-mile-long bridge there! It takes about half an hour to get across.

2 If you like to look way, way down when you cross a bridge, you should go to Colorado. A bridge there stands more than a thousand feet above a river. A 75-story building could fit under that bridge!

3 If you do not like to look down, get in the middle lane of a bridge in Australia. It has eight lanes for cars, two train tracks, a bike path, and a sidewalk.

4 Finally, if you like crowds and bridges, go to India. A bridge there carries 100,000 cars and trucks every day, plus thousands of walkers.

Chapter 5: Reading

1. How does the text help you understand how long a 24-mile-long bridge is?

2. How does the text help you understand how high the bridge in Colorado is?

3. If you do not like to look over the side of a bridge, why would the bridge in Australia be a good one to cross?

4. Why is the bridge in India a bridge to remember?

5. Name three things, other than cars, that cross bridges in the selection.

6. What do some people do if they are nervous on a bridge?

Chapter 5: Reading

Those Were the Days

What does Lorna learn about the past?

1 "Who's that in the picture?" Lorna asked. She pointed to a woman with white hair. Her mother looked more closely.

2 "That's your greatgrandmother Lucy."

3 Lorna looked closer too. "How did she ride her air scooter in that thing she's wearing?"

4 Lorna's mother smiled. "That 'thing' is a dress. And they didn't have air scooters. People drove cars to get around."

5 "Oh, I remember reading about those," Lorna nodded. "How did people get them up to their houses?"

6 Lorna's mother smiled again. "People's houses were on the ground back then."

7 Lorna made a face. "That would be weird."

Chapter 5: Reading

Some of these sentences are about **real** things. Write **R** by them.
The other sentences are about **make believe** things. Write **M** by them.

1. ______ Houses are not on the ground.

2. ______ Children wear space suits.

3. ______ People look at old pictures.

4. What do you learn about Lorna from the picture?

____

____

5. Why does Lorna ask about getting a car up to a house?

____

____

6. Look at the picture. What do you like best about Lorna's world?

____

7. Do you think Lorna lives in the past or in the future? Explain.

____

____

8. What is the setting for this story?

____

9. Why do you think Lorna feels that having a house on the ground is weird?

____

____

10. In the photo, Lorna's great grandma is wearing a ______________________.

Chapter 5: Reading

One City Block

Read to see who lives on Rachel's block.

1 Mama says the whole world lives right here on our block. Everyone is different, and I'll always like it that way.

2 Right down the hall is Mrs. Rotollo. She and her husband speak Italian, but when they see me, they always say "hello" in English. When Mama was sick once, Mrs. Rotollo helped me make dinner. It turned out yummy!

3 Upstairs is Philip. He takes dancing lessons. When I hear his feet thumping in the morning, I know it is time to get up.

4 Next door is Mr. Tran's grocery. Mama sends me over for fresh vegetables and fruit. Mr. Tran always picks out the best ones for me.

5 On the first floor of our building is Mrs. Moya's shop. I love the colors! I always know when it's going to rain because she takes her piñatas down.

Chapter 5: Reading

Write one thing you know about each of Rachel's neighbors.

1. Mr. and Mrs. Rotollo ______________________________

2. Philip ______________________________

3. Mr. Tran ______________________________

4. Mrs. Moya ______________________________

5. Look at the picture and the story. Which neighbor seems most interesting to you? Write why.

   ____

6. In the picture, who is Rachel? How do you know?

   ____

   ____

7. Would you like to live in an apartment like Rachel's? Why or why not?

   ____

   ____

8. How does Rachel know it is time to get up in the morning?

   ____

9. In the first paragraph, why does Mama say "the whole world lives right here on our block?"

   ____

   ____

Chapter 5: Reading

What Is a City?

What kinds of people, buildings, and jobs make up your hometown?

1 A city is made up of people. They live and work in the city. Some of them work to make sure the city is a good place to live. They make rules for the people in the city. One rule might be, "Don't throw trash in the street." What rules does your city have?

2 Other people try to make sure there are things to do in a city. They run restaurants, movie theaters, and sports centers. The bigger a city is, the more things there are to do. What is there to do where you live?

3 If a city is going to be a nice place to live, the people who live there must agree to follow the city's rules. They must also pay taxes. Taxes pay for things such as cleaning the streets, running schools, and filling the public library with books. Is your city a nice place to live?

Chapter 5: Reading

1. This article is mostly about

   ______ what makes a city.

   ______ how to live in a city.

   ______ America's largest cities.

2. What is your favorite thing to do in your city or in a nearby city? Write about it.

   ____

3. The person who wrote this article is the ______________________________.

4. Do you think this article is meant to give information or to make you laugh? Write why.

   ____

5. Would you most like to live in a city, in a small town, or in the country? Explain.

   ____

6. Which of the following would taxes NOT pay for?

   ______ library books

   ______ a new clothing store

   ______ street cleaning

7. If you made the rules for a city, what rule would be most important to you?

   ____

8. **It is more fun to live in a city than in the country.** Is this a fact or an opinion?

   ____

Chapter 5: Reading

Two Boys, Big Plans

Read to see what Sam and Kent are planning.

1 "Okay, I'm going to ask my parents right now. Are you?" Sam waited for Kent's reply over the phone.

2 "I think so," said Kent after a moment. "My dad just got home a little while ago. Are you bringing crackers?"

3 Sam laughed. Kent was always hungry. "Yes, I'll bring the crackers," he said. "And be sure to tell them that we'll turn the lights out by 9:30. Okay?"

4 "Nine-thirty. Right," Kent agreed. "Okay, I'm going to go ask. I'll talk to you in a little bit."

5 "Okay," answered Sam, and he hung up. *Now, if only we can talk our parents into letting us do this,* he thought to himself. He put on a big smile and entered the family room.

6 "Dad?" said Sam quietly so he wouldn't make his father jump. "I cleaned up those grass clippings for you."

7 "Oh, good," nodded Mr. Hume. "Thanks, Sam."

8 "Mom? Dad?" started Sam again. Both his parents looked up from their reading. The words rushed out of Sam. "Kent and I were wondering if we could sleep out in the tent tonight. We'd be warm enough in our sleeping bags, and we won't eat too much, and it'll be lights out at 9:30, we promise."

9 Mr. and Mrs. Hume blinked, then looked at each other. *How do they talk to each other without saying anything?* wondered Sam.

10 "Did Kent's parents say it was okay?" asked Mrs. Hume.

11 "He's asking right now." Sam shifted from one foot to the other. Another look passed between his parents.

12 Mr. Hume nodded. "If Kent's parents say it's okay, it's okay with us."

13 "Thanks, Dad! Thanks, Mom!" called Sam as he dashed for the phone. He dialed and held his breath. Then, he heard Kent's voice.

14 "Okay?" asked Sam.

15 "Okay!" said Kent.

Chapter 5: Reading

1. This story is mostly about

_____ a sleepover.

_____ Sam's parents.

_____ two boys' plans.

2. At the beginning, when Sam and Kent are talking on the phone, what did you think they might be talking about?

____

____

3. In the story, when did you find out what the boys are planning?

____

4. Why do you think Sam told his dad about the grass clippings?

____

____

5. Why does Sam mention being warm enough and when the lights will be turned out?

____

____

6. Now that the boys have permission, what do you think they will do next?

____

____

7. In paragraph 5, why are the words *Now, if we can only talk our parents into letting us do this* in italics?

____

8. What is the author's purpose in writing this selection?

____

9. Have you ever been worried about asking your parents to do something? What was it, and how did you ask them?

____

____

Chapter 5: Reading

One Tent, Lots of Stuff

What do the boys need for their night in the tent?

1 "Lantern?"

2 "Got it."

3 "Sleeping bags?"

4 "Got it—both of them."

5 "Pillows?"

6 "Two fat ones."

7 "Crackers?"

8 "Three kinds."

9 "Three kinds? Great!"

10 Sam and Kent had made a list of all the things they needed for sleeping out in the tent. Now, they were sitting cross-legged in the tent, checking things off the list.

11 "Are you going to bring a bathrobe and slippers?" Kent asked Sam.

12 "Oh, no! We're camping. Those are just for in the house," answered Sam, looking as if he knew all about camping.

13 "Oh, right," said Kent, who had never been camping before. He didn't think Sam had been camping before either. Still, it was Sam's dad's tent, so he must know.

14 "Oh, I almost forgot. Can you bring your baseball glove?" Sam looked very serious.

15 Kent couldn't figure this one out. "My baseball glove? What do we need that for?"

16 "Well, we just might. You never know," said Sam with mystery and authority.

17 "Okay," shrugged Kent, "I'll bring it when I come after supper. What time do you think you'll be able to come out?"

18 Sam thought for a moment. "We usually eat at 5:45. Then, I have to clear the table. I should be done by 6:30. What about you?"

19 "My dad doesn't get home until six o'clock," said Kent, regretfully. "Maybe if I offer to help Mom with supper, things will go quickly."

20 Sam shrugged. "It's worth a try. Come out as soon as you can." Sam looked around the tent. "Okay, I think everything's ready. I'll see you later."

21 "See you later," said Kent, and the boys both ran home.

Chapter 5: Reading

1. One of the boys usually has the ideas. The other one seems to go along with those ideas. Which boy is the "leader"?

2. What details from the story helped you answer question 1?

3. Kent says he might help his mom with supper. What does that tell you about Kent?

4. Based on what you know about camping, how do you feel about all the stuff the boys have in their tent? List what you think they need and what they don't need.

   What They Need

   What They Don't Need

5. In some stories, the author tells you what is happening. In this story, the author uses mostly dialogue, what the characters say, to let you know what is going on. Choose one line of dialogue and write what it helps you know about the character.

   Dialogue: ______

6. Why does Kent think that Sam knows more about camping?

7. How do you think the boys feel about camping out together? Explain your answer.

Chapter 5: Reading

How to Pitch a Tent

Follow these instructions to learn how to pitch a tent.

These general instructions should allow anyone to pitch any size or style of tent. Keep in mind that pitching a tent alone, even if you have experience, is difficult.

1. Choose a flat area on which to pitch your tent. Remove any stones or rocks that might poke through the tent's floor.
2. Take the tent and all equipment out of the storage bag. Lay everything on the ground neatly.
3. Spread a groundcloth over the chosen spot. Then, lay the tent floor over the groundcloth. Fold the edges of the groundcloth under, so they do not stick out from the edges of the tent.

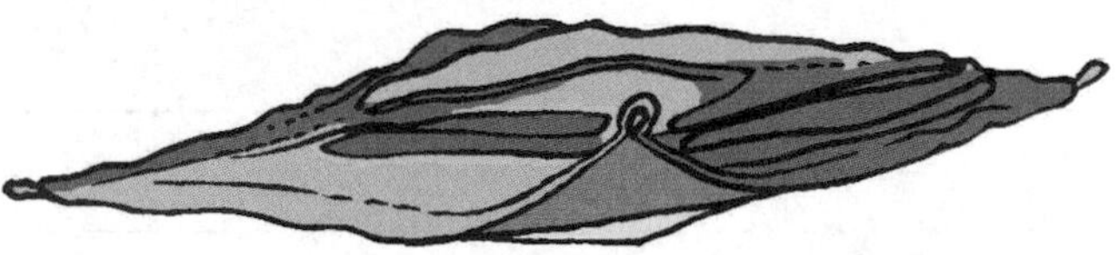

4. Make sure the tent door is zipped shut. Then, pound a stake through each loop, pulling snugly as you go so the floor gets stretched to its full size.

5. Put together the tent poles, if necessary. Thread each one through its loops or channels. Do not step or walk on the tent to do this. If necessary, crawl or lie down on your stomach to reach the center of the tent.

6. Raise the poles. If you have a partner, work on opposite sides of the tent.

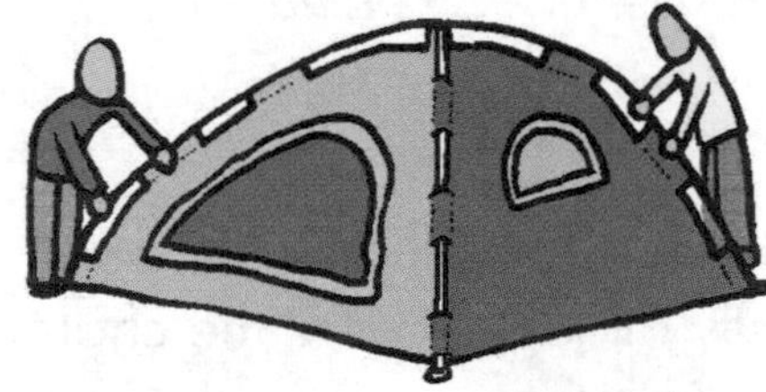

7. Pull the guy lines straight out from the sides of the tent. Peg each one.

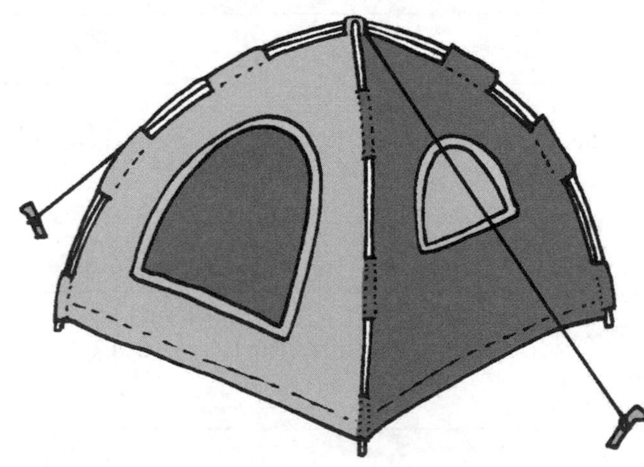

Chapter 5: Reading

1. What do you know about pitching a tent? Do you have anything to add to these instructions?

____

____

2. Number the sentences to show the order of steps to pitch a tent.
   _____ Spread out groundcloth.
   _____ Tighten and peg guy lines.
   _____ Choose and clear an area.
   _____ Put together tent poles.
   _____ Lay out equipment.
   _____ Pound stakes through loops.
   _____ Raise the poles.

3. If you don't know or understand what a guy line is, which illustration helps you figure it out? Tell how.

____

____

4. Choose one illustration. Explain what it shows.

____

____

____

5. In the first paragraph, the author says that pitching a tent alone is difficult. Why do you think this is?

____

____

6. What is the purpose of a groundcloth?

____

7. Which two steps explain what to do with the poles?

_____________________ and _____________________

8. After reading these instructions, do you think you could pitch a tent? Why or why not?

____

____

Chapter 5: Reading

One Tent...What Next?

What do the boys expect to happen?

1 "Then, there was the time my brother and I nearly got blown away with the tent! Did I tell you about that one?" Sam shook his head and tried not to look impatient. His dad had been telling camping stories for almost an hour. *How can I get him to stop without saying anything?* thought Sam to himself. He really wanted to get out to the tent.

2 Finally, his dad stopped for a bite of dessert, and Sam asked to be excused. When his mom nodded her head okay, it took only four trips to clear the table. Then, he was off and across the backyard.

3 "Caught you!" yelled Sam as he flipped back the tent flap. Kent jumped and turned red. "Ha! I knew it! In the crackers already." Then, he laughed. "Have you been waiting long?"

4 Kent shook his head because his mouth was full. Finally, he said, "Not long. My dad got home late."

5 Sam shrugged. "Oh, well. We're here now. Let's get ready."

6 "Ready for what?" asked Kent.

7 "For whatever's going to happen," answered Sam. *Well, he must know*, thought Kent. He helped Sam straighten the sleeping bags and stash stuff in the corners. They played catch across the tent for a little while. *Ah, the baseball glove*, thought Kent. They played badminton with crackers, but then Sam discovered crumbs in his sleeping bag, so they stopped.

8 They turned on the lantern and read. After a while, Sam retold some of his dad's camping stories. Then, Kent turned out the light, and they listened for noises in the dark. They didn't hear any for a very long time.

9 Finally, Kent heard something at the tent flap. He half crawled and half flew across the tent to warn Sam. Sam yelled when Kent landed on top of him.

10 "Hey, are you guys all right?" It was Sam's mom. "Breakfast is ready."

11 Sam and Kent looked at each other in disbelief. They had slept through the whole night, and nothing had happened.

Chapter 5: Reading

1. Which sentence best describes this story?

   _____ Nothing exciting happens to the boys in the tent.

   _____ The boys have a crazy night in the tent.

   _____ In the morning, Kent plays a trick on Sam and scares him.

2. Why did the boys stop playing badminton?

   ____

   ____

3. Read the sentences below. Write **F** next to sentences that are facts and **O** next to sentences that are opinions.

   _____ Kent eats too many crackers.

   _____ Sam's dad had been telling camping stories for almost an hour.

   _____ Breakfast is ready.

   _____ Sam's dad tells the best camping stories.

4. What do you think the boys were hoping would happen?

   ____

   ____

   ____

5. In paragraph 3, why does Kent turn red?

   ____

   ____

6. Write **C** next to the sentence below that is the cause. Write **E** next to the sentence that is the effect.

   _____ Kent landed on top of Sam.

   _____ Sam's mom startled the boys.

7. This story has two settings. What are they?

   ____________________ and ____________________

Chapter 5: Reading

Night Lights

What is keeping Mikki awake?

1 There were lights flashing outside. No matter what I did, I could see those lights. I couldn't figure out what they were, so I started worrying.

2 I turned away from the window and closed my eyes. But then I had to open them, just a crack, to see if the lights were still there. *Flash-flash, off, flash!*

3 I rolled toward the window and watched. Maybe I could figure it out. I started listing things. Car lights? Not bright enough. Police car flashers? Not blue and red enough. Spaceships? Not likely. All right, this is really bugging me. I have to go ask Mom, I finally concluded.

4 I padded downstairs where my mom was reading a magazine. She was a little surprised to see me.

5 "The lights are flashing upstairs," I said.

6 "They are?" She said it with that "this is a great excuse for being out of bed" look on her face.

7 "I can't figure out what it is," I continued, hoping for some comfort. To my relief, she put down her magazine and steered me back upstairs.

8 We lay across my bed on our stomachs and watched out the window. Mom knew right away.

9 "Mikki, do you remember driving up to visit Uncle Walt last month?" she asked. I nodded. "Do you remember how long it took?" I nodded again. "Well, Uncle Walt is having a thunderstorm way up north where his house is. The lightning is sort of shining off the clouds, so we can see the flashing down here, even though the storm is far away from us."

10 "Oh," I said. I thought to myself, *Well, that makes sense.* After all, what else causes lights to flash in the sky? Aliens? Not likely.

Chapter 5: Reading

1. What is causing Mikki to worry?

____

2. What does Mikki do to try to get to sleep?

First, she ____

____

Then, she ____

____

3. What is causing the flashing lights?

____

____

4. Have you ever been kept awake at night by something that bothered or puzzled you? Write about it.

____

____

5. From whose point of view is this story told?

_____ Mom's _____ Mikki's _____ Uncle Walt's

6. Which word best describes Mom in the story?

_____ impatient _____ confused _____ kind

7. Is this story realistic? Why or why not?

____

____

8. Name three things that Mikki thinks the lights could be.

_______________ _______________ _______________

Chapter 5: Reading

Thunder and Lightning

What causes thunder and lightning?

1 The story of thunder and lightning is a lesson on electricity. Lightning is really just a giant electrical spark. Thunder is a direct result of the activity of that spark.

Lightning First

2 Imagine a single water droplet high above Earth. It is in a cloud among millions of other water droplets. As this water droplet falls toward Earth, it gets bigger by collecting more moisture. When the droplet gets to just about the size of a pea, it splits. This splitting action causes an electrical charge to build up on the two new droplets.

3 If the droplets fall straight to Earth, the electrical charge is very small and will have no effect. If the droplets get swept upward by air currents, however, the whole process begins again. The droplets fall, grow, split, and become more strongly charged with electricity each time.

4 In time, the electrical charge in the droplets becomes so strong that it has to discharge itself. The result is a huge spark. It may leap from a cloud to the ground in less than one-tenth of a second. We know it as lightning.

Thunder Second

5 When lightning flashes, the air is suddenly heated, and then it quickly cools. These rapid changes in the air cause the cracking sound of thunder. During a storm, we see lightning first, and then wait to hear the thunder. That's because light travels faster than sound. We see the lightning as it happens, but the sound of the thunder may take any number of seconds to reach us, depending on how far away the lightning was. The rumbling sound of thunder is actually an echo from the sound waves bouncing off Earth or off the clouds.

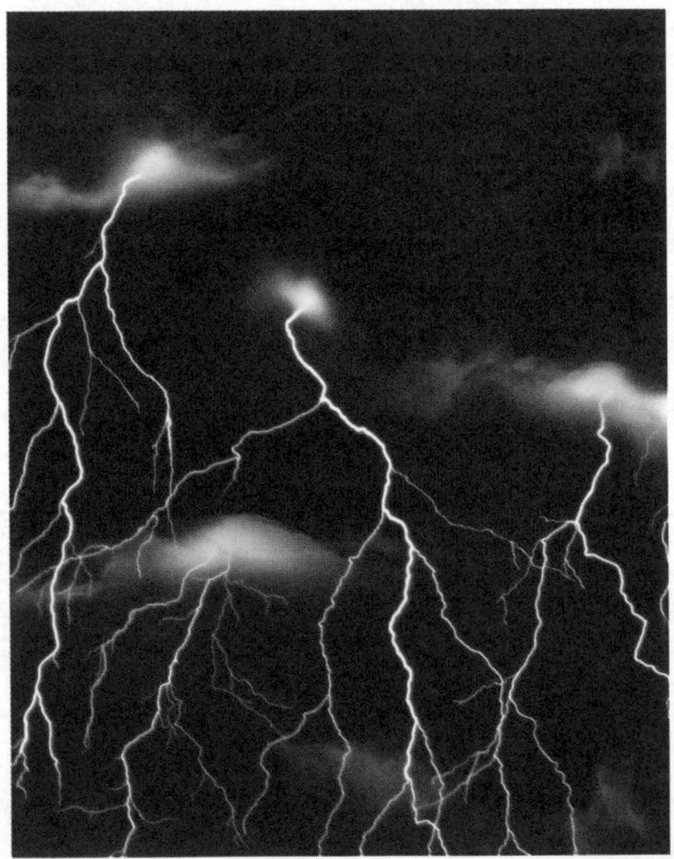

Chapter 5: Reading

1. The author wrote this article to
   _____ entertain.
   _____ give information.
   _____ persuade.

2. Which comes first, thunder or lightning?

   ____

3. What causes lightning? Give a brief answer.

   ____

   ____

   ____

4. How does lightning cause thunder?

   ____

   ____

   ____

5. If you read only the two headings in this article, what would you learn?

   ____

   ____

   ____

6. Write **T** for true or **F** for false next to each statement below.
   _____ Thunder always takes the same amount of time to reach Earth.
   _____ Light travels faster than sound.
   _____ Thunder and lightning are not related to each other.

7. What is the main idea of paragraph 4?

   ____

   ____

   ____

8. Which of the following is the purpose of paragraph 1?

   _____ introduction _____ author's purpose _____ conclusion

Chapter 5: Reading

Smokey the Bear

Read to find out how Smokey the Bear became famous.

1 Smokey the Bear's story doesn't start with a bear. It starts with a problem, a solution, and then a drawing.

2 In the 1940s, during World War II, the leaders of the United States had a problem. They were worried about having enough wood to build ships and other equipment for the war. The solution: To protect America's forests (and the wood that might be needed for ships), the U.S. Forest Service started a campaign to prevent forest fires.

3 The Forest Service created posters reminding people about fire safety. The posters featured a deer named Bambi from a popular movie. Before long, however, the poster images were switched to a popular toy animal—a bear. An illustrator, Albert Staehle, drew that first bear with a park ranger's hat in 1944 and named him *Smokey*.

4 Six years later, while fighting a forest fire in New Mexico, firefighters found a black bear cub clinging to a tree. They rescued the cub and called it Hotfoot. Soon, however, the cub was renamed Smokey after the drawings on the posters.

5 Once he recovered from his injuries, Smokey was taken to the National Zoo in Washington, D.C. Thousands of people visited him there until he died in 1976. Smokey was 26 years old. His message is still with us, however, as we see him reminding us to prevent forest fires all across the nation.

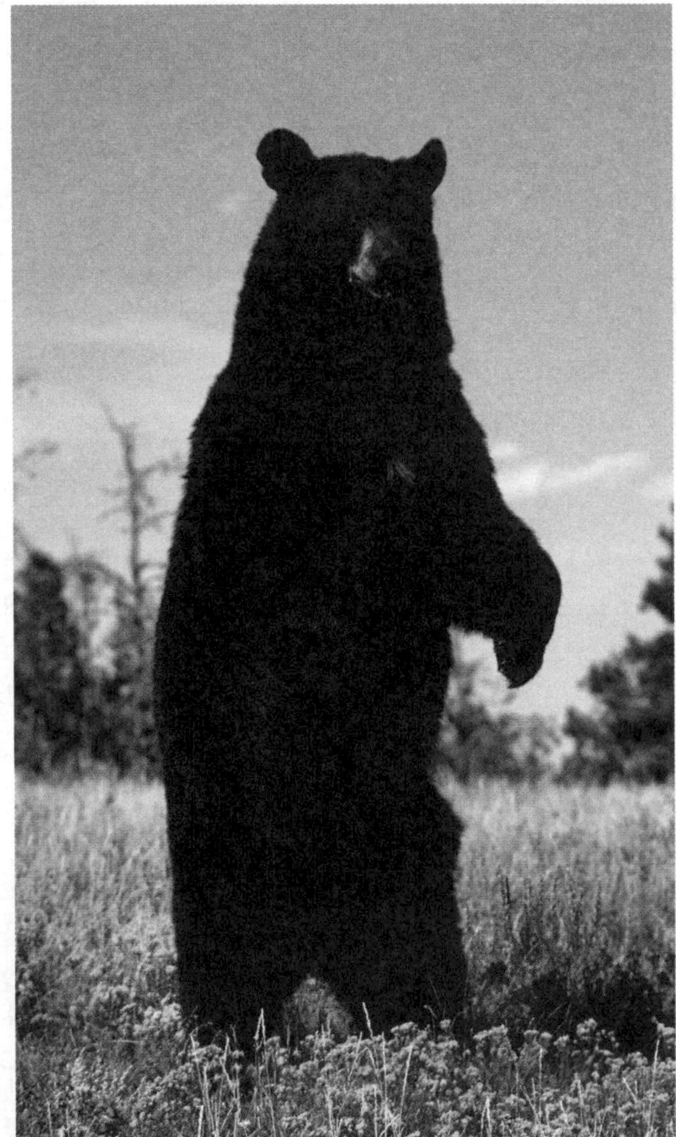

Chapter 5: Reading

Put a check next to the sentences that are true.

1. _____ The idea for Smokey the Bear started in the 1940s.
2. _____ Smokey the Bear lives in New Mexico.
3. _____ The Forest Service made posters in honor of a bear cub that died in a fire.
4. _____ Smokey the Bear was a drawing first, and then a real bear.

Write **M** next to the sentences that tell about make-believe things.

5. _____ Smokey the Bear lived in a zoo for many years.
6. _____ Smokey the Bear speaks to campers about the danger of forest fires.
7. _____ Smokey the Bear used to help firefighters put out fires.
8. Why was Smokey the Bear created? Write the phrase or sentence from the article that tells you.

    ____

    ____

    ____

9. In paragraph 2, what problem did U.S. leaders have?

    ____

10. What was the solution?

    ____

11. What organization created the fire safety posters?

    ____

12. In the posters, did Smokey the Bear look realistic? Explain.

    ____

    ____

Chapter 5: Reading

Planting Dreams

What does Rosa dream about?

1 She was walking home from work one evening when she got the idea. Rosa didn't like her job at the factory, but it was better than no job at all. So, while she was trying not to think about work, she saw the pots stacked up in an alley. They were cheap plastic pots, but there were dozens of them piled up behind the flower shop. *Such a waste*, she thought. When the pots were still there three days later, Rosa went in and asked if she could take some. The flower shop lady said she didn't mind, so Rosa carried home a tower of pots, pretending she was a circus performer on the way.

2 At home, Rosa set the pots on the fire escape outside her tiny apartment. And there they sat. Once, a gust of wind sent them clattering to the street three floors below, and she had to go and chase them before the gathering storm.

3 Every day, Rosa went to work and thought about her pots. She was waiting for something, but she had patience.

4 At last, the newspaper brought good news. A hardware store had a sale on potting soil. Rosa carefully counted her money, and then she walked the six blocks to the store. She bought six bags and carried them home. She bought seeds, too. Rosa slept well that night and dreamed of masses of flowers and fat, glowing fruits.

5 Sundays were always good days. Rosa didn't have to work on Sundays. But Rosa couldn't remember when she had had *such* a good Sunday. She got up early and ate her breakfast on the fire escape with her pots. Then, she began to scoop dirt into the pots. She hummed a little song until all six of her bags of soil were empty. Then, she laid her precious seed packets out and planned her garden. Tomatoes for the biggest pots, and peppers for the next-biggest ones. Flowers in all the rest.

6 At the end of the day, Rosa sat in her garden and watched the sunset. *Soon*, she thought, *there will be masses of flowers and fat, glowing fruits.*

Chapter 5: Reading

A **fact** is something that can be proven true. An **opinion** is what someone thinks or feels. Check the sentences that are facts.

1. _____ Vegetables can be grown in pots.

2. _____ Creating a garden on a fire escape is difficult.

3. _____ Any garden is beautiful.

4. _____ Plants need soil and water.

5. Number the sentences to show the order in which things happened.

_____ Rosa bought potting soil.

_____ Rosa took the pots home.

_____ Rosa planted her seeds.

_____ Rosa saw the pots.

6. Check the words or phrases that best describe Rosa.

_____ selfish

_____ tends to waste time

_____ likes the outdoors

_____ appreciates beauty

7. Why do you think Rosa slept well the night after she bought seeds and soil?

____

____

____

8. The author repeats a line from paragraph 4 in the last paragraph. What line is it? Why do you think the author repeats it?

____

____

____

9. Have you ever planted something and watched it grow? Tell about how it made you feel.

____

____

____

____

Chapter 5: Reading

Dreaming of the Harvest

Read to see how Rosa's garden is doing.

1 Rosa hurried home from work. She knew it had been quite warm that day, and it hadn't rained since last week. She was worried that her tiny seedlings might have gotten too much sun. When she got to her building, she raced up the stairs, two at a time, up to the third floor.

2 Rosa was still panting when she stepped out onto the fire escape. *Oh, you poor things!* was all she could think. Even her strongest, tallest tomato plant looked as if it had just given up. It was pale and dry looking, not green and smooth like it had been this morning. Rosa got her watering can and went right to work. She watered each pot until it began to drip out the holes in the bottom. She made sure each plant got just the right amount. Then, she went in to fix something to eat.

3 In the kitchen, Rosa bit into an apple and imagined that it was a big, juicy tomato. She chopped a carrot and imagined that it was a shiny, green pepper getting ready to join some tomatoes in a pot of rich, spicy sauce.

4 She carried her dinner out to the fire escape. The apartment building across the street cast its shadow on her garden, letting it rest from the day's hot sun. Rosa leaned against the wall and closed her eyes. She let her hard day of work at the factory fade away as she imagined taking her flowers to her friends at work. Just think how surprised they would be. They would think she had robbed the flower shop!

5 Rosa watched her garden grow until after dark. Then, she went inside and dreamed of running her own shop filled with trays of fresh vegetables and baskets of flowers fresh from her own garden.

Chapter 5: Reading

1. Why is Rosa worried about her plants on this day?

____

____

Write **T** if the sentence is true. Write **F** if the sentence is false.

2. _____ This story is mostly about Rosa worrying about her garden.
3. _____ Rosa is careless about her garden.
4. _____ Rosa plans to share her flowers with others.
5. _____ Too much sun causes Rosa's plants to dry up.

Compare how things really are with how they used to be, or with what Rosa imagines.

6. The strongest, tallest tomato plant is _______________________.

   It had been _______________________.
7. Rosa bites into an _______________________.

   She imagines that it is a _______________________.
8. She chops a _______________________.

   She imagines that it is a _______________________.
9. For now, Rosa works at a _______________________.

   She dreams of _______________________.
10. Why do you think Rosa spends so much time daydreaming?

    ____

    ____
11. What details from the story helped you answer question 10?

    ____

    ____
12. Which of these is most likely to be true?

    _____ Rosa lives in the country.

    _____ Rosa lives in a city.

Chapter 5: Reading

Peppers

Which kind of pepper do you like best?

1 What comes in many colors and is high in vitamins A and C? Some people like them hot; some prefer them mild. They are a common sight in backyard gardens throughout the United States. Have you guessed yet? They are peppers.

2 Whether green, yellow, or red, peppers add flavor to many types of foods. People eat them raw, pickled, or cooked. They go in salads, in sauces, on sandwiches, and, of course, on pizza.

Bell Peppers

3 The mildest variety of pepper is the bell pepper. They are sometimes called *sweet peppers*, but they are not sweet like sugar. They are simply less spicy, or hot, than other types of peppers. The round, apple-sized fruits of bell pepper plants are green, yellow, or red. Some people eat them before they get fully ripe. Bell peppers are by far the most common pepper found in gardens and on grocery store shelves.

Chili Peppers

4 "Chili pepper" is a general name for a number of quite spicy peppers that come in many sizes and appear red, yellow, or green. These hotter peppers tend to be long and skinny. Chili peppers don't actually burn your mouth, but they can cause pain. A certain chemical in the fruit causes this feeling. Chili peppers, whether fresh or dried, add an almost fiery zing to foods. Dishes from Mexico, India, and Africa are noted for including the hottest types of peppers. Eating these foods may take some getting used to. In addition to the discomfort in your mouth, hot peppers may cause your eyes to water, your nose to run, and your ears to feel warm.

5 Whatever their color or flavor, peppers add variety and spice to fancy or even everyday foods. When was the last time you had a pepper?

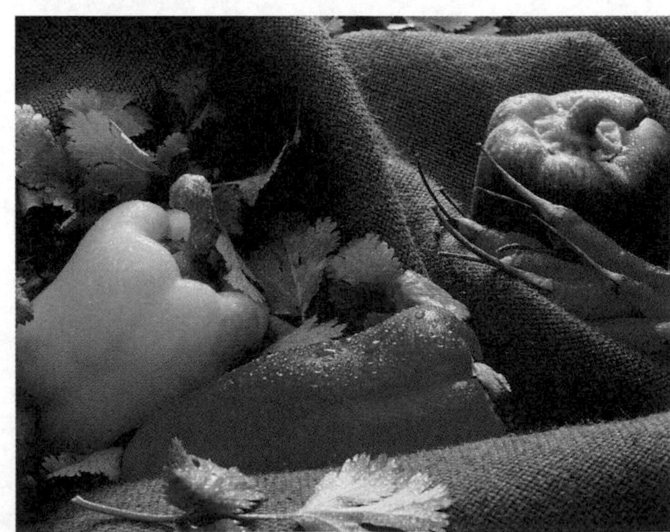

Chapter 5: Reading

1. What do you know about peppers, or what experiences have you had growing or eating peppers?

____

____

2. Do you like peppers? Write why or why not.

____

3. How are bell peppers and chili peppers the same? How are they different? Write what the article tells you about each kind.

Bell Peppers

Size ______________

Shape ______________

Color ______________

Flavor ______________

Chili Peppers

Size ______________

Shape ______________

Color ______________

Flavor ______________

4. What two headings does the author divide the article into? How is this helpful?

____

____

5. Write **T** for true or **F** for false next to each statement below.

   _____ Hot peppers can make your eyes water.

   _____ Bell peppers are very spicy.

   _____ Peppers can be prepared in many ways.

   _____ Bell peppers are red, and chili peppers are green.

6. What makes chili peppers burn your mouth?

____

7. What two vitamins are peppers high in?

____________________ and ____________________

Chapter 5: Reading

Soccer Blues

Why is Perry so unhappy about soccer practice?

1 "Okay, everybody, come over here and listen up!" Coach's voice carried across the soccer field. Kids of all sizes and shapes stopped what they were doing and walked or trotted toward the coach. When the several dozen boys and girls were in a ring around him, the coach continued. "I want all of you to practice dribbling on your own for at least half an hour a day outside of practice. Okay?"

2 "Okay, Coach!" yelled the circle. Everyone smiled. Coach always liked answers to his questions.

3 Satisfied with the response, Coach went on. "Most of the passing we do in games is when we're only 10, maybe 20, yards apart. We need to be able to deliver the ball within that range *every time we pass*," Coach explained. "Now, we're going to do a one-on-one passing exercise. One partner over here, the other over there," he said, pointing to one touch line and another invisible line about halfway across the field. "What I want you to do is...."

4 Around the circle, heads nodded as eager players listened to Coach. One head, though, wasn't nodding; it was bobbing. Perry was so tired and hungry that his knees felt shaky. He was sure he had dribbled his soccer ball a hundred miles already this afternoon. He felt as if one more passing exercise would pretty much finish him off. Somehow, he stumbled through. He was pretty sure he did not impress Coach, though, when one of his passes went wildly across the field.

5 At the end of practice, Perry flopped into the back seat of the car and buckled his seatbelt. He didn't even wait for his mom's usual question.

6 "Practice was awful," said Perry without even opening his eyes. "I don't ever want to go back."

Chapter 5: Reading

1. In most stories, a character has a problem. What is Perry's problem?

____

2. What information in the story helped you answer question 1?

____

____

3. **Dialogue** is what the characters in a story say. What did you learn about Perry from his dialogue?

____

____

4. Find a line of the coach's dialogue. What does it tell you about the coach?

   Dialogue: _______________________________________

   ____

   What it tells: ___________________________________

   ____

5. Coach thinks that a passing exercise is important because

____

____.

6. What is the setting for this story?

____

7. **Practice was awful.** Is this a fact or an opinion?

____

8. The last line of paragraph 5 says that Perry didn't even wait for his mom's usual question. What do you think her question is?

____

9. Which word or phrase best describes Perry in this story?

   _____ confident _____ full of energy _____ exhausted

10. Have you ever wished you could quit an activity? Tell about it.

____

____

Chapter 5: Reading

Mom to the Rescue

Have you ever solved a mystery?

1 Mrs. Rothman was speechless. The only thing Perry had talked about all winter was soccer. Now, Perry wanted to quit soccer. Not knowing whether to laugh or cry, she drove home and fixed dinner.

2 After dinner, Mrs. Rothman tried to get to the bottom of the problem.

3 "Do you think Coach is too tough?"

4 "No."

5 "Are you having trouble with one of the other kids?"

6 "No."

7 "Did you get hurt?"

8 "No."

9 "Do you feel as if you're not good enough? If that's the case, you should talk to Coach...."

10 "Well, that's sort of it. I just felt so weak during practice. My knees were shaky. I could hardly lift my feet." Perry shook his head. "I just don't have what it takes. A soccer player has to run and run and not even get winded."

11 *Hmm,* thought Mrs. Rothman. *Weak? Shaky knees?* She softened her questioning a little. "Did you have a good lunch today?"

12 Perry thought for a second. "Um, yes, I guess so. Oh, except that there was a fire drill, and I didn't get to finish."

13 *Aha, that's it! A boy can't make it through school and soccer practice without the proper fuel.*

14 "I'll tell you what, Perry," said Mrs. Rothman, patting his knee. "Why don't you try it for one more day. I'll meet you after school with a power snack, and we'll see if that helps." Perry agreed, but he wondered what a power snack was and how it could possibly help.

Chapter 5: Reading

1. Mrs. Rothman is speechless because

____.

2. Check two words that tell how Perry probably felt.

_____ disappointed

_____ proud

_____ eager

_____ frightened

3. Perry says he wants to quit soccer because

____.

4. Have you ever tried to do something that was hard, or that you had to work at? What was it?

____

____

Did you get discouraged? Did you quit?

____

____

5. Do you think Perry's decision is reasonable, or do you think he is giving up too easily? Explain.

____

____

6. Mrs. Rothman probably feels

_____ surprised _____ angry _____ entertained

7. What problem does Mrs. Rothman think Perry is having?

____

8. How does she plan to help Perry?

____

____

9. What do you think would be a good example of a power snack? Explain your choice.

____

____

Chapter 5: Reading

Power Snack

Have you ever had a power snack?

Energy Bars

1 c. brown sugar
1 c. vegetable oil
2 eggs
2 c. oats
$1\frac{1}{2}$ c. flour
1 c. raisins
1 c. peanuts (optional)
1 c. coconut (optional)
$1\frac{1}{2}$ tsp. ground cinnamon
$1\frac{1}{2}$ tsp. ground cloves
1 tsp. baking soda
$\frac{1}{4}$ tsp. salt

Heat oven to 350° F. Grease 11″ x 17″ pan. Mix brown sugar, oil, and eggs until smooth. Stir in remaining ingredients. Spread mixture into pan, pressing with fingers until even. Bake until center is set, but not firm, 16–22 minutes. Remove from oven and cool for 15 minutes. Drizzle honey glaze* over bars. Let cool completely. Cut into squares. Store covered for two weeks. Or, wrap tightly and freeze for up to six months.

*Directions for honey glaze: Place $\frac{1}{4}$c. honey and 2 T. butter or margarine in a sauce pan. Heat and stir until well blended and heated through. Drizzle over bars.

(Note: Always ask a grown-up for help in the kitchen.)

Chapter 5: Reading

Write these steps in the correct order. (Not all of the recipe's steps are here.)

- spread mixture into pan
- drizzle glaze
- grease the pan
- mix sugar, oil, and eggs
- remove from oven and cool

1. ______________________________

2. ______________________________

3. ______________________________

4. ______________________________

5. ______________________________

6. How long do the directions say to bake the bars?

____

7. The directions say to "drizzle honey glaze over bars." How did you know what honey glaze was?

____

Recipes often use short forms of words called **abbreviations**. Match the common recipe words in the box with their abbreviations.

cup	**Fahrenheit**	**teaspoon**	**tablespoon**

8. T. ______________________ **10.** F ______________________

9. c. ______________________ **11.** tsp. ______________________

12. The directions say, "Bake until center is set but not firm." What does this mean?

____

____

13. How long do the energy bars need to cool?

____

14. What is the longest you could keep these bars? What would you need to do to them?

____

____

Chapter 5: Reading

And It's Out of the Park!

What happens at the soccer game?

1 "Okay, everybody listen up!" Coach said. It took only a moment for the team to gather. It was the first game of the season. Perry could tell that everyone was nervous and excited, just like he was.

2 "This is where all those drills pay off. You guys have dribbled to the moon and back since we started practice. You've done a good job. Now, let's remember everything we learned and play a good game. Okay?"

3 "Okay!" the team yelled, and Coach smiled. He liked their spirit.

4 "All right! Let's go, Bobcats!" Perry and his teammates roared onto the field and took their positions.

5 It seemed as if Coach's hopes were coming true. The midfielders stayed in position. The center backs defended the goal well. Coach even heard some of the other team's parents admiring how his team handled the ball.

6 Neither team scored in the first half. During the second half, there was a great play that almost put a goal on the scoreboard in the final seconds.

7 There was a terrific jumble around the ball. Perry and another player were down, leaving two other players battling it out. Perry rolled out of the way and scrambled to his feet. Just then, the ball somehow broke free and came his way. Without hesitating for a moment, he reeled back and kicked.

8 *Now that was a solid kick*, Perry thought to himself. Time seemed to stop as everyone on the field watched the arc of the ball's flight. It was beautiful. When the ball disappeared from sight, someone in the crowd yelled, "It's a home run!" The crowd and the players exploded in laughter. In the midst of all the end-of-game confusion, Perry's only thought was, *Wow, those power snacks really work.*

Chapter 5: Reading

1. When you read the story's title, did you guess about how the story ended? Was your guess close to being correct? Explain.

2. Circle the word that best describes the coach's words before the game.

   angry   encouraging

3. Have you ever been in a sporting event or a performance that didn't turn out the way you expected? Did something funny or weird happen? Write about it.

4. At the end of paragraph 2, Coach says that the players have "dribbled to the moon and back." This is a figure of speech. What does it mean?

5. Give one example of dialogue in the story.

   Now, give one example of a character's thought that is not spoken out loud.

6. How are the two examples in question 5 written differently from each other?

7. Why is it funny that someone in the crowd says, "It's a home run!"?

History of Soccer

Read to see how soccer had its start.

Earliest Record

1 The earliest written evidence of a soccer-like game comes from China. More than 2,000 years ago, Chinese soldiers took part in an activity that involved kicking a ball into a small net. Historians think the game was a skill-building exercise for the soldiers.

Years of Development

2 In ancient Greece and Rome, teams of up to 27 players played a soccer-type game. In Britain hundreds of years later, during the 1200s, whole villages played against each other. With hundreds of people playing, these games were both long and rough. Kicking, punching, and biting were common and allowed.

3 In 1331, English king Edward III passed a law in an attempt to put a stop to the popular but violent game. The king of Scotland spoke against the game a hundred years later. Queen Elizabeth I, during the late 1500s, passed a law that called for a week of jail for anyone caught playing "football," or soccer, as we call it. But the game could not be stopped.

The Modern Game Emerges

4 Two hundred and fifty years later, people in Britain were still playing a game we would recognize as soccer. A well-known English college, Eton, developed a set of rules in 1815. A number of other colleges soon agreed to use the same rules, and those schools played against each other. Finally, 50 years later, a formal association formed to oversee the playing of the game and its rules. In 1869, a rule against handling the ball with the hands transformed the game into the sport of soccer that is wildly popular all around the world.

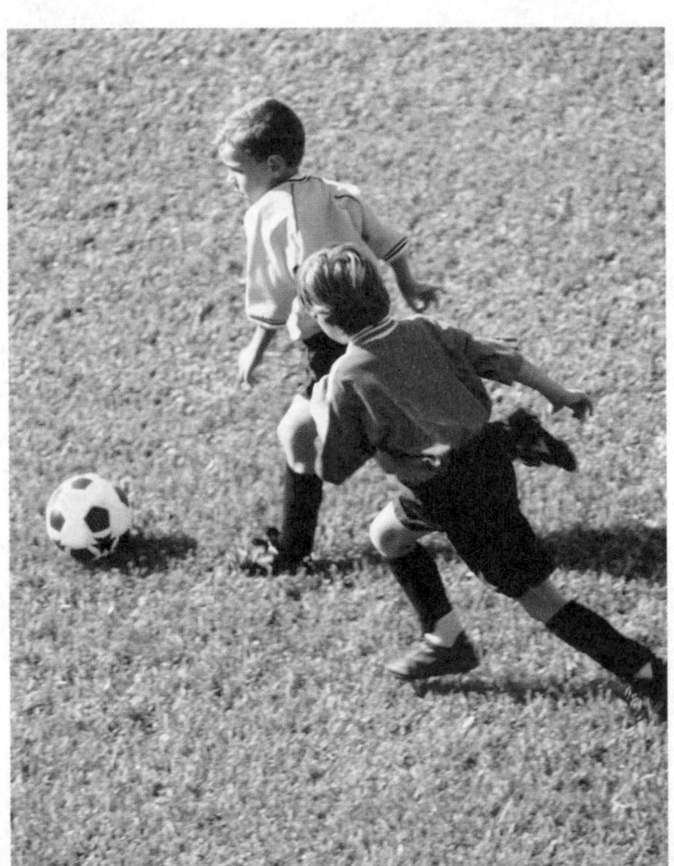

Chapter 5: Reading

1. This article is mostly about
   _____ how soccer was named.
   _____ the rules of soccer.
   _____ soccer's history.

2. Historians think that soccer might have started out as a

   ____.

3. Why did King Edward III pass a law against soccer?

   ____

   ____

4. What punishment did Queen Elizabeth have for soccer players?

   ____

5. What important rule change made the game into what we know as soccer? When did it happen?

   ____

   ____

6. If you wanted to find out about the beginnings of soccer, under which heading should you look?

   ____

7. Under which heading would you find information about soccer during the last century or so?

   ____

8. Write **T** for **true** or **F** for **false** next to each statement below.
   _____ Today, you are allowed to touch the ball with your hands in soccer.
   _____ Kicking and biting were common in soccer games long ago.
   _____ In Britain, soccer is called "football."

9. At the end of paragraph 3, it says, "the game could not be stopped." Why do you think this was true?

   ____

   ____

10. What was the author's purpose for writing this article?

   ____

Chapter 5: Reading

Why Soccer?

Why do you think soccer is so popular?

1 On what topic do millions of American kids agree? Soccer! The U.S. Youth Soccer Association registers about 3 million players each year. Add all other ages into the mix, and you come up with more than 24 million Americans playing soccer. What makes soccer so popular?

2 First, I think there's the international appeal. Americans see that people in many other countries in the world are wildly excited about soccer. The excitement must be catching.

3 Second, soccer takes less equipment than some other sports, especially football. For that reason, it's not very costly for a kid to join a soccer team.

4 Third, parents view soccer as a safer sport than some other sports. Though accidents may occur, body contact isn't supposed to be part of the game. Therefore, fewer injuries occur.

5 Fourth, soccer appeals to both boys and girls. Though soccer was at first only a male sport (just like all other sports), soccer has caught on with girls. This is good for the sport, I think. Interest in the sport extends to whole families, so there are more players, more fans, more coaches, and so on.

6 Finally, I think there is the running factor. Running up and down a field chasing a ball is such a healthy, all-American thing to do. Kids love it, and few parents can object to it.

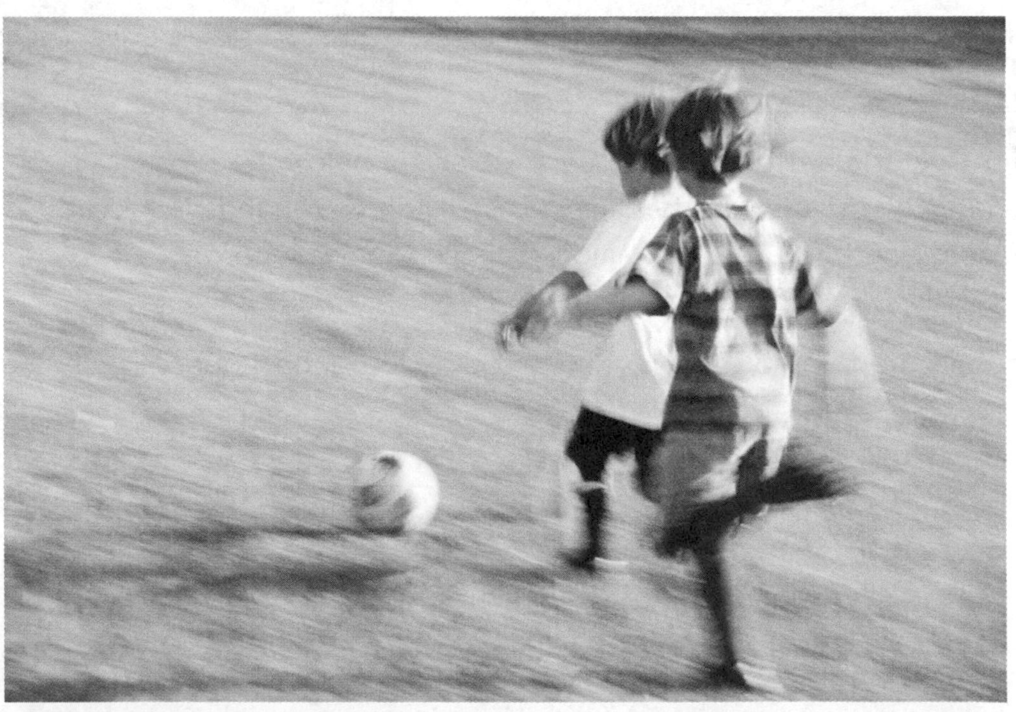

Chapter 5: Reading

1. The person who wrote this article is the **author**. The author probably wrote this article to

_____ make you laugh.

_____ give information.

_____ persuade you to do something.

The author states some facts in the article. She also gives her opinion. Write **F** next to each sentence that is a fact. Write **O** next to each sentence that gives an opinion.

2. _____ The U.S. Youth Soccer Association registers about 3 million players each year.

3. _____ First, I think there's the international appeal.

4. _____ Though accidents may occur, body contact isn't supposed to be part of the game.

5. _____ And finally, I think there is the running factor.

6. Look back at the sentences you marked as opinions. What do you notice about them?

____

____

7. What is the main idea of paragraph 5?

_____ Soccer is only for boys, just like other sports.

_____ Soccer is a good sport for both boys and girls.

_____ Soccer has caught on with girls.

8. Why is soccer less expensive than some other sports?

____

____

9. Look at the focus question under the title. What do you think its purpose is?

____

____

10. Have you ever played soccer? If so, tell about your experience. If not, explain why you would or would not like to try it.

____

____

Chapter 5: Reading

A Teacher's Journal

Do you think the girls will be able to work together?

April 14

1 When my students work together on projects, everything usually works out. I had my doubts today, though, when I put Sharla, Tess, and Lee together to make a volcano. At one point, I knew something was going to blow up, and it wasn't the volcano!

2 I knew the girls weren't good friends, but I encourage my students to learn to work with all of their classmates. I could tell they felt a little shy when they sat down for their first planning meeting. Students in other groups had questions, so I didn't notice the girls for quite a few minutes. When I looked back in their direction, one looked mad, one looked sad, and one was nearly in tears. Good grief!

3 As I approached, they all started talking at once. Tess didn't want to have to touch "that icky paste" to build the volcano. Sharla had some design ideas that she couldn't get across to the other two. Lee thought they should just stop talking and get to work.

4 I calmed the girls down and suggested that they make a list of things on which they agreed. They agreed they were making a volcano out of flour, salt, and water, and that's all. They couldn't agree on the size, on a base for the volcano, or on who should get to mix the paste. Each girl had her own ideas and would not budge for the sake of working together or moving ahead.

5 By this time, the work session was over and it was time for lunch. The girls had made very little progress, and I was wondering if I had made a big mistake. Maybe this was one group of students who just couldn't work together.

Chapter 5: Reading

1. Do you think Sharla, Tess, and Lee will be able to work together? Write why or why not.

____

____

2. Think of times when you worked with classmates on projects. Was it hard or easy? Explain.

____

____

____

3. Would you say that you are more like Sharla—full of ideas—or more like Lee—eager to stop talking and get to work? Write why.

____

____

4. Does the teacher who is writing the journal seem thoughtful or worn out? Write why you think so.

____

____

5. At the end of the first paragraph, the teacher says, "I knew something was going to blow up, and it wasn't the volcano." What does she mean?

____

____

6. From whose point of view is this selection told?

_____ Sharla _____ Lee _____ the teacher

7. What do you predict will happen next in the story?

____

____

8. If you wrote a journal entry, what would you write about?

____

____

Chapter 5: Reading

A Student's Journal

Read to see how the girls are moving ahead with their volcano.

April 16

1 Tess and Lee and I have to make a volcano together. Mrs. Holt put us in a group on Tuesday, and we had such a big argument! Tess was fussing about the paste, and Lee didn't want to plan anything. She just wanted to jump in and start working. It was awful. We didn't get anything done. Yesterday, Mrs. Holt made us stay in during recess so we could finish planning our volcano. Missing recess was so unfair!

2 Anyway, we finally said we would make the volcano about a foot high, and we'd add a little village around the base. That way, Tess can make the little village since she refuses to touch the volcano paste. (I think Mrs. Holt should make her.)

3 Today, Lee and I mixed up the paste. It was really goopy but kind of fun. We set up a plastic water bottle and some wadded-up aluminum foil as a base for the volcano. Then, we started plopping paste on. Tess just watched (no fair).

4 I was making my side all nice and smooth. I told Lee she should smooth out her side, too. She said, "No, Sharla, it should look lumpy, like a real mountain," just as if she were the boss. I said it would just look messy and that we should make it smooth. Well, the whole thing went downhill from there. Our paste started to dry out, and we didn't have time to finish. I suppose that means we'll have to miss recess again tomorrow, and it's all Lee's fault.

Chapter 5: Reading

This story is written in the form of a journal entry. The person who is writing uses *I* to refer to herself. She is the **narrator**, or the person telling the story.

1. Find a sentence that tells you that the narrator actually took part in the action of the story. Write the sentence here.

   ____

   ____

2. The narrator, Sharla, disagreed with Lee about

   ____.

3. Sharla was upset because

   ____

   ____

4. Did you expect this journal to be written by Mrs. Holt, the teacher? Why or why not?

   ____

   ____

5. Why did the girls decide to make a village around the base?

   ____

6. Which of these words best describes Sharla's attitude toward the other two girls?

   _____ impatient _____ understanding _____ comforting

7. Explain how the picture adds to your understanding of the story.

   ____

   ____

8. Write **C** next to the sentence below that is the cause. Write **E** next to the sentence that is the effect.

   _____ The girls didn't make much progress on their volcano.

   _____ Mrs. Holt made the girls stay in at recess.

The Great Volcano Debate

What is the great volcano debate all about?

1 "Sharla? Lee? Tess? Can you come here for a minute, please?" Mrs. Holt called the girls to her desk. It was Friday morning.

2 "Now, you know today is the last work session on our projects, right?" she asked.

3 The girls all nodded.

4 "Are you ready to finish up?"

5 No one answered.

6 "Is there a problem?" Mrs. Holt asked, knowing perfectly well that there was a problem. She wanted the girls to put it in their own words, though.

7 Sharla glanced at the other two, and then began. "Well, I think the volcano should be smooth so it looks nice."

8 "And," jumped in Lee, "I think it should look rough and rocky, like a real mountain."

9 "I see," said Mrs. Holt, stalling for time. "What do you think, Tess?"

10 "Well, I've been making buildings for the village," she said quickly, to make sure Mrs. Holt knew she had been helping. "I think it would be neat if we could show lava flowing down toward the village, sort of like Pompeii...."

11 "Hey," cut in Sharla, "that's a great idea! The flowing lava would be smooth. Right, Mrs. Holt?"

12 "Yes, I guess so." Mrs. Holt had never actually seen flowing lava, but it seemed reasonable.

13 Sharla continued. "The other side of the mountain, where there's no lava, would look rocky and bumpy. Right?"

14 Tess caught on. "So one side can be smooth, and the other side can be rough. Come on, you guys, let's go finish!"

15 Mrs. Holt wasn't sure, but she thought the girls might have solved their own problem.

Chapter 5: Reading

1. In most stories, the characters have a problem. What problem do the characters in this story have?

____

2. What caused Mrs. Holt to call the girls up to her desk?

____

3. What is Tess's idea?
   _____ to show flowing lava
   _____ to make both sides smooth
   _____ to make the village larger

4. What is the result of Tess's idea?

____

____

5. Where in the story do we learn that the teacher, Mrs. Holt, knows the girls are not getting along?

____

____

6. What is the main difference in the way this story is written, compared to the other two about the same characters?
   _____ This story is told from Lee's point of view.
   _____ Sharla is not a character in this story.
   _____ It is not written as a journal entry.

7. How do you think Mrs. Holt feels about the girls solving their own problem? Explain.

____

____

8. What is the setting for this story?

____

9. The girls learned how to build a volcano by doing this project. What else do you think they learned?

____

____

Chapter 5: Reading

The End of a Volcano Tale

What did the girls learn from their project?

1 Sharla, Tess, and Lee stood proudly behind their model volcano. Tess straightened a tiny building in the village at the base of the mountain.

2 Mrs. Holt quieted the class. "Girls, you may begin."

3 Lee felt something wiggly in her stomach. She was supposed to go first.

4 "This is our volcano," she said. *Oh, that was stupid*, thought Lee, trying not to roll her eyes. *They can probably figure that out.* "We made it this shape because that's how a lot of volcanoes are shaped."

5 Next, Sharla told about what happens when a volcano erupts. After that, Tess told about a famous volcano and the town nearby that got covered up with ash and mud.

6 When it looked as if they were done, Mrs. Holt had a question. "Can you tell about the steps you went through to complete your project, girls?"

7 The girls looked at each other. They hadn't expected this. Sharla felt her face turn red, but she spoke up.

8 "Well, at first we didn't agree about what we wanted and how we wanted to do it." Sharla shrugged. "It took us a while to make a plan and get it done."

9 Tess went on. "We figured out that everybody had a job to do."

10 "And everybody has good ideas, even if they're not what you expect," added Lee.

11 Mrs. Holt looked pleased. *It only took one volcano and two explosions to figure out how to work together*, she thought. *Not bad.*

Chapter 5: Reading

1. This story is mostly about
   _____ becoming best friends after working together.
   _____ what the girls learned from their project.
   _____ how a teacher helped the girls get along.

2. How do the girls feel about their volcano project?

   ____

   ____

3. When it is Lee's turn to speak, she feels
   _____ nervous.
   _____ happy.
   _____ cross.

4. Why did Sharla's face turn red when Mrs. Holt asked about how they completed their project?

   ____

   ____

5. What experiences have you had working with other people? Were there times when you didn't agree or get along? Write about it.

   ____

   ____

   ____

6. When it is Tess's turn to speak, what does she tell about?

   ____

   ____

7. Make a check mark next to the thing that happened first.
   _____ Mrs. Holt had a question.
   _____ Lee said, "This is our volcano."
   _____ Mrs. Holt looked pleased.

8. If the girls had to work together again, how do you think they would do? Explain.

   ____

   ____

Chapter 5: Reading

Volcanoes

Read to find out why volcanoes erupt.

1 The surface of Earth is not a solid place. There are many holes, some of which allow magma to reach Earth's surface from deep inside.

2 Magma comes from deep inside Earth where it's hot. It's so hot that rocks melt. Magma is **molten**, or melted, rock. Because of the heat, there is also pressure. When things such as air, gases, or molten rock get hot, they **expand**, or get bigger. That means they need space. Weak parts of Earth's crust get pushed aside, or opened up. The magma follows the easiest path, usually along **fissures**, or cracks, toward the surface.

3 When it does reach the surface, magma is called *lava*. If there is a great deal of pressure behind the magma, it explodes through the crust's surface, sending dust, ash, lava, and rocks high into the air. When there is only a little pressure, the magma may simply bubble up and form a lava flow that spreads across the land.

4 A volcano may be **active**, or experience eruptions, on a fairly regular basis. Or it may lie **dormant**, or inactive, for hundreds of years. Scientists, called *volcanologists*, are always ready to learn more because each volcano is unique and may teach them something new about the inner workings of Earth.

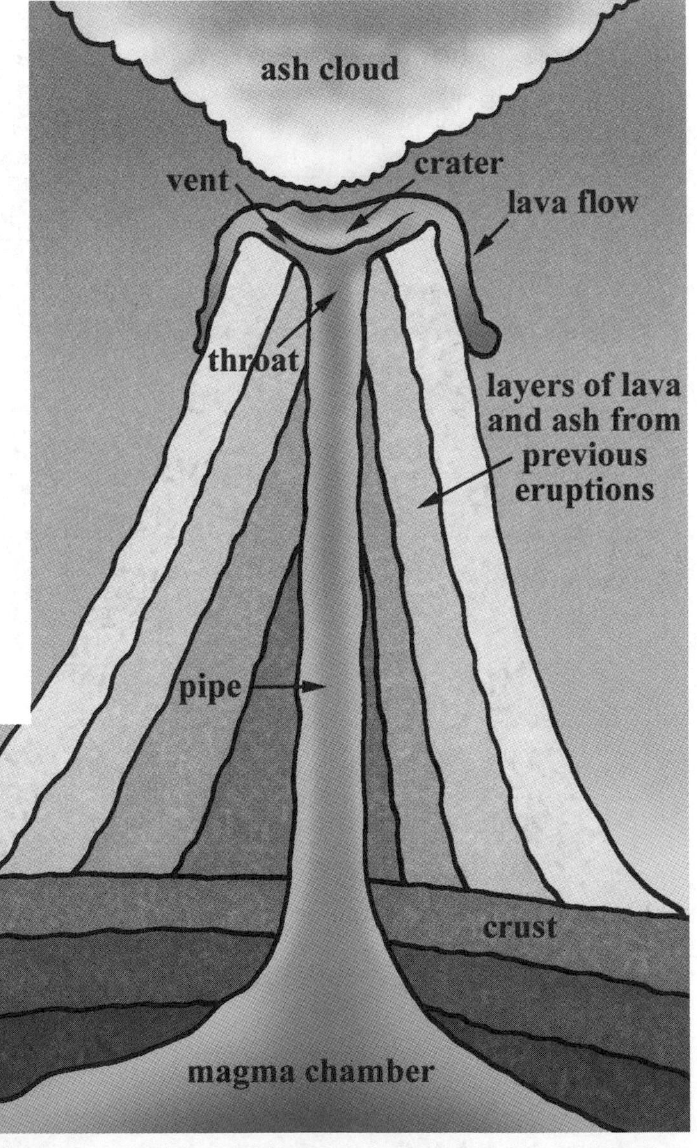

Chapter 5: Reading

In nonfiction writing, the author sometimes calls attention to words that the reader may not know. Those words appear in **bold** type. The author usually gives the meaning of the bold word in the same sentence.

Below are the bold words from the article. Write the meaning of each word.

1. molten ______________________________
2. expand ______________________________
3. fissures ______________________________
4. active ______________________________
5. dormant ______________________________

Write **F** next to each sentence that is a fact. Write **O** next to each sentence that is an opinion.

6. _____ Volcanic eruptions are one of the most striking natural events.
7. _____ A volcanic eruption is more frightening than a hurricane.
8. _____ Volcanoes are located in many places in the world.
9. What does the illustration show?

   ____

   ____

10. Trace with your finger the path that magma would take from under Earth's crust to the surface. Describe the path in your own words.

    ____

    ____

11. Write **C** next to the sentence below that is the cause. Write **E** next to the sentence that is the effect.

    _____ Parts of Earth's crust open up.

    _____ The molten rock gets very hot and expands.

12. What are scientists who study volcanoes called?

    ____

Chapter 5: Reading

Forest Mammals

Do you know what a mammal is?

Common Characteristics

1 What does a moose have in common with a porcupine? How about a bear with a mouse? How can more than 4,000 different kinds of mammals have much of anything in common? In fact, mammals have four distinct characteristics:

1. Mammals have warm blood, which means they can maintain a steady body temperature.
2. Mammals have backbones.
3. Female mammals produce milk to feed their babies.
4. Mammals have fur or hair, though the amount of it varies widely.

North American Forest Dwellers

2 Forest mammals are alike in that they live in the same natural conditions, or **habitat**. Trees and the leafy undergrowth provide shelter and food for the many types of mammals that live in a North American forest.

3 **Insect eaters:** Moles and shrews are just two types of **insectivores** that live on or under the forest floor. They find insects in the dirt or in rotting tree trunks or leaf matter.

4 **Gnawing animals:** This large family of mammals, called **rodents**, includes beavers, squirrels, mice, and porcupines. Whether on the ground or in trees, these animals gnaw on nuts, seeds, and branches with their strong front teeth.

5 **Hare-like animals:** Rabbits and hares make up this group. Leafy sprouts and sometimes the bark of young trees are the main diet of these animals.

6 **Meat eaters:** In North America, the largest meat eaters, or **carnivores**, are bears and mountain lions. Wolves and coyotes are also members of this group. They eat smaller mammals such as rabbits, mice, and moles.

7 **Hoofed animals:** In North America, moose and deer are the most common forest-dwelling hoofed animals. The forest provides both shelter and food for them.

Chapter 5: Reading

1. What four common characteristics do mammals have?

____

____

In the article, the author showed some words in bold type. The meanings of those words are given as well. Find the meanings of the words, and write them here.

2. habitat ____

____

3. insectivores ____

____

4. rodents ____

____

5. carnivores ____

____

6. Hoofed animals are named for the kind of ____________ they have.

7. Give one example of each kind of forest dweller.

insect eaters: ____________ gnawing animals: ____________

hare-like animals: ____________ meat eaters: ____________

hoofed animals: ____________

8. Why do you think a forest is a good habitat for many different kinds of mammals?

____

____

9. Think about what you know about mammals. Name two kinds of mammals that are not mentioned in the article.

____________________ and ____________________

10. **Meat eaters eat smaller mammals, such as rabbits, mice, and moles.** Is this sentence a fact or an opinion?

____

Chapter 5: Reading

Snakes: Love Them or Leave Them?

Why do you think snakes are not popular?

1 I think it is safe to say that most people really don't like snakes. It would be hard to find a person who is neutral, or simply doesn't care one way or the other. What I can't figure out is why something that doesn't even have any legs causes such alarm.

2 Snakes are reptiles, of course, not mammals. Do you think there is some ancient hatred between mammals and reptiles? Maybe their cold-bloodedness is what makes us dislike snakes. Or perhaps age-old stories about frightening creatures with scales cause us to turn away from our neighbors, the snakes.

3 Snakes are quite useful, but that doesn't seem to matter. Snakes help control the rodent population. Without snakes, perhaps we would be overrun with mice. Most of us, however, would rather see a mouse than a snake.

4 The poison argument is a strong one. Some snakes are poisonous, and people all over the world do die from snake bites each year. However, the poisonous varieties are only a small percentage of the world's snakes. We can't say the whole batch is bad just because of a few rotten ones.

5 And what do we do with the people who really like snakes? They like snakes even more strongly than we dislike them. These people learn about them, seek them out, and observe them. Why? The only reason I can think of is that these people are truly generous and open-minded. They are able to put aside differences and welcome the snake as a fellow living being.

6 Whatever the reason for our like or dislike, snakes are a vital part of the circle of life. They would prefer to be left alone, and that is what we should do. If you're lucky, you might not run across more than a few of them in an entire lifetime. That would be fine with most of us.

Chapter 5: Reading

The author of this article chose to share her own point of view. Find a sentence in which the author uses the word *I*. What idea is the author sharing in that sentence?

1. The sentence begins with

____

The author is saying ______________________________

______________________________.

2. Do you think the author likes snakes, dislikes snakes, or is neutral? Write a sentence from the article that supports your answer.

____

____

Write **F** next to each sentence that is a fact. Write **O** next to each sentence that is an opinion.

3. _____ People dislike snakes because they have no legs.

4. _____ Snakes control the rodent population.

5. _____ Not meeting many snakes is a good thing.

6. Name one difference between mammals and reptiles.

____

____

7. What is one way in which snakes are useful?

____

8. What is the main idea of paragraph 4?

_____ If you get bitten by a poisonous snake, seek medical help.

_____ Some snakes are poisonous, but that's not a good reason to dislike all snakes.

_____ Poisonous snakes are very vicious.

9. Tell how you feel about snakes and why.

____

____

____

Chapter 5: Reading

Redwood Giants

Read to learn about America's biggest trees.

1 From a seed that is smaller than a pea grows the tallest of trees. The coast redwood is the unchallenged giant of North America's trees.

What's special about redwoods?

2 Redwoods are special for a couple of reasons. The first is their size. Imagine standing next to a tree that is the height of a 20- or 30-story building. The second is their age. Redwoods commonly make it to 600 years or so. Some have been found that are more than 2,000 years old.

Where do redwoods grow?

3 To find a coast redwood, you'll have to go to Oregon or California. A strip of coastline about 450 miles long and up to 35 miles wide is home to the redwoods. Coast redwoods do not grow anywhere else in the world.

Why do redwoods grow there?

4 The coast of the Pacific Ocean provides a special environment for the redwoods. Cool, moist air comes off the ocean and keeps the trees moist all year. That is important because almost all of the area's rain falls between October and May. During the dry summer months, the trees depend on moisture from the thick fog that often hangs over the coast.

How do redwoods survive?

5 Redwoods have a couple of built-in protection systems. Most of a redwood's branches and leaves are high up on the tree. This keeps them safe from forest fires. Also, the bark of a mature redwood tree is as much as 12 inches thick. The thick covering protects the lower part of the tree from fire damage. Redwoods are safe from insect damage because the wood contains a bitter-tasting chemical called *tannin*.

What should I do?

6 If you ever get a chance, visit a redwood forest. Look among the tree trunks and imagine who might have camped there a thousand years ago. Look upward and just imagine how high the trees might grow if we preserve and protect them.

Chapter 5: Reading

1. To see a redwood tree, you have to go to ______________________________.

2. Why do redwoods grow there?

____

____

3. What might happen if someone tried to grow a redwood tree in Kansas or Missouri, for example?

____

____

4. What do you think is most special about redwood trees? Write why.

____

____

5. Why do you think the author chose to use questions for the headings?

____

____

6. If you want to find out what conditions redwoods need to grow, under which heading would you look?

____

7. If you wonder what the big deal is about redwoods, under which heading should you look?

____

8. What three objects are shown in the diagram?

____

9. What is the author's purpose for writing this selection?

_____ to entertain

_____ to persuade

_____ to inform

10. About how long can a redwood live?

____

Chapter 5: Reading

Problem Solved

What will Miss Eller decide the class should study?

1 So far, Miss Eller's idea had worked out. Her students had done some research on whatever they wanted to know about the natural world. They had all really enjoyed uncovering facts about snails or redwood trees or grasshoppers. And Enzo's plastic snakes had been a big hit.

2 Now, it all fell back to Miss Eller, though. She had to decide whose ideas to accept and whose to reject. She thought back on the students' reports and tried to sort them into groups. Furry things in this group, and crawling things in that group? No, that didn't really work.

3 Suddenly, her gaze shifted and she realized that the answer was right in front of her. A poster on the wall showed a lush woodland scene that included many different kinds of trees, forest creatures, birds, and, yes, even some snakes and crawly things. Miss Eller smiled. *A picture is worth a thousand words—or a thousand ideas*, she thought. She had the solution.

4 After lunch, the students gathered on the meeting rug. "What if I told you that we are going to have one topic, but that you are all going to be able to study what you want?"

5 "How can that be?" questioned Tara. "We all had different ideas."

6 Miss Eller shrugged. "It all depends on how you group things together. What if our topic is 'Redwood Forests'? What do you suppose lives in a redwood forest?"

7 Hands shot up left and right. Everything the students could think of fit into Miss Eller's topic: redwood trees, of course, cute and fuzzy mammals, snails, snakes—you name it.

8 Within a few weeks, the classroom had been transformed. A sign appeared outside the classroom door.

Welcome to our
redwood forest.
If something lives, grows, eats, breathes, or crawls in a redwood forest, we know all about it.
Come on in.

Chapter 5: Reading

Complete each sentence with the correct word.

author	dialogue	narrator

1. When characters speak, their words make up the story's ____________________.

2. The person who wrote the story is the ____________________.

3. Within the story, the person or character who tells the story is the ____________________.

4. In most stories, the main character has a problem. Miss Eller's problem is that

   ____

5. Look at the illustration. What did Miss Eller's students do during their study of redwood forests?

   ____

   ____

   ____

6. Where did Miss Eller get the idea of how to solve the problem?

   ____

7. How do you think Miss Eller's class feels about the project?

   _____ excited

   _____ worried

   _____ upset

8. The last paragraph says that the classroom had been transformed. What does this mean?

   ____

9. Write **C** next to the sentence below that is the cause. Write **E** next to the sentence that is the effect.

   _____ Students raise their hands to answer the question.

   _____ Miss Eller asks what lives in a redwood forest.

Chapter 5: Reading

Magic with Flowers

What are Josh and Gary trying to do?

1 *"Ala-ka-ZAM!"* said Gary, trying to make his voice sound big. He waved his arms in and out in what he hoped was a fancy pattern, and then tapped the box sitting on the table with a magic wand. He held his breath. The box jiggled a little. Then, the table jiggled a little.

2 *"Ahhhhh!"* The exclamation erupted from under the table.

3 "What's the matter?" called Gary. "Did it work?"

4 Gary's friend Josh came out from under the table. His hair was wet. His shirt was wet. He was holding a vase of fake flowers. "Well, it worked if you don't count spilling water all over," Josh grumbled. The boys had put water in the vase because they thought it would make it all seem more real.

5 "Maybe we should use real flowers," suggested Gary.

6 "They'd just wilt," Josh shook his head.

7 Gary shrugged. "Yeah, I guess so. Aside from spilling, how did it go under there?"

8 Josh told what had happened. When Gary tapped the box, Josh was supposed to open the secret door on the bottom of the box and pull the vase of flowers down, and then close up the box again. But the bottom had gotten stuck and the vase had tipped. The boys sat down to rethink their plan.

9 The boys had thought the old broken table was almost too good to be true. Its worn-out wicker top had a hole that was just the right size for covering with the box as well as for making stuff disappear by pulling it through.

10 "This whole magic thing just isn't as easy as I thought it would be," noted Gary.

11 "Yeah, I know," Josh agreed. "How do you suppose the real magicians did it? They made stuff disappear all the time."

12 An idea popped into Gary's head and his face brightened. "Maybe it is the fake flowers. The real ones used real stuff, like rabbits. We need a rabbit. Go get Wiggles!"

Chapter 5: Reading

1. This story is mostly about

   _____ two boys trying to do a magic trick.

   _____ a boy teaching another boy a magic trick.

   _____ how to do a magic trick.

2. Josh got wet because ____

   ____.

3. Why was Josh under the table?

   ____

   ____

4. Write **C** next to the sentence below that is the cause. Write **E** next to the sentence that is the effect.

   _____ The vase tipped and got Josh wet.

   _____ The bottom of the box got stuck.

5. Why were the boys so excited about the old table they found?

   ____

   ____

6. Doing magic is (easier, harder) than the boys had expected.

7. Gary thinks that he and Josh need real things, so he tells Josh to go get a real

   ____

8. Read the sentences below. Write **F** next to sentences that are facts and **O** next to sentences that are opinions.

   _____ Gary held his breath.

   _____ The boys should use real flowers.

   _____ Being a magician is hard work.

   _____ Josh's hair was wet.

9. What do you think will happen next?

   ____

   ____

   ____

Chapter 5: Reading

Magic with Wiggles

Read to see whether Josh and Gary's new trick works.

1 *Well, okay,* thought Josh. Every magician they had ever read about had used rabbits. Josh couldn't believe they hadn't thought of Wiggles earlier. He had a good feeling about this.

2 Gary put a lettuce leaf in the box, and then Josh put Wiggles in the box and closed one of the top flaps. Josh got into position under the table so he could pull Wiggles through the hole in the bottom of the box and make him disappear.

3 Gary cleared his throat and raised his arms slowly. *"Ala-ka-...."*

4 "Hey, wait," called Josh from underneath the table. He crawled partway out. "Maybe we should try a new word. A rabbit-y word."

5 "A rabbit-y word?" Gary looked doubtful. "Like what?"

6 "Well, I don't know." Josh thought for a moment. "How about *rabbit-o-zam*?

7 *"Rabbit-o-ZAM!"* Gary tried it out. Both boys shook their heads.

8 Josh tried again. *"Shish-rabbit-ka-zam!"* Nope.

9 *"Abra-ca-DAB-rabbit!"* tried Gary.

10 "Abra-ca-DAB-rabbit?" Josh was laughing so hard he could barely get the word out.

11 After a good laughing spell, the boys got back down to business. They agreed to go back to good old *abracadabra*.

12 Josh took his position, and Gary did his part, complete with arms waving and stick tapping. The box jiggled a tiny bit. The table jiggled.

13 *"Ahhhhh!"* The cry from under the table was truly alarming.

14 "Now what's wrong?" cried Gary.

15 *"It worked!"* screamed Josh, scrambling out from under the table. *"It worked! Wiggles is gone!"*

16 "It worked?" cried Gary, and he dived under the table in disbelief. When he came out, the boys did a little dance, and then they bowed to the imaginary crowd, quite certain that they heard wild clapping.

17 Wiggles had, indeed, disappeared.

Chapter 5: Reading

1. How was the magic trick supposed to work?

____

2. What actually happened?

____

____

Write the best word to complete each sentence below.

3. They should have thought of Wiggles ____________. (brighter, sooner, calmer)

4. The magic words made the boys ____________ so hard. (laugh, lame, learn)

5. It made Gary feel like a real magician when he ____________ his arms. (waved, cried, tapped)

6. The boys couldn't ____________ Wiggles was gone. (agree, scramble, believe)

7. Write **R** next to the sentences that tell about something real. Write **M** next to the sentences that are about made-up things.

_____ Rabbits eat lettuce.

_____ Rabbits disappear and reappear.

_____ Magicians say magic words.

8. In the story, who is the magician, and who is the assistant?

____

____

9. Do you think the boys were surprised that Wiggles was actually gone? Why or why not?

____

____

10. Which words best describe the boys?

_____ good-natured

_____ sneaky

_____ irritated

11. What do you think will happen next in the story?

____

____

Chapter 5: Reading

Houdini

What made Harry Houdini so great?

1 Do you believe in magic? The greatest magician of all time didn't. Harry Houdini was known as "The King of Cards" and "The Great Escape Artist." But he was the first to say that his magic tricks were tricks, not magic.

2 Houdini's early interest in magic tricks led him to read about famous magicians. He studied and then practiced and practiced. His first magic shows, begun when he was 17, included mostly card tricks. He added new tricks, such as escaping from an ordinary box, once he had perfected them.

3 From those simple beginnings, Houdini's magic tricks became more showy and more daring. He escaped from handcuffs. Then, he allowed audience members to bring their own handcuffs to prove he could escape from *any* pair of handcuffs. Then, he escaped from a straitjacket, hanging upside down by his ankles.

4 How can a performer top his own top performance? Think of a trick that seems truly impossible. Houdini had himself locked into a crate and thrown into a river. He also had himself sealed into a lead coffin, which was placed into a hotel swimming pool. An hour later, Houdini waved to the waiting fans and newspaper reporters.

5 Houdini strongly supported the work of magicians but just as strongly spoke against "fake" magicians who claimed that they had special powers or communicated with "spirits." Houdini would expose these false magicians by visiting their shows and then writing magazine or newspaper articles to reveal how they fooled their audiences.

6 To set himself apart from the "spiritual" magicians, Houdini practiced his tricks, perfected them, and then practiced again. Though Harry Houdini died almost a hundred years ago, the man and his tricks have never been matched.

Chapter 5: Reading

1. The author wrote this article to

_____ persuade.

_____ make you laugh.

_____ give you information.

Write **F** next to each sentence that is a fact. Write **O** next to each sentence that is an opinion.

2. _____ Harry Houdini died almost a hundred years ago.
3. _____ Houdini could escape from handcuffs.
4. _____ Harry Houdini was the only "real" magician.
5. _____ Houdini's magic tricks were wonderful.
6. The article gives details about Houdini and his life. Number the details in the order in which the author tells about them.

_____ He escaped from a straitjacket, hanging upside down.

_____ Houdini had his first magic shows when he was 17.

_____ Houdini exposed "fake" magicians.

_____ Houdini's magic tricks became more showy and daring.

7. Which of these old sayings would Houdini have agreed with?

_____ Practice makes perfect.

_____ You are what you eat.

_____ A watched pot never boils.

8. **Houdini believed he had special powers and could talk to spirits.** Is this statement true or false?

____

Chapter 5: Reading

David Copperfield

What kind of a magician is David Copperfield?

1 An illusion is something that fools the senses or the mind. An illusion may make you think something exists when it really does not. It may be something that appears to be one thing, but is really something else. David Copperfield calls himself an *illusionist*. He is someone who makes or creates illusions.

2 Many people are interested in magic, but most of them are not performing and getting paid for it by age 12. Nor are they teaching college-level classes in magic at age 16. Copperfield was the youngest person ever to be allowed to join the Society of American Magicians. When he got to college himself, Copperfield got the leading part in a play called *The Magic Man*. In addition to acting and singing, he created all the magic in the show. The show ran for longer than any other musical in Chicago's history.

3 Copperfield is a huge success as a showy illusionist, but he has other projects as well. He says that his best work is Project Magic. Copperfield developed a number of tricks done with the hands. These tricks help hospital patients who need to improve their hand strength or coordination to move and control their fingers. Learning to do the tricks also builds confidence. Patients in the program can boast that they can do tricks that able-bodied people can't do.

4 Like many magicians, Copperfield has an interest in the history of magic. He has created a museum and library in which books, articles, and old magic props, or equipment, are stored and displayed. By keeping track of history, Copperfield hopes to save magic for future generations.

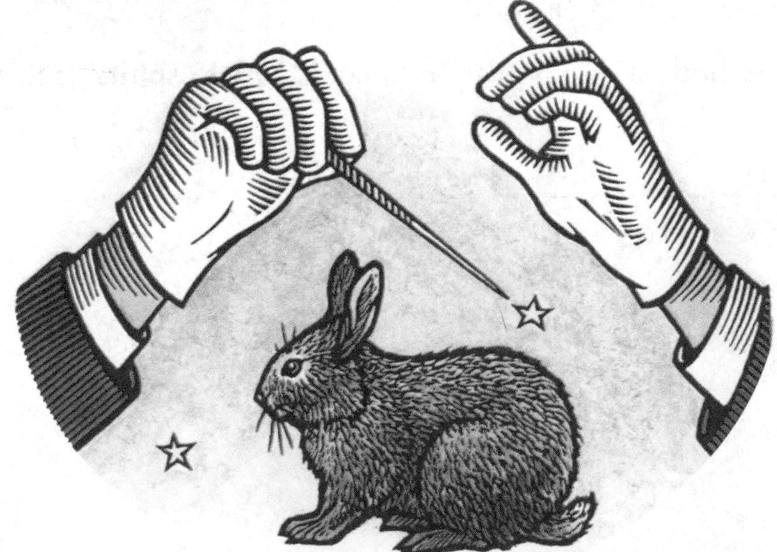

Chapter 5: Reading

1. David Copperfield is an ______________.

2. What did he start doing at age 12?

____

3. What was he doing by age 16?

____

Check all answers that are correct.

4. Which of these words do you think best describe Copperfield?
   _____ thoughtless
   _____ lazy
   _____ hard-working
   _____ talented

5. What do you think a magician could learn from Copperfield's collection of old magic books and equipment?

____

____

6. If you were a magician or an illusionist, what kinds of tricks would you like to do?

____

____

7. The headings below belong in this article. To which paragraph does each heading belong?
   Copperfield's Beginnings _____
   What Is an Illusion? _____
   Saving Magic for the Future _____
   Project Magic _____

8. In your own words, explain what an illusion is.

____

____

9. The youngest person ever to be allowed to join the Society of American Magicians was ______________________.

10. Why do you think Copperfield believes that his best work is Project Magic?

____

____

Chapter 5: Reading

Wiggles Reappears

How do the boys get Wiggles back?

1 "Which word do you think did it?" asked Josh.

2 "What do you mean?" asked Gary, still feeling great because their magic trick had worked. They had finally gotten something to disappear.

3 "Was it *shish-rabbit-ka-zam* or *abra-ca-dab-rabbit*?" Josh asked, working hard to repeat the magic words they had thought up.

4 Gary laughed again, remembering the words. "Oh, I think it was definitely *abra-ca-dab-rabbit*, don't you?"

5 "I don't know," shrugged Josh. "I guess we'll have to try each of them backward to get him back."

6 All of a sudden, it was very quiet. Gary looked at Josh. How in the world were they going to get Wiggles back?

7 "I think I remember all the words," Gary said, trying to encourage Josh. Wiggles was Josh's pet, after all.

8 The boys sat down on the back steps of Josh's house to figure out how to say the words backward so the magic would work the other way.

9 "Okay," said Gary, thinking hard. "We have *zam-ka-rabbit-shish* and *rabbit-dab-ca-abra*."

10 Josh continued, "And *zam-o-rabbit* and just plain old *dabra-ca-abra*."

11 Gary nodded, "I think that's it."

12 *"Ahhhhh!"* The cry came from around the corner of the house. It was Josh's mom.

13 "Mom? What's the matter?" called Josh, as both boys went running.

14 "Now, how many times have I told you not to chew on my…" Josh heard his mom's voice. Just around the corner, both boys stopped short.

15 "Wiggles! He reappeared!" Josh cried.

16 Mom looked at the boys. "Wiggles? Reappeared? Who's going to make my flowers reappear?"

17 The boys looked at each other, smiled, and nodded. They waved their arms and said, in their best magician voices, *"Zam-ka-flowers-SHISH!"*

Chapter 5: Reading

1. Number the sentences to show the order in which events happened in the story.

   _____ Gary laughed about their magic words.

   _____ The boys heard Josh's mom.

   _____ The boys discovered Mom and Wiggles.

   _____ The boys figured out how to say the words backward.

   _____ Gary felt great because their trick worked.

   _____ The boys tried to make Mom's flowers reappear.

2. What problem do the boys have in this story?

   ____

   ____

3. What problem does Mom have?

   ____

   ____

4. How do the boys try to help Mom? Do you think it will work?

   ____

   ____

   ____

5. Who does Wiggles belong to?

   ____

6. Do you think Wiggles has escaped before? What details in the story helped you answer this question?

   ____

   ____

   ____

7. Do you think the boys will continue working on their magic tricks? Why or why not?

   ____

   ____

   ____

Chapter 5: Reading

Caught in Traffic

What happens on the way back from the field trip?

1 Jason was winning. He and his friends had been trying to see who could list the most cool things that they had seen on the field trip. Jason had 27 so far. Steven was starting to catch up, though.

2 As Luisa thought up more ideas, she gazed out the bus window and realized that the bus wasn't moving. She saw long lines of cars beside them and stretching around a curve in front of them.

3 "Hey, I wonder what's happening," she said, pointing out the window. "Everyone is stopped."

4 The bus driver heard Luisa and nodded his head. "This often happens on the outer edges of the city, especially on Friday afternoons. Everyone has to be somewhere, and right now they're all right here," he said, turning to frown, but in a friendly way, at Luisa.

5 Jason was a little worried. "What if we don't get back to school on time?"

6 "Oh, we have plenty of time," Mrs. Mason quickly assured him. "And if it does get late, I'll just call the school and let them know what's happening. It'll be all right."

7 "Just look at them all," said Luisa, still gazing out the window. "How many do you think there are?"

8 "Let's see!" suggested Steven. "One, two, three, four, five, six, seven, eight...."

9 "Okay, okay," cut in Luisa, waving a hand at Steven, "that's annoying." She grinned at Steven, and Steven grinned right back.

10 Jason had a different thought. "I wonder where they're all going and where they came from." The three friends all looked out the window at the cars disappearing into the distance. Each of them wondered about all the different kinds of people and all of their different reasons for being here right now, clogging up the highway.

Chapter 5: Reading

Write the best word to complete each sentence below.

1. Up ahead, the line of cars went around a ______________. (curve, ledge, movement)
2. Jason was worried about the bus being ______________. (hard, late, extra)
3. Steven wanted to ______________ the cars. (spin, read, count)
4. Have you ever been stuck in traffic? Write about how it felt.

____

____

____

____

5. What might cause a traffic jam? List as many reasons as you can.

____

____

____

6. How do you think the bus driver feels about the traffic jam?

_____ amused

_____ joyful

_____ frustrated

7. If the bus is late, what will Mrs. Mason do?

____

____

8. Write **C** next to the sentence below that is the cause. Write **E** next to the sentence that is the effect.

_____ Lots of cars are on the highway at the same time.

_____ The cars are causing a traffic jam.

Chapter 5: Reading

How Many Are There?

Read to see why we count things.

1 Look in any newspaper and you are likely to see numbers. We like to know how many inches of rain we've had, or how many students are in our schools. We want to know how much the city government is spending, or how many people have voted. We like to see numbers.

2 Fortunately, many people like to count or keep track of things. They count traffic accidents and help us decide where to put stop signs and traffic lights. They count people to help us decide when we need more houses or more schools. They count how many people catch the flu and tell us when to get shots.

3 Some numbers help us see that we need to change something. Other numbers show how things are changing. The numbers in the graph on this page show how the population and the number of cars in the United States have changed. How has the growth in population affected or changed the United States? How has the increase in the number of cars affected the country? Think about how this growth has affected you and your community.

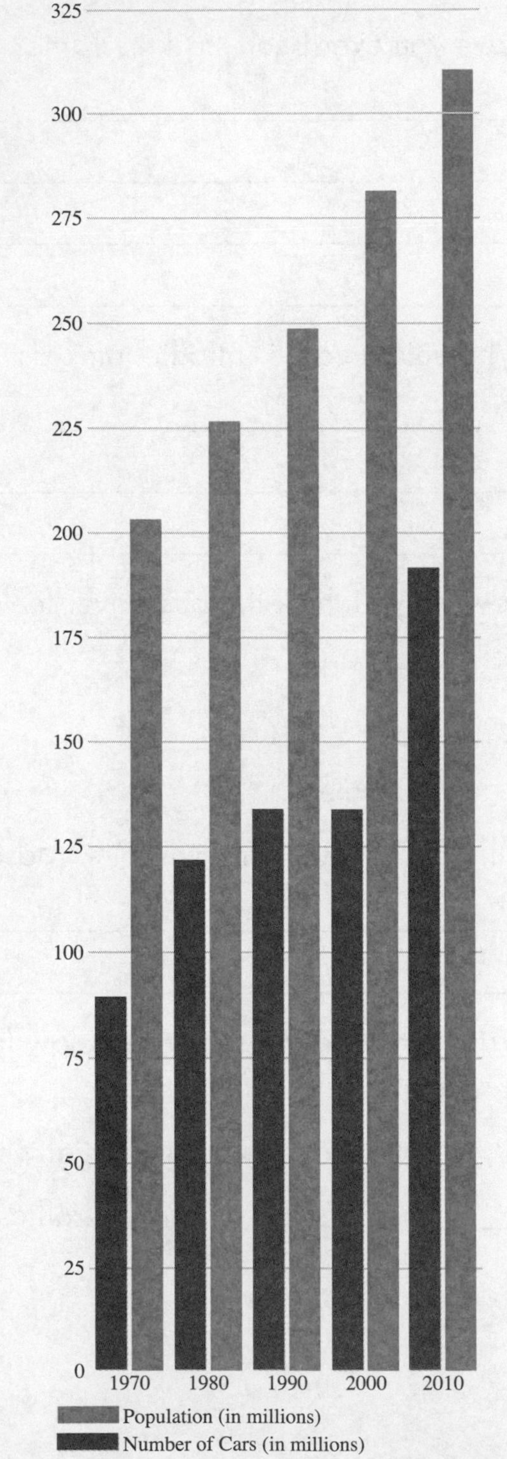

Chapter 5: Reading

1. What kinds of things do we count? List two examples from the article.

2. What do we learn from counting things?

3. How do you think the information shown in this graph affects you and your community?

4. What can the number of traffic accidents tell us?

5. How many years does this chart cover?

6. Why is the title of the chart important?

Use the bar graph to answer these questions.

7. For each year, which is greater, the population or the number of cars?

8. If you want population data for 1950, would this graph help you? How can you tell?

9. What was the population of the United States in 1970?

10. How many cars were there in 1990?

Chapter 5: Reading

Sidewalk Art

How do a sister and brother fill a long, hot afternoon?

1 I feel like a cactus. No, that's too dry. I feel like the glass greenhouse at the city park, all steamy and cloudy inside because the plants like it warm and moist. I feel like…

2 Oh, it's no use. I don't feel like anything. I'm just hot. It's hot outside. It's hot inside. There is nothing to do. I sit on the front steps of our building, trying to stay in a small triangle of shade. At the same time, I try to touch as little of the step as possible because everything feels hot and sticky, including my own skin.

3 I squint toward the sun to make bright, fuzzy patterns with my eyelashes. I watch a tree across the street. I can count on the fingers of one hand the number of leaves moving in the breeze. That's how weak the breeze is.

4 I try to think of something to do. I give myself a deadline. When the shade of my building gets to that crack in the sidewalk, I will do something. It happens slowly, just like everything else in the heat. When it gets close, I go down to the crack and watch. Yes, it's time. What should I do?

5 My brother Fujio's box of chalk is sitting forgotten at the bottom of the steps. I take out a piece of yellow chalk and make a blazing sun on the sidewalk. I surround it with white, then with every color in the chalk box.

6 Fujio appears at my side. "What's that, Tatsu?" he asks.

7 I don't say anything, but I write "Heat" at the bottom of my drawing. He just shrugs. Then, he gets the black chalk (his favorite color) and starts coloring. He fills a whole square of the sidewalk.

8 "What's that?" I ask.

9 "Shade," he says.

10 "Fujio, that's not…," I begin to say, but then I stop. It doesn't really matter. It's something to do, and that's a bonus on a hot day.

Chapter 5: Reading

1. Tatsu is sitting in the shade on the front steps because

____.

2. Tatsu titles her drawing "Heat" because

____

____.

3. Write **R** next to the sentences that tell about something real. Write **M** next to the sentences that are about made-up things.

_____ A person can make shade by drawing a picture of it.

_____ A person can draw a picture of heat.

_____ A person can draw a picture of the sun.

The **narrator** is the person who tells a story. Answer these questions.

4. Because the narrator is also a character, she uses the words *I* and *me* to tell her story. Find a place in the story where one of these words is used. Write the sentence here.

____

____

5. Where in the story do you discover what the narrator's name is?

____

6. Do you think Tatsu and Fujio live in the city, in the country, or in a small town? Why?

____

____

7. From whose point of view is the story told?

_____ Tatsu's _____ Fujio's _____ Not enough information is given.

8. The author uses lots of descriptions to tell how hot it is. List three details from the story that help you imagine the heat.

____

____

____

9. What do you like to do on a super hot summer day?

____

Chapter 5: Reading

Wishes on the Sidewalk

How do the children try to cool themselves off?

1 It's late afternoon now, and it's getting a little better. The heat, I mean. The shade came around to the front of the building, so at least the sidewalk doesn't burn you anymore.

2 I tease Fujio about drawing a picture of shade. He's pretty cool about it. He just says, "It helped me think about not being hot."

3 I look at my own picture of the hot, hot sun. Maybe I should have tried it Fujio's way. Maybe my sun picture just makes it hotter here.

4 I see our neighbors Mario and Katie coming down the sidewalk. They stop and look at our pictures. Mario points at Fujio's black square and raises his eyebrows.

5 "Shade," sighs Fujio, as if he is tired of being an artist who is not understood. Mario wrinkles his brow for a moment, and then bends down and picks up the blue chalk. He begins at a corner, just like Fujio did, and covers a square with blue.

6 It's too hot to talk, so we just wait. We figure he'll explain. When Mario is done, he stands up and gives a little bow. "Cool water," he says. Fujio and I smile. Then, Katie jumps up and grabs the white chalk.

7 "Watch this, Tatsu," she says to me. Mario steps aside as Katie begins in the middle of a square. The square fills with white as the chalk gets smaller and smaller.

8 Finally, she stands. "A snow bank," she announces.

9 Fujio, Mario, and I cheer and clap. "Bravo! Bravo!"

10 Katie sits back down on the steps and leans back. I can tell she and the boys are thinking cool thoughts. I get up and make a big black "X" across my hot sun picture. Then, I go and sit right in the middle of Katie's snow bank. It's so cool it doesn't even melt.

Chapter 5: Reading

1. Why do Mario and Katie choose to draw pictures of cool water and a snow bank?

___

___

2. Why does Tatsu cross out her own picture of the sun?

___

___

3. Which word best describes the group of friends?

_____ energetic

_____ creative

_____ anxious

4. Mario doesn't use words to ask Fujio what he drew. How does he ask instead?

___

5. What is the author's purpose in writing this story?

_____ to teach _____ to persuade _____ to entertain

6. Why is the story titled "Wishes on the Sidewalk"?

___

___

___

7. Do you think that thinking about cool things can help a person cool down? Write why or why not.

___

___

___

8. Can you remember a hot day? How did it feel? Describe it so that someone else can imagine it easily.

___

___

___

Chapter 5: Reading

Drawings on the Wall

What might you have been doing if you lived 17,000 years ago?

1 The year, if anyone were counting, would be around 15,000 B.C. You were probably looking for food, maybe using an animal skin to carry water, and possibly tending a fire to keep warm. Oh, and there's one other thing. You might have been drawing pictures on the walls of your cave.

2 We don't know why you drew the pictures. You had to go deep into the cave to do it, so you must have had a plan. You probably took a lamp made out of animal fat with you. Some of us think you drew pictures to bring good luck when you hunted. Others think the spears in some of the pictures mean that you were teaching other people to hunt.

3 For paint, you mixed animal fat with various things, such as dirt or berries. You used the ragged end of a stick to brush or dab the paint onto the wall. Sometimes, you didn't feel like using any color and you used the end of a stick that had been burned in the fire. It made broad black marks, much like modern artists make with chalk.

4 You drew what you saw around you—animals such as buffalo, deer, horses, and sometimes birds and fish. You drew people, but not very often. Sometimes, you made handprints or basic shape patterns on the wall.

5 You'll be happy to know that we think your pictures are really quite good. The buffalo look strong and powerful. And many of the horses and deer look graceful. You drew their shapes well.

6 We have found your drawings in more than 130 caves, mostly in France and England. We wonder if there are more that we haven't found yet. We wonder so many things, but we'll just have to satisfy ourselves with admiring your drawings. We're glad you made them.

Chapter 5: Reading

1. This article is mostly about

   _____ animals that lived thousands of years ago.

   _____ early cave art.

   _____ how early people survived.

2. What did early cave artists use for paint?

   ____

3. Where did early artists make their drawings?

   ____

4. Early cave art has been found in more than _______ caves.

5. How do you like the cave art shown on this page? How is it the same or different from other drawings you have seen of mammoths?

   ____

   ____

   ____

6. Who is the author addressing, or talking to, in this article?

   _____ the reader

   _____ the people who made the cave paintings

   _____ artists of today

7. Why is this an unusual way to write the article?

   ____

   ____

   ____

8. Most of the cave drawings have been found in ____________ and ____________.

9. What is the main idea of paragraph 4?

   ____

   ____

10. About how many years ago were the cave paintings made?

    ____

Math Answers

Chapter 1

page 8

1. 5 **2.** 16 **3.** 7 **4.** 8 **5.** 3 **6.** 14
7. 9 **8.** 6 **9.** 9 **10.** 11 **11.** 7 **12.** 13
13. 7 **14.** 11 **15.** 14 **16.** 11 **17.** 14 **18.** 6
19. 0 **20.** 11 **21.** 14 **22.** 7 **23.** 8 **24.** 12

page 9

1. 5 **2.** 6 **3.** 1 **4.** 5 **5.** 7 **6.** 5
7. 3 **8.** 3 **9.** 3 **10.** 8 **11.** 9 **12.** 2
13. 5 **14.** 3 **15.** 6 **16.** 3 **17.** 7 **18.** 7
19. 11 **20.** 1 **21.** 16 **22.** 8 **23.** 5 **24.** 13

page 10

1. 39 **2.** 33 **3.** 30 **4.** 28 **5.** 88 **6.** 76
7. 27 **8.** 48 **9.** 27 **10.** 83 **11.** 92 **12.** 55
13. 26 **14.** 47 **15.** 59 **16.** 80 **17.** 77 **18.** 44
19. 59 **20.** 55 **21.** 56 **22.** 48 **23.** 69 **24.** 69

page 11

1. 11 **2.** 64 **3.** 22 **4.** 20 **5.** 81 **6.** 32
7. 52 **8.** 70 **9.** 21 **10.** 42 **11.** 12 **12.** 56
13. 41 **14.** 22 **15.** 27 **16.** 13 **17.** 44 **18.** 30
19. 41 **20.** 21 **21.** 12 **22.** 22 **23.** 21 **24.** 12

page 12

1. 41 **2.** 91 **3.** 90 **4.** 52 **5.** 81 **6.** 48
7. 63 **8.** 91 **9.** 64 **10.** 80 **11.** 83 **12.** 72
13. 81 **14.** 81 **15.** 45 **16.** 32 **17.** 56 **18.** 70
19. 81 **20.** 45 **21.** 81 **22.** 31 **23.** 90 **24.** 54

page 13

1. 8 **2.** 3 **3.** 25 **4.** 14 **5.** 36 **6.** 59
7. 17 **8.** 6 **9.** 34 **10.** 19 **11.** 17 **12.** 19
13. 35 **14.** 15 **15.** 46 **16.** 29 **17.** 25 **18.** 24
19. 7 **20.** 40 **21.** 59 **22.** 67 **23.** 35 **24.** 19

page 14

1. 84 **2.** 92 **3.** 64 **4.** 68 **5.** 48 **6.** 90
7. 98 **8.** 72 **9.** 60 **10.** 53 **11.** 71 **12.** 84
13. 83 **14.** 52 **15.** 19 **16.** 91 **17.** 74 **18.** 85
19. 96 **20.** 92 **21.** 93 **22.** 66 **23.** 91 **24.** 89

page 15

1. 118 **2.** 103 **3.** 140 **4.** 118 **5.** 110 **6.** 162
7. 94 **8.** 119 **9.** 105 **10.** 113 **11.** 158 **12.** 114
13. 102 **14.** 119 **15.** 161 **16.** 115 **17.** 127 **18.** 121
19. 114 **20.** 104 **21.** 119 **22.** 102 **23.** 105 **24.** 170
25. 100 **26.** 107 **27.** 120 **28.** 111 **29.** 139 **30.** 86

page 16

1. 140 **2.** 61 **3.** 151 **4.** 111 **5.** 94 **6.** 92
7. 81 **8.** 110 **9.** 104 **10.** 111 **11.** 121 **12.** 145
13. 141 **14.** 44 **15.** 120 **16.** 93 **17.** 91 **18.** 111
19. 81 **20.** 134 **21.** 121 **22.** 94 **23.** 62 **24.** 80

page 17

1. 89 **2.** 78 **3.** 88 **4.** 86 **5.** 77 **6.** 39
7. 79 **8.** 79 **9.** 67 **10.** 66 **11.** 68 **12.** 86
13. 26 **14.** 8 **15.** 48 **16.** 89 **17.** 69 **18.** 88
19. 78 **20.** 58 **21.** 69 **22.** 86 **23.** 59 **24.** 76

page 18

1. 685 **2.** 1,153 **3.** 933 **4.** 1,123
5. 444 **6.** 1,656 **7.** 1,175 **8.** 1,030
9. 1,570 **10.** 1,042 **11.** 1,280 **12.** 868
13. 1,282 **14.** 1,001 **15.** 681 **16.** 973
17. 1,356 **18.** 1,194 **19.** 982 **20.** 944
21. 367 **22.** 404 **23.** 414 **24.** 1,234

page 19

1. 212 **2.** 593 **3.** 489 **4.** 120
5. 480 **6.** 148 **7.** 408 **8.** 206
9. 279 **10.** 106 **11.** 377 **12.** 190
13. 331 **14.** 399 **15.** 519 **16.** 189
17. 577 **18.** 321 **19.** 114 **20.** 208
21. 529 **22.** 171 **23.** 448 **24.** 220

Math Answers

page 20

1. 369 **2.** 901 **3.** 417 **4.** 732
5. 521 **6.** 290 **7.** 1,108 **8.** 606
9. 1,075 **10.** 1,005 **11.** 397 **12.** 476
13. 847 **14.** 711 **15.** 931 **16.** 550
17. 531 **18.** 506

page 21

1. 570 **2.** 238 **3.** 33 **4.** 326 **5.** 165 **6.** 222
7. 121 **8.** 15 **9.** 226 **10.** 112 **11.** 129 **12.** 296
13. 399 **14.** 220 **15.** 106 **16.** 263 **17.** 264 **18.** 405

page 22

1. 18 **2.** 20 **3.** 31 **4.** 44 **5.** 97 **6.** 16
7. 133 **8.** 153 **9.** 123 **10.** 83 **11.** 142 **12.** 150
13. 251 **14.** 120 **15.** 120 **16.** 223 **17.** 157 **18.** 55
19. 163 **20.** 183 **21.** 188 **22.** 39 **23.** 120 **24.** 212

page 23

1. 1,040 **2.** 1,594 **3.** 650 **4.** 1,794
5. 1,616 **6.** 914 **7.** 1,612 **8.** 973
9. 2,417 **10.** 445 **11.** 1,100 **12.** 723
13. 2,027 **14.** 2,158 **15.** 1,489 **16.** 1,673
17. 1,239 **18.** 1,867 **19.** 660 **20.** 1,612
21. 1,285 **22.** 1,279 **23.** 1,802 **24.** 1,353

page 24

1. 135; 213; 159; 507
2. 186; 175; 182; 543

page 25

1. 9,057 **2.** 9,873 **3.** 7,389 **4.** 7,464
5. 9,469 **6.** 9,803 **7.** 3,764 **8.** 9,990
9. 9,311 **10.** 7,296 **11.** 9,793 **12.** 8,052
13. 7,757 **14.** 9,281 **15.** 8,405 **16.** 4,065
17. 9,173 **18.** 8,485 **19.** 8,420 **20.** 9,465
21. 3,578 **22.** 8,874 **23.** 9,717 **24.** 9,512
25. 7,413

page 26

1. 1,523; 1,695; 3,218
2. 1,200; 1,320; 2,520
3. 2,122

page 27

1. 7,483 **2.** 6,736 **3.** 4,661 **4.** 1,742
5. 894 **6.** 1,882 **7.** 8,080 **8.** 6,982
9. 7,882 **10.** 3,872 **11.** 4,092 **12.** 595
13. 1,582 **14.** 5,291 **15.** 7,481 **16.** 6,891
17. 2,795 **18.** 7,492 **19.** 3,493 **20.** 2,791

page 28

1. 2,532; 1,341; 1,191
2. 1,250; 495; 755
3. 1986; 103; 1883

page 29

1. 960 **2.** 150 **3.** 190 **4.** 4,030
5. 130 **6.** 3,450 **7.** 8,660 **8.** 7,990
9. 8,800 **10.** 1,000 **11.** 3,300 **12.** 7,900
13. 500 **14.** 1,300 **15.** 800 **16.** 4,400
17. 8,600 **18.** 1,900 **19.** 360 **20.** 1,540
21. 1,900 **22.** 770 **23.** 900 **24.** 90

page 30

1. 540 **2.** 900 **3.** 480 **4.** 960
5. 5,700 **6.** 9,650 **7.** 4,400 **8.** 1,610
9. 600 **10.** 90 **11.** 5,400 **12.** 980
13. 4,930 **14.** 9,700 **15.** 600 **16.** 700
17. 1,100 **18.** 7,090 **19.** 7,450 **20.** 1,140
21. 4,600 **22.** 3,900 **23.** 5,100 **24.** 600

page 31

1. 70 **2.** 30 **3.** 110
4. 170 **5.** 260 **6.** 250
7. 500 **8.** 500 **9.** 1,100
10. 1,600 **11.** 6,200 **12.** 5,300
13. 5,000 **14.** 13,000 **15.** 12,000

Math Answers

page 32
1. 900 **2.** 30 **3.** 800

page 33
1. 20 **2.** 40 **3.** 10
4. 930 **5.** 730 **6.** 480
7. 200 **8.** 400 **9.** 300
10. 2,400 **11.** 4,100 **12.** 7,000
13. 5,000 **14.** 6,000 **15.** 1,000

page 34
1. 20 **2.** 100 **3.** 200 **4.** 110

Chapter 2

page 37
1. 6 **2.** 14 **3.** 12 **4.** 18 **5.** 16
6. 4 **7.** 2 **8.** 15 **9.** 18 **10.** 9
11. 6 **12.** 3 **13.** 12 **14.** 21 **15.** 8
16. 16 **17.** 4 **18.** 20 **19.** 36 **20.** 32
21. 12 **22.** 8 **23.** 10 **24.** 24 **25.** 27

page 38
1. 10 **2.** 15 **3.** 3 **4.** 4 **5.** 12 **6.** 10
7. 0 **8.** 1 **9.** 15 **10.** 4 **11.** 0 **12.** 12
13. 16 **14.** 10 **15.** 20 **16.** 6 **17.** 25 **18.** 0
19. 8 **20.** 0 **21.** 9 **22.** 16 **23.** 6 **24.** 2
25. 0 **26.** 9 **27.** 8 **28.** 0 **29.** 6 **30.** 20

page 39
1. 4; 5; 20 **2.** 3; 2; 6
3. Answers may vary—solution is 5
4. Answers may vary—solution is 12

page 40
1. 0 **2.** 27 **3.** 30 **4.** 4 **5.** 5 **6.** 18
7. 18 **8.** 40 **9.** 40 **10.** 0 **11.** 18 **12.** 12
13. 24 **14.** 21 **15.** 6 **16.** 14 **17.** 15 **18.** 4
19. 12 **20.** 25 **21.** 9 **22.** 8 **23.** 21 **24.** 0
25. 0 **26.** 18 **27.** 35 **28.** 30 **29.** 6 **30.** 8

page 41
1. 27 **2.** 42 **3.** 20 **4.** 63 **5.** 48 **6.** 0
7. 12 **8.** 40 **9.** 36 **10.** 0 **11.** 35 **12.** 18
13. 5 **14.** 24 **15.** 16 **16.** 48 **17.** 0 **18.** 0
19. 3 **20.** 24 **21.** 18 **22.** 12 **23.** 18 **24.** 30
25. 24 **26.** 18 **27.** 42 **28.** 81 **29.** 32 **30.** 15

page 42
1. 6; 5; 30 **2.** 7; 9; 63
3. Answers may vary—solution is 35
4. Answers may vary—solution is 36

page 43
1. 90 **2.** 20 **3.** 90 **4.** 240
5. 160 **6.** 490 **7.** 200 **8.** 400
9. 540 **10.** 80 **11.** 400 **12.** 480
13. 180 **14.** 50 **15.** 140 **16.** 150
17. 210 **18.** 150 **19.** 80 **20.** 30
21. 360 **22.** 630 **23.** 120 **24.** 250

page 44
1. 100 **2.** 150 **3.** 30 **4.** 40
5. 120 **6.** 100 **7.** 150 **8.** 40
9. 180 **10.** 40 **11.** 210 **12.** 120
13. 160 **14.** 160 **15.** 240 **16.** 140
17. 300 **18.** 250 **19.** 320 **20.** 0
21. 350 **22.** 360 **23.** 60 **24.** 80
25. 140 **26.** 240 **27.** 180 **28.** 300
29. 480 **30.** 320

page 45
1. 60; 3; 180 **2.** 20; 4; 80
3. 30; 4; 120 **4.** 20

page 46
1. 84 **2.** 70

Math Answers

Chapter 3

page 49

1. 12; 2 **2.** 24; 3 **3.** 4; 8; 2 **4.** 7; 35; 5
5. 20; 4 **6.** 27; 3 **7.** 3; 15; 5 **8.** 2; 14; 7

page 50

1. 4; 4; 4 × 3 = 12
2. 3; 3; 3 × 4 = 12
3. 4; 5; 5; 5 × 4 = 20
4. 5; 4; 4; 4 × 5 = 20
5. 12; 2; 6; 6; 6 × 2 = 12
6. 12; 6; 2; 2; 2 × 6 = 12

page 51

1. 2; 3 × 2 = 6 **2.** 7; 2 × 7 = 14
3. 5; 1 × 5 = 5 **4.** 2; 2 × 2 = 4
5. 4; 1 × 4 = 4 **6.** 9; 3 × 9 = 27
7. 3; 1 × 3 = 3 **8.** 9; 2 × 9 = 18
9. 7; 1 × 7 = 7 **10.** 7; 3 × 7 = 21
11. 4; 3 × 4 = 12 **12.** 8; 2 × 8 = 16
13. 5; 1 × 5 = 5 **14.** 6; 3 × 6 = 18
15. 5; 2 × 5 = 10 **16.** 6; 1 × 6 = 6
17. 8; 1 × 8 = 8 **18.** 4; 2 × 4 = 8
19. 2; 1 × 2 = 2 **20.** 1; 1 × 1 = 1

page 52

1. 9; 6 × 9 = 54 **2.** 9; 3 × 9 = 27
3. 8; 6 × 8 = 48 **4.** 5; 5 × 5 = 25
5. 9; 4 × 9 = 36 **6.** 6; 5 × 6 = 30
7. 6; 4 × 6 = 24 **8.** 8; 4 × 8 = 32
9. 6 **10.** 7 **11.** 7 **12.** 4 **13.** 7
14. 9 **15.** 2 **16.** 8 **17.** 8 **18.** 3
19. 4 **20.** 8 **21.** 3 **22.** 9 **23.** 3

page 53

1. 24; 6; 4 **2.** 30; 6; 5
3. 42; 6; 7 **4.** 3

page 54

1. 1; 7 × 1 = 7 **2.** 4; 6 × 4 = 24
3. 7; 8 × 7 = 56 **4.** 5; 6 × 5 = 30
5. 8; 8 × 8 = 64 **6.** 2; 6 × 2 =12
7. 5; 7 × 5 = 35 **8.** 3; 8 × 3 = 24
9. 7 **10.** 9 **11.** 8 **12.** 7 **13.** 3
14. 2 **15.** 2 **16.** 3 **17.** 6 **18.** 5
19. 7 **20.** 2 **21.** 3 **22.** 1 **23.** 6

page 55

1. 72; 9; 8 **2.** 40; 8; 5 **3.** 16; 8; 2 **4.** 9

page 56

1. 5 **2.** 4 **3.** 3 **4.** 9 **5.** 3
6. 9 **7.** 9 **8.** 8 **9.** 7 **10.** 1
11. 8 **12.** 7 **13.** 4 **14.** 7 **15.** 9
16. 2 **17.** 2 **18.** 5 **19.** 3 **20.** 3
21. 6 **22.** 5 **23.** 1 **24.** 9 **25.** 3
26. 4 **27.** 9 **28.** 4 **29.** 6 **30.** 9
31. 1 **32.** 8 **33.** 6 **34.** 9 **35.** 8

page 57

1. 2 **2.** 2 **3.** 9 **4.** 9 **5.** 9 **6.** 2
7. 5 **8.** 6 **9.** 3 **10.** 3 **11.** 8 **12.** 4
13. 8 **14.** 3 **15.** 4 **16.** 7 **17.** 1 **18.** 6
19. 100 **20.** 60 **21.** 320 **22.** 20 **23.** 50 **24.** 270
25. 42 **26.** 300 **27.** 400 **28.** 90 **29.** 280 **30.** 80
31. 60 **32.** 70 **33.** 350 **34.** 480 **35.** 180 **36.** 18

page 58

1. 6 **2.** 40

Chapter 4

page 61

1. $\frac{1}{3}$ **2.** $\frac{3}{4}$ **3.** $\frac{4}{5}$
4. $\frac{1}{10}$ **5.** $\frac{3}{8}$ **6.** $\frac{1}{2}$
7. $\frac{2}{3}$ **8.** $\frac{4}{8}$ **9.** $\frac{2}{5}$
10. $\frac{2}{4}$ **11.** $\frac{3}{5}$ **12.** $\frac{4}{10}$

Math Answers

page 62

1. $\frac{4}{5}$ 2. $\frac{1}{4}$ 3. $\frac{4}{8}$
4. $\frac{1}{2}$ 5. $\frac{1}{10}$ 6. $\frac{2}{3}$
7. ▲▲△△ ▲▲△△ 8. ●● ●○ 9. ■■■□□ □□□□□ 10. ▲△△ △△

page 63

1. $\frac{1}{4} < \frac{3}{4}$ 2. $\frac{1}{2} = \frac{2}{4}$ 3. $\frac{2}{3} > \frac{1}{2}$
4. $\frac{7}{10} > \frac{3}{5}$ 5. $\frac{3}{8} < \frac{3}{4}$ 6. $\frac{1}{3} < \frac{5}{8}$
7. $\frac{1}{5} = \frac{2}{10}$ 8. $\frac{3}{4} > \frac{1}{2}$ 9. $\frac{6}{10} > \frac{2}{5}$

page 64

1. $\frac{1}{2} = \frac{2}{4}$ 2. $\frac{2}{3} < \frac{3}{4}$ 3. $\frac{1}{5} < \frac{2}{5}$
4. $\frac{3}{4} < \frac{7}{8}$ 5. $\frac{2}{3} > \frac{1}{4}$ 6. $\frac{5}{8} < \frac{2}{3}$
7. $\frac{4}{5} = \frac{8}{10}$ 8. $\frac{1}{2} < \frac{3}{4}$ 9. $\frac{5}{8} < \frac{8}{10}$

page 65

1. 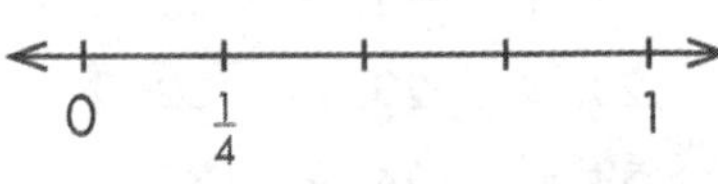

2. 0 $\frac{1}{3}$ 1

3. 0 $\frac{2}{3}$ 1

4. 0 $1 = \frac{4}{4}$

page 66

1. no; $\frac{2}{8}$ and $\frac{1}{4}$ or $\frac{4}{8}$ and $\frac{2}{4}$ or $\frac{6}{8}$ and $\frac{3}{4}$
2. no; $\frac{1}{3}$ and $\frac{2}{6}$ or $\frac{2}{3}$ and $\frac{4}{6}$

page 67

1. $\frac{4}{4}$ 2. $\frac{3}{3}$ 3. $\frac{2}{2}$ 4. $\frac{5}{5}$ 5. $\frac{10}{10}$ 6. $\frac{8}{8}$

Chapter 5

page 70

1. 90 kilograms 2. 500 liters
3. 5,000 grams 4. 1 gram
5. 46 6. 2
7. 7 8. 10

page 71

1. 600 liters 2. 1 gram
3. 1 liter 4. 3,000 grams
5. 36 6. 100
7. 24 8. 5

page 72

Flowers In My Garden

Daisies	✿ ✿ ✿ ✿
Roses	✿ ✿ ½✿
Sunflowers	✿

Key: ✿ = 2 flowers

15 total flowers

Math Answers

page 73

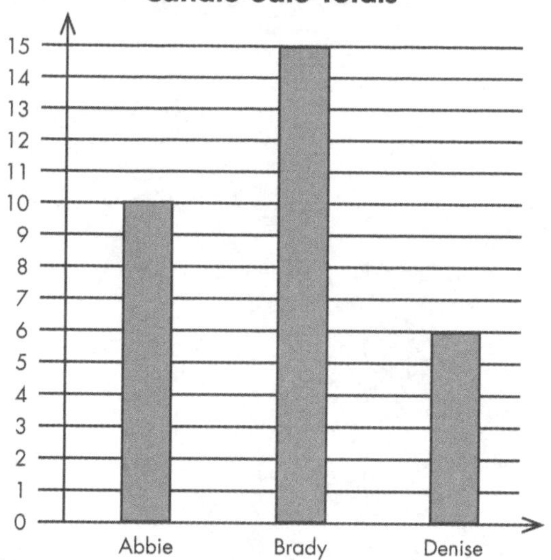

9 more candles

page 74

1. $4\frac{1}{4}$ **2.** $4\frac{1}{2}$ **3.** $5\frac{1}{4}$ **4.** $4\frac{1}{2}$ **5.** $5\frac{1}{4}$

6. $5\frac{1}{4}$ **7.** $4\frac{1}{4}$ **8.** $5\frac{1}{4}$ **9.** $4\frac{1}{4}$

10.

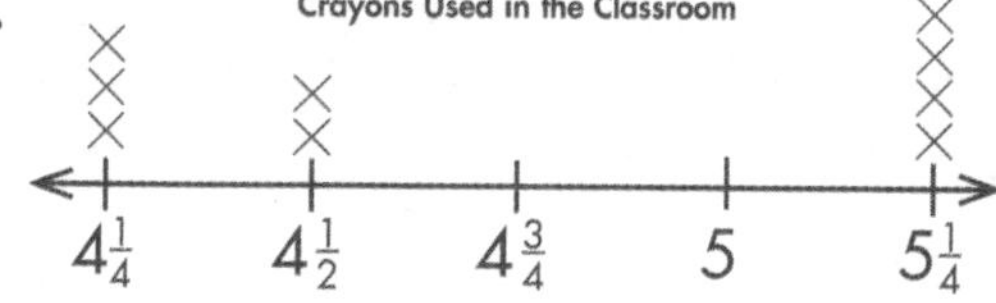

page 75

1. $2\frac{1}{2}$ **2.** $3\frac{1}{4}$ **3.** $2\frac{1}{2}$ **4.** $2\frac{1}{4}$ **5.** $2\frac{1}{4}$

6. $2\frac{1}{2}$ **7.** $3\frac{1}{4}$

8.

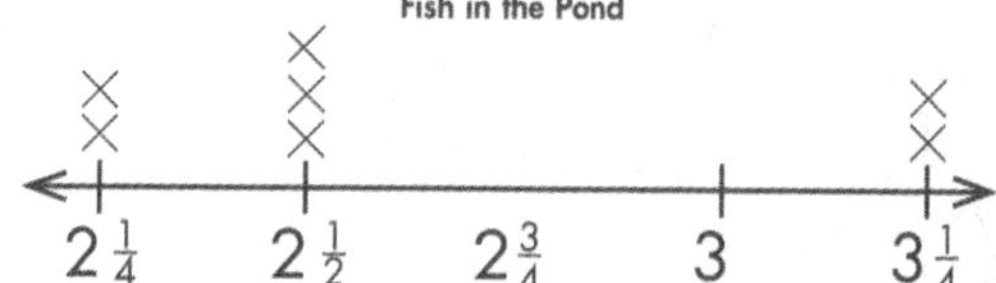

page 76

1. 12 **2.** 10 **3.** 24 **4.** 28 **5.** 7 **6.** 12

page 77

1. 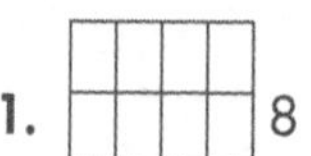 8 **2.** 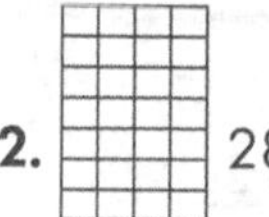 28 **3.** 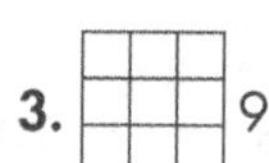 9

4. 3 **5.** 4 **6.** 5

page 78

1. 75 **2.** 56 **3.** 40 **4.** 300

5. 175 **6.** 40 **7.** 160 **8.** 160

page 79

1. ; 8 x 3 = 24; 24 **2.** ; 2 x 2 = 4; 4

3. ; 1 x 4 = 4; 4

4. ; 9 x 3 = 27; 27

page 80

1. Drawings may vary; 25

2. Drawings may vary; 41

3. Drawings may vary; 24

4. Drawings may vary; 27

page 81

1. 80 **2.** 90 **3.** 450 **4.** 81

page 82

1. 14 **2.** 28

3. 225 **4.** 30

5. 5 **6.** 30

page 83

1. 25 **2.** 100 **3.** 52 **4.** 306

Math Answers

Chapter 6

page 86

1. 15; 6 **2.** 10; 12
3. 50; 7 **4.** 10; 8
5. 45; 12 **6.** 15; 1
7. 4:20 **8.** 6:13 **9.** 7:10
10. 6:45 **11.** 8:09 **12.** 12:30

page 87

1. 2:00 2:30 2:15 2:20
2. 9:00 8:30 8:30 8:36

3.

4.

5.

6.

page 88

1. 5:45 pm — 6:00 pm — 9:00 pm — 9:10 pm
15 min. 3 hrs. 10 min.
3 hours, 25 minutes

2. 7:45 am — 8:00 am — 4:00 pm — 4:15 pm
15 min. 8 hrs. 15 min.
8 hours, 30 minutes

Chapter 7

page 91

1. **2.** **3.** **4.**

	a	b	c	d	e
5.	0	4	3	4	3
6.	0	4	1	4	0
7.	0	0	2	0	3

page 92

1. 6; 0; 0 **2.** 0; 6; 0 **3.** 1; 0; 4 **4.** 0
5. 8 **6.** 12 **7.** 12 **8.** 5
9–14. Answers may vary.

page 93

1.
2.
3.
4.
5.
6. square

page 94

1. $\frac{1}{2}$ $\frac{1}{2}$

2. $\frac{1}{3}$ $\frac{1}{3}$ $\frac{1}{3}$

3. $\frac{1}{3}$ $\frac{1}{3}$ $\frac{1}{3}$

4. $\frac{1}{2}$ $\frac{1}{2}$

5. $\frac{1}{4}$ $\frac{1}{4}$ $\frac{1}{4}$ $\frac{1}{4}$

6. $\frac{1}{5}$ $\frac{1}{5}$ $\frac{1}{5}$ $\frac{1}{5}$ $\frac{1}{5}$

7. $\frac{1}{2}$ $\frac{1}{2}$

8. $\frac{1}{4}$ $\frac{1}{4}$ $\frac{1}{4}$ $\frac{1}{4}$

Chapter 8

page 97

	a	b	c
1.	8	10	12
2.	7	9	11
3.	14	12	10
4.	6	3	1
5.	10	9	8
6.	20	25	30
7.	12	15	18
8.	70	110	160
9.	7	4	1
10.	7	6	5

page 98

1. 4 **2.** 6 **3.** 0
4. 2 **5.** 5 **6.** 1
7. 2 **8.** 4 **9.** 1
10. 5 **11.** 3 **12.** 5
13. 4 **14.** 6 **15.** 2
16. 5 **17.** 5 **18.** 2
19. 3 **20.** 6 **21.** 2

page 99

1. 3 x 5 = 15; 15 x 2 = 30; d = 30
2. 2 x 9 = 18; 18 x 1 = 18; h = 18
3. 4 x 6 = 24; 24 x 2 = 48; e = 48
4. 7 x 4 = 28; 28 x 2 = 56; g = 56
5. 6; 24 + 24; 48
6. 6; 24 + 18; 42
7. 10; 18 + 20; 38
8. 9; 35 + 45; 80

Language Arts Answers

Chapter 1: Grammar

Common and Proper Nouns

A **common noun** can be a person, place, or thing.

teacher (person) *museum* (place)
notebook (thing)

A **proper noun** is a noun that names a specific person, place, or thing. Proper nouns are capitalized to show that they are important.

Here are some examples of common and proper nouns:

Common nouns	Proper nouns
school	Hickory Hills Elementary School
zoo	Memphis Zoo
brother	Alexander
city	Tallahassee
day	Sunday
cat	Sasha

Complete It

Complete the sentences below with a noun from the box. If there is a **P** after the space, use a proper noun. If there is a **C** after the space, use a common noun.

Walnut High School	Saturday	town
dog	Jordan Lake	brother

1. Uncle Dale is taking me fishing at **Jordan Lake** (P).
2. We will leave early on **Saturday** (P) morning.
3. My **brother** (C), Kris, is coming with us.
4. Uncle Dale lives an hour away in a **town** (C) called Rockvale.
5. He is a math teacher at **Walnut High School** (P).
6. Uncle Dale's **dog** (C), Patches, always comes fishing with us.

GRADE 3 102 SPECTRUM COMPLETE LEARNING + VIDEOS

102

Chapter 1: Grammar

Common and Proper Nouns

Identify It

Underline the nouns in the sentences below. The number in parentheses will tell you how many nouns there are. Above each noun, write **P** for *proper* or **C** for *common*.

1. Patches (P) jumped into the rowboat (C). (2)
2. Kris (P) and I put on our life jackets (C). (2)
3. Last August (P), we went to Griggs Lake (P). (2)
4. We stopped at Elmwood Historic Car Museum (P) on the way home (C). (2)
5. We caught six fish (C) on our trip (C). (2)
6. Uncle Dale (P) cooked them on the grill (C). (2)
7. Mom (P) made some coleslaw (C) and potatoes (C). (3)

Try It

1. Write a sentence using at least two common nouns. Circle the nouns.

Answers will vary.

2. Write a sentence using two proper nouns and one common noun. Circle the common noun. Underline the proper nouns.

Answers will vary.

GRADE 3 103 SPECTRUM COMPLETE LEARNING + VIDEOS

103

Chapter 1: Grammar

Abstract Nouns

Abstract nouns are nouns that you can't experience with your five senses. They are feelings, concepts, and ideas. Some examples are *friendship, childhood, bravery, hope,* and *pride.*

Identify It

Underline the abstract noun or nouns in each sentence below.

1. Maya's honesty is one of the reasons we are best friends.
2. Martin Luther King, Jr., wanted to change hate and injustice in the world.
3. Darius's patriotism is the reason he joined the army.
4. I love the delight on my sister's face on her birthday.
5. Your kindness will not be forgotten.
6. Benji felt great pride when his team won the championship.
7. What are your parents' best stories about their childhood?
8. It is important to me that you always tell the truth.

GRADE 3 104 SPECTRUM COMPLETE LEARNING + VIDEOS

104

Chapter 1: Grammar

Abstract Nouns

Complete It

Fill in each blank below with an abstract noun from the box.

wisdom	liberty	freedom	knowledge
courage	joy	kindness	

1. Our country was founded on the ideas of **liberty** and **freedom** for all.
2. It took great **courage** to rebuild after the hurricane.
3. Uncle Zane's **knowledge** of birds amazes me.
4. The room was filled with **joy** when Will found his lost puppy.
5. Neighbors showed us much **kindness** when my baby sister was born.
6. Grandpa has the **wisdom** that comes with a long life.

Try It

Write three sentences that use abstract nouns. You may use abstract nouns from the exercises or think of your own.

1.
2.
3.

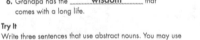

Answers will vary.

GRADE 3 105 SPECTRUM COMPLETE LEARNING + VIDEOS

105

Language Arts Answers

Chapter 1: Grammar

Pronouns

A **pronoun** is a word that takes the place of a noun. Pronouns keep you from using the same noun or nouns over and over again.

Some pronouns take the place of a single person or thing: *I, me, you, he, she, him, her,* and *it.* Other pronouns take the place of plural nouns: *we, us, they,* and *them.*

In the examples below, pronouns take the place of the underlined nouns.

The grizzly bears waded into the stream.
They waded into the stream.
Molly finished her report at noon.
She finished her report at noon.
Put the bowl on the table.
Put *it* on the table.

Identify It
Read the paragraphs below. Circle each pronoun. You should find 15 pronouns.

Sonja Henie was an amazing figure skater. (She) was born in Oslo, Norway, in 1912. When Sonja was only five years old, (she) won (her) first skating contest. (It) was the start of a great career. (She) was a world champion for ten years. People around the world became interested in skating. (They) followed the career of the talented young girl.

Sonja also wanted to be a movie star. (She) moved to Hollywood and began acting. (She) also performed in a traveling ice show. (It) was very popular. Huge crowds came to watch Sonja perform. (They) could not get enough of (her). Sonja enjoyed (her) fame and the money (it) brought (her). But (her) first and greatest love was always skating.

GRADE 3 106 SPECTRUM COMPLETE LEARNING + VIDEOS

106

Chapter 1: Grammar

Pronouns

Rewrite It
Read the sentences below. Rewrite each sentence using a pronoun in place of the underlined noun or nouns.

Example: David kicked the ball toward the goal.
He kicked the ball toward the goal.

1. Bryan and Anna had their first skating lesson on Tuesday.
   They had their first skating lesson on Tuesday.
2. Bryan had never skated before.
   He had never skated before.
3. The ice was slick and shiny.
   It was slick and shiny.
4. The teacher helped Anna tighten her skates.
   The teacher helped her tighten her skates.
5. The teacher told Bryan and Anna that they did a great job.
   The teacher told them that they did a great job.

Try It
1. Think about the first time you tried something new. Write a sentence about your experience. Circle the pronoun.
   Answers will vary.
2. Write a sentence using the pronoun *he, she,* or *it.*
   Answers will vary.

GRADE 3 107 SPECTRUM COMPLETE LEARNING + VIDEOS

107

Chapter 1: Grammar

Verbs

Verbs are often action words. They tell what happens in a sentence. Every sentence has a verb.

Ramon *put* on his running shoes. He *grabbed* his headphones. He *opened* the door and *took* a deep breath. Ramon *stretched* for a few minutes. Then, he *ran* down the street toward the park.

Complete It
A verb is missing from each sentence below. Complete the sentences with verbs from the box.

breathed	moved	attached	invented
gave	kept	carried	helped

1. In 1819, August Siebe **invented** the first diving suit.
2. The large helmet **attached** to a leather and canvas suit.
3. Weights **helped** divers stay underwater.
4. The divers underwater **breathed** air through hoses.
5. Later on, rubber suits **kept** divers dry.
6. The invention of scuba gear **gave** divers more freedom.
7. Divers **moved** from place to place on their own.
8. They **carried** their air with them.

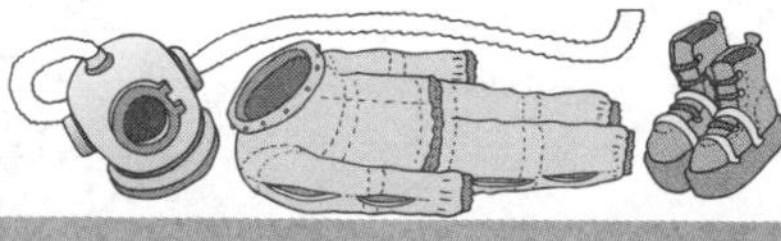

GRADE 3 108 SPECTRUM COMPLETE LEARNING + VIDEOS

108

Chapter 1: Grammar

Verbs

Identify It
Circle the 10 action verbs in the paragraphs below.

Jacques Cousteau (explored) many of Earth's oceans. In 1950, he (bought) a ship called *Calypso*. On the *Calypso*, Jacques (traveled) to bodies of water around the world. He (wrote) many books and (made) many movies about his travels. He (won) prizes for some of his work. Jacques also (invented) things, like an underwater camera and the first scuba equipment.

Jacques Cousteau (believed) it was important to protect ocean life. He (created) a group called the *Cousteau Society*. More than 300,000 people (belong) to the Cousteau Society today.

Try It
1. Write a sentence about a place you would like to visit one day. Circle the verb.
   Answers will vary.
2. Write a sentence about your favorite thing to do during the weekend. Circle the verb.
   Answers will vary.

GRADE 3 109 SPECTRUM COMPLETE LEARNING + VIDEOS

109

Language Arts Answers

Chapter 1: Grammar

Linking Verbs

A **linking verb** links the subject to the rest of the sentence. Linking verbs are not action words.

The verb *to be* is a linking verb. Some different forms of the verb *to be* are *is, am, are, was,* and *were*. Some other linking verbs are *become, feel,* and *seem*.

Identify It

Read the sentences below. Underline the linking verbs. Circle the action verbs. Some sentences may have more than one verb.

1. My grandmother is a marine biologist.
2. She studies undersea life.
3. She was always a good student.
4. She loved the ocean and animals as a child.
5. It was hard for her to become a scientist.
6. When she was young, some people felt women could not be good at science.
7. My grandma proved she was smart and hardworking.
8. One day, I might become a marine biologist myself.

110

Chapter 1: Grammar

Linking Verbs

Solve It

Use the linking verbs from the box to complete each sentence. Some may work for more than one sentence. Then, look for the linking verbs in the word search puzzle. Circle each word you find.

feels	am	became
was	is	

1. Today, my grandfather **is** a stage actor.
2. He first **became** a movie star at the age of 22.
3. He **feels** lucky to have had such an amazing career.
4. I **am** going to see him in a Broadway play next week.
5. When my dad **was** little, he was in one of Grandpa's movies.

a	d	r	j	k	f	p
b	e	c	a	m	e	i
d	w	a	s	b	e	y
a	f	v	c	u	l	p
m	u	f	q	i	s	g

Try It

1. Write a sentence using a linking verb.
   Answers will vary.
2. Write a sentence using a linking verb and an action verb.
   Answers will vary.

111

Chapter 1: Grammar

Adjectives and Articles

Adjectives are words that describe. They give more information about nouns. Adjectives answer the questions *What kind?* and *How many?* They often come before the nouns they describe.

Fat raindrops bounced off the umbrella. (what kind of raindrops?)

Adjectives can also appear other places in the sentence. If you are not sure a word is an adjective, look for the noun you think it describes.

The robot was *helpful*. The package is *huge!*

An **article** is a word that comes before a noun. *A, an,* and *the* are articles.

Use *the* to talk about a specific person, place, or thing.

the computer *the* jacket *the* bicycle *the* starfish

Use *a* or *an* to talk about any person, place, or thing. If the noun begins with a consonant sound, use *a*. If it begins with a vowel sound, use *an*.

a wig *a* bed *an* apple *an* envelope

Complete It

Complete each item below with an adjective from the box.

shy electric prickly warty smelly seve[n] ... [howl]ed

Answers will vary. Possible answers:

1. the **prickly** porcupine
2. the **warty** toad
3. the **electric** eel
4. the gray, **wrinkled** elephant
5. the **tiny** hummingbird
6. the tall, **skinny** giraffe
7. the **smelly** skunk
8. the **shy** deer
9. the **howling** wolf
10. **seven** flamingos

112

Chapter 1: Grammar

Adjectives and Articles

Rewrite It

The sentence[s] ... the sentences. Add at least ...

Answers will vary. Possible answers:

1. The dog barked at the squirrel as it ran up the tree.
   The small, fierce dog barked at the gray squirrel as it ran up the old, gnarled tree.
2. The dolphin dove into the waves and swam toward the sunset.
   The friendly dolphin dove into the gentle waves and swam toward the colorful sunset.

Proof It

Read the paragraph below. Circle the 20 articles you find. Six of the articles are incorrect. Cross them out, and write the correct articles above them.

A time capsule is ~~a~~ **an** interesting way to communicate with people in ~~a~~ **the** future. A time capsule is a group of items from the present time. ~~An~~ **The** items tell something about a person, a place, or a moment in time. They are sealed in a container. A glass jar or ~~the~~ **a** plastic box with a tight lid works well. Then, the capsule is buried or put in ~~an~~ **a** safe place. An attached note should say when the capsule will be opened. Some capsules are opened in ~~the~~ **a** year or in ten years. Others will stay buried or hidden for a thousand or even five thousand years!

113

Language Arts Answers

Chapter 1: Grammar

Adverbs

Adverbs are words that describe verbs. Adverbs often answer the questions *When? Where?* or *How?*

She *joyfully* cheered for them. — *Joyfully* tells *how* she cheered.
Yesterday, I had a picnic. — *Yesterday* tells *when* I had a picnic.
Brady put the box *downstairs*. — *Downstairs* tells *where* Brady put the box.

Adverbs can also describe adjectives. They usually answer the question *How?*
Sierra was ***too*** *late*. The sunset was ***really*** *beautiful*.

Adverbs can describe other adverbs, too.
Luke spoke ***extremely*** *quietly*. Shawn ***very*** *sadly* said good-bye.

Complete It
An adverb is missing from each sentence below. Choose the adverb from the box that best completes each sentence. Write it on the line. Then, circle the word the adverb describes.

loudly	brightly	often
beside	suddenly	completely

1. Dylan (sat) **beside** Amina at the school play.
2. The two friends **often** (went) to plays together.
3. The room was **completely** (dark.)
4. **Suddenly**, the curtain (opened.)
5. The scenery onstage was **brightly** (painted.)
6. The children (said) their lines **loudly** so that everyone could hear them.

114

Chapter 1: Grammar

Adverbs

Solve It
Read the sentences below. Find the adverb in each sentence. Write it on the lines after the sentence.

1. The prince slowly climbed Rapunzel's long hair.
s l o (w) l y
2. Little Red Riding Hood safely returned home.
(s) a f e l y
3. The wolf hid outside. **(o) u t s i d e**
4. Jack climbed down the beanstalk to escape the giant.
(d) o w n
5. The cast proudly bowed at the end of the play.
p r (o) u d l y

Write the circled letters from your answers on the lines below.
w s o d o

Unscramble the letters to find the missing word in the title of the play.
Into the **Woods**

Try It
Write two sentences about a fairy tale. Use an adverb from the box in each sentence. Circle the adverb. Then, underline the word the adverb describes.

quickly	carefully	softly	completely
suddenly	gently	sadly	

1. **Answers will vary.**
2. **Answers will vary.**

115

Chapter 1: Grammar

Conjunctions

A **conjunction** joins together words, phrases, and parts of sentences. The most common conjunctions are *and, or,* and *but.* Other conjunctions are *since, because, although, if, while, unless,* and *however.*

Chloe loves Brussels sprouts, *but* Haley won't eat them.
Since you play soccer, can you give me some tips?

Complete It
Choose a conjunction to complete each sentence. Write it on the line.

1. Do you want to play the violin **or** the piano? (or, but)
2. Mr. Randall canceled Lucy's lesson **because** he had a cold. (unless, because)
3. Let's play a duet at the recital **if** we can learn it in time. (while, if)
4. Owen plays the drums, **and** Marcus plays the trombone. (and, or)
5. Mrs. Klein likes to knit **while** Ezra practices singing. (however, while)
6. Liam always practices his scales, **but** Alla never does. (but, if)
7. Jade can buy a drum set, **however** her parents want her to help pay for it. (however, or)
8. **Although** Vikram's lesson is at 11:00, he often arrives at 10:30. (While, Although)

116

Chapter 1: Grammar

Conjunctions

Rewrite It
Combine each pair of se[ntences] ... may be more than one correct answer for each i[tem].

Possible answers:

1. Jack wants to take violin lessons. His sister has been taking them for years.
Jack wants to take violin lessons since his sister has been taking them for years.
2. Nora plays piano by ear. She can't read notes at all.
Nora plays piano by ear, but she can't read notes at all.
3. Dion enjoys listening to music. He doesn't play any instruments yet.
Although Dion enjoys listening to music, he doesn't play any instruments yet.
4. Mr. Santiago hums. He practices every afternoon.
Mr. Santiago hums while he practices every afternoon.

Try It
Write a short paragraph about music. Use at least four conjunctions, and circle them.

Answers will vary. Conjunctions should be circled.

117

Language Arts Answers

Chapter 1: Grammar

Statements and Commands

A **statement** is a sentence that begins with a capital letter and ends with a period. A statement gives information.

Diego will be 13 in April. Sudan is a country in Africa.

Commands are sentences that tell you to do something. Commands also begin with a capital letter and end with a period.

Use the bright blue marker. Chop the onions.

Tip: Statements usually begin with a noun or a pronoun. Commands often begin with a verb.

Complete It

The statements below are missing periods. Add periods where they are needed. Circle each period you add so that it is easy to see.

Monday, July 16

Dear Diary,

On Saturday, Shi-Ann and I set up a lemonade stand. We made colorful signs to hang around the neighborhood. Dad helped us make cookies and chocolate pretzels. We wanted to make sure our customers would be thirsty.

At the store, we bought a tablecloth, cups, and napkins. Dad let us borrow some money to use in our change box. Once we opened for business, we had tons of customers. Shi-Ann and I had to keep making fresh lemonade all day.

We each made ten dollars from our lemonade stand. I had fun, but now I know that owning a business is a lot of work.

GRADE 3 118 SPECTRUM COMPLETE LEARNING + VIDEOS

118

Chapter 1: Grammar

Statements and Commands

Identify It

Read the sentences below. If a sentence is a statement, write **S** in the space. If it is a command, write **C** in the space.

1. It is simple and fun to make your own lemonade. S
2. Ask an adult to cut ten lemons in half. C
3. Use a juicer to squeeze the juice from the lemons. C
4. Mix the lemon juice with six cups of water. C
5. The amount of sugar you add depends on how sweet you like your lemonade. S
6. I use one cup of sugar. S
7. Stir in the sugar until it dissolves. C
8. Add some ice, and enjoy a glass of cool, refreshing lemonade. C

Try It

1. Write a command you might use to advertise a lemonade stand. Remember, a command usually begins with a verb.

   Example: Buy some cold, sweet lemonade today.

   Answers will vary.
2. Write a statement about a business that you could start on your own.

   Answers will vary.

GRADE 3 119 SPECTRUM COMPLETE LEARNING + VIDEOS

119

Chapter 1: Grammar

Questions

Questions are sentences that ask something. When a person asks a question, he or she is looking for information. A question begins with a capital letter and ends with a question mark.

Will you go to the party with me?

What is the weather like in Phoenix?

Rewrite It

Read each statement below. Then, rewrite it as a

Answers will vary. Possible answers:

Example: It was cold and rainy on Saturday.

What was the weather like on Saturday?

1. The largest frog in the world is called the Goliath frog.

   What is the largest frog in the world?
2. The skin of a toad feels dry and bumpy.

   How does a toad's skin feel?
3. Gliding leaf tree frogs can glide almost 50 feet in the air.

   How far can gliding leaf tree frogs glide?
4. The poison-dart frog lives in Colombia, South America.

   Where does the poison-dart frog live?
5. There are more than 4,000 species of frogs in the world.

   How many species of frogs are there?

Tip: Questions often begin with the words *who, what, where, when, how,* or *why.*

GRADE 3 120 SPECTRUM COMPLETE LEARNING + VIDEOS

120

Chapter 1: Grammar

Questions

Proof It

Read the following paragraphs. There are seven incorrect end marks. Cross out the mistakes. Then, write the correct end marks above them.

Have you ever heard someone say it was "raining frogs"? You might have thought that it was just a figure of speech. But in rare cases, it has actually rained frogs! How could this happen? It sounds impossible. During a tornado or a powerful thunderstorm, water from a pond or lake can be sucked into the air. This includes anything that is in the water.

The storm continues to move. As it travels, it releases the water into the air. Does this mean that frogs and fish come raining down from the sky? Yes, this is exactly what happens.

Cases of strange things falling from the sky have been reported for many years. People have seen small frogs, fish, grasshoppers, and snails drop from the sky in places like France, India, Louisiana, and Kansas. Are animals the only things that get swept up by storms? No. In fact, in 1995, it rained soda cans in the Midwest.

Try It

1. Write a question you would like to ask a frog expert.

   Answers will vary.
2. Write a question you would like to ask a weather expert.

   Answers will vary.

GRADE 3 121 SPECTRUM COMPLETE LEARNING + VIDEOS

121

Language Arts Answers

Chapter 1: Grammar

Exclamations

Exclamations are sentences that show excitement or surprise. Exclamations begin with a capital letter and end with an exclamation point.

The Gold Nuggets won the championship!

We missed the bus!

Sometimes an exclamation can be a single word. Sometimes it can contain a command.

Oops!   Uh-oh!   Watch out!   Come back!

Complete It

Read the advertisement below. Some of the end marks are missing. Write the correct end marks on the lines.

Kirby's Toy Store
is closing.
Get new toys while they last !
Our store is open every night until 9:00 .
We are located at the corner of Nelson Road and Ash Street .
Tell your friends ! Tell your neighbors !
Prices are being slashed every day!
Toys are 50%–75% off !
Don't miss out on the best toy sale of the year !

122

Chapter 1: Grammar

Exclamations

Proof It

Read the sentences below. If the end mark is correct, make a check mark (✓) on the line. If the end mark is not correct, cross it out and write the correct end mark in the space.

1. Watch out. x !
2. Did you take the dog for a walk! x ?
3. Luis is going to learn how to play the trumpet? x .
4. We won the game. x !
5. I lost my wallet? x !
6. How old is Ella. x ?
7. My grandma had 16 brothers and sisters! ✓
8. Harry wore a new suit to the wedding. ✓

Try It

Imagine that you were going on a jungle animal safari. Think of two exclamations you might make. Write them on the lines below.

Examples: Watch out for that big snake!

That leopard runs really fast!

Answers will vary.

123

Chapter 1: Grammar

Parts of a Sentence: Subject

The **subject** of a sentence is what a sentence is about. In a statement, the subject is usually found at the beginning of the sentence before the verb. A subject can be a single word or it can be several words.

The entire team cheered when the winning goal was scored.

Irina loves to eat oatmeal for breakfast.

Brian Adams and Brian Rowley are in the same class.

Four raccoons, three chipmunks, and an opossum live in my backyard.

Identify It

Underline the subject in each sentence below.

1. The Golden Gate Bridge is located in San Francisco, California.
2. The bridge was built in 1937.
3. It was the longest suspension bridge in the world until 1964.
4. A suspension bridge is a bridge that hangs from cables.
5. Joseph Strauss was the engineer who designed the amazing bridge.
6. The Verrazano Narrows Bridge and the Mackinac Bridge are two other famous bridges.
7. The bridge's orange color was chosen so that it would be easy to see on foggy days.
8. Many movies and TV shows have included views of the bridge.
9. You can walk or bike across the Golden Gate Bridge during the day.

124

Chapter 1: Grammar

Parts of a Sentence: Subject

Complete It

Each sentence below is missing a subject. Find the subject in the box that best fits each sentence. Write the subject on the line.

The Golden Gate Bridge	A statue of Joseph B. Strauss
People and cars	Maria
The cost to build the bridge	About nine million people

1. Maria learned all about different kinds of bridges from her teacher.
2. The Golden Gate Bridge is 1.7 miles long.
3. A statue of Joseph B. Strauss celebrates the famous engineer.
4. About nine million people visit the bridge every year.
5. People and cars that travel north on the bridge do not have to pay a toll.
6. The cost to build the bridge was 27 million dollars.

Try It

1. Write a sentence in which the subject is a person's name. Underline the subject.

   Answers will vary.

2. Write a sentence in which the subject is more than one word. Underline the subject.

   Answers will vary.

125

Language Arts Answers

Chapter 1: Grammar

Parts of a Sentence: Predicate

A **predicate** tells what happens in a sentence. It tells what the subject is or does. The predicate always includes the verb. Finding the verb in a sentence can help you identify the predicate.

In the sentences below, the verbs are in bold type. The predicates are in italics.

Evelina ***recycles*** *all her cans and bottles.*
The seagull ***soared*** *above the stormy waters.*
Jermaine ***took*** *a picture of the dog with his camera.*

Identify It
Read the paragraph below. Underline the predicate in each sentence.

In the United States, April 22 is Earth Day. On Earth Day, people celebrate the planet Earth. They take the time to remember that the environment is fragile. The first Earth Day was held in 1970. About 20 million Americans celebrated that year. Today, more than 500 million people around the world take part in Earth Day activities.

On Earth Day, people learn about different types of pollution. They also learn what they can do to help save the planet. Many people recycle things. Paper, glass, and aluminum can be reused in new ways. Some groups plant trees to help keep the air clean. Others pick up litter in their parks and neighborhoods. For some caring people, every day is Earth Day!

GRADE 3 126 SPECTRUM COMPLETE LEARNING + VIDEOS

126

Chapter 1: Grammar

Parts of a Sentence: Predicate

Rewrite It
One box below is filled with subjects. One box is filled with predicates. Draw a line to match each subject to a predicate. Then, write the complete sentences on the lines below. (There is more than one correct way to match the subjects and predicates.)

Subjects	Predicates
Roma and Patrick	held an Earth Day 5K Run.
Alexis	cleaned up litter at McCoy Park.
Ms. Piazza's class	...euse
My sister an...	
The students at Waxhill Elementary	donated ten dollars to a fund for endangered animals.
	planted eight small trees on Earth Day.

Answers will vary.

1.
2.
3.
4.
5.

Answers will vary.

Try It
Write two sentences about something you can do every day to protect the planet. Underline the predicate in each sentence.

Answers will vary.

GRADE 3 127 SPECTRUM COMPLETE LEARNING + VIDEOS

127

Chapter 1: Grammar

Sentence Fragments and Run-On Sentences

A sentence is a group of words that contains a complete thought or idea. All sentences have a subject and a predicate. Part of a sentence, or an incomplete sentence, is called a **sentence fragment**. Sentence fragments cannot stand alone.

Examples: *Drove to the store.* (no subject)
Because the sun. (group of words)
The girls on the porch. (no predicate)

Run-on sentences are sentences that are too long. They are hard to follow, so they need to be split into two separate sentences. If the two sentences are about the same idea, they can be joined with a comma and a conjunction like *and* or *but*.

Clare likes cheese her brother Miles does not. (run-on)
Clare likes cheese. *Her* brother Miles does not. (split into two sentences)
Clare likes cheese, *but* her brother Miles does not. (combined with a comma and conjunction)

Identify It
Read each item below. If it is a complete sentence, write **C** on the line. If it is a sentence fragment, write **F** on the line.

1. F Threw the ball.
2. F After Madeline made a basket.
3. C James scored a goal.
4. F Cheered, clapped, and yelled.
5. C The volleyball bounced off the net.

GRADE 3 128 SPECTRUM COMPLETE LEARNING + VIDEOS

128

Chapter 1: Grammar

Sentence Fragments and Run-On Sentences

Proof It
Read the paragraphs below. There are four run-on sentences. Make a slash (/) where you would break the run-on sentences into two sentences.

Example: The clown wore enormous shoes / he had a large, red nose.

There are many different breeds of dogs/each one has a special personality. Basset hounds are often thought of as hunting dogs. They have long, floppy ears and wrinkly skin/they can be loyal, friendly, and stubborn. Some people think their droopy eyes are sweet/others think these hounds always look sad.

Cocker spaniels are good dogs for families. They are friendly and good with children/they have beautiful, long silky ears. Cocker spaniels are usually tan or black in color.

Try It
On a separate piece of paper, write two sentence fragments. Trade papers with a classmate. On the lines below, turn your classmate's fragments into complete sentences.

1. Answers will vary.
2. Answers will vary.

GRADE 3 129 SPECTRUM COMPLETE LEARNING + VIDEOS

129

Language Arts Answers

Chapter 1: Grammar

Combining Sentences: Subjects and Objects

Sometimes sentences that tell about the same thing can be combined. Then, the writer does not have to repeat words. Instead, the writer can combine two sentences into one by using the word *and*.

Terrence likes popcorn. Peter likes popcorn.
Terrence *and* Peter like popcorn.

Because the subject (Terrence and Peter) is plural, the verb form has to change from *likes* to *like*.

In the example below, both sentences tell about what Jill read, so they can be combined.

Jill read a new book. Jill read a magazine.
Jill read a new book *and* a magazine.

Identify It

Read each pair of sentences below. If the sentences tell about the same thing and can be combined with the word *and*, make a check mark (✓) on the line. If they tell about different things and cannot be combined, make an **X** on the line.

1. ✓ Snakes are reptiles. Lizards are reptiles.
2. X Cheetahs are mammals. Toads are amphibians.
3. ✓ The robin ate some berries. The robin ate a worm.
4. ✓ Tarantulas are spiders. Black widows are spiders.
5. X The dolphin swam beside its baby. The whale headed for deeper waters.

GRADE 3 130 SPECTRUM COMPLETE LEARNING + VIDEOS

130

Chapter 1: Grammar

Combining Sentences: Subjects and Objects

Rewrite It

Combine each pair of sentences below into one sentence. Write the new sentence on the line.

1. Bobcats live in the mountains of Virginia. Bears live in the mountains of Virginia.
   Bobcats and bears live in the mountains of Virginia.
2. The deer drinks from the stream. The coyote drinks from the stream.
   The deer and the coyote drink from the stream.
3. The airplane startled the rabbit. The airplane startled the owl.
   The airplane startled the rabbit and the owl.
4. It is rare to spot mountain lions. It is rare to spot bald eagles.
   It is rare to spot mountain lions and bald eagles.
5. Andy saw a deer at dusk. Andy saw a raccoon at dusk.
   Andy saw a deer and a raccoon at dusk.

Try It

Write two sentences about wild animals you have seen. Then, combine your sentences into a single sentence.

Example: I saw a wild turkey. I saw a woodpecker.
I saw a wild turkey and a woodpecker.

Answers will vary.

GRADE 3 131 SPECTRUM COMPLETE LEARNING + VIDEOS

131

Chapter 1: Grammar

Combining Sentences: Verbs

When two sentences tell about the same thing, they can sometimes be combined using the word *and*. The first two sentences below are about what Veronica did at breakfast, so they can be combined.

Veronica ate some cereal. Veronica drank a glass of orange juice.
Veronica ate some cereal *and* drank a glass of orange juice.

Some sentences can be combined using the word *or*. Use *or* if there are several choices about what might happen. In the example below, we do not know which choice Habib will make, so the word *or* is used.

Habib might walk home. Habib might ride his bike home. Habib might run home.
Habib might walk, ride his bike, *or* run home.

If you list several things in a row, place a comma after each one except the last.

Complete It

Read the sentences below. Fill in each blank with the missing word.

1. Grandpa spread out the tent. Grandpa hammered the stakes.
   Grandpa spread out the tent and hammered the stakes.
2. Will might look for sticks. Will might cook dinner.
   Will might look for sticks or cook dinner.
3. Will put the pillows in the tent. Will unrolled the sleeping bags.
   Will put the pillows in the tent and unrolled the sleeping bags.
4. Grandpa and Will might make sandwiches. Grandpa and Will might grill hamburgers.
   Grandpa and Will might make sandwiches or grill hamburgers.

GRADE 3 132 SPECTRUM COMPLETE LEARNING + VIDEOS

132

Chapter 1: Grammar

Combining Sentences: Verbs

Rewrite It

Combine each set of sentences below into one sentence. Write the new sentence on the line.

1. Grandpa stacked the wood. Grandpa found the matches. Grandpa lit the fire.
   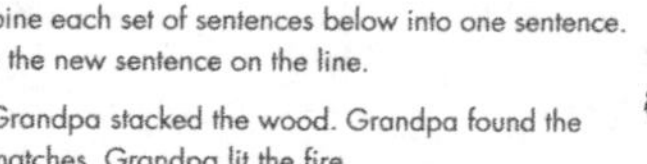
   Grandpa stacked the wood, found the matches, and lit the fire.
2. Grandpa toasted a marshmallow. Grandpa placed it between two graham crackers.
   Grandpa toasted a marshmallow and placed it between two graham crackers.
3. Will read in the tent with a flashlight. Will finished his book.
   Will read in the tent with a flashlight and finished his book.
4. Grandpa and Will looked at the night sky. Grandpa and Will found the Big Dipper.
   Grandpa and Will looked at the night sky and found the Big Dipper.
5. Next summer, they might sail down the coast. Next summer, they might go fishing.
   Next summer, they might sail down the coast or go fishing.

Try It

1. Write two sentences that tell about things you do in the morning. Use a different verb in each sentence.
   Answers will vary.
2. Now, combine the two sentences you wrote using the word *and*.
   Answers will vary.

GRADE 3 133 SPECTRUM COMPLETE LEARNING + VIDEOS

133

Language Arts Answers

Chapter 1: Grammar

Combining Sentences: Adjectives

Sometimes, sentences can be combined.

The leaves are green. They are shiny. They are large.

The adjectives *green, shiny,* and *large* all describe *leaves.* The sentences can be combined into one by using the word *and.* Remember to use a comma after each adjective except the last.

The leaves are green, shiny, *and* large.

In the example below, only a comma is needed to combine the two sentences. Both sentences describe the jacket.

The red jacket is Amelia's favorite. The jacket is warm.

The warm, red jacket is Amelia's favorite.

Identify It

Read each set of sentences below. If the adjectives describe the same thing, the sentences can be combined. Make a check mark (✓) on the line. If they describe different things, the sentences cannot be combined. Make an **X** on the line.

1. ✓ The strawberries are red. They are juicy.
2. X The lemons are tart. The lemonade is sweet.
3. ✓ I like wild blueberries. I like fresh blueberries.
4. ✓ The grapes are ripe. They are dark purple. They are plump.
5. ✓ The fuzzy kiwi is on the table. It is round.
6. X Oranges are tropical. Apples can be red, green, or yellow.

GRADE 3 134 SPECTRUM COMPLETE LEARNING + VIDEOS

134

Chapter 1: Grammar

Combining Sentences: Adjectives

Rewrite It

Combine each set of sentences below into one sentence. Write the new sentence on the line.

1. Cucumbers are long. They are thin. They are green.
   Cucumbers are long, thin, and green.
2. Sam grew some huge tomatoes in his garden. They were juicy.
   Sam grew some huge, juicy tomatoes in his garden.
3. The rabbits seem to love Mom's lettuce. It is leafy.
   The rabbits seem to love Mom's leafy lettuce.
4. The seedlings are tiny. The seedlings are pale green.
   The seedlings are tiny and pale green.
5. Rohan's peppers were small. They were spicy.
   Rohan's peppers were small and spicy.

Try It

1. Write two sentences that describe a piece of clothing you are wearing. Use a different adjective in each sentence.
   Example: I am wearing a new shirt. My shirt is striped.
   Answers will vary.
2. Now, write a sentence that combines the two sentences you wrote.
   Example: I am wearing a new, striped shirt.
   Answers will vary.

GRADE 3 135 SPECTRUM COMPLETE LEARNING + VIDEOS

135

Chapter 2: Mechanics

Capitalizing the First Word in a Sentence

The first word of a sentence always begins with a **capital letter**. A capital letter is a sign to the reader that a new sentence is starting.

I live on the third floor of the apartment building.
Do you like green beans?
Here comes the parade!
Maya grinned at Jeff.

Proof It

Read the paragraphs below. The first word of every sentence should be capitalized. To capitalize a letter, underline it three times (≡). Then, write the capital letter above it.

Example: my (M) sister taught me a new computer game.

have (H) you ever played golf? if (I) you have, you know that it can be harder than it looks. golfer (G) Michelle Wie West makes it look pretty easy. that's (T) because she can hit a golf ball more than 300 yards! at (A) the age of 13, Michelle became the youngest winner ever of the Women's Amateur Public Links. she (S) has even played on the famous men's golf tour, the PGA Tour. some (S) people think that this amazing six-foot-tall golfer will be the next Tiger Woods.

GRADE 3 138 SPECTRUM COMPLETE LEARNING + VIDEOS

138

Chapter 2: Mechanics

Capitalizing the First Word in a Sentence

Rewrite It

Rewrite each sentence below. Make sure your sentences begin with a capital letter.

1. michelle Wie West's family is Korean.
   Michelle Wie West's family is Korean.
2. she started beating her parents at golf when she was about eight.
   She started beating her parents at golf when she was about eight.
3. today, Michelle plays regularly on the LPGA Tour.
   Today, Michelle plays regularly on the LPGA Tour.
4. *competitive* and *determined* are two words that describe Michelle.
   ***Competitive* and *determined* are two words that describe Michelle.**
5. david Leadbetter was Michelle's coach for years.
   David Leadbetter was Michelle's coach for years.
6. what kind of golfing records will Michelle set in the future?
   What kind of golfing records will Michelle set in the future?

Try It

1. What sports do you like to play or watch? Begin your sentence with a capital letter.
   Answers will vary.
2. What sports figure do you most admire? Begin your sentence with a capital letter.
   Answers will vary.

GRADE 3 139 SPECTRUM COMPLETE LEARNING + VIDEOS

139

Language Arts Answers

Chapter 2: Mechanics

Capitalizing Names and Titles

Capitalize the **specific names of people and pets.**

My cousin *Umeko* moved here from Japan.
We named the puppy *George.*

A **title** is a word that comes before a person's name. A title gives more information about who a person is. Titles that come before a name are capitalized.

Grandpa Bruce | *Aunt* Juliet
Captain Albrecht | *President* Abraham Lincoln
Senator Barbara Boxer | *Judge* Naser

Titles of respect are also capitalized.

Mr. Watterson | *Miss* Newton | *Mrs.* Cohen
Dr. Gupta | *Ms.* Liang

Tip: If a title is not used with a name, it is not capitalized. My *aunt* is funny. The *judge* was here. But, if a title is used as a name, it is capitalized. Tell *Mom* I am going to the park. *Grandpa* will fix the computer.

Complete It

Complete each sentence below with the words in parentheses ( ). Some of the words will need to be capitalized. Others will not.

1. Kelly took her dog, **Abby**, for a walk to the park. (abby)
2. My school has a new **principal**. (principal)
3. On Tuesday, **Grandma** is coming to visit. (grandma)
4. The best teacher I ever had was **Mr. Butler**. (mr. butler)
5. The baby dolphin at the zoo is named **Michi**. (michi)

GRADE 3 140 SPECTRUM COMPLETE LEARNING + VIDEOS

140

Chapter 2: Mechanics

Capitalizing Names and Titles

Proof It

Read the letter below. There are ten mistakes. To capitalize a letter, underline it three times, and write the capital letter above it. To lowercase a letter (or change it from a capital letter to a small letter), make a slash through it. Then, write the small letter above it.

Example: Olivia and matt (M) asked their Grandma (g) if she knew mr. (M) Buckman.

April 12

Dear mayor (M) Hendricks,

My name is annie (A) Chun. My aunt and Uncle (u) live near Pebblebrook Creek. When I visited them last week, we went wading. We were looking for rocks for a science project I am doing in mrs. sutton's (M S) class. We found the rocks, but we found many other things, too. For example, aunt (A) Rose found several soda cans. Uncle Richard found some candy wrappers. Their dog, louie (L), discovered an old bottle. He thought it was a bone.

I would like to organize a cleanup of Pebblebrook Creek. I know the environment is important to you as the town Mayor (m). Can you help me organize this event? Maybe the next time my Aunt (a), uncle, Louie, and I go wading, we won't find anything but rocks.

Sincerely,
Annie chun (C)

GRADE 3 141 SPECTRUM COMPLETE LEARNING + VIDEOS

141

Chapter 2: Mechanics

Capitalizing Place Names

The **names of specific places** always begin with a capital letter.

Madison, Wisconsin | *Rocky Mountains*
Italy | *Liberty Avenue*
Science Museum of Minnesota | *Jupiter*
Jones Middle School | *Los Angeles Public Library*

Complete It

Complete each sentence below with the word or words in parentheses ( ). Remember to capitalize the names of specific places.

1. There are many **towns** (towns) across **America** (america) that have interesting names.
2. Have you ever heard of Okay, **Arkansas** (arkansas)?
3. Some towns are named after foods, like Avocado, California, and **Two Egg** (two egg), Florida.
4. Some names, like Chickasawhatchee and **Goochland** (goochland) are fun to say.
5. A person from **Russia** (russia) might be surprised to find a town named Moscow in Vermont.
6. If you're on your way to visit **Mount Rushmore** (mount rushmore), look for Igloo, South Dakota.
7. Would you like to go to **Boring Elementary School** (boring elementary school) in Boring, Oregon?

Tip: In the names of specific places, some words are not capitalized. All the important words begin with a capital letter. Small words, like *of, the, and,* and *a,* do not begin with a capital letter unless they are at the beginning of a sentence.

GRADE 3 142 SPECTRUM COMPLETE LEARNING + VIDEOS

142

Chapter 2: Mechanics

Capitalizing Place Names

Proof It

Read the directions below. Capitalize the names of specific places. To capitalize a letter, underline it three times (≡), and write the capital letter above it.

- Take wilbur (W) street (S) to preston (P) parkway (P), and turn left.
- Travel about two miles on preston (P) parkway (P).
- You will pass montgomery (M) library (L) and the talbot (T) recreation (R) center (C).
- At the light, turn right onto solomon (S) road (R).
- You will drive over haystack (H) bridge (B) and pass a gas station.
- children's (C) playhouse (P) is located on the west side of the street.
- The address is 1548 solomon (S) road (R).

Try It

On the lines below, write your own set of directions from your home to a friend's house. Be sure to include street names and any landmarks like schools, libraries, parks, and so on.

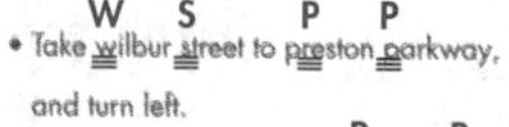

GRADE 3 143 SPECTRUM COMPLETE LEARNING + VIDEOS

143

Language Arts Answers

Chapter 2: Mechanics

Capitalizing Dates and Holidays

The **days of the week** each begin with a capital letter.
Monday, Tuesday, Wednesday, Thursday, Friday, Saturday, Sunday

The **months of the year** are capitalized.
January, February, March, April, May, June, July, August, September, October, November, December

The **names of holidays** are capitalized.
Memorial Day, Mother's Day, Thanksgiving, Kwanzaa

Complete It

Complete the sentences below with the name of a day, month, or holiday. Remember to use capital letters where needed.

1. I was born in the month of **Answers will vary.**
2. On **New Year's Eve**, many people stay up until midnight to welcome the new year.
3. My favorite day of the week is **Answers will vary.**
4. On **Father's Day**, Austin made a card for his dad and washed his dad's car.
5. **Wednesday** is the middle of the week.
6. In northern states, it often snows in **Answers will vary.**
7. The groundhog did not see his shadow on **Groundhog Day** this year.
8. Independence Day is on **July** 4th every year.

Tip: The names of the seasons (*spring, summer, autumn,* and *winter*) are not capitalized unless they appear at the beginning of a sentence.

144

Chapter 2: Mechanics

Capitalizing Dates and Holidays

Rewrite It

Rewrite the sentences below. Capitalize the names of days, months, and holidays.

1. presidents' day is on monday, february 21.
   Presidents' Day is on Monday, February 21.
2. If the weather is nice, we will have a cookout on labor day.
   If the weather is nice, we will have a cookout on Labor Day.
3. thanksgiving day always falls on a thursday.
   Thanksgiving Day always falls on a Thursday.
4. Ty gave a valentine to every person in his class on valentine's day.
   Ty gave a valentine to every person in his class on Valentine's Day.
5. Jessy is having a pool party on saturday, june 20.
   Jessy is having a pool party on Saturday, June 20.

Try It

1. What is your favorite holiday? Why?
   Answers will vary.
2. What is the coldest month of the year where you live? What is the warmest month?
   Answers will vary.

145

Chapter 2: Mechanics

Capitalizing Book, Movie, and Song Titles

The titles of books, movies, and songs are capitalized. Small words, like *of, the, and, in, to, a, an,* and *from,* do not begin with a capital letter unless they are the first or last word of a title.

Books	Movies	Songs
Stuart Little	Epic	"Down by the Bay"
Ramona the Brave	The Secret Garden	"Pop Goes the Weasel"
A Light in the Attic	Jumanji	"When You Wish Upon a Star"

Rewrite It

Rewrite the sentences below. Capitalize the names of books, movies, and song titles.

1. It took Shakhil only two days to read the book how to eat fried worms.
   It took Shakhil only two days to read the book How to Eat Fried Worms.
2. Sara is sleeping over tonight, and we are going to watch toy story 2.
   Sara is sleeping over tonight, and we are going to watch Toy Story 2.
3. The song "let it go" is from the movie frozen.
   The song "Let It Go" is from the movie Frozen.
4. I love the poems in Bruce Lansky's book no more homework, no more tests.
   I love the poems in Bruce Lansky's book No More Homework, No More Tests.
5. Devon listened to the song "yellow submarine" on his mom's music playlist.
   Devon listened to the song "Yellow Submarine" on his mom's music playlist.

146

Chapter 2: Mechanics

Capitalizing Book, Movie, and Song Titles

Proof It

Read the sentences below. There are 24 words that should begin with a capital letter but do not. To capitalize a letter, underline it three times. Then, write the capital letter above it.

1. I love to sing "hakuna matata" from the Lion King because the words are fun to say. (**H M T**)
2. Have you seen the old version or the new version of The parent trap? (**P T**)
3. Felipe borrowed the way things work by David Macaulay from the library. (**T W T W**)
4. If you watch Schoolhouse Rock, you can learn the song "conjunction junction." (**C J**)
5. Last week, Lottie read Freckle juice and Chocolate fever. (**J F**)
6. madeline is the name of a book and a movie. (**M**)
7. Reading the great kapok tree by Lynne Cherry is a good way to learn about rain forests. (**T G K T**)
8. My little sister sings "shake your sillies out" every morning. (**S Y S O**)
9. Paul and Tyler saw walking with dinosaurs three times in the movie theater! (**W D**)

Try It

1. Imagine that you were shipwrecked on a desert island. If you could bring only one book with you, what would it be?
   Answers will vary.
2. What is the funniest movie you have seen in the last year?
   Answers will vary.

147

Language Arts Answers

Chapter 2: Mechanics

Periods

A **period** is an end mark that follows a statement or a command.

Put your bike in the garage. Natalie has four brothers.

Periods are also used after initials. An **initial** is a letter that stands for a name.

Darren B. Johnson *P. L.* Travers *J. P.* O'Bryan

The **days of the week** are often written as abbreviations, or in a shorter form. A period follows the abbreviation.

Mon. Tues. Wed. Thurs. Fri. Sat. Sun.

The **months of the year** can also be abbreviated. May, June, and July are not abbreviated because their names are short.

Jan. Feb. Mar. Apr. Aug. Sept. Oct. Nov. Dec.

People's titles are usually abbreviated when they come before a name.

Mrs. = mistress *Mr.* = mister *Dr.* = doctor

Types of streets are written as abbreviations in addresses.

St. = street *Ave.* = avenue *Dr.* = drive *Ln.* = lane
Rd. = road *Blvd.* = boulevard *Ct.* = court *Cir.* = circle

Match It

Write the letter of the correct abbreviation on the line.

1. __a__ October 2 **a.** Oct. 2 **b.** Octob. 2
2. __b__ John Fitzgerald Kennedy **a.** John F Kennedy **b.** John F. Kennedy
3. __b__ Tuesday **a.** Tu. **b.** Tues.
4. __b__ Chester Avenue **a.** Chester Avn. **b.** Chester Ave.
5. __a__ December 19 **a.** Dec. 19 **b.** Dcmbr. 19
6. __b__ Madison Anne Hall **a.** Madison A Hall **b.** Madison A. Hall

GRADE 3 148 SPECTRUM COMPLETE LEARNING + VIDEOS

148

Chapter 2: Mechanics

Periods

Proof It

Read the schedule below. Cross out words that can be written as abbreviations. Write the correct abbreviations above them.

Mon. Mar. ~~Monday, March~~ 7	Hot Potatoes concert at 422 Lakeshore Dr. ~~Drive~~—7:00
Thurs. Apr. ~~Thursday, April~~ 14	Cassie's dentist appointment with Dr. ~~Doctor~~ Phillips—10:00
Fri. Apr. ~~Friday, April~~ 29	Meeting with Mr. ~~Mister~~ Haddad—noon
Sat. ~~Saturday~~, May 21	Drop-off costumes at Mrs. ~~Mistress~~ Jensen's house—1668 Dublin Ln. ~~Lane~~
Tues. Aug. ~~Tuesday, August~~ 30	Jimmy Ortega's birthday party—46 Brentwood Blvd. ~~Boulevard~~
Sun. Sept. ~~Sunday, September~~ 18	Brunch with Mr. ~~Mister~~ Sato—11:00

Try It

1. Write a sentence about what you would do if someone gave you a hundred-dollar bill. End your sentence with a period.

   Answers will vary.

2. Ask three friends when their birthdays are. Write the dates on the line using abbreviations for the names of the months.

   Answers will vary.

Tip: Abbreviations for days, months, and types of streets are used only in addresses and casual writing. For example, you might abbreviate the name of a day or month in a calendar or a note. Do not use these abbreviations in the body of a letter, a report, or a story.

GRADE 3 149 SPECTRUM COMPLETE LEARNING + VIDEOS

149

Chapter 2: Mechanics

Question Marks

Use a **question mark** to end a sentence that asks a question.

Would you like some fruit punch? How many books did you read?
Where is Connor going? Can all birds fly?

Complete It

Read each answer below. Then, write the question that goes with the answer.

Example: **Q:** _ Answers will vary. Possible answers:
A: Mr

1. **Q:** How many moons does Jupiter have?
   A: Jupiter has at least 63 known moons.
2. **Q:** What is the largest body in the solar system?
   A: The sun is the largest body in the solar system.
3. **Q:** Is Mars or Saturn closer to the sun?
   A: Mars is closer to the sun than Saturn.
4. **Q:** When did Galileo make his first telescope?
   A: Galileo made his first telescope in 1608.
5. **Q:** How long has Shannon Lucid spent in space?
   A: Astronaut Shannon Lucid has spent more than 200 days in space.
6. **Q:** What is the smallest planet?
   A: Mercury is the smallest planet.

GRADE 3 150 SPECTRUM COMPLETE LEARNING + VIDEOS

150

Chapter 2: Mechanics

Question Marks

Proof It

Read the paragraphs below. Cross out the six incorrect end marks. Add the correct end marks, and circle them.

Have you ever visited the Sleeping Bear Dunes(?) ~~.~~ They are located along the shore of Lake Michigan. The enormous dunes, or sand hills, are more than 400 feet tall in places. Many people travel to Michigan every year to climb the dunes(.) ~~?~~ Most visitors come in the summer, but some people come in the winter, instead. Why would they visit the icy shores of the lake in the winter(?) ~~.~~ Sledding down the steep slopes can be a lot of fun!

Do you know where the dunes got their name(?) ~~.~~ A Native American legend says that a mother bear lay on the beach to watch for her cubs after a fire. Over time, sand covered the bear(.) ~~?~~ Some people still think they can see the shape of a bear sleeping on the beach. This is how the dunes came to be called the Sleeping Bear Dunes(.) ~~?~~

Try It

On the lines below, write a question you could ask a park ranger at Sleeping Bear Dunes National Lakeshore.

Answers will vary.

GRADE 3 151 SPECTRUM COMPLETE LEARNING + VIDEOS

151

Language Arts Answers

Chapter 2: Mechanics

Exclamation Points

An **exclamation point** is used to end a sentence that is exciting or expresses strong feeling. Sometimes exclamation points are used to show surprise or fear.

That pan is hot! Lindsay won first prize!
I can't believe you broke the chair! There's a snake!

Proof It
Read the diary entry below. Five of the periods should be exclamation points. Find the five incorrect periods, and cross them out. Then, add exclamation points where they are needed.

Saturday, May 6

Dear Diary,
Something interesting happened today. I am going to be in a movie! The movie The Time Travelers is being filmed in my town. My mom works at the library. The director was learning about the history of the town at the library. My mom helped the director find what she needed. The director saw my picture on my mom's desk. She asked my mom if I would be interested in a small part in the movie. Would I ever!
I will have only two lines to say. Mom said she will help me memorize them. My scene will last about five minutes. Do you know what the best part is? I get to work with my favorite actor! I can't wait to start filming! Who knows? Maybe I'll be famous one day!

GRADE 3 152 SPECTRUM COMPLETE LEARNING + VIDEOS

152

Chapter 2: Mechanics

Exclamation Points

Complete It
The sentences below are missing end marks. Add the correct end mark in the space following each sentence. You should add four periods, two question marks, and three exclamation points.

1. Evan and Tanner have been jumping on the trampoline all morning **.**
2. Have you read the book A Cricket in Times Square **?**
3. Kazuki's swimming lesson was cancelled **.**
4. Watch out **!**
5. Please clean your room before bedtime **.**
6. The Bradview Tigers won the championship **!**
7. Would you like cheese on your sandwich **?**
8. There's a huge spider in my bed **!**
9. Tereza traded stickers with her little brother **.**

Try It

1. Write a sentence that shows excitement. Your sentence should end with an exclamation point.
   Answers will vary.
2. Write a sentence that shows fear. Your sentence should end with an exclamation point.
   Answers will vary.

GRADE 3 153 SPECTRUM COMPLETE LEARNING + VIDEOS

153

Chapter 2: Mechanics

Commas with Dates, Cities, States, and Addresses

Commas are used in dates. They are used in between the day and the year.

March 4, 2006 September 22, 1750 June 1, 1991

Commas are also used in between the names of cities and states or cities and countries.

Portland, Oregon Paris, France Minneapolis, Minnesota

When the names of cities and states (or countries) are in the middle of a sentence, a comma goes after the state or country, too.

Bethany stopped in Burlington, Vermont, on her way home.

In an address, a comma is used between the city name and state abbreviation.

Richmond, VA Juneau, AK

Proof It
Read the sentences below. Add commas by using this symbol (^).

Example: The Rock and Roll Hall of Fame is in Cleveland, Ohio.

1. Basketball star LeBron James was born on December 30, 1984.
2. Sarah Hughes skated in the Winter Olympics in Salt Lake City, Utah.
3. Tennis stars Serena and Venus Williams won the doubles event at the Olympics in August 2012.
4. Olympic swimmer Michael Phelps was born in Baltimore, Maryland, in 1985.

Tip	When only a month and year are given, do not separate them with a comma. August 1999 February 2014 December 1941

GRADE 3 154 SPECTRUM COMPLETE LEARNING + VIDEOS

154

Chapter 2: Mechanics

Commas with Dates, Cities, States, and Addresses

Identify It
There are two choices below for each item. Choose the correct version, and write the letter in the space.

1. **b** a. October, 12 1954 b. October 12, 1954
2. **a** a. Omaha, NE b. Omaha NE
3. **b** a. August, 2007 b. August 2007
4. **a** a. January 24, 1936 b. January, 24, 1936
5. **b** a. Amarillo Texas b. Amarillo, Texas
6. **a** a. September 30, 2015 b. September 30 2015,
7. **a** a. Nashville, Tennessee, is 284 miles from Shreveport, Louisiana.
   b. Nashville Tennessee, is 284 miles from Shreveport, Louisiana.
8. **a** a. The ship traveled from Crete, Greece, to the shores of Turkey.
   b. The ship traveled from Crete, Greece to the shores of Turkey.

Try It
Ask two people in your class or your family the questions below. Record their answers on the lines.

1. In what city and state were you born?
   Answers will vary.
2. What is your birth date?
   Answers will vary.

GRADE 3 155 SPECTRUM COMPLETE LEARNING + VIDEOS

155

Language Arts Answers

Chapter 2: Mechanics

Commas in a Series

A **series** is a list of words. Use a comma after each word in a series except the last word.

Ms. Pinckney asked Alonzo, Erica, and Charley to work on the project together.
Dakota put a sandwich, an apple, and a granola bar in her lunchbox.
Our neighbors have two dogs, three cats, seven chickens, and a goat.

Proof It
Read the note below. Twelve commas are missing. Add commas where they are needed by using this symbol (^).

Dear Dillon,

Please go to the store for me when you get home from school. Tonight we are going to make muffins for Grandad's birthday breakfast. We will need blueberries^ eggs^ sugar^ and lemon juice. I left some money on the kitchen table.

Ellie is going swimming with Rob^ Aliya^ Eve^ and Hunter. She will be home around 4:00. Please remind her to let the dog out^ hang up her swimsuit^ and start her homework.

I made a list of the things you said you will need for your science project. I put glue^ sand^ newspaper^ vinegar^ and baking soda on the list. Is anything missing? We can go shopping tomorrow afternoon.

See you in a couple of hours!

Love,

Mom

GRADE 3 156 SPECTRUM COMPLETE LEARNING + VIDEOS

156

Chapter 2: Mechanics

Commas in a Series

Rewrite It
The numbered sentences are missing commas. Rewrite each numbered sentence in the recipe, using commas where needed.

Lemony Blueberry Muffins

1 ½ cups flour
¾ cup yellow cornmeal
½ cup sugar
1 ½ teaspoons baking powder
½ teaspoon baking soda
¼ teaspoon salt
¾ cup milk
½ cup plain yogurt
3 tablespoons oil
1 tablespoon lemon juice
1 egg
1 cup blueberries

*Always have an adult help you when you are cooking.

- (1) You will also need cooking spray a muffin tin a measuring cup two bowls a teaspoon a tablespoon and a wooden spoon.
  You will also need cooking spray, a muffin tin, a measuring cup, two bowls, a teaspoon, a tablespoon, and a wooden spoon.
- Preheat the oven to 400°F. Spoon the flour into the measuring cup.
- (2) Combine the flour cornmeal sugar baking powder baking soda and salt.
  Combine the flour, cornmeal, sugar, baking powder, baking soda, and salt.
- (3) In the other bowl, combine the milk yogurt oil lemon juice and egg.
  In the other bowl, combine the milk, yogurt, oil, lemon juice, and egg.
- Add the wet mixture to the flour mixture. Stir until moist. Fold in the blueberries.
- Spoon the batter into the muffin tin. Bake at 400°F for 20 minutes.
- (4) Remove the muffins from the pan place them on a wire rack and let them cool.
  Remove the muffins from the pan, place them on a wire rack, and let them cool.

GRADE 3 157 SPECTRUM COMPLETE LEARNING + VIDEOS

157

Chapter 2: Mechanics

Commas in Compound Sentences

A **simple sentence** tells about one complete thought. A **compound sentence** is made of two or more simple sentences. To form a compound sentence, use a comma and the conjunction *and*, *or*, or *but* to join the simple sentences.

In the examples below, the underlined parts of each compound sentence can stand alone as simple sentences. Notice that a comma follows the first simple sentence.

Sadie likes orange juice, *but* her brother prefers apple juice.
Do you want to go to the zoo, *or* would you rather go to the art museum?
Alejandro collects baseball cards, *and* Adam collects coins.

Identify It
Read each sentence below. If it is a simple sentence, write **S** on the line. If it is a compound sentence, write **C** on the line. Then, underline each simple sentence in the compound sentence.

1. S Have you noticed birds in your yard or your neighborhood?
2. C Feeding birds can be fun, and it can be educational.
3. C Some birds like birdseed, but others like suet, a type of fat.
4. S In the winter, many birds prefer fatty foods, like peanut butter.
5. C Bird food placed on the ground will attract birds, but it will also attract other animals.
6. S Squirrels are known for eating bird food and scaring birds away.
7. S Once birds notice that you are feeding them, they will come to visit often.
8. C Finches love thistle seed, and orioles love oranges.

GRADE 3 158 SPECTRUM COMPLETE LEARNING + VIDEOS

158

Chapter 2: Mechanics

Commas in Compound Sentences

Proof It
Read the paragraph below. Three commas are missing from compound sentences. Add each comma by using this symbol (^).

If you have a plastic soda bottle, you can make your own bird feeder. With an adult's help, make two holes on opposite sides of the bottle^ and push a twig through each hole. Small birds can perch on the twig. Then, make several other holes in the bottle. The birds will be able to eat seeds from these holes. Tie some string around the neck of the bottle^ and hang it from a sturdy tree branch. Enjoy watching the birds from a window^ but don't forget to feed them.

Try It

1. Write a simple sentence about birds you have seen at a park or in your neighborhood.
   Answers will vary.
2. Write a compound sentence about other city wildlife you have seen.
   Answers will vary.

GRADE 3 159 SPECTRUM COMPLETE LEARNING + VIDEOS

159

Language Arts Answers

Chapter 2: Mechanics

Punctuating Dialogue

The exact words a person says are called **dialogue**. One set of quotation marks is used before the first word of dialogue. A second set of quotation marks is used after the last word of dialogue.

"I love to sail." "Is the fruit ripe?"

If the dialogue does not end the sentence, put a comma (not a period) inside the quotation marks. The period belongs at the very end of the sentence.

"I love to sail," Chloe said. "The fruit isn't ripe," said Geoff.

If the dialogue is a question and does not end the sentence, keep the question mark inside the quotation marks.

"Do you love sailing?" Chloe asked.
"Are the bananas ripe?" asked Geoff.

If part of the sentence comes before the dialogue, put a comma after that part of the sentence. The period at the end of the sentence belongs inside the quotation marks.

Chloe said, "I love to sail." Geoff asked, "Is the fruit ripe?"

Proof It

Read each sentence below. If the sentence is correct, make a check mark on the line (✓). If it is not correct, make an **X** on the line. Then, use the proofreading marks in the box to show the changes.

^ = insert comma
○ = insert period
" = insert quotation marks

Example: X "Our suitcases are in the attic," said Dad.

1. X "This summer, I am going to take Spanish lessons," said Mackenzie.
2. ✓ "My family is driving all the way across the country in an RV," Ryan said.
3. X Nicolae said, "I plan to go swimming at the lake every day."

160

Chapter 2: Mechanics

Punctuating Dialogue

Rewrite It

The sentences below are missing commas, periods, and quotation marks. Rewrite each sentence. Add punctuation marks where needed.

1. I have never been to a farm before replied Audrey
   "I have never been to a farm before," replied Audrey.
2. Neither have I agreed Nicolae
   "Neither have I," agreed Nicolae.
3. My grandparents have cows, horses, goats, and barn cats said Van
   "My grandparents have cows, horses, goats, and barn cats," said Van.
4. He added I stay with them every summer, and there is always something to do
   He added, "I stay with them every summer, and there is always something to do."
5. I would love to learn how to ride a horse or milk a cow said Audrey
   "I would love to learn how to ride a horse or milk a cow," said Audrey.
6. Van grinned at Audrey and said My grandparents can always use an extra hand
   Van grinned at Audrey and said, "My grandparents can always use an extra hand."

Try It

Ask two of your classmates what they plan to do next summer. Record their answers on the lines below. Remember to use quotation marks to show the exact words your classmates use.

1. **Answers will vary, but quotation marks should be used correctly.**
2. **Answers will vary, but quotation marks should be used correctly.**

161

Chapter 2: Mechanics

Punctuating Titles

Titles of books, movies, and plays are underlined.

Lucas did a book report on Two Heads Are Better Than One.
The movie Two Brothers is an adventure about twin tiger cubs.
For Dionne's birthday, her family went to see the play Peter Pan.

Titles of songs, poems, and stories are set in quotation marks.

Judith Viorst wrote the poem "If I Were in Charge of the World."
The story "The Emperor's Clothes" is in my book of fairy tales.
My favorite song is "Bright Eyes" by Remy Zero.

Complete It

Read each sentence below. Underline the titles of books, movies, and plays. Put quotation marks around the titles of songs, stories, and poems.

1. Before the first softball game of the season, we always sing "Take Me Out to the Ballgame."
2. Scotty Smalls is the main character in the movie The Sandlot.
3. My favorite poem is "Eletelephony" by Laura E. Richards.
4. In the play Annie, Bridget McCabe had the lead role.
5. Laura Ingalls Wilder wrote Little House in the Big Woods.
6. The movie The Incredibles won an award for Best Animated Film.
7. When it was time for bed, Dad told me a story called "Gregory and Grandpa's Wild Balloon Ride."
8. I memorized Edward Lear's poem "The Owl and the Pussycat."
9. Singing the song "Purple People Eater" makes my sister laugh.

Tip	Remember to place periods inside quotation marks if a title comes at the end of a sentence.

162

Chapter 2: Mechanics

Punctuating Titles

Proof It

Read the diary entry below. Find the titles, and underline them or place them in quotation marks. To add quotation marks, use this symbol (").

Thursday, October 8

Dear Diary,

I had a very busy week. On Monday, I went to the library after school. I worked on the story I am writing. It is called "The Mystery of the Golden Toothbrush." I borrowed the books Summer of the Sea Serpent, Stone Fox, and Pink and Say. I am going to write a book report on one of them, but I haven't decided which one.

On Wednesday, I recited two poems for Poetry Week. I chose "The Shadow" by Robert Louis Stevenson and "Jellyfish Stew" by Jack Prelutsky. After school, I tried out for the play The Princess and the Pea. I hope I land the role of the princess.

On Friday night, Ankit and Kendra came over to watch some movies. We rented Antz and My Neighbor Totoro. Antz is Kendra's favorite movie. My parents made subs and popcorn for us. We had a lot of fun, but I'm glad this crazy week is over!

Try It

1. What is your favorite song? Write the title on the line.
   Answers will vary, but the song title should be set in quotation marks.
2. Think of an idea for a story you could write. Then, write two possible titles for your story on the lines below.
   Answers will vary, but both titles should be set in quotation marks.

163

Language Arts Answers

Chapter 3: Usage

Subject-Verb Agreement: Adding s and es

The **subject** of a sentence tells who or what the sentence is about. When the subject is **singular**, it is only one person, place, or thing. When there is a singular subject, the verb ends with **s** or **es**.

Add **s** to most regular verbs that have a single subject.

The boat sail**s** close to shore. *The woman* water**s** the flower.

Add **es** to regular verbs that have a single subject and end in **sh**, **ch**, **s**, **x**, and **z**.

Gran kiss**es** us good-bye. *Jake* crunch**es** his cereal loudly.

When the subject is **plural**, it is more than one person, place, or thing. When the subject is plural, the verb does not end with **s** or **es**.

The kittens sleep on the sofa. *Zared and Nina* latch the gate.

Proof It

Read the paragraph below. Underline the subjects. Find the verbs that do not agree with their subjects. Add or delete **s** or **es** from the verbs so that they agree with their subjects. Use this symbol (^) to add a letter or letters. Cross out letters that don't belong.

Mr. Ruskin wash^(es) his historic car on Saturdays. Aaron and Ali help~~s~~ him. Mr. Ruskin sprays the old car with warm water. He scrub^(s) every inch of the car with a big sponge. The children polish~~es~~ the windshield and the mirrors. They use clean, soft rags. Aaron wax^(es) the beautiful red car. It shine^(s) in the sunlight. He wishes to have a car just like his dad's one day. Mr. Ruskin take^(s) Aaron and Ali for a drive in the shiny car every Saturday afternoon. They buy ice-cream cones. Then, they walk~~s~~ in the park.

GRADE 3 166 SPECTRUM COMPLETE LEARNING + VIDEOS

166

Chapter 3: Usage

Subject-Verb Agreement: Adding s and es

Complete It

Read each sentence below. Then, read the pair of verbs in parentheses ( ). Choose the correct verb form. Write it on the line.

1. Emily and Mateo **toss** a ball in the backyard. (toss, tosses)
2. The Jorgensons **harvest** their pumpkins every autumn. (harvest, harvests)
3. My little brother **brushes** his teeth with an electric toothbrush. (brush, brushes)
4. Britta **bikes** ten miles a day when she is in training for the race. (bike, bikes)
5. The blender **mixes** the ingredients. (mix, mixes)
6. The Guzmans **camp** near a crystal-clear mountain lake every summer. (camp, camps)
7. The shaggy Irish setter **catches** the ball each time I throw it. (catch, catches)
8. Aunt Celeste **lives** about two hours away. (live, lives)

Try It

1. Write a sentence using one of the following verbs: *climb, skate, twirl, travel, race, point,* or *bake*. Underline the subject in your sentence, and circle the verb. Make sure that the subject and the verb agree.

   Answers will vary.

2. Write a sentence using one of the following verbs: *push, crash, finish, pitch, watch, miss,* or *fix*. Underline the subject in your sentence, and circle the verb. Make sure that the subject and the verb agree.

   Answers will vary.

GRADE 3 167 SPECTRUM COMPLETE LEARNING + VIDEOS

167

Chapter 3: Usage

Irregular Verbs: *Am, Is, Are*

Am, is, and *are* are all different forms of the verb *to be*.

Am is used only with the subject *I*.

I ***am*** sleepy. *I* ***am*** hungry. *I* ***am*** under the bed.

Is is used when the subject is singular.

Mickey ***is*** sixteen. *Annabelle* ***is*** tall. *The beach* ***is*** rocky.

Are is used with the subject *you*.

You ***are*** very funny. *You* ***are*** correct. *You* ***are*** first in line.

Are is also used when the subject is plural.

Haley Joel Osment and Dakota Fanning ***are*** actors.

The boys ***are*** at home.

Rewrite It

Rewrite each sentence below. If it has a plural subject, rewrite it with a single subject. If it has a single subject, rewrite it with a plural subject. Remember that the form of the verb must agree with the subject and verb.

Example: The salad dressing and the salad are on the table.
The salad dressing is on the table.

1. Nissa and Toby are eight.

   Nissa is eight. OR Toby is eight.

2. The photograph is in an album.

   The photographs are in an album.

3. The books on the shelf are from the library.

   The book on the shelf is from the library.

4. We are excited about traveling to Mexico.

   Possible answer: I am excited about traveling to Mexico.

GRADE 3 168 SPECTRUM COMPLETE LEARNING + VIDEOS

168

Chapter 3: Usage

Irregular Verbs: *Am, Is, Are*

Proof It

Read the paragraphs below. There are 11 mistakes with the verbs *am, is,* and *are*. Cross out each mistake. Then, write the correct form of the verb above it.

A topiary (*toe pee air ee*) ~~are~~ **is** a kind of sculpture made from plants. Topiaries ~~is~~ **are** cut to look like many different things. Some ~~am~~ **are** shaped like animals. For example, a topiary can look like an elephant, a bear, a horse, or even a dinosaur. Other topiaries ~~is~~ **are** trimmed to look like castles, cones, or mazes.

A topiary gardener ~~are~~ **is** an artist. He or she can turn simple shrubs into beautiful sculptures. Boxwood, holly, bay laurel, and yew ~~am~~ **are** some of the best plants to use for topiary. They ~~is~~ **are** easy to train and to trim.

In May, I ~~are~~ **am** going to visit the Green Animals Topiary Garden in Rhode Island. It ~~am~~ **is** one of the oldest topiary gardens in the country. There ~~am~~ **are** 80 pieces of topiary there! It ~~are~~ **is** fun to imagine all the green animals coming to life and roaming the gardens.

Try It

Write three sentences on the lines below. Use the verbs *am, is,* or *are* in each sentence.

Answers will vary.

GRADE 3 169 SPECTRUM COMPLETE LEARNING + VIDEOS

169

Language Arts Answers

Chapter 3: Usage

Irregular Verbs: *Has, Have*

Has and *have* are different forms of the verb *to have.*

Have is used when the subject is *I* or *you.*

I **have** a cold. *You* **have** two brothers.

Have is also used with plural subjects.

We **have** a book about dinosaurs.
Roberto and Chiara **have** a baby sister.
They **have** a yellow house. *Both cars* **have** flat tires.

Has is used when there is a single subject like *he, she,* or *it.*

She **has** blonde hair. *The librarian* **has** a cheerful smile.
A male deer **has** antlers.

Complete It
Complete each sentence below with the word *has* or *have.* Write the correct word in the space.

1. Gus and Emily **have** a shell collection.
2. A horse conch **has** a cone shape and can grow to be almost two feet long.
3. Shells **have** value when they are beautiful or rare.
4. The shapes of some shells **have** interesting names, like helmet, basket, lamp, frog, and trumpet.
5. Oysters and clams **have** shells that are hinged at the back.
6. Emily **has** a necklace made from polished pieces of shell.
7. Cowrie shells **have** been used as money on Indian and Pacific islands.
8. If Gus **has** more than one of a certain shell, he will trade it with other collectors.

GRADE 3 170 SPECTRUM COMPLETE LEARNING + VIDEOS

170

Chapter 3: Usage

Irregular Verbs: *Has, Have*

Proof It
Read the letter below. There are eight mistakes with the verbs *have* and *has.* Cross out each incorrect verb. Then, write the correct form of the verb above it.

August 6, 2015

Dear Kyra,

How is life at home in Massachusetts? We are having a great time in Florida. Gus and I ~~has~~ **have** 40 new shells to add to our collection! We ~~has~~ **have** been busy searching the beaches here. Gus and I already ~~has~~ **have** labels for our new shells. We don't want to forget their names by the time we get home.

Some shells still ~~has~~ **have** animals living in them. We never collect those shells. Our parents ~~has~~ **have** helped us look in rock crevices and tide pools. That is how we found a true tulip shell. It ~~have~~ **has** a pretty peachy color and an interesting pattern. I ~~has~~ **have** a surprise to bring home for you. You ~~has~~ **have** never seen a shell like this. I can't wait to see you. Wish you were here!

Your friend,

Emily

GRADE 3 171 SPECTRUM COMPLETE LEARNING + VIDEOS

171

Chapter 3: Usage

Forming the Past Tense by Adding ed

Verbs in the **present tense** tell about things that are happening right now. Verbs in the **past tense** tell about things that have already happened.

Add **ed** to a regular verb to change it to the past tense. If the verb already ends in **e**, just add **d**.

The concert end**ed** at 9:00. It snow**ed** 16 inches yesterday!
Uncle Donny taste**d** the pudding. The waitress smile**d** at the girl.

If a verb ends in **y**, change the **y** to **i** and add **ed**.

We hurr**y** to catch the bus. We hurr**ied** to catch the bus.
I dr**y** the laundry outside. I dr**ied** the laundry outside.

Complete It
Read the sentences below. Complete each sentence with the past tense of the verb in parentheses ( ).

1. Leonardo da Vinci **painted** the mysterious *Mona Lisa.* (paint)
2. Women and children often **posed** for artist Mary Cassatt. (pose)
3. The Impressionists **showed** the world that not all paintings had to look realistic. (show)
4. Grandma Moses **loved** to paint cheerful pictures of life in the country. (love)
5. Jackson Pollack, who made colorful paint-splattered paintings, **studied** with Thomas Hart Benton. (study)
6. Vincent van Gogh **created** more than 800 oil paintings during his lifetime! (create)
7. Chinese artist Wang Yani **started** painting when she was only two. (start)

GRADE 3 172 SPECTRUM COMPLETE LEARNING + VIDEOS

172

Chapter 3: Usage

Forming the Past Tense by Adding ed

Rewrite It
Read the sentences below. They are all in the present tense. Underline the verb in each sentence. Then, rewrite the sentences in the past tense.

1. Norman Rockwell <u>lives</u> from 1894 until 1978.
   Norman Rockwell lived from 1894 until 1978.
2. Norman <u>studies</u> at the National Academy of Design in New York.
   Norman studied at the National Academy of Design in New York.
3. He <u>illustrates</u> issues of children's magazines, like *Boys' Life.*
   He illustrated issues of children's magazines, like *Boys' Life.*
4. Norman <u>paints</u> scenes from everyday small-town life.
   Norman painted scenes from everyday small-town life.
5. Norman <u>calls</u> himself a storyteller.
   Norman called himself a storyteller.
6. A fire <u>destroys</u> many of Norman's paintings.
   A fire destroyed many of Norman's paintings.
7. Norman Rockwell <u>receives</u> the Presidential Medal of Freedom in 1976.
   Norman Rockwell received the Presidential Medal of Freedom in 1976.

Try It

1. Write a sentence in the present tense that describes a piece of art you have seen or made.
   Answers will vary.
2. Now, rewrite the same sentence in the past tense.
   Answers will vary.

GRADE 3 173 SPECTRUM COMPLETE LEARNING + VIDEOS

173

Language Arts Answers

Chapter 3: Usage

Irregular Past-Tense Verbs: *Ate, Said, Grew, Made, Rode*

Some verbs do not follow the pattern of regular verbs. The past tenses of these verbs are different. To form the past tense, do not add **ed** or **d** to these verbs. Instead, you must change the entire word.

Present tense	Past tense
She *eats* a snack every day.	She *ate* a snack every day.
Mario *says* it will rain tonight.	Mario *said* it will rain tonight.
The tiny pine tree *grows* quickly.	The tiny pine tree *grew* quickly.
Catalina *makes* bracelets.	Catalina *made* bracelets.
I *ride* the bus downtown.	I *rode* the bus downtown.

Proof It

Some of the verbs below are in the wrong tense. Cross out the verbs in bold type. Use this symbol (^), and write the correct word above it.

When my mom was a little girl, her family owned a bakery. Mom ~~says~~ said that she loved the sweet smell of bread and pastries baking in the ovens. Every morning, Mom ~~eats~~ ate a cinnamon roll for breakfast. She ~~rides~~ rode her bike to school when the weather was nice. In her bag, she carried fresh muffins for her teachers and her friends.

In the afternoon, she and her dad ~~make~~ made crusty rolls and chewy bagels. Grandpa put all the ingredients in a big bowl. He and Mom took turns kneading the dough. Then, he covered it with a clean towel. The dough ~~grows~~ grew and ~~grows~~ grew. Mom ~~says~~ said she loved to punch it down. Finally, she and Grandpa shaped the dough and popped it into the ovens. Mom's family ~~eats~~ ate fresh bread with dinner every night!

174

Chapter 3: Usage

Irregular Past-Tense Verbs: *Ate, Said, Grew, Made, Rode*

Solve It

Read each sentence below. On the line, write the past tense of the underlined verb.

1. Grandma always eats a blueberry bagel with cream cheese for breakfast. **ate**
2. The Larsons say that Hot Cross Buns was the best bakery in town. **said**
3. Mom's cousin, Eddie, rides his bike around town and delivered bread. **rode**
4. Mom grows up helping her parents at the bakery. **grew**
5. Every Saturday, Mom and Grandpa make 12 loaves of wheat bread, 15 loaves of French bread, and 100 dinner rolls. **made**

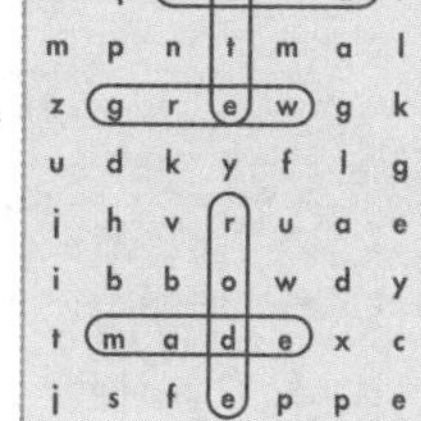

h	q	s	a	i	d	r
m	p	n	t	m	a	l
z	g	r	e	w	g	k
u	d	k	y	f	l	g
j	h	v	r	u	a	e
i	b	b	o	w	d	y
t	m	a	d	e	x	c
j	s	f	e	p	p	e

Now, find each past-tense verb in the word search puzzle. Circle the words you find. Words are written across and down.

Try It

1. What did you eat for dinner last night? Use a complete sentence to answer the question.
   Answers will vary.
2. Write a sentence that uses the past tense of one of these words: *say, grow, make,* or *ride.*
   Answers will vary.

175

Chapter 3: Usage

Irregular Past-Tense Verbs: *Gave, Flew, Brought, Thought, Wrote*

The past tenses of some verbs do not follow the patterns of regular verbs. To form the past tense, do not add **ed** or **d**. Instead, you must change the entire word.

Present tense	Past tense
Franklin *gives* her an orange.	Franklin *gave* her an orange.
The goose *flies* over the pond.	The goose *flew* over the pond.
Marisa *brings* some games.	Marisa *brought* some games.
Beth *thinks* she got an A.	Beth *thought* she got an A.
I *write* a letter to my grandma.	I *wrote* a letter to my grandma.

Rewrite It

The sentences below are all in the present tense. Rewrite them in the past tense.

1. Ms. Lucetta gives the class an assignment.
   Ms. Lucetta gave the class an assignment.
2. Nicholas and Liv write a play about a giant who lives in the forest.
   Nicholas and Liv wrote a play about a giant who lived in the forest.
3. They think the giant should be kind, not scary.
   They thought the giant should be kind, not scary.
4. A small bluebird flies many miles to save the kind giant.
   A small bluebird flew many miles to save the kind giant.
5. The bluebird brings him an important message.
   The bluebird brought him an important message.
6. The giant gives the bluebird shelter in his cave.
   The giant gave the bluebird shelter in his cave.

176

Chapter 3: Usage

Irregular Past-Tense Verbs: *Gave, Flew, Brought, Thought, Wrote*

Proof It

Some of the verbs below are in the wrong tense. Cross out the underlined verbs. Use this symbol (^), and write the correct past-tense verbs above them.

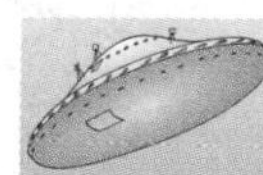

Pradeep and Kent ~~write~~ wrote a play for Ms. Lucetta's class. Their play was about a brother and sister who ~~think~~ thought that an alien spaceship landed near their house. They named the brother and sister Harry and Carrie. In the play, something very large ~~flies~~ flew over Harry and Carrie's house one night. It made a loud whirring noise. Its lights flashed on and off.

Carrie ran to the window. She ~~thinks~~ thought it was a helicopter until she saw how big it was. Harry ran into the backyard. He ~~brings~~ brought his camera with him. Harry took as many photos as he could. Then, the ship grew silent and quickly ~~flies~~ flew away.

Pradeep and Kent ~~think~~ thought the play they ~~write~~ wrote was fun and exciting. They were not sure how to end it though. Did aliens actually visit Harry and Carrie's house? Was it all a dream? They knew they would have to decide before they ~~give~~ gave their play to Ms. Lucetta.

Try It

In the selection above, why did the spaceship fly away? Use the past tense of the verb *fly* in your answer.

Answers will vary.

177

Language Arts Answers

Chapter 3: Usage

Forming the Future Tense

To write or speak about something that is happening right now, use the **present tense**. When something has already happened, use the **past tense**. When something has not happened yet, use the **future tense**.

Past: I *used* all the shampoo.
Present: I *use* all the shampoo.
Future: I *will use* all the shampoo.

The future tense is formed by using the word *will* with a verb. The word *will* means that something has not taken place yet, but it will happen in the future.

Seamus *will come* home in three days.
The plumber *will fix* the leaky pipe.
The water *will boil* in a minute or two.
Ms. Webster *will make* lasagna for dinner.

Complete It
Complete each sentence with the future tense of the verb in parentheses ( ).

1. Charlotte **will be** a doctor when she grows up. (be)
2. Fernando **will learn** to speak eight languages. (learn)
3. Maddy **will train** for the Olympics. (train)
4. Travis **will find** a cure for a serious disease. (find)
5. Akio **will photograph** wild animals. (photograph)
6. Elena **will travel** all around the world. (travel)

GRADE 3 178 SPECTRUM COMPLETE LEARNING + VIDEOS

178

Chapter 3: Usage

Forming the Future Tense

Rewrite It
On the line, write **PA** if a sentence takes place in the past. Write **PR** if it takes place in the present. Then, rewrite each sentence in the future tense.

Example: PA The movie ended at 8:00.
The movie will end at 8:00.

1. **PA** The sheepdog barked at the mail carrier.
The sheepdog will bark at the mail carrier.
2. **PR** The gardener picks flowers from her wildflower garden.
The gardener will pick flowers from her wildflower garden.
3. **PR** The robin pulls a fat earthworm from the soil.
The robin will pull a fat earthworm from the soil.
4. **PA** A ladybug landed on Layla's shoulder.
A ladybug will land on Layla's shoulder.

Try It
1. Write a sentence about someplace you have been in the past. Underline the verb.
Answers will vary.
2. Write a sentence about where you are right now. Underline the verb.
Answers will vary.
3. Write a sentence about somewhere you will go or something you will do in the future. Underline the verb.
Answers will vary.

GRADE 3 179 SPECTRUM COMPLETE LEARNING + VIDEOS

179

Chapter 3: Usage

Contractions with *Not, Will,* and *Have*

A **contraction** is a short way of saying something by combining two words into one. An apostrophe (') takes the place of the missing letters.

Many contractions are formed when a verb and the word *not* are combined. The apostrophe takes the place of the letter **o** in *not*.

is not = isn't	are not = aren't	was not = wasn't
were not = weren't	does not = doesn't	did not = didn't
do not = don't	can not = can't	

Some contractions can be formed with pronouns and the verb *will*. An apostrophe takes the place of the letters **wi** in *will*.

I will = I'll	it will = it'll	you will = you'll
we will = we'll	she will = she'll	they will = they'll
he will = he'll		

Contractions can also be made with the verb *have*. An apostrophe takes the place of the letters **ha** in *have*.

I have = I've	we have = we've
you have = you've	they have = they've

Proof It
Cross out the five incorrect contractions below. Use this proofreading mark (^), and write the correct contraction above it.

My neighborhood is having a giant yard sale on Saturday. ~~We'l~~ **We'll** post signs all around town. This week, ~~I'll~~ **I'll** go through the boxes under my bed and in the attic. There are many things I know we ~~do'nt~~ **don't** need. At first, my little brother ~~did'nt~~ **didn't** want to help. Then, I told him all the money would go to the animal shelter where we got our dog Maisy. I think ~~he'ill~~ **he'll** be happy to help now.

GRADE 3 180 SPECTRUM COMPLETE LEARNING + VIDEOS

180

Chapter 3: Usage

Contractions with *Not, Will,* and *Have*

Rewrite It
Circle the two words in each sentence that could be combined to make a contraction. Then, rewrite the sentences using contractions.

1. We (were not) even open for business yet when the first customers arrived.
We weren't even open for business yet when the first customers arrived.
2. "(I will) give you 15 dollars for the tricycle," said Mrs. Smythe.
"I'll give you 15 dollars for the tricycle," said Mrs. Smythe.
3. "(You will) find many great bargains," Justin told our customers.
"You'll find many great bargains," Justin told our customers.
4. Our free lemonade (did not) last long.
Our free lemonade didn't last long.
5. (We have) raised hundreds of dollars for the animal shelter!
We've raised hundreds of dollars for the animal shelter!
6. Maisy and I (can not) wait to give the check to the shelter's director.
Maisy and I can't wait to give the check to the shelter's director.

Try It
1. Write a sentence about something you do not like doing. Use a contraction with *not* in your sentence. Circle the contraction.
Answers will vary.
2. Write a sentence about something you will do in the future. Use a contraction with *will* in your sentence. Circle the contraction.
Answers will vary.

GRADE 3 181 SPECTRUM COMPLETE LEARNING + VIDEOS

181

Language Arts Answers

Chapter 3: Usage

Contractions with *Am, Is, Are,* and *Would*

Contractions can be made with different forms of the verb *to be*. The apostrophe takes the place of the first vowel in *am, is,* and *are.*

I am = I'm	it is = it's
you are = you're	we are = we're
he is = he's	they are = they're
she is = she's	

Contractions formed with the word *would* are a little different. The apostrophe takes the place of the entire word, except for the **d**.

I would = I'd	it would = it'd
you would = you'd	we would = we'd
he would = he'd	they would = they'd
she would = she'd	

Match It

Match each pair of underlined words with its contraction. Write the letter of the contraction in the space.

1. __d__ I am going to take gymnastics lessons with my friend, Elise.
2. __g__ She is a year older than I am.
3. __b__ Elise said she would show me some warm-up stretches.
4. __f__ Our class meets on Wednesdays. It is in an old building on Fourth Street.
5. __a__ We are going to carpool to class.
6. __c__ Elise's dad teaches gymnastics. He is also the high school coach.
7. __e__ I would like to be on his team when I am in high school.

a. We're
b. she'd
c. He's
d. I'm
e. I'd
f. It's
g. She's

GRADE 3 182 SPECTRUM COMPLETE LEARNING + VIDEOS

182

Chapter 3: Usage

Contractions with *Am, Is, Are,* and *Would*

Complete It

Fill in each blank below with a contraction from the box.

I'm	It's	He's	It'd
We're	she'd	I'd	She's

1. __I'd__ like to meet Olympic gymnast Simone Biles one day.
2. __She's__ from my hometown of Spring, Texas.
3. I think __she'd__ be a great gymnastics coach one day.
4. Elise's favorite gymnast is Sam Mikulak. __He's__ a three-time Olympic gymnast.
5. __We're__ each going to write a letter to Simone and Sam.
6. __I'm__ sure they will write back to us when they hear what big fans we are.
7. __It'd__ be an amazing experience to see the Olympic Games live.
8. __It's__ my dream to travel to the Olympics.

Try It

1. Write a sentence about a famous person you would like to meet. Use a contraction in your sentence. Underline the contraction.

   Answers will vary.

2. Write a sentence that includes a contraction with the word *am, is,* or *are.* Underline the contraction.

   Answers will vary.

GRADE 3 183 SPECTRUM COMPLETE LEARNING + VIDEOS

183

Chapter 3: Usage

Negative Words and Double Negatives

Negative words are words like *no, none, never, nothing, nobody, nowhere,* and *no one.* The word *not* and contractions that use *not* are also negative words. A sentence needs only one negative word. It is incorrect to use a **double negative**, or more than one negative word, in a sentence.

Correct: There were *not* any oranges in the refrigerator.
There were *no* oranges in the refrigerator.
Incorrect: There were *not no* oranges in the refrigerator.

Correct: Kevin *never* saw anyone he knew at the store.
Kevin saw *no one* he knew at the store.
Incorrect: Kevin *never* saw *no one* he knew at the store.

Correct: *None* of the students were born in another country.
Incorrect: *None* of the students *weren't* born in another country.

Proof It

Read the paragraphs below. There are five double negatives. Cross out one negative word or phrase in the incorrect sentences to correct them.

If you haven't ~~never~~ heard of Jellyfish Lake, you should learn more about it. This amazing saltwater lake is in Palau, an island in the Philippines. You do not ~~never~~ want to get too close to a jellyfish in the ocean. Ocean jellyfish sting their prey. The jellyfish of Jellyfish Lake do not have ~~no~~ stingers. Instead, they use algae and sunlight to get the nutrients they need.

These jellyfish have only one predator—the sea anemone. This is why there are so many of them. No one can ~~never~~ swim in the lake without seeing millions of these jellyfish. It is a special experience for humans. ~~Not~~ Nowhere else in the world can people swim surrounded by more than 25 million harmless jellyfish.

GRADE 3 184 SPECTRUM COMPLETE LEARNING + VIDEOS

184

Chapter 3: Usage

Negative Words and Double Negatives

Complete It

Read each sentence below. Circle the word or words from the pair in parentheses ( ) that correctly complete each sentence.

1. The jellyfish don't (never, **ever**) stop moving.
2. They don't do (**anything,** nothing) but follow the sun across the lake all day long.
3. My aunt said there (**is,** is not) nowhere on Earth she would rather go snorkeling.
4. People who swim with the jellyfish shouldn't (**ever,** never) lift or throw the delicate animals.
5. There aren't (no, **any**) jellyfish without stingers in the oceans of the world.
6. Because the jellyfish don't have to hunt for their food, there (**was,** was not) no need for stingers.
7. The beautiful jellyfish don't (never, **ever**) seem to be too bothered by human visitors.
8. El Niño brought high temperatures to Palau in the late 1990s. Suddenly, there weren't (**any,** no) jellyfish in the lake.

Try It

1. Write a sentence using one of these negative words: *no, none, never, nothing, nobody, nowhere, no one,* or *not.*

   Answers will vary.

2. On another piece of paper, write a sentence using a double negative. Trade papers with a classmate. On the line below, write your classmate's sentence correctly.

   Answers will vary.

GRADE 3 185 SPECTRUM COMPLETE LEARNING + VIDEOS

185

Language Arts Answers

Chapter 3: Usage

Forming Plurals with s and es

The word **plural** means *more than one*. To make many nouns plural, add **s**.

one egg → two eggs — one dog → six dogs
one pencil → many pencils — one photo → nine photos

If a noun ends in **sh**, **ch**, **s**, or **x**, form the plural by adding **es**.

one bush → three bushes — one peach → five peaches
one fox → two foxes — one bus → several buses

If a noun ends with a consonant and a **y**, drop the **y** and add **ies** to form the plural.

one baby → all the babies — one city → many cities

Complete It
Read each sentence below. Complete it with the plural form of the word in parentheses ( ).

1. Ethan made two **wishes** as he blew out his birthday candles. (wish)
2. All the **branches** in the yard came down during the huge thunderstorm last week. (branch)
3. Jacob takes care of the **cats** next door when our neighbors go out of town. (cat)
4. We need about six ripe **apples** to make apple pie. (apple)
5. Hallie left her **glasses** at a friend's house. (glass)
6. Claudia and Crista picked sour **cherries** from the tree in the yard. (cherry)
7. Please recycle the **boxes** in the garage. (box)
8. Four **families** have volunteered to organize the book sale. (family)

186

Chapter 3: Usage

Forming Plurals with s and es

Solve It
Read the clues below. Find the word in the box that matches each clue. Then, make the word plural, and write it in the numbered space in the crossword puzzle.

airplane	dress
bed	beach
giraffe	fox
dish	baby

Across
2 very young people — babies
4 machines that let people fly in the sky — airplanes
5 sandy places near lakes or oceans — beaches
6 red animals with pointy ears and fluffy tails — foxes
7 pieces of clothing worn by girls — dresses

Down
1 tall animals with long, skinny necks — giraffes
3 cups, plates, and bowls — dishes
5 soft pieces of furniture that you sleep in — beds

Try It
1. Write a sentence using the plural form of one of these words: *peach, watch, wish, bush, dress, class,* or *box*.
Answers will vary.
2. Write a sentence using the plural form of any word. Circle the plural word.
Answers will vary.

187

Chapter 3: Usage

Irregular Plurals

Some plural words do not follow the rules. Instead of adding an ending to these words, you need to remember their plural forms.

one *man*, seven *men* — one *foot*, two *feet*
one *woman*, five *women* — one *goose*, ten *geese*
one *ox*, six *oxen* — one *child*, a lot of *children*
one *mouse*, many *mice* — one *die*, two *dice*

Some words do not change at all. The singular and plural forms are the same.

one *deer*, six *deer* — one *fish*, forty *fish*
one *moose*, two *moose* — one *sheep*, a dozen *sheep*
one *trout*, five *trout* — one *series*, three *series*
one *species*, nine *species*

Match It
Match each phrase below to the correct plural form. Write the letter on the line.

1. **b** one woman — **a.** fifty womans — **b.** fifty women
2. **a** one die — **a.** six dice — **b.** six dies
3. **a** a moose — **a.** many moose — **b.** many mooses
4. **a** the trout — **a.** hundreds of trout — **b.** hundreds of trouts
5. **a** one species — **a.** eight species — **b.** eight specieses
6. **b** the goose — **a.** four gooses — **b.** four geese
7. **b** one ox — **a.** a herd of oxes — **b.** a herd of oxen
8. **b** a child — **a.** most childs — **b.** most children

188

Chapter 3: Usage

Irregular Plurals

Solve It
On the lines below, write the plural form of each word in the box.

foot **feet**	ox **oxen**	deer **deer**
man **men**	mouse **mice**	sheep **sheep**

Use the words in the box to complete the rhymes below.

1. The room was filled with 25 **men**, and every single man's name was Ken.
2. "Hurry, hurry, hurry!" said all of the **sheep**. "Walking's too slow, let's take the jeep!"
3. I am only one tiny gray **mouse**, and yet there are dozens of cats in this house.
4. Please do me a favor and move your **feet**. I do not want footprints all over my seat!
5. In the garden I see dozens of **deer**, and they've eaten all of my lettuce, I fear.
6. The man scratched his head and looked at the **ox**. "Was it you who ate my bagel and lox?"
7. If I've told you once, I've told you twice. There's no room in this house for any more **mice**!

Try It
On the lines below, make up two of your own rhymes using one of the plurals from the exercise above.
1. **Answers will vary.**
2. **Answers will vary.**

189

Language Arts Answers

Chapter 3: Usage

Singular Possessives

When something belongs to a person or thing, they *possess* it. An apostrophe (') and the letter **s** at the end of a word show that the person or thing is the owner in a **possessive**.

Julianne**'s** violin	the school**'s** gym
Ichiro**'s** basketball	the tiger**'s** stripes
the park**'s** gates	Trent**'s** sister

Proof It

The possessives below are missing apostrophes. To add an apostrophe, use this symbol (ˇ).

1. The White House's address is 1600 Pennsylvania Avenue.
2. Two fires almost destroyed the home of the nation's president.
3. The President's House, the President's Palace, and the Executive Mansion were early names for the White House.
4. The Oval Office's shape was chosen by President Taft.
5. Some of the world's best artists have work displayed in the White House.
6. President Bush's dogs, Barney and Miss Beazley, were Scottish terriers.

GRADE 3 190 SPECTRUM COMPLETE LEARNING + VIDEOS

190

Chapter 3: Usage

Singular Possessives

Rewrite It

Rewrite the sentences below. Replace the underlined words in each sentence with a possessive.

Example: The capital of Hawaii is Honolulu.
Hawaii's capital is Honolulu.

1. The hometown of Ronald Reagan was Tampico, Illinois.
   Ronald Reagan's hometown was Tampico, Illinois.
2. The nickname of Benjamin Harrison was "Little Ben."
   Benjamin Harrison's nickname was "Little Ben."
3. Theodore Roosevelt was the youngest president of the nation.
   Theodore Roosevelt was the nation's youngest president.
4. Michelle Obama, the wife of President Obama, is an advocate for healthy eating.
   Michelle Obama, President Obama's wife, is an advocate for healthy eating.
5. The 39th president of America was Jimmy Carter.
   America's 39th president was Jimmy Carter.
6. Before he became president, one of the jobs of Harry Truman was farming.
   Before he became president, one of Harry Truman's jobs was farming.

Try It

Write a sentence about a well-known figure from history. Use a possessive in your sentence.

Answers will vary.

GRADE 3 191 SPECTRUM COMPLETE LEARNING + VIDEOS

191

Chapter 3: Usage

Plural Possessives

To form the **possessive of a plural** word that ends in **s**, add an apostrophe after the **s**.

the girls**'** room	the monkeys**'** food
the berries**'** juice	the teachers**'** decision

For plural words that do not end in **s**, add an apostrophe and an **s** to form the possessive.

the people**'s** goals	the men**'s** clothes

Complete It

Read each sentence below. Replace the words in parentheses ( ) with a possessive. Write the possessive in the space.

1. (The thick white fur of polar bears) **The polar bears' thick white fur** keeps them warm during Arctic winters.
2. (The mother of the bear cubs) **The bear cubs' mother** protects her babies from wolves and other predators.
3. (The coats of caribous) **The caribous' coats** change colors, depending on the seasons.
4. (The flippers of seals) **The seals' flippers** make them strong, speedy swimmers.
5. When the young girl listened quietly, she could hear (the songs of walruses) **the walruses' songs**.

Tip

Apostrophes are the key to telling the difference between a plural and a possessive.

Plural	Possessive
thousands of bugs	a bug's wings
several boys	the boys' clubhouse
four watermelons	the watermelon's seeds

GRADE 3 192 SPECTRUM COMPLETE LEARNING + VIDEOS

192

Chapter 3: Usage

Plural Possessives

Identify It

Read each phrase below. If it is plural, write **PL** on the line. If it is plural possessive, write **PP**.

1. **PL** the playful baby seals
2. **PP** the igloos' walls
3. **PL** the floating icebergs
4. **PL** the Arctic rivers
5. **PL** hundreds of salmon
6. **PP** the puffins' brightly-colored beaks
7. **PP** the explorers' route
8. **PP** the people's warm clothing

Try It

Write two sentences that include plural words.

1. **Answers will vary.**
2. **Answers will vary.**

Now, write two sentences that use the possessive form of the plural words from above.

3. **Answers will vary.**
4. **Answers will vary.**

GRADE 3 193 SPECTRUM COMPLETE LEARNING + VIDEOS

193

Language Arts Answers

Chapter 3: Usage

Subject and Object Pronouns

Pronouns are words that take the places of nouns and proper nouns. **Subject pronouns** take the place of subjects in sentences. Some subject pronouns are *I, you, he, she, it, we,* and *they.*

Eduardo likes to rollerblade.	*He* likes to rollerblade.
The mall was crowded.	*It* was crowded.
Serena and Libby were in the newspaper.	*They* were in the newspaper.

Object pronouns often follow action words or words like *to, at, from, with,* and *of.* Some object pronouns are *me, you, him, her, it, us,* and *them.*

The horse ***jumped*** *the fence.*	The horse ***jumped*** *it.*
Joey went ***with*** *Mr. Simms.*	Joey went ***with*** *him.*
I put the letter on top ***of*** *the dresser.*	
I put the letter on top ***of*** *it.*	

Identify It

Read the sentences below. Underline each pronoun. Write **SP** above it if it is a subject pronoun. Write **OP** above it if it is an object pronoun.

1. The librarian gave him (OP) the book.
2. Heather and Chase took the puppy with them (OP).
3. It (SP) will be sunny and 65 degrees today.
4. The children sang the song to her (OP).
5. I (SP) will ask the owner tomorrow.
6. Ngozi received all the information from you (OP).

Tip When you are talking about yourself and another person, always put the other person before you.
Jaya and I   Lee and me   He and I

194

Chapter 3: Usage

Subject and Object Pronouns

Proof It

Read the sentences below. Cross out the incorrect pronouns. Then, use this symbol (^), and write the correct pronouns above them.

1. The students in Ms. Curry's class are going on a field trip. ~~Them~~ They are going to the museum.
2. Ms. Curry told ~~we~~ us that the museum is her favorite field trip.
3. The bus will leave at 8:30 in the morning. ~~She~~ It will be parked in the school's west lot.
4. Casey and Allison will sit together. ~~Them~~ They are best friends.
5. Ibrahim or Peter might sit with ~~I~~ me.
6. The Goose Creek museum is not far away. It did not take ~~we~~ us long to drive to ~~him~~ it.
7. Michael forgot to bring his lunch. Ms. Curry gave ~~he~~ him half of her sandwich and an apple.
8. ~~Me~~ I loved seeing all the fossils.

Try It

1. Write a sentence using a subject pronoun. Circle the pronoun.
   Answers will vary.
2. Write a sentence using an object pronoun. Circle the pronoun.
   Answers will vary.

195

Chapter 3: Usage

Comparative Adjectives

Adjectives can be used to compare people or things that are similar. Add **er** to an adjective to compare two things.

"The medium chair is hard**er** than the small chair," said Little Red Riding Hood.

Add **est** to compare three or more things.

Papa Bear's bed is soft. Mama Bear's bed is soft**er**. Baby Bear's bed is soft**est**.

For adjectives that end in **e**, just add **r** or **st**.

nice, nice**r**, nice**st**   close, close**r**, close**st**   gentle, gentle**r**, gentle**st**

For adjectives that end in a consonant and a **y**, drop the **y** and add **ier** or **iest**.

tiny, tin**ier**, tin**iest**   spicy, spic**ier**, spic**iest**   busy, bus**ier**, bus**iest**

Identify It

Read the sentences below. Choose the correct adjective from the pair in parentheses, and circle it.

4th Annual Fitness Challenge a Success!

Here are the results from last week's Fitness Challenge.

- Brad Dexter and Ariela Vega were the (faster, **fastest**) sprinters.
- The (**youngest**, young) student to participate was six-year-old Emily Yu.
- Most students said the obstacle course this year was (hardest, **harder**) than the one last year.
- Everyone agreed that the (easyest, **easiest**) event was the beanbag toss.
- The weather was both (sunnyer, **sunnier**) and (coldest, **colder**) than last year.
- The (stranger, **strangest**) thing that happened all week was when the clown made a homerun at the kickball game. No one knows who was wearing the clown costume!
- The cafeteria was (busiest, **busier**) after the challenges than it usually is at lunchtime.
- Morgan Bonaventure won the award for (**Greatest**, Greater) Overall Performance.

196

Chapter 3: Usage

Comparative Adjectives

Complete It

Read each sentence below. Complete it with the correct comparative form of the adjective in parentheses ( ).

1. I wish it had been **windier** during the Kite Race. (windy)
2. The **loudest** cheers came at the end of the day when Principal Sneed did jumping jacks wearing a suit. (loud)
3. Micah is **taller** than Jack, but Jack can sink more basketballs. (tall)
4. The **closest** race was between Nadia and Kyle. (close)
5. It is much **safer** to ride a bike wearing a helmet than to ride a bike without one. (safe)
6. This year's awards were even **nicer** than they have been in other years. (nice)

Try It

1. Write a sentence using a comparative adjective to compare two types of animals.
   Answers will vary.
2. Write a sentence using a comparative adjective to compare two things that you can see from where you are sitting.
   Answers will vary.

197

Language Arts Answers

Chapter 3: Usage

Comparative Adverbs

Adverbs can be used to make comparisons. Some adverbs follow the same rules that adjectives do. For most one-syllable adverbs, add **er** or **est** to make a comparison.

The boy in the blue shorts ran *faster* than I did.
Over the summer, Katherine grew *taller* than Jane.

To make a comparison using adverbs that end in **ly**, use the words *more* or *most*.

Aunt Peg read the book *more slowly* than Uncle Calvin.
My sister sang *most beautifully* of all the girls in her class.

Complete It

Fill in the spaces in the chart with the correct adverbs. Remember that some comparative adverbs need to be used with the words *more* or *most*.

slowly	**more slowly**	most slowly
fast	faster	**fastest**
skillfully	**more skillfully**	**most skillfully**
happily	more happily	**most happily**
patiently	more patiently	most patiently
late	**later**	latest
safely	**more safely**	most safely
playfully	**more playfully**	**most playfully**

GRADE 3 198 SPECTRUM COMPLETE LEARNING + VIDEOS

198

Chapter 3: Usage

Comparative Adverbs

Proof It

Read the diary entry below. There are seven comparative adverb mistakes. Cross out each mistake. To add a word, use this symbol (^) and write the correct word above it.

Saturday, September 24

Dear Diary,

Today was the first day of Flannery's obedience class. We got there ~~soonest~~ **sooner** than most of the other dogs and owners. Flannery sniffed and greeted the dogs as they arrived. She wagged her tail ~~most~~ **more** cheerfully than any other dog.

The class leader helped everyone teach their dogs some basic commands. He laughed ~~more~~ harder than anyone when Flannery stole a treat out of his pocket. I'm sure he will hide them ~~carefullier~~ **more carefully** next time. The little dachshund standing next to us fetched ~~more~~ **most** eagerly of all the dogs. She had short little legs, but she could run ~~more fast~~ **faster** than many of the bigger dogs. At the end of the class, Mom and I clapped ~~most~~ loudest of all the owners! Flannery will get her diploma in no time!

Try It

1. Write a sentence comparing two or more people or things. Use some form of the adverb *playfully*.
   Answers will vary.

GRADE 3 199 SPECTRUM COMPLETE LEARNING + VIDEOS

199

Chapter 3: Usage

Synonyms and Antonyms

Synonyms are words that have the same, or almost the same, meanings. Using synonyms in your writing can help you avoid using the same words over and over. They can make your writing more interesting.

quick, fast	present, gift	sad, unhappy
close, near	jump, hop	tired, sleepy

Antonyms are words that have opposite meanings.

old, young	wide, narrow	true, false
never, always	funny, serious	smile, frown

Complete It

Read each sentence below. If the sentence is followed by the word *synonym*, write a synonym for the underlined word on the line. If it is followed by the word *antonym*, write an antonym for the underlined word.

1. The rocks in the walls of the Grand Canyon are millions of years old. (antonym)
   young
2. Limestone is the top layer in the nine layers of rocks. (antonym)
   bottom
3. The waters of the Colorado River formed the enormous canyon. (synonym)
   Possible answers: huge, giant
4. Francisco Vásquez de Coronado led the first Europeans to see the canyon. (antonym) **last**
5. American Indians lived in the canyon before Europeans arrived. (antonym)
   after
6. If you yell into the canyon, you will hear echoes of your voice. (synonym)
   Possible answers: scream, shout, holler
7. People like taking burro rides through the canyon. (synonym) **enjoy**

GRADE 3 200 SPECTRUM COMPLETE LEARNING + VIDEOS

200

Chapter 3: Usage

Synonyms and Antonyms

Solve It

Write a synonym from the box beside each word in numbers 1–5. Write an antonym from the box beside each word in numbers 6–10.

difficult	wrong	destroy	sleepy	giggle
close	cheap	speak	loose	same

1. laugh **giggle**
2. wreck **destroy**
3. talk **speak**
4. shut **close**
5. tired **sleepy**
6. right **wrong**
7. expensive **cheap**
8. tight **loose**
9. easy **difficult**
10. different **same**

r	t	j	d	e	g	h	o	s	q	d
f	d	i	f	f	i	c	u	l	t	g
j	e	i	b	w	g	h	m	e	y	y
o	s	a	m	e	g	e	d	e	u	r
a	t	w	b	k	l	a	e	p	z	n
w	r	o	n	g	e	p	n	y	u	o
l	o	o	s	e	k	c	l	o	s	e
g	y	c	l	n	s	p	e	a	k	d

Now, find the words from the box in the word search puzzle. Circle each word you find. Words are written across and down.

Try It

1. Write a sentence using a synonym for *terrific*.
   Answers will vary.
2. Write a sentence using an antonym for *boring*.
   Answers will vary.

GRADE 3 201 SPECTRUM COMPLETE LEARNING + VIDEOS

201

Language Arts Answers

Chapter 3: Usage

Homophones

Homophones are words that sound alike but have different spellings and meanings. Here are some examples of homophones.

Did you *hear* that noise?	The party is *here*.
Connor *knew* it would rain today.	I like your *new* haircut.
There is only *one* pancake left.	I *won* the raffle!
Our family is very large.	Pick Sam up in an *hour*.
Your mom speaks Spanish.	*You're* my best friend.

Identify It

Read each sentence below. If the word in **bold** type is used correctly, make a check mark (✓) on the line. If it is not used correctly, write its homophone on the line.

1. knew Mei **new** the best way to get from Seattle, Washington, to Portland, Oregon.
2. ✓ We are meeting for lunch an **hour** before we go up in the Space Needle.
3. Your **You're** sister said that it rains a lot in Seattle.
4. ✓ The Seattle Mariners **won** the game on Friday night!
5. Our **Hour** class is going on a field trip to Pike Place Market.
6. ✓ Is **your** boat docked in Puget Sound?
7. here The 1962 World's Fair was held **hear** in Seattle.
8. new The **knew** Seattle Central Library is a beautiful glass and steel building located downtown.

202

Chapter 3: Usage

Homophones

Complete It

Read the following sentences. Complete each sentence with a word from the pair of homophones in parentheses. Write the word on the line.

1. Jada knew they would take the Washington State Ferry to Bainbridge Island. (knew, new)
2. Our family moved to Seattle because Mom works with computers. (Hour, Our)
3. I can see the Cascade Mountains from here! (hear, here)
4. I am excited that you're going hiking at Mount Rainier this weekend. (your, you're)
5. One of Seattle's most famous residents is computer giant Bill Gates. (Won, One)
6. Brendan did not hear the guide say that Smith Tower was Seattle's first skyscraper. (hear, here)
7. The Seattle Seahawks moved into their new football stadium in 2002. (new, knew)
8. Does your uncle still work at the Seattle Children's Museum? (you're, your)

Try It

On the lines below, write two sentences. Use the word *won* in the first sentence. Use the word *one* in the second sentence.

1. Answers will vary.
2. Answers will vary.

203

Chapter 3: Usage

Multiple-Meaning Words

Multiple-meaning words are words that are spelled the same but have different meanings. Look at how the word is used in the sentence to figure out which meaning it has.

In the first sentence below, the word *trunk* means *an elephant's snout*. In the second sentence, it means *a sturdy box used for storage*.

The elephant used its *trunk* to pick up the stick.
Grandpa's old photos are stored in a *trunk* in the attic.

In the first sentence below, the word *fair* means *a carnival*. In the second sentence, it means *equal* or *just*.

Jonah rode on a Ferris wheel at the county *fair*.
It is not *fair* that I have to go to bed an hour earlier than Amanda.

Find It

The dictionary entry below shows two different meanings for the same word. Each meaning is a different part of speech. Use the dictionary entry to answer the questions below.

watch *noun*: a small device that is worn on the wrist and used to keep time
verb: to look at or follow with one's eyes

1. Mikayla's grandparents gave her a watch for her birthday. Which definition of *watch* is used in this sentence? a
   a. the first definition **b.** the second definition
2. Did you watch the movie you rented? Which definition of *watch* is used in this sentence? b
   a. the first definition **b.** the second definition
3. What part of speech is *watch* when it is used to mean *a device used to keep time*? a
   a. a noun **b.** a verb

204

Chapter 3: Usage

Multiple-Meaning Words

Match It

Read each sentence below. Choose the definition that matches the way the word in **bold** type is used in the sentence. Write the letter of the definition on the line.

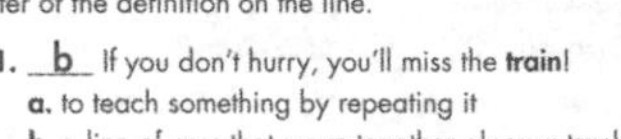

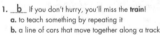

1. b If you don't hurry, you'll miss the **train**!
   a. to teach something by repeating it
   b. a line of cars that move together along a track
2. b Mark scored a **goal** in the second half of the game.
   a. something that people work hard to achieve
   b. a score in a game when a puck or ball is shot into a certain area
3. a Eloise is the **second** child in a family of four girls.
   a. number two; the one that comes after the first
   b. a moment in time; a small part of a minute
4. b We dropped pennies in the **well** and made a wish for each one.
   a. healthy; good
   b. a deep hole in the ground, used to get water or oil
5. a Gabrielle's piano teacher is **patient** when she makes mistakes.
   a. not easily irritated or annoyed
   b. someone who is getting medical treatment

Try It

1. Write a sentence using one of the multiple-meaning words from the exercise above (*train, goal, second, well, patient*).
   Answers will vary.
2. Now, write a sentence using the other meaning of the word you chose.
   Answers will vary.

205

Language Arts Answers

Chapter 5: Reading

1. What kinds of bridges does Dad build?
   heavy, strong ones and light ones
2. Why is Dad nervous?
   It is his first day at a new job.
3. How does the boy know that Dad is nervous?
   He almost poured milk in his juice.
4. What kind of bridge did the boy and Dad make at home?
   They filled the boy's room with bridges made from boxes, blocks, and pans.
5. From whose point of view is the story told?
   the boy
6. The last line of the story says that Dad is going to make one more bridge at home. What does he use to make it?
   things on the breakfast table

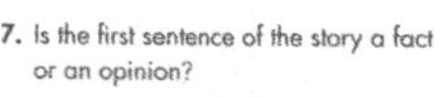

7. Is the first sentence of the story a fact or an opinion?
   an opinion

GRADE 3 219 SPECTRUM COMPLETE LEARNING + VIDEOS

219

Chapter 5: Reading

1. This passage is mostly about
   ______ old bridges.
   __X__ kinds of bridges.
   ______ making bridges.
2. The author wrote this selection to
   ______ make you laugh.
   __X__ help you learn.
3. Think about what you already know about bridges. What are bridges for?
   to get across or to get over something; to carry things across
4. This passage tells about another use for bridges. What is it?
   Some bridges were made to carry water.
5. Are all bridges made by humans? What might a natural bridge be made of?
   No. Possible answer: A natural bridge could be made of rocks or a log.
6. How are bridges with arches and beams different?
   Bridges with arches have curved supports. Bridges with beams have straight supports.
7. *The Golden Gate Bridge is the prettiest bridge in the U.S.* Is this a fact or an opinion?
   an opinion

GRADE 3 221 SPECTRUM COMPLETE LEARNING + VIDEOS

221

Chapter 5: Reading

1. How does the text help you understand how long a 24-mile-long bridge is?
   It takes half an hour to go across.
2. How does the text help you understand how high the bridge in Colorado is?
   It says that a 75-story building could fit under the bridge.
3. If you do not like to look over the side of a bridge, why would the bridge in Australia be a good one to cross?
   because it is very wide
4. Why is the bridge in India a bridge to remember?
   It is a very busy bridge, with cars and trucks and walking traffic.
5. Name three things, other than cars, that cross bridges in the selection.
   Possible answers: trucks, trains, bikes, walkers
6. What do some people do if they are nervous on a bridge?
   They hold their breath until they get to the other side.

GRADE 3 223 SPECTRUM COMPLETE LEARNING + VIDEOS

223

Chapter 5: Reading

Some of these sentences are about **real** things. Write **R** by them.
The other sentences are about **make believe** things. Write **M** by them.

1. __M__ Houses are not on the ground.
2. __M__ Children wear space suits.
3. __R__ People look at old pictures.
4. What do you learn about Lorna from the picture?
   Possible answer: Her house looks like a spaceship. It is high off the ground.
5. Why does Lorna ask about getting a car up to a house?
   Possible answer: Her house is up off the ground, so she thinks houses were always that way.
6. Look at the picture. What do you like best about Lorna's world?
   Answers will vary.
7. Do you think Lorna lives in the past or in the future? Explain.
   Possible answer: future; She didn't know much about cars or dresses. The picture looks like something from the future.
8. What is the setting for this story?
   Lorna's and her mom's house
9. Why do you think Lorna feels that having a house on the ground is weird?
   Possible answer: In the future, houses are up high.
10. In the photo, Lorna's great grandma is wearing a __**dress**__.

GRADE 3 225 SPECTRUM COMPLETE LEARNING + VIDEOS

225

Language Arts Answers

Chapter 5: Reading

Write one thing you know about each of Rachel's neighbors.

1. Mr. and Mrs. Rotollo **Italian, helped make dinner**
2. Philip **dancer, lives above Rachel, wakes her up**
3. Mr. Tran **runs grocery, gives Rachel best food**
4. Mrs. Moya **runs shop, takes down piñatas when it rains**
5. Look at the picture and the story. Which neighbor seems most interesting to you? Write why.
   Answers will vary.
6. In the picture, who is Rachel? How do you know?
   the blonde girl; Possible answer: Philip, the dancer, lives above her. You can see him in the picture.
7. Would you like to live in an apartment like Rachel's? Why or why not?
   Answers will vary.
8. How does Rachel know it is time to get up in the morning?
   She hears Philip dancing upstairs.
9. In the first paragraph, why does Mama say "the whole world lives right here on our block?"
   Possible answer: People from all around the world live on their block.

GRADE 3 227 SPECTRUM COMPLETE LEARNING + VIDEOS

227

Chapter 5: Reading

1. This article is mostly about
   X what makes a city.
   ____ how to live in a city.
   ____ America's largest cities.
2. What is your favorite thing to do in your city or in a nearby city? Write about it.
   Answers will vary.
3. The person who wrote this article is the **author**.
4. Do you think this article is meant to give information or to make you laugh? Write why.
   To give information; reasons will vary.
5. Would you most like to live in a city, in a small town, or in the country? Explain.
   Answers will vary.
6. Which of the following would taxes NOT pay for?
   ____ library books
   X a new clothing store
   ____ street cleaning
7. If you made the rules for a city, what rule would be most important to you?
   Answers will vary.
8. **It is more fun to live in a city than in the country.** Is this a fact or an opinion?
   opinion

GRADE 3 229 SPECTRUM COMPLETE LEARNING + VIDEOS

229

Chapter 5: Reading

1. This story is mostly about
   ____ a sleepover.
   ____ Sam's parents.
   X two boys' plans.
2. At the beginning, when Sam and Kent are talking on the phone, what did you think they might be talking about?
   Answers will vary.
3. In the story, when did you find out what the boys are planning?
   when Sam asks his parents for permission
4. Why do you think Sam told his dad about the grass clippings?
   Answers will vary.
5. Why does Sam mention being warm enough and when the lights will be turned out?
   Answers will vary.
6. Now that the boys have permission, what do you think they will do next?
   Answers will vary.
7. In paragraph 5, why are the words *Now, if we can only talk our parents into letting us do this* in italics?
   Sam is not speaking out loud. He is thinking those words.
8. What is the author's purpose in writing this selection?
   to entertain
9. Have you ever been worried about asking your parents to do something? What was it, and how did you ask them?
   Answers will vary.

GRADE 3 231 SPECTRUM COMPLETE LEARNING + VIDEOS

231

Chapter 5: Reading

1. One of the boys usually has the ideas. The other one seems to go along with those ideas. Which boy is the "leader"?
   Sam
2. What details from the story helped you answer question 1?
   Answers will vary.
3. Kent says he might help his mom with supper. What does that tell you about Kent?
   Answers will vary.
4. Based on what you know about camping, how do you feel about all the stuff the boys have in their tent? List what you think they need and what they don't need.
   What They Need
   Answers will vary.
   What They Don't Need
   Answers will vary.
5. In some stories, the author tells you what is happening. In this story, the author uses mostly dialogue, what the characters say, to let you know what is going on. Choose one line of dialogue and write what it helps you know about the character.
   Dialogue: **Possible answer: "Oh, no! We're camping. Those are just for in the house..."**
   Answers will vary.
6. Why does Kent think that Sam knows more about camping?
   Possible answer: The tent belongs to Sam's dad, so Kent figures Sam knows something about camping.
7. How do you think the boys feel about camping out together? Explain your answer.
   Answers will vary.

GRADE 3 233 SPECTRUM COMPLETE LEARNING + VIDEOS

233

Language Arts Answers

Chapter 5: Reading

1. What do you know about pitching a tent? Do you have anything to add to these instructions?
   Answers will vary.
2. Number the sentences to show the order of steps to pitch a tent.
   3 Spread out groundcloth.
   7 Tighten and peg guy lines.
   1 Choose and clear an area.
   5 Put together tent poles.
   2 Lay out equipment.
   4 Pound stakes through loops.
   6 Raise the poles.
3. If you don't know or understand what a guy line is, which illustration helps you figure it out? Tell how.
   The illustration that goes with Step 7; the guy lines are stretched out, just as the text describes.
4. Choose one illustration. Explain what it shows.
   Answers will vary.
5. In the first paragraph, the author says that pitching a tent alone is difficult. Why do you think this is?
   Possible answer: It is hard to put in the poles and raise the tent alone.
6. What is the purpose of a groundcloth?
   Possible answer: to protect the bottom of the tent
7. Which two steps explain what to do with the poles?
   5 and **6**
8. After reading these instructions, do you think you could pitch a tent? Why or why not?
   Answers will vary.

GRADE 3 235 SPECTRUM COMPLETE LEARNING + VIDEOS

235

Chapter 5: Reading

1. Which sentence best describes this story?
   X Nothing exciting happens to the boys in the tent.
   ____ The boys have a crazy night in the tent.
   ____ In the morning, Kent plays a trick on Sam and scares him.
2. Why did the boys stop playing badminton?
   Sam finds crumbs in his sleeping bag.
3. Read the sentences below. Write F next to sentences that are facts and O next to sentences that are opinions.
   O Kent eats too many crackers.
   F Sam's dad had been telling camping stories for almost an hour.
   F Breakfast is ready.
   O Sam's dad tells the best camping stories.
4. What do you think the boys were hoping would happen?
   Answers will vary.
5. In paragraph 3, why does Kent turn red?
   Answers will vary.
6. Write C next to the sentence below that is the cause. Write E next to the sentence that is the effect.
   E Kent landed on top of Sam.
   C Sam's mom startled the boys.
7. This story has two settings. What are they?
   Sam's kitchen and **the tent**

GRADE 3 237 SPECTRUM COMPLETE LEARNING + VIDEOS

237

Chapter 5: Reading

1. What is causing Mikki to worry?
   She sees lights flashing outside.
2. What does Mikki do to try to get to sleep?
   First, she **turns away from the window and closes her eyes.**
   Then, she **rolls toward the window and tries to figure out what it is.**
3. What is causing the flashing lights?
   There is a thunderstorm far in the distance. Mikki is seeing only the lightning.
4. Have you ever been kept awake at night by something that bothered or puzzled you? Write about it.
   Answers will vary.
5. From whose point of view is this story told?
   ____ Mom's **X** Mikki's ____ Uncle Walt's
6. Which word best describes Mom in the story?
   ____ impatient ____ confused **X** kind
7. Is this story realistic? Why or why not?
   yes; Possible answer: The things that happen in the story could happen in real life.
8. Name three things that Mikki thinks the lights could be. **Possible answers:**
   car lights **police car flashers** **spaceships**

GRADE 3 239 SPECTRUM COMPLETE LEARNING + VIDEOS

239

Chapter 5: Reading

1. The author wrote this article to
   ____ entertain.
   X give information.
   ____ persuade.
2. Which comes first, thunder or lightning?
   Lightning comes first.
3. What causes lightning? Give a brief answer.
   a build-up of electricity on water droplets
4. How does lightning cause thunder?
   Possible answer: When lightning strikes, the air heats, then cools. The sudden changes in air temperature cause the sound.
5. If you read only the two headings in this article, what would you learn?
   Lightning happens before thunder.
6. Write T for true or F for false next to each statement below.
   F Thunder always takes the same amount of time to reach Earth.
   T Light travels faster than sound.
   F Thunder and lightning are not related to each other.
7. What is the main idea of paragraph 4?
   Possible answer: Lightning happens when the electrical charge in droplets has to discharge.
8. Which of the following is the purpose of paragraph 1?
   X introduction ____ author's purpose ____ conclusion

GRADE 3 241 SPECTRUM COMPLETE LEARNING + VIDEOS

241

Language Arts Answers

Chapter 5: Reading

Put a check next to the sentences that are true.

1. ✓ The idea for Smokey the Bear started in the 1940s.
2. _____ Smokey the Bear lives in New Mexico.
3. _____ The Forest Service made posters in honor of a bear cub that died in a fire.
4. ✓ Smokey the Bear was a drawing first, and then a real bear.

Write **M** next to the sentences that tell about make-believe things.

5. _____ Smokey the Bear lived in a zoo for many years.
6. M Smokey the Bear speaks to campers about the danger of forest fires.
7. M Smokey the Bear used to help firefighters put out fires.
8. Why was Smokey the Bear created? Write the phrase or sentence from the article that tells you.
   to protect America's forests
9. In paragraph 2, what problem did U.S. leaders have?
   They were worried about having enough wood for the war.
10. What was the solution?
   to start a campaign to prevent forest fires
11. What organization created the fire safety posters?
   the Forest Service
12. In the posters, did Smokey the Bear look realistic? Explain.
   Possible answer: No, he was wearing a park ranger's hat.

GRADE 3 243 SPECTRUM COMPLETE LEARNING + VIDEOS

243

Chapter 5: Reading

A **fact** is something that can be proven true. An **opinion** is what someone thinks or feels. Check the sentences that are facts.

1. ✓ Vegetables can be grown in pots.
2. _____ Creating a garden on a fire escape is difficult.
3. _____ Any garden is beautiful.
4. ✓ Plants need soil and water.
5. Number the sentences to show the order in which things happened.
   3 Rosa bought potting soil.
   2 Rosa took the pots home.
   4 Rosa planted her seeds.
   1 Rosa saw the pots.
6. Check the words or phrases that best describe Rosa.
   _____ selfish
   _____ tends to waste time
   ✓ likes the outdoors
   ✓ appreciates beauty
7. Why do you think Rosa slept well the night after she bought seeds and soil?
   Possible answer: She felt happy and content.
8. The author repeats a line from paragraph 4 in the last paragraph. What line is it? Why do you think the author repeats it?
   masses of flowers and fat, glowing fruits; Possible answer: It's something Rosa likes to repeat to herself to remind her of what her garden will be like.
9. Have you ever planted something and watched it grow? Tell about how it made you feel.
   Answers will vary.

GRADE 3 245 SPECTRUM COMPLETE LEARNING + VIDEOS

245

Chapter 5: Reading

1. Why is Rosa worried about her plants on this day?
   She is afraid the heat and lack of rain will hurt her plants.

Write **T** if the sentence is true. Write **F** if the sentence is false.

2. F This story is mostly about Rosa worrying about her garden.
3. F Rosa is careless about her garden.
4. T Rosa plans to share her flowers with others.
5. T Too much sun causes Rosa's plants to dry up.

Compare how things really are with how they used to be, or with what Rosa imagines.

6. The strongest, tallest tomato plant is **pale and dry looking**.
   It had been **green and smooth**.
7. Rosa bites into an **apple**.
   She imagines that it is a **big, juicy tomato**.
8. She chops a **carrot**.
   She imagines that it is a **shiny green pepper**.
9. For now, Rosa works at a **factory**.
   She dreams of **running her own flower shop**.
10. Why do you think Rosa spends so much time daydreaming?
   Possible answer: She doesn't like her job, and her life is not very colorful or interesting.
11. What details from the story helped you answer question 10?
   Answers will vary.
12. Which of these is most likely to be true?
   _____ Rosa lives in the country.
   ✓ Rosa lives in a city.

GRADE 3 247 SPECTRUM COMPLETE LEARNING + VIDEOS

247

Chapter 5: Reading

1. What do you know about peppers, or what experiences have you had growing or eating peppers?
   Answers will vary.
2. Do you like peppers? Write why or why not.
   Answers will vary.
3. How are bell peppers and chili peppers the same? How are they different? Write what the article tells you about each kind.
   Bell Peppers
   Size **apple-sized**
   Shape **round**
   Color **red, yellow, or green**
   Flavor **less spicy**
   Chili Peppers
   Size **many sizes**
   Shape **long and skinny**
   Color **red, yellow, or green**
   Flavor **hot or spicy**
4. What two headings does the author divide the article into? How is this helpful?
   bell peppers and chili peppers; Possible answer: The sections help you know where to look for information in the article.
5. Write **T** for true or **F** for false next to each statement below.
   T Hot peppers can make your eyes water.
   F Bell peppers are very spicy.
   T Peppers can be prepared in many ways.
   F Bell peppers are red, and chili peppers are green.
6. What makes chili peppers burn your mouth?
   a chemical in them
7. What two vitamins are peppers high in?
   A and **C**

GRADE 3 249 SPECTRUM COMPLETE LEARNING + VIDEOS

249

Language Arts Answers

Chapter 5: Reading

1. In most stories, a character has a problem. What is Perry's problem?
   He feels awful during soccer practice.
2. What information in the story helped you answer question 1?
   Answers will vary.
3. **Dialogue** is what the characters in a story say. What did you learn about Perry from his dialogue?
   He doesn't ever want to go back to soccer practice.
4. Find a line of the coach's dialogue. What does it tell you about the coach?
   Dialogue: **Answers will vary.**
   What it tells: **Answers will vary.**
5. Coach thinks that a passing exercise is important because
   the players need to be able to pass the ball well during a game.
6. What is the setting for this story?
   the soccer field
7. **Practice was awful.** Is this a fact or an opinion?
   an opinion
8. The last line of paragraph 5 says that Perry didn't even wait for his mom's usual question. What do you think her question is?
   Possible answer: How was practice?
9. Which word or phrase best describes Perry in this story?
   ____ confident ____ full of energy **✓** exhausted
10. Have you ever wished you could quit an activity? Tell about it.
    Answers will vary.

GRADE 3 251 SPECTRUM COMPLETE LEARNING + VIDEOS

251

Chapter 5: Reading

1. Mrs. Rothman is speechless because
   Perry has just said he wants to quit soccer.
2. Check two words that tell how Perry probably felt.
   ✓ disappointed
   ____ proud
   ____ eager
   ✓ frightened
3. Perry says he wants to quit soccer because
   he is weak; doesn't have what it takes.
4. Have you ever tried to do something that was hard, or that you had to work at? What was it?
   Answers will vary.
   Did you get discouraged? Did you quit?
   Answers will vary.
5. Do you think Perry's decision is reasonable, or do you think he is giving up too easily? Explain.
   Answers will vary.
6. Mrs. Rothman probably feels
   ✓ surprised ____ angry ____ entertained
7. What problem does Mrs. Rothman think Perry is having?
   He didn't have a good lunch, so he was low on energy.
8. How does she plan to help Perry?
   She's going to make him a power snack to eat right before the next practice.
9. What do you think would be a good example of a power snack? Explain your choice.
   Answers will vary.

GRADE 3 253 SPECTRUM COMPLETE LEARNING + VIDEOS

253

Chapter 5: Reading

Write these steps in the correct order. (Not all of the recipe's steps are here.)

- spread mixture into pan
- drizzle glaze
- grease the pan
- mix sugar, oil, and eggs
- remove from oven and cool

1. **grease the pan**
2. **mix sugar, oil, and eggs**
3. **spread mixture into pan**
4. **remove from oven and cool**
5. **drizzle glaze**
6. How long do the directions say to bake the bars?
   16 to 22 minutes
7. The directions say to "drizzle honey glaze over bars." How did you know what honey glaze was?
   Answers will vary.

Recipes often use short forms of words called **abbreviations**. Match the common recipe words in the box with their abbreviations.

cup	Fahrenheit	teaspoon	tablespoon

8. T. **tablespoon**
10. F **Fahrenheit**
9. c. **cup**
11. tsp. **teaspoon**
12. The directions say, "Bake until center is set but not firm." What does this mean?
    Possible answer: The middle should not be gooey, but it should not be overbaked either.
13. How long do the energy bars need to cool?
    They need to cool completely.
14. What is the longest you could keep these bars? What would you need to do to them?
    six months; freeze them

GRADE 3 255 SPECTRUM COMPLETE LEARNING + VIDEOS

255

Chapter 5: Reading

1. When you read the story's title, did you guess about how the story ended? Was your guess close to being correct? Explain.
   Answers will vary.
2. Circle the word that best describes the coach's words before the game.
   angry **(encouraging)**
3. Have you ever been in a sporting event or a performance that didn't turn out the way you expected? Did something funny or weird happen? Write about it.
   Answers will vary.
4. At the end of paragraph 2, Coach says that the players have "dribbled to the moon and back." This is a figure of speech. What does it mean?
   Possible answer: They have dribbled a great distance.
5. Give one example of dialogue in the story.
   Possible answer: "Okay, everybody listen up!"
   Now, give one example of a character's thought that is not spoken out loud.
   Possible answer: Now that was a solid kick.
6. How are the two examples in question 5 written differently from each other?
   The first one is in quotation marks, and the second one is in italics.
7. Why is it funny that someone in the crowd says, "It's a home run!"?
   Possible answer: There are no home runs in soccer. The person was confusing soccer with baseball.

GRADE 3 257 SPECTRUM COMPLETE LEARNING + VIDEOS

257

Language Arts Answers

Chapter 5: Reading

1. This article is mostly about
   _____ how soccer was named.
   _____ the rules of soccer.
   __✓__ soccer's history.
2. Historians think that soccer might have started out as a
   skill-building exercise for soldiers.
3. Why did King Edward III pass a law against soccer?
   The game was rough or violent.
4. What punishment did Queen Elizabeth have for soccer players?
   a week of jail
5. What important rule change made the game into what we know as soccer? When did it happen?
   In 1869, a rule against handling the ball with the hands was made.
6. If you wanted to find out about the beginnings of soccer, under which heading should you look?
   Earliest Record
7. Under which heading would you find information about soccer during the last century or so?
   The Modern Game Emerges
8. Write **T** for **true** or **F** for **false** next to each statement below.
   __F__ Today, you are allowed to touch the ball with your hands in soccer.
   __T__ Kicking and biting were common in soccer games long ago.
   __T__ In Britain, soccer is called "football."
9. At the end of paragraph 3, it says, "the game could not be stopped." Why do you think this was true?
   Possible answer: It was popular, and people loved it too much to stop playing.
10. What was the author's purpose for writing this article?
    to tell about the history of soccer

GRADE 3 259 SPECTRUM COMPLETE LEARNING + VIDEOS

259

Chapter 5: Reading

1. The person who wrote this article is the **author**. The author probably wrote this article to
   _____ make you laugh.
   _____ give information.
   __X__ persuade you to do something.

The author states some facts in the article. She also gives her opinion. Write **F** next to each sentence that is a fact. Write **O** next to each sentence that gives an opinion.

2. __F__ The U.S. Youth Soccer Association registers about 3 million players each year.
3. __O__ First, I think there's the international appeal.
4. __F__ Though accidents may occur, body contact isn't supposed to be part of the game.
5. __O__ And finally, I think there is the running factor.
6. Look back at the sentences you marked as opinions. What do you notice about them?
   They both contain the word "I."
7. What is the main idea of paragraph 5?
   _____ Soccer is only for boys, just like other sports.
   __✓__ Soccer is a good sport for both boys and girls.
   _____ Soccer has caught on with girls.
8. Why is soccer less expensive than some other sports?
   You don't need a lot of equipment.
9. Look at the focus question under the title. What do you think its purpose is?
   Possible answer: It tells you something to look for or think about as you read.
10. Have you ever played soccer? If so, tell about your experience. If not, explain why you would or would not like to try it.
    Answers will vary.

GRADE 3 261 SPECTRUM COMPLETE LEARNING + VIDEOS

261

Chapter 5: Reading

1. Do you think Sharla, Tess, and Lee will be able to work together? Write why or why not.
   Answers will vary.
2. Think of times when you worked with classmates on projects. Was it hard or easy? Explain.
   Answers will vary.
3. Would you say that you are more like Sharla—full of ideas—or more like Lee—eager to stop talking and get to work? Write why.
   Answers will vary.
4. Does the teacher who is writing the journal seem thoughtful or worn out? Write why you think so.
   Answers will vary.
5. At the end of the first paragraph, the teacher says, "I knew something was going to blow up, and it wasn't the volcano." What does she mean?
   Possible answer: She knows that the girls may end up having a fight.
6. From whose point of view is this selection told?
   _____ Sharla _____ Lee __✓__ the teacher
7. What do you predict will happen next in the story?
   Answers will vary.
8. If you wrote a journal entry, what would you write about?
   Answers will vary.

GRADE 3 263 SPECTRUM COMPLETE LEARNING + VIDEOS

263

Chapter 5: Reading

This story is written in the form of a journal entry. The person who is writing uses *I* to refer to herself. She is the **narrator**, or the person telling the story.

1. Find a sentence that tells you that the narrator actually took part in the action of the story. Write the sentence here.
   Answers will vary.
2. The narrator, Sharla, disagreed with Lee about
   whether to make the sides of the volcano smooth or rough.
3. Sharla was upset because
   she thought it was unfair to have to stay inside at recess.
4. Did you expect this journal to be written by Mrs. Holt, the teacher? Why or why not?
   Answers will vary.
5. Why did the girls decide to make a village around the base?
   Tess could do something without touching the volcano paste.
6. Which of these words best describes Sharla's attitude toward the other two girls?
   __✓__ impatient _____ understanding _____ comforting
7. Explain how the picture adds to your understanding of the story.
   Possible answer: I can get an idea of what the volcano will look like. I can see that Tess is not really helping.
8. Write **C** next to the sentence below that is the cause. Write **E** next to the sentence that is the effect.
   __C__ The girls didn't make much progress on their volcano.
   __E__ Mrs. Holt made the girls stay in at recess.

GRADE 3 265 SPECTRUM COMPLETE LEARNING + VIDEOS

265

Language Arts Answers

Chapter 5: Reading

1. In most stories, the characters have a problem. What problem do the characters in this story have?
   They had disagreed about how to finish their project.
2. What caused Mrs. Holt to call the girls up to her desk?
   They weren't done with their project.
3. What is Tess's idea?
   X to show flowing lava
   ____ to make both sides smooth
   ____ to make the village larger
4. What is the result of Tess's idea?
   The girls agree to make one side smooth and one side rough. Sharla and Lee can both get what they want.
5. Where in the story do we learn that the teacher, Mrs. Holt, knows the girls are not getting along?
   Where it says, "knowing perfectly well that there was a problem."
6. What is the main difference in the way this story is written, compared to the other two about the same characters?
   ____ This story is told from Lee's point of view.
   ____ Sharla is not a character in this story.
   ✓ It is not written as a journal entry.
7. How do you think Mrs. Holt feels about the girls solving their own problem? Explain.
   Answers will vary.
8. What is the setting for this story?
   a school classroom
9. The girls learned how to build a volcano by doing this project. What else do you think they learned?
   Possible answer: They learned how to get along and work as a team.

GRADE 3 267 SPECTRUM COMPLETE LEARNING + VIDEOS

267

Chapter 5: Reading

1. This story is mostly about
   ____ becoming best friends after working together.
   X what the girls learned from their project.
   ____ how a teacher helped the girls get along.
2. How do the girls feel about their volcano project?
   They are proud of it.
3. When it is Lee's turn to speak, she feels
   X nervous.
   ____ happy.
   ____ cross.
4. Why did Sharla's face turn red when Mrs. Holt asked about how they completed their project?
   She was embarrassed.
5. What experiences have you had working with other people? Were there times when you didn't agree or get along? Write about it.
   Answers will vary.
6. When it is Tess's turn to speak, what does she tell about?
   a famous volcano and a town that got covered by mud and ash
7. Make a check mark next to the thing that happened first.
   ____ Mrs. Holt had a question.
   ✓ Lee said, "This is our volcano."
   ____ Mrs. Holt looked pleased.
8. If the girls had to work together again, how do you think they would do? Explain.
   Answers will vary.

GRADE 3 269 SPECTRUM COMPLETE LEARNING + VIDEOS

269

Chapter 5: Reading

In nonfiction writing, the author sometimes calls attention to words that the reader may not know. Those words appear in **bold** type. The author usually gives the meaning of the bold word in the same sentence.

Below are the bold words from the article. Write the meaning of each word.

1. molten melted
2. expand get bigger
3. fissures cracks
4. active experience eruptions
5. dormant inactive

Write **F** next to each sentence that is a fact. Write **O** next to each sentence that is an opinion.

6. O Volcanic eruptions are one of the most striking natural events.
7. O A volcanic eruption is more frightening than a hurricane.
8. F Volcanoes are located in many places in the world.
9. What does the illustration show?
   the inside of a volcano
10. Trace with your finger the path that magma would take from under Earth's crust to the surface. Describe the path in your own words.
    Answers will vary.
11. Write **C** next to the sentence below that is the cause. Write **E** next to the sentence that is the effect.
    E Parts of Earth's crust open up.
    C The molten rock gets very hot and expands.
12. What are scientists who study volcanoes called?
    volcanologists

GRADE 3 271 SPECTRUM COMPLETE LEARNING + VIDEOS

271

Chapter 5: Reading

1. What four common characteristics do mammals have?
   warm blood, backbones, milk fed to babies, and hair or fur

In the article, the author showed some words in bold type. The meanings of those words are given as well. Find the meanings of the words, and write them here.

2. habitat natural conditions
3. insectivores insect eaters
4. rodents gnawing animals
5. carnivores meat eaters
6. Hoofed animals are named for the kind of feet they have.
7. Give one example of each kind of forest dweller. Possible answers:
   insect eaters: moles
   gnawing animals: beavers
   hare-like animals: rabbits
   meat eaters: coyotes
   hoofed animals: moose
8. Why do you think a forest is a good habitat for many different kinds of mammals?
   Possible answer: There are lots of trees to provide shelter.
9. Think about what you know about mammals. Name two kinds of mammals that are not mentioned in the article. Possible answers:
   dogs and dolphins
10. **Meat eaters eat smaller mammals, such as rabbits, mice, and moles.** Is this sentence a fact or an opinion?
    a fact

GRADE 3 273 SPECTRUM COMPLETE LEARNING + VIDEOS

273

Language Arts Answers

Chapter 5: Reading

The author of this article chose to share her own point of view. Find a sentence in which the author uses the word *I*. What idea is the author sharing in that sentence?

1. The sentence begins with Answers will vary.
   The author is saying Answers will vary.
2. Do you think the author likes snakes, dislikes snakes, or is neutral? Write a sentence from the article that supports your answer.
   Answers will vary.

Write **F** next to each sentence that is a fact. Write **O** next to each sentence that is an opinion.

3. O People dislike snakes because they have no legs.
4. F Snakes control the rodent population.
5. O Not meeting many snakes is a good thing.
6. Name one difference between mammals and reptiles.
   Possible answer: Mammals are warm-blooded, and reptiles are cold-blooded.
7. What is one way in which snakes are useful?
   They help control the rodent population.
8. What is the main idea of paragraph 4?
   ___ If you get bitten by a poisonous snake, seek medical help.
   ✓ Some snakes are poisonous, but that's not a good reason to dislike all snakes.
   ___ Poisonous snakes are very vicious.
9. Tell how you feel about snakes and why.
   Answers will vary.

GRADE 3 275 SPECTRUM COMPLETE LEARNING + VIDEOS

275

Chapter 5: Reading

1. To see a redwood tree, you have to go to Oregon or California.
2. Why do redwoods grow there?
   They need moisture from the ocean.
3. What might happen if someone tried to grow a redwood tree in Kansas or Missouri, for example?
   Answers will vary.
4. What do you think is most special about redwood trees? Write why.
   Answers will vary.
5. Why do you think the author chose to use questions for the headings?
   Answers will vary.
6. If you want to find out what conditions redwoods need to grow, under which heading would you look?
   Why do redwoods grow there?
7. If you wonder what the big deal is about redwoods, under which heading should you look?
   What's special about redwoods?
8. What three objects are shown in the diagram?
   a building, a tree, and a van
9. What is the author's purpose for writing this selection?
   ___ to entertain
   ___ to persuade
   ✓ to inform
10. About how long can a redwood live?
    more than 2,000 years

GRADE 3 277 SPECTRUM COMPLETE LEARNING + VIDEOS

277

Chapter 5: Reading

Complete each sentence with the correct word.

author dialogue narrator

1. When characters speak, their words make up the story's dialogue.
2. The person who wrote the story is the author.
3. Within the story, the person or character who tells the story is the narrator.
4. In most stories, the main character has a problem. Miss Eller's problem is that she needs to find a topic that will make everyone happy.
5. Look at the illustration. What did Miss Eller's students do during their study of redwood forests?
   Answers will vary.
6. Where did Miss Eller get the idea of how to solve the problem?
   She saw a poster of a woodland scene on the wall.
7. How do you think Miss Eller's class feels about the project?
   ✓ excited
   ___ worried
   ___ upset
8. The last paragraph says that the classroom had been transformed. What does this mean?
   Possible answer: It has been changed to look like something else.
9. Write **C** next to the sentence below that is the cause. Write **E** next to the sentence that is the effect.
   E Students raise their hands to answer the question.
   C Miss Eller asks what lives in a redwood forest.

GRADE 3 279 SPECTRUM COMPLETE LEARNING + VIDEOS

279

Chapter 5: Reading

1. This story is mostly about
   X two boys trying to do a magic trick.
   ___ a boy teaching another boy a magic trick.
   ___ how to do a magic trick.
2. Josh got wet because the flower vase tipped and spilled.
3. Why was Josh under the table?
   to pull the flower vase down; to make the flowers disappear
4. Write **C** next to the sentence below that is the cause. Write **E** next to the sentence that is the effect.
   E The vase tipped and got Josh wet.
   C The bottom of the box got stuck.
5. Why were the boys so excited about the old table they found?
   It was perfect for doing magic tricks because of the hole.
6. Doing magic is (easier, (harder)) than the boys had expected.
7. Gary thinks that he and Josh need real things, so he tells Josh to go get a real rabbit.
8. Read the sentences below. Write **F** next to sentences that are facts and **O** next to sentences that are opinions.
   F Gary held his breath.
   O The boys should use real flowers.
   O Being a magician is hard work.
   F Josh's hair was wet.
9. What do you think will happen next?
   Answers will vary.

GRADE 3 281 SPECTRUM COMPLETE LEARNING + VIDEOS

281

Language Arts Answers

Chapter 5: Reading

1. How was the magic trick supposed to work?
   Josh would pull Wiggles down through the bottom of the box.
2. What actually happened?
   Wiggles got out without the boys noticing.

Write the best word to complete each sentence below.

3. They should have thought of Wiggles **sooner**. (brighter, sooner, calmer)
4. The magic words made the boys **laugh** so hard. (laugh, lame, learn)
5. It made Gary feel like a real magician when he **waved** his arms. (waved, cried, tapped)
6. The boys couldn't **believe** Wiggles was gone. (agree, scramble, believe)
7. Write **R** next to the sentences that tell about something real. Write **M** next to the sentences that are about made-up things.
   R Rabbits eat lettuce.
   M Rabbits disappear and reappear.
   R Magicians say magic words.
8. In the story, who is the magician, and who is the assistant?
   Gary is the magician, and Josh is the assistant.
9. Do you think the boys were surprised that Wiggles was actually gone? Why or why not?
   Answers will vary.
10. Which words best describe the boys?
    ✓ good-natured
    ___ sneaky
    ___ irritated
11. What do you think will happen next in the story?
    Answers will vary.

GRADE 3 283 SPECTRUM COMPLETE LEARNING + VIDEOS

283

Chapter 5: Reading

1. The author wrote this article to
   ___ persuade.
   ___ make you laugh.
   X give you information.

Write **F** next to each sentence that is a fact. Write **O** next to each sentence that is an opinion.

2. **F** Harry Houdini died almost a hundred years ago.
3. **F** Houdini could escape from handcuffs.
4. **O** Harry Houdini was the only "real" magician.
5. **O** Houdini's magic tricks were wonderful.
6. The article gives details about Houdini and his life. Number the details in the order in which the author tells about them.
   3 He escaped from a straitjacket, hanging upside down.
   1 Houdini had his first magic shows when he was 17.
   4 Houdini exposed "fake" magicians.
   2 Houdini's magic tricks became more showy and daring.
7. Which of these old sayings would Houdini have agreed with?
   ✓ Practice makes perfect.
   ___ You are what you eat.
   ___ A watched pot never boils.
8. **Houdini believed he had special powers and could talk to spirits.** Is this statement true or false?
   false

GRADE 3 285 SPECTRUM COMPLETE LEARNING + VIDEOS

285

Chapter 5: Reading

1. David Copperfield is an **illusionist**.
2. What did he start doing at age 12?
   performing magic
3. What was he doing by age 16?
   teaching college-level classes

Check all answers that are correct.

4. Which of these words do you think best describe Copperfield?
   ___ thoughtless
   ___ lazy
   ✓ hard-working
   ✓ talented
5. What do you think a magician could learn from Copperfield's collection of old magic books and equipment?
   Answers will vary.
6. If you were a magician or an illusionist, what kinds of tricks would you like to do?
   Answers will vary.
7. The headings below belong in this article. To which paragraph does each heading belong?
   Copperfield's Beginnings **2nd**
   What Is an Illusion? **1st**
   Saving Magic for the Future **4th**
   Project Magic **3rd**
8. In your own words, explain what an illusion is.
   Possible answer: An illusion is like a trick on the eyes or the senses.
9. The youngest person ever to be allowed to join the Society of American Magicians was **David Copperfield**.
10. Why do you think Copperfield believes that his best work is Project Magic?
    Possible answer: It's something he has done that helps other people and makes a difference in their lives.

GRADE 3 287 SPECTRUM COMPLETE LEARNING + VIDEOS

287

Chapter 5: Reading

1. Number the sentences to show the order in which events happened in the story.
   2 Gary laughed about their magic words.
   4 The boys heard Josh's mom.
   5 The boys discovered Mom and Wiggles.
   3 The boys figured out how to say the words backward.
   1 Gary felt great because their trick worked.
   6 The boys tried to make Mom's flowers reappear.
2. What problem do the boys have in this story?
   They can't find Wiggles the rabbit.
3. What problem does Mom have?
   Wiggles has eaten her flowers.
4. How do the boys try to help Mom? Do you think it will work?
   They try to do a magic trick to make her flowers reappear.
5. Who does Wiggles belong to?
   Josh
6. Do you think Wiggles has escaped before? What details in the story helped you answer this question?
   Yes, because Josh's mom says, "Now how many times . . ." This sounds as though Wiggles has escaped and eaten flowers many times before.
7. Do you think the boys will continue working on their magic tricks? Why or why not?
   Answers will vary.

GRADE 3 289 SPECTRUM COMPLETE LEARNING + VIDEOS

289

Language Arts Answers

Chapter 5: Reading

Write the best word to complete each sentence below.

1. Up ahead, the line of cars went around a **curve**. (curve, ledge, movement)
2. Jason was worried about the bus being **late**. (hard, late, extra)
3. Steven wanted to **count** the cars. (spin, read, count)
4. Have you ever been stuck in traffic? Write about how it felt.
   Answers will vary.
5. What might cause a traffic jam? List as many reasons as you can.
   Answers will vary.
6. How do you think the bus driver feels about the traffic jam?
   ___ amused
   ___ joyful
   ✓ frustrated
7. If the bus is late, what will Mrs. Mason do?
   call the school to let them know
8. Write **C** next to the sentence below that is the cause. Write **E** next to the sentence that is the effect.
   C Lots of cars are on the highway at the same time.
   E The cars are causing a traffic jam.

GRADE 3 291 SPECTRUM COMPLETE LEARNING + VIDEOS

291

Chapter 5: Reading

1. What kinds of things do we count? List two examples from the article.
   Ex.: inches of rain, students, government spending, voters, traffic accidents, etc.
2. What do we learn from counting things?
   Ex.: to see how things need to change or how things are changing
3. How do you think the information shown in this graph affects you and your community?
   Answers will vary.
4. What can the number of traffic accidents tell us?
   where new stop signs and lights should go
5. How many years does this chart cover?
   40 years
6. Why is the title of the chart important?
   It tells you what the chart shows.

Use the bar graph to answer these questions.

7. For each year, which is greater, the population or the number of cars?
   the population
8. If you want population data for 1950, would this graph help you? How can you tell?
   No. The title says that the graph includes data only for 1970–2010.
9. What was the population of the United States in 1970?
   just over 200 million
10. How many cars were there in 1990?
    about 130 million

GRADE 3 293 SPECTRUM COMPLETE LEARNING + VIDEOS

293

Chapter 5: Reading

1. Tatsu is sitting in the shade on the front steps because
   it is a very hot day.
2. Tatsu titles her drawing "Heat" because
   the sun is what is making her so hot.
3. Write **R** next to the sentences that tell about something real. Write **M** next to the sentences that are about made-up things.
   M A person can make shade by drawing a picture of it.
   M A person can draw a picture of heat.
   R A person can draw a picture of the sun.

The **narrator** is the person who tells a story. Answer these questions.

4. Because the narrator is also a character, she uses the words *I* and *me* to tell her story. Find a place in the story where one of these words is used. Write the sentence here.
   Answers will vary.
5. Where in the story do you discover what the narrator's name is?
   when her brother asks her a question
6. Do you think Tatsu and Fujio live in the city, in the country, or in a small town? Why?
   a city; Possible answer: They live in an apartment building. The picture looks like a city, with lots of concrete.
7. From whose point of view is the story told?
   ✓ Tatsu's ___ Fujio's ___ Not enough information is given.
8. The author uses lots of descriptions to tell how hot it is. List three details from the story that help you imagine the heat.
   Possible answers: Everything feels hot and sticky, including my own skin; I feel like the glass greenhouse at the city park; I can count on the fingers of one hand the number of leaves moving in the breeze.
9. What do you like to do on a super hot summer day?
   Answers will vary.

GRADE 3 295 SPECTRUM COMPLETE LEARNING + VIDEOS

295

Chapter 5: Reading

1. Why do Mario and Katie choose to draw pictures of cool water and a snow bank?
   because it helps them think about being cool on a hot day
2. Why does Tatsu cross out her own picture of the sun?
   She thinks it might be making things feel hotter.
3. Which word best describes the group of friends?
   ___ energetic
   ✓ creative
   ___ anxious
4. Mario doesn't use words to ask Fujio what he drew. How does he ask instead?
   He raises his eyebrows.
5. What is the author's purpose in writing this story?
   ___ to teach ___ to persuade ✓ to entertain
6. Why is the story titled "Wishes on the Sidewalk"?
   Possible answer: The kids draw pictures on the sidewalk of things they are wishing for.
7. Do you think that thinking about cool things can help a person cool down? Write why or why not.
   Answers will vary.
8. Can you remember a hot day? How did it feel? Describe it so that someone else can imagine it easily.
   Answers will vary.

GRADE 3 297 SPECTRUM COMPLETE LEARNING + VIDEOS

297

Language Arts Answers

Chapter 5: Reading

1. This article is mostly about
   _____ animals that lived thousands of years ago.
   __X__ early cave art.
   _____ how early people survived.
2. What did early cave artists use for paint?
   animal fat mixed with dirt or berries
3. Where did early artists make their drawings?
   on walls deep inside caves
4. Early cave art has been found in more than __130__ caves.
5. How do you like the cave art shown on this page? How is it the same or different from other drawings you have seen of mammoths?
   Answers will vary.
6. Who is the author addressing, or talking to, in this article?
   _____ the reader
   __✓__ the people who made the cave paintings
   _____ artists of today
7. Why is this an unusual way to write the article?
   Possible answer: Those people have been dead for thousands of years. They are not reading the article.
8. Most of the cave drawings have been found in __France__ and __England__.
9. What is the main idea of paragraph 4?
   People drew what they saw around them.
10. About how many years ago were the cave paintings made?
    about 17,000 years

299

Password Tracker

Website:

Username: ______

Password: ______

Email: ______

Notes: ______

______

______

Website:

Username: ______

Password: ______

Email: ______

Notes: ______

______

______

Website:

Username: ______

Password: ______

Email: ______

Notes: ______

______

______

Website:

Username: ______

Password: ______

Email: ______

Notes: ______

______

______

Website:

Username: ______

Password: ______

Email: ______

Notes: ______

______

______

Website:

Username: ______

Password: ______

Email: ______

Notes: ______

______

______

Password Tracker

Website:

Username: ______________________

Password: ______________________

Email: ______________________

Notes: ______________________

____

____

Website:

Username: ______________________

Password: ______________________

Email: ______________________

Notes: ______________________

____

____

Website:

Username: ______________________

Password: ______________________

Email: ______________________

Notes: ______________________

____

____

Website:

Username: ______________________

Password: ______________________

Email: ______________________

Notes: ______________________

____

____

Website:

Username: ______________________

Password: ______________________

Email: ______________________

Notes: ______________________

____

____

Website:

Username: ______________________

Password: ______________________

Email: ______________________

Notes: ______________________

____

____

Weekly

Monday

Tuesday

Friday

Saturday

Fall Schedule

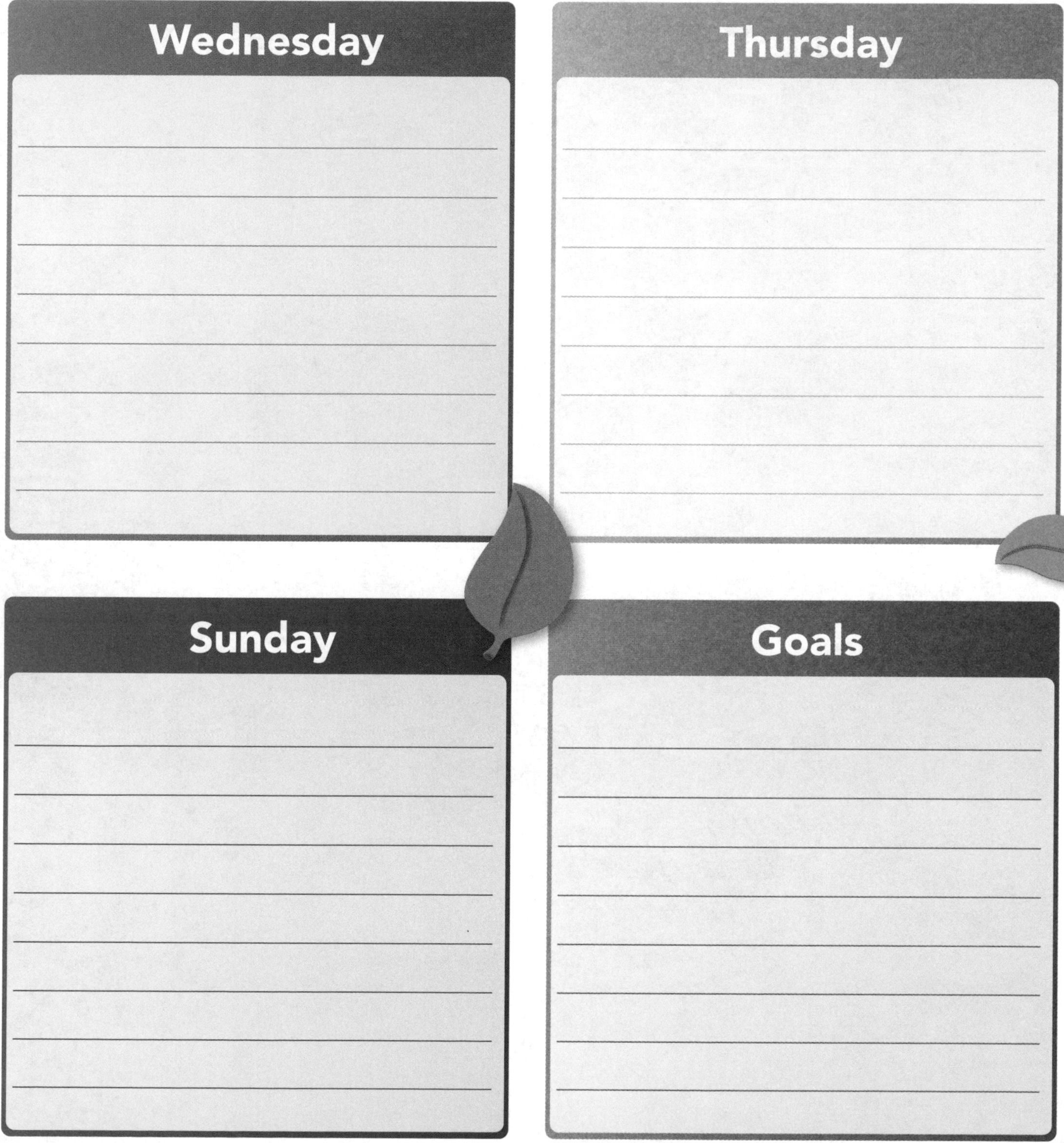

Monday

Tuesday

Friday

Saturday

Winter Schedule

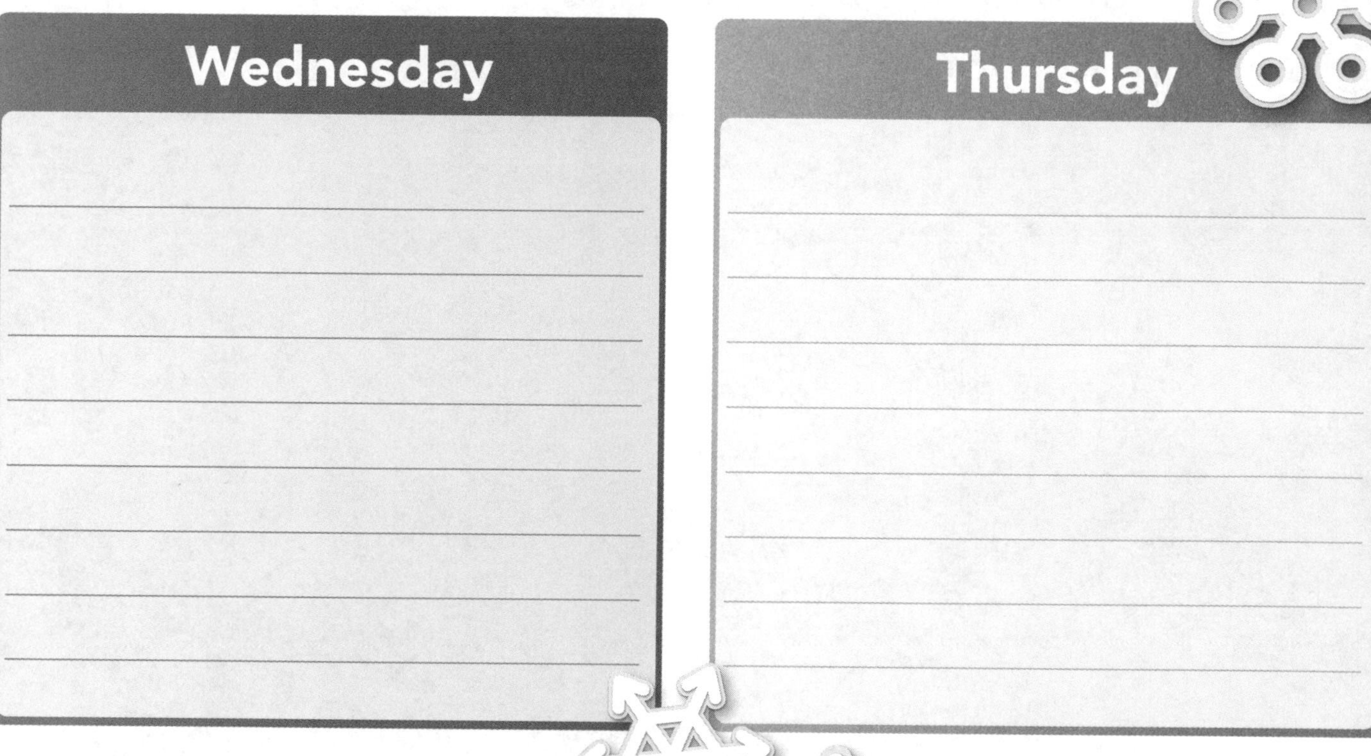

Monday

Tuesday

Friday

Saturday

Spring Schedule

Wednesday

Thursday

Sunday

Goals

Summer Goals

Goals for School

Fun Activities

Reading List

Places to Go